T0288046

Buying & Selling a Home For Canadians

5th edition

by Douglas Gray, LLB, and Peter Mitham

A Wiley Brand

Buying & Selling a Home For Canadians For Dummies®, 5th edition

Published by: **John Wiley & Sons, Inc.,** 111 River Street, Hoboken, NJ 07030-5774, www.wiley.com

Copyright © 2021 by John Wiley & Sons, Inc., Hoboken, New Jersey

Published simultaneously in Canada

No part of this publication may be reproduced, stored in a retrieval system or transmitted in any form or by any means, electronic, mechanical, photocopying, recording, scanning or otherwise, except as permitted under Sections 107 or 108 of the 1976 United States Copyright Act, without the prior written permission of the Publisher. Requests to the Publisher for permission should be addressed to the Permissions Department, John Wiley & Sons, Inc., 111 River Street, Hoboken, NJ 07030, (201) 748-6011, fax (201) 748-6008, or online at https://www.wiley.com/go/permissions.

Trademarks: Wiley, For Dummies, the Dummies Man logo, Dummies.com, Making Everything Easier, and related trade dress are trademarks or registered trademarks of John Wiley & Sons, Inc., and may not be used without written permission. All other trademarks are the property of their respective owners. John Wiley & Sons, Inc., is not associated with any product or vendor mentioned in this book.

LIMIT OF LIABILITY/DISCLAIMER OF WARRANTY: WHILE THE PUBLISHER AND AUTHOR HAVE USED THEIR BEST EFFORTS IN PREPARING THIS BOOK, THEY MAKE NO REPRESENTATIONS OR WARRANTIES WITH RESPECT TO THE ACCURACY OR COMPLETENESS OF THE CONTENTS OF THIS BOOK AND SPECIFICALLY DISCLAIM ANY IMPLIED WARRANTIES OF MERCHANTABILITY OR FITNESS FOR A PARTICULAR PURPOSE. NO WARRANTY MAY BE CREATED OR EXTENDED BY SALES REPRESENTATIVES OR WRITTEN SALES MATERIALS. THE ADVICE AND STRATEGIES CONTAINED HEREIN MAY NOT BE SUITABLE FOR YOUR SITUATION. YOU SHOULD CONSULT WITH A PROFESSIONAL WHERE APPROPRIATE. NEITHER THE PUBLISHER NOR THE AUTHOR SHALL BE LIABLE FOR DAMAGES ARISING HEREFROM.

For general information on our other products and services, please contact our Customer Care Department within the U.S. at 877-762-2974, outside the U.S. at 317-572-3993, or fax 317-572-4002. For technical support, please visit https://hub.wiley.com/community/support/dummies.

Wiley publishes in a variety of print and electronic formats and by print-on-demand. Some material included with standard print versions of this book may not be included in e-books or in print-on-demand. If this book refers to media such as a CD or DVD that is not included in the version you purchased, you may download this material at http://booksupport.wiley.com. For more information about Wiley products, visit www.wiley.com.

Library of Congress Control Number: 2020947493

ISBN: 978-1-119-71591-7

ISBN 978-1-119-71619-8 (ebk); ISBN 978-1-119-71620-4 (ebk)

Manufactured in the United States of America

SKY10022012_102820

Contents at a Glance

Table of Contents

Introduction

Buying or selling a home is an incredibly enormous undertaking, but at the same time it shouldn't be the cause of shortness of breath, dizziness, or an extended hospital stay. However, it does involve some of the most important financial decisions you'll ever make, as chances are your home is the biggest asset you'll ever own. But it's not so bad — especially with this book in hand. Armed with information about everything from mortgages to heating systems, you can calmly face the real estate world and see how it works. With this book, you get to know what fixed-rate, open-term mortgages are. You find out just how important a home inspection can be. And most important, you discover what your priorities are, and how to match them with a home — a home of your own.

If you're considering buying a home, you've come to the right place! Self-promotion aside, we tell you what you need to think about before making that huge decision, how to make your choices in a realistic and informed way, and how to avoid unexpected problems, crumbling foundations, and street parking.

If you're selling, we share all kinds of information about what your buyer expects from you, how to get the most money for your home, and how to manage the details so you don't overlook anything. If you're thinking about selling your home yourself, you can find lots of tips to help you out. Selling your home is a long, intense process that many people do as a full-time job; we try to help you see whether you're really up for that kind of do-it-yourself challenge.

Buying a new home or leaving an old and cherished one involves a lot of decisions and considerations. In this book, we outline them all and help you move on to your new home, wherever that may be.

About This Book

Some of you are buyers, some of you are sellers, and some of you are both at the same time. This new edition of *Buying & Selling a Home For Canadians For Dummies* builds on the valuable information published in the previous editions, dividing the book into two key parts:

» Read the first half if you're looking to buy a home.

» Read the second half if you're trying to sell one.

Because it's good to know what's happening on both sides of the transaction, this handy guide groups a lot of the basic information about buying and selling a home up front in a new Part 1 before getting into the nitty-gritty of either process, and we've extensively updated the text throughout with the latest information. We cover diverse topics like assembling the team of key experts who will make sure you hit a home run with your home purchase. We discuss finding the right mortgage for you, shopping for a new home, and selling your property whether you're trading up, downsizing, or a change in job or life circumstances requires it.

Wherever you start reading, we guarantee you can find information that's useful and easy to absorb. We do our best to keep it simple, but sometimes you just can't get around using the A-word (amortization). Consider those moments like a stress test (another concept we discuss in the mortgage chapter).

Foolish Assumptions

When we revised this book, we made the following assumptions about you:

» **You're interested in buying or selling a home.** We're also fairly certain you're more interested in owning a home than renting it, which means we focus on how you can buy and sell a home for you, your family, your parents, and your children. This book spends very little time on tenants (also known as mortgage helpers) and home-based businesses. You can find other books to help you understand those activities.

» **You're fairly close to buying a home and using this book as part of the planning process.** You may even be on the fence about whether you're ready to be a homeowner. If so, we help you navigate the pros and cons of buying and renting and explain the financial benefits that can be yours from investing in your own home. If you already have a home, this book is a great refresher course on how to handle all the details involved in choosing a new home. If this is your first time on the home-buying market, we take you through all the key decisions to make and the steps to take to get yourself into the right home at the right price.

>> **You're getting ready to buy a home.** Selling your current home is often an extremely tough decision, and we don't ignore the fact that you may not feel completely ready to slap a For Sale sign on the front lawn. This book helps you determine whether you're ready to say good-bye to your present home. If you've already decided on moving to a bigger and better (or a smaller and less expensive) home, we take you through the nuts and bolts of getting your home sold. We include pointers on working with a selling agent or handling the sale yourself. Everything from writing your listing, to making your home irresistible to buyers, to negotiating the best-selling conditions is all here.

Icons Used in This Book

As you read through this book, you'll see a few icons lurking on the left-hand side. Here's a guide to what they mean:

TIP

Extra-helpful information to help you survive in the real estate jungle.

WARNING

A heads-up about potential problems and pitfalls in your path.

REMEMBER

Reminders of important information that you don't want to lose sight of in your home hunt or purchasing pursuit.

TECHNICAL STUFF

Definitions of terms, technical information, and stuff that you don't necessarily need to know but may want to anyway.

Where to Go from Here

We introduce you to some of the key people who can help you navigate the purchase and sale process in Chapter 2. After you've made your decision to buy or sell a home, make them the next stop on your journey. We discuss the basics here, so now you're ready to put that knowledge to work and find the home of your dreams! We won't be far away, of course, if you have questions or need to refresh your memory of things you might have forgotten in the excitement! Or, if you're not sure where to start, peruse the Table of Contents or index to find a topic that piques your interest.

You can also find a tonne of information online about buying and selling a home that will help keep you informed as you consider your options. In addition, check out www.dummies.com and search for "Buying & Selling a Home For Canadians" for a handy Cheat Sheet with lots of helpful information you can reference as needed. With so many things to remember along the way, it's sure to be a handy reference for you.

Of course, your final destination is a home of your own. When you reach it, we hope you enjoy it. And when it's time to move on, may the next one be even better!

1

Getting Started Buying and Selling a Home

Get a handle on the big picture of buying and selling a home, get oriented to the adventure that lies ahead as you scout properties, and then find a buyer when you're ready to move on.

Find a good team backing you up and locate a real estate agent, appraiser, and lawyer that fits your needs.

Examine the pros and cons of selling your house without the use of an agent.

Chapter **1**

Buying and Selling a Home: Just the Basics

Any deal involving a home, whether it's buying or selling, is usually a milestone moment in your life. It can be a step into adulthood, the moment you finally move out of our parents' basement, or perhaps a new phase of your career. People often trade up in the size of their home when they change jobs or have children, and they often trade down to a smaller home when their kids leave and retirement beckons. Some people are nomads or serial renovators and buy several homes over a lifetime; others are small-time investors, trading in homes like other people trade stocks.

This chapter gives you a taste of what's to come and helps you navigate the wealth of information we have to offer. Consider it your jumping-off point into the world of buying and selling a home. We introduce you to the key players in the game of residential real estate and the steps in the process. We also raise some of the key questions you'll want to ask yourself when you're thinking about buying a home or selling the one you have.

Knowing the Cast of Characters When Buying or Selling

Buying a home may not involve a cast of thousands, but it's not a solo adventure, either. Several key figures are involved in helping you do the deal, and many of the same people also help you sell your property. Even though you're the one making the decisions, you can count on guidance from experts in the areas of finance, law, and, of course, real estate.

Recognizing who's important when buying

The obvious goal when you're buying a home is finding a property that provides you with the amenities that meet your present and future needs at a price that meets your affordability criteria. You want a peach of a deal, not a lemon. That's where it pays having these people on your side who know how to find what you're looking for, making your money go further, and giving you peace of mind that your purchase is free of defects and won't need immediate expensive repairs.

The real estate agent

The *real estate agent*, also known by the trademarked term Realtor, is a professional with an intimate knowledge of the market and the types of homes available in a certain market. Working with a knowledgeable agent can mean the difference between a short search and a good deal or a long process that ends up being more trouble than it's worth. We discuss the role of the real estate agent and how to find a good one in Chapter 2.

The lender

Most people require financial help to buy a home. That help usually comes in the form of a loan, known as a *mortgage*. Having a *lender* who can provide you with a mortgage that suits your needs is important. Whether you work with a bank, credit union, or mortgage broker, securing a mortgage will be critical to your getting the kind of house you want at a price you can afford. We discuss your options for mortgages, including which source is right for you in Chapter 5.

The appraiser

Most people won't deal directly with an appraiser when they're buying a home, but appraisers are the folks who confirm that the price you're paying is the one you should be paying. The *appraiser* assesses the fair market value of properties, helping you size up the kind of offer you should make and, more important, letting the lender know whether the home is worth the mortgage you're asking for. Chapter 2 focuses on the role of the appraiser.

The property inspector

The *property inspector* is a key to avoiding trouble when buying a home. You may think the home has no issues, but the property inspector may tell quite a different story. That could be the difference between saving a few thousand on the purchase price and paying out tens of thousands on repairs. We discuss property inspections in Chapter 10.

The lawyer

Because a home purchase involves a legally binding contract, you'll want to have a lawyer review it. A *lawyer* — or in some provinces, a notary — will also handle *conveyancing*, ensuring the documents documenting the transfer of title into your name are in good order. A lawyer focused on real estate will ensure the property you're buying meets the legal description and is free of liens or encumbrances. The lawyer will also help protect you from real estate fraudsters (alas, they exist). Chapter 2 examines the role of a lawyer when buying a home.

Identifying who's essential when selling

Many of the same experts who assist home buyers in purchasing a home (the possible exception is a lender) also assist home sellers. The experts will represent the property in the best possible light to attract the best offers, enabling the seller to pocket some or reinvest the proceeds in their next dream home. Here are the important people:

The real estate agent

A real estate agent can help take a load off your mind by handling the transaction for you. The agent's role includes making sure that potential buyers know that your house is for sale, coordinating viewings, and generally making sure you can focus on preparing for the move. The professional assistance a real estate agent offers will help you achieve the best possible market value for the home in the shortest period of time. Chapter 2 looks closer at the agent's role when selling your property.

The home stager

You may think your home looks awesome, but those mauve curtains aren't everyone's cup of tea. A *home stager* will prep your home for sale, making it look like something from a TV show, helping it live up to the listing description (and price).

Even though a home doesn't need to be staged or furnished with the latest styles to sell, a home stager can help it command a higher price than it would otherwise. We discuss home stagers in Chapter 15.

The appraiser

The appraiser also plays a critical role when selling, because an appraiser's specialty is in determining the property's fair market value. An appraisal will help you establish a fair list price for the property and provide documentation that validates the suggested list price. The appraiser can also let you know about market factors that will help you position the property for sale. We discuss the appraiser's role in selling a home in Chapter 14.

The lawyer

The lawyer, even more than the real estate agent, is critical when selling a home. The lawyer handles conveyancing documents including discharge of the mortgage. If you're selling your home yourself, without a real estate agent's help, a lawyer can review the contract documents and ensure that you haven't exposed yourself to future claims or liabilities. Chapter 2 focuses on the lawyer's role when selling your house.

Preparing to Buy a Home

Buying a home can take a few days or a few weeks, but the typical process has a few key steps that remain the same, including arranging financing, finding a property, making an offer, and closing the deal. These sections look closer at these processes.

Arranging financing

How much home you can afford depends on how much cash you have for a down payment and how large a mortgage you can obtain. Knowing how much you can put towards a down payment and multiplying the amount five times will indicate the size of conventional mortgage you'll need.

REMEMBER

For example, a down payment of $100,000 would cover 20 percent of a home bought for $500,000. The corresponding conventional mortgage would be $400,000. However, a variety of other factors may mean the lender only approves you for a mortgage of $300,000. By pre-qualifying for a mortgage, you'll know the price range that will guide your purchasing process. We discuss down payments and preapprovals in Chapter 4.

Finding a home

After you know how much home you can afford, scout the listings to see what's available and where different homes are located. Work with a real estate agent who knows what you're looking for; the agent may be able to give you a head start on your dream home. Chapter 7 discusses the ins and outs of shopping for a home.

Making an offer

Have you found a home you seriously love and that fits your budget? If so, it's time to make an offer. The negotiating process may take a few days, and during this stage you and the seller will hammer out a contract that gets you the home you want at a price that pleases both sides on a timeline that makes everyone happy. We discuss the fine art of making an offer in Chapter 9.

Doing the due diligence

A deal isn't done just because your offer is accepted. There's still plenty of work to do, as we discuss in Chapters 10 and 11. You'll need to make sure that the conditions you've put on the offer are satisfied, including a comprehensive property inspection that doesn't reveal serious issues with the property that may lead you to walk away and obtaining financing. You need to make sure that the property the seller is offering is the property you're getting and that you won't face any headaches afterwards. After you're satisfied that this home is right for you, you can remove the conditions and proceed to close the deal.

Closing the deal

Closing, or completing, the purchase involves a lot of paperwork. Ideally, if your real estate agent, lender, and lawyer are on the same page, it will go smoothly. Sometimes it doesn't, so make sure the closing date isn't the same day as the possession date, let alone the moving date. We discuss what's involved in Chapter 12 and how you can manage the process so that it involves as few hassles as possible.

Considering Some Important Questions to Ask When You're Ready to Buy

Never feel timid about asking questions, because questions lead to a deeper understanding of the process, your obligations, and the obligations of others. Here are some sample questions to consider as you begin your buying journey.

What is this going to cost me?

In addition to the purchase price, a home purchase comes with plenty of additional costs, including closing costs. Your lender will likely factor them in as part of your mortgage qualification process, but knowing what your costs will be will help you understand what loan amount the lender will be prepared to extend to you.

Closing costs include legal fees, sales taxes, property transfer taxes, and various adjustments that can add significantly to the purchase price. Then you have ongoing costs of ownership, including maintenance fees (charged monthly for condo dwellers), property taxes, home insurance, and of course mortgage costs. A smart buyer will also budget for special levies, extraordinary expenses, and other costs, ideally by setting aside a contingency fund.

In short, there's plenty of costs beyond the cost of a home. Know what to expect by reading Chapter 4.

This is the right home, but is this the right neighbourhood?

You're not just buying a home, you're also buying into a community. We discuss neighbourhood priorities and how to size up neighbourhoods in Chapter 7.

TIP

For example, if you have visions of living in a place where everybody knows your name, be sure to talk to the neighbours before you move in. Visit the local park and bike trails and find out what they're like. Do people greet you on the street, or do they wander around with eyes glued to a screen and ear buds blocking out the world?

Perhaps you don't crave social interaction, but you love the amenities a community has to offer. What are the shops, restaurants, and so on like, and does the transportation infrastructure allow you to get around, either by car or public transit? Can you live life on your terms, or will you be caught waiting for a bus that comes every half hour at 40 below? (We've been there, and we don't recommend it.)

Don't forget to factor in the hidden annoyances like the summer music fest that attracts thousands of nonresidents to the local park with music blasting until late at night. What about the regional transit loop at the end of the street with the constant coming and going of diesel buses? Be sure to visit your neighbourhood at all hours to make sure it's a place you want to live.

What kind of changes can I make?

Your house, your rules, right? Sadly, that's not always the case. Sometimes, the structure of the home or site conditions prevent you from making the kinds of changes you want to make. You may want to add a guest suite in the basement, for example, but the reality is that there's not enough headroom for it to be a legal suite. Alternatively, zoning bylaws may prevent you from expanding the home or adding certain uses. Other restrictions may relate to the heritage status of the building, which can seriously hamper your efforts to upgrade the property. Chapter 8 discusses several of the changes you can't make that might be deal-breakers.

How much should I budget for maintenance?

Because every property is different, depending on age and upkeep, we can't answer this question for you. A property inspection will give you some tips that will help you draft a budget, however. The inspection report you receive as part of your due diligence will help you understand the condition of the home you're buying and flag areas of specific concern. You can then begin to budget for the repairs, potentially even asking for a discount off the purchase price if the seller is unwilling to undertake the repairs prior to sale.

The inspection report will guide you in developing a contingency fund you can put towards annual repairs, if not a full-blown renovation or replacement of key items such as the roof, windows, heating systems, and so forth. We discuss the cost of various renovations in Chapter 8, but individual circumstances will vary as will labour costs.

What's my exit strategy?

Thinking about leaving your home before you've even bought it may seem premature. However, nothing lasts forever, so consider how and when you might like to eventually sell your place. Knowing how long you plan to be somewhere, or under what circumstances you'd consider moving, can help you determine how to structure your financing and may allow you to settle for a starter home if you're planning on moving after three or five years.

Although a home can be a shelter from the storms of the world, some people keep trying to pay a mortgage long after economic shocks strike. Being ready to sell can help you avoid default if, for example, you lose your job and can no longer pay your mortgage. It sometimes pays to cut your losses rather than get so far into arrears that you lose all the equity you built in your home. We discuss the various factors you should take into account when determining the right time to sell in Chapter 13.

Knowing What Happens When You Sell

Selling a home is the flip side of the process of buying a home. If you're moving to a new home, you'll quickly discover just how different the process is. You won't prequalify for a mortgage, but you'll have to prepare the home to appeal to buyers. These sections give you a quick overview of the process.

Deciding to sell

Several factors play into the decision to sell, as we discuss in Chapter 13. Sometimes you have no choice, as when you change jobs, your family grows, or your financial circumstances change. The decision may be sudden or you may have thought it out. Regardless, after you make the decision to sell, the sales process begins.

Preparing the home

Preparing your home for sale involves two related activities:

>> You need to prepare to move, in which case it pays to read up in Chapter 12 on decluttering your home and packing only what you need.

>> You want to give the home a makeover, addressing any problems and making the cosmetic changes that will boost its curb appeal. This may include minor landscaping, a paint job, and of course a general cleaning. Chapter 15 offers plenty of tips on how to make your house shine.

Listing the home

Whether you're working with an agent or selling the home yourself, you'll need to make sure it gets in front of the right people. A real estate agent has the experience needed to develop a listing that brings in the right buyers, though you can also use sites that allow you to post your own ad. In some cases, an agent will promote your property in exchange for a finder's fee. We discuss the various options available for listing a property in Chapter 16.

Negotiating the sale contract

When a buyer decides your property meets her needs, she'll submit an offer. As the seller, you can present a counteroffer that includes your terms for the sale. Or you may accept or reject the buyer's offer outright. You can also specify a timeline for the sale that meets your needs as part of the negotiating process. Because you're selling the home, the onus is on the buyer to get you to part with it (unless, of course, you're a motivated seller). We discuss the negotiating tricks in Chapter 18.

Closing the deal

After you and the buyer have hammered out the sale contract to your mutual satisfaction, and all the conditions of sale have been removed, the stage is set for closing. The buyer will typically have more to do than you at this point, but as the seller you'll have to pay the listing agent a commission for the hard work she's put in to selling the property.

You'll also have various fees associated with the discharge of the mortgage and the paperwork required to complete the transaction. The story's not over till these fees are paid, and you've received the net proceeds from the sale. After they're in hand, you can move onto your next home purchase or whatever the future holds.

Answering Some Questions You May Have When Selling

"Why are you selling?" is among the most common questions people get asked when a For Sale sign appears on their property. But it also pays to ask yourself these questions to make sure you're confident that you're making the right decision.

Does this home meet my needs?

Sometimes you just need to purge years of stuff to realize that you haven't outgrown your home. Taking a close look at how you're using your house (or condo) and making some simple changes can convince you a move is unnecessary. Other times, a growing family or a progressive disease such as multiple sclerosis or Parkinson's requires people to consider an alternative living situation. You may want a larger home or one with rooms all on one level with universal design features that make it safe for you to age in place. Perhaps the kids have moved out and you're left with more home than you need, and the accumulated equity will be put to better use elsewhere.

Determining whether or not a house meets your needs, a question we discuss in Chapter 13, will be key to deciding whether or not it's time to sell and whether there's a better option available.

Will moving be more trouble than it's worth?

When the time comes to pack, many people are overwhelmed. Or, perhaps the commission they'll have to pay an agent is daunting. Alternatively, a penalty may be owing for early discharge of the mortgage. Really, is it all worth it?

The questions all factor into the decision to sell, something we discuss in Chapter 13, but being able to pin down some of the answers can help you understand if selling really is worthwhile or just a lot of trouble. If you're selling to move to a more manageable home, one that suits your lifestyle, or one that will allow you to continue building equity, then no, the move won't be too much trouble (in retrospect, anyway).

How much will this cost me?

Between commissions, home staging, and mortgage costs, not to mention moving to a new home, selling a home is a considerable expense. We discuss the price of selling in Chapter 14, but don't forget that the proceeds from the sale will likely cover them.

REMEMBER

The final payment you receive when the dust settles will be net of most of those expenses, meaning that the costs won't hurt you as much as if you paid them straight out of your pocket. Focus on maximizing the proceeds and putting them towards what the future holds.

Are last-minute renovations worth the cost?

Will that $10,000 renovation add $20,000 to the sale price of your home? It all depends on where you're spending it, and whether or not it's making up for a major deficiency. Some renovations may be perceived as window dressing, whereas others amount to, ahem, deferred maintenance.

Buyers expect your property will be in good condition, meaning just a few renovations have the wow factor that add significant value to a property. A renovation worth doing is one worth enjoying well before it comes time to sell. Chapter 8 includes a table of common renovations and the value they add to a resale property.

What are the chances I'll be homeless if I sell?

You won't end up sleeping rough if you sell your home. Most sales contracts can include a clause that makes the sale contingent on the seller finding a new home or providing for a closing date that coincides with a new purchase.

TIP

In a worst-case scenario, arrange for temporary accommodation while you're waiting to take possession of your new home. Alternatively, you can obtain *bridge financing* (a short-term loan designed for temporary financing needs) to enable you to buy a new home before the proceeds from the old one's sale become available. Both options are extra expenses you may not want, but getting the short-term bridge financing is probably better than sleeping in the local park. We discuss the various contingency plans in Chapters 12 and 13.

Chapter **2**

Introducing the Key Players

Whether you're buying or selling your first home, moving to a new city or downsizing, more than likely you have plenty of questions. (That's one of the reasons you've picked up this book, right?) The good news is that lots of experienced people besides us can help you. Many of them are the people you'll need to complete the big deal.

This chapter introduces you to many of the common professionals needed to guide you through the purchase and sale of your home. Picking a good team can pay off, so don't be afraid to ask a lot of questions and shop around until you find people who can relate to you and help ease your nerves. Some of the key players on your home-buying team include

>> A real estate agent

>> An appraiser

>> A lawyer

A fourth key member of your team is, above all, your lender. A home is one of the biggest purchases you'll ever make, and you'll need someone to keep you on the right financial track. Because financing is such a critical part of the process, we devote Chapters 4 and 5 to the topic, including the selection of a lender.

This chapter discusses the opportunities for representing yourself during the purchase or sale of a home, too. Even though this approach has the potential to save you money, make sure you have your ducks in a row or your goose might be cooked!

Understanding the Real Estate Agent's Role

Lots of real estate agents will want to work with you, so make sure you find one you want to work with when buying or selling your home. You'll rely on your agent for information about the real estate market, both regional and local, and advice about your specific situation. Your agent deals with both buyers and sellers, negotiates for you, and advises you throughout the process. When you pick an agent to work with, make sure that you're a good fit, personality-wise.

The following sections explain the difference between the brokerage and the agent, and help you understand the role each play in your real estate dealings. We also give you tips on finding an agent who will help you achieve your goal, whether it's finding a dream home or selling your old one.

Identifying important agent qualities when buying or selling a house

Buying or selling a house without the right team behind you is a lot like playing hide-and-seek . . . blindfolded. So, when you decide to work with an agent, here are some of the key qualities to look for:

» **Knowledge:** Your agent must be familiar with the neighbourhoods you like and the style and price range of house you are looking for. So, if you want to buy a condo in Toronto, you probably won't want to rely on that agent friend of yours in Ottawa.

» **Experience:** Your agent should be someone who has worked with clients like you before, who knows how to help you buy the house you want for a fair price, and who can anticipate problems before they come up.

» **Time:** Your agent must be willing to spend time to give you the support and direction you need . . . when you need it. If you place a call to your agent and don't hear back within 24 hours (but preferably much less!), you may not get the service you need.

>> **Contacts:** Your agent should have a list of colleagues and advisers to call in when you need financial advice or assistance, legal work, appraisals, and so on.

>> **Ethics:** The relationship you have with your agent is guided by a code of ethics, available online at www.crea.ca/realtor-members/realtor-code/. Reading the code will help you understand what to expect of your agent.

>> **Established broker/office manager:** The managing broker of the office where the agent is based should be a respected and well-connected broker. The broker provides backup to the agent and, if a serious problem arises in the conduct of the sale, can be an indispensable ally for you, too.

>> **Multimedia skills:** Even though your agent may not be the star of a dedicated YouTube channel or have 10,000 followers on Twitter or Instagram, you still want to make sure you're on the same wavelength when it comes to tech smarts. Your agent should be comfortable with online and multimedia marketing tools and familiar with how to use them to find properties that suit you and market your home to potential buyers.

Sorting out the basics to the broker-agent relationship

We know, you thought the relationships in your life were already complicated. Well, the relationships between you, your agent, and the agent's broker can be no less confusing. But help is on the way! In this section, we examine the roles and responsibilities of the agent and the agent's team:

>> **Real estate agent (also sometimes referred to as *salesperson, Realtor representative,* or *sales representative*):** Subcontracted by the broker to work on behalf of the buyer or seller or occasionally both (provided buyer and seller agree; the arrangement is known as dual agency, something we discuss in the next section).

>> **Broker or managing broker/nominee:** Legal agent who works on behalf of the buyer or seller, or both; usually serves as an office manager overseeing daily operations and also reviews all transactions.

When you decide to work with a real estate agent, you're effectively engaging the services of the agent's broker as well, regardless of whether you meet that individual. The broker is the person you can turn to if things go terribly, terribly wrong and your agent can't manage the situation. A skilled broker is able to negotiate bureaucratic roadblocks or procedural questions issues or assist if a transaction spirals into a nasty legal dispute (they're not common, but they happen).

Some real estate agents also have the qualifications to legally call themselves brokers, but they tend to use the more commonly understood term of *agent* or even *representative*. In many provinces, a broker's (or managing broker's) licence requires additional training and testing and a licence designation beyond that of a salesperson. With this extra education, an individual can own a brokerage or run an office (be the *nominee* for the office) and ensure that the salespeople and all the office's trust accounts adhere to the requirements of the provincial Real Estate Act.

REMEMBER

A broker or brokerage company, and by extension a real estate agent, may be a seller's agent or a buyer's agent. In some cases, real estate agents working for the same broker will represent both the seller and the buyer in a deal. Although each party has its own real estate agent, because both agents work for the same broker or legal agent, the situation is referred to as *dual agency*. The agent that you're working with to find a home may show you a property that is listed with her office. If you buy that property, you'll have to agree to enter into a limited dual-agency agreement.

TECHNICAL
STUFF

Another term you'll encounter is *Realtor*. This term is a trademark of the Canadian Real Estate Association (www.crea.ca). Only brokers and real estate agents who are CREA members may use this term to describe themselves professionally. Extensive training and continuing education are required. Realtors are expected to follow a very strict Code of Ethics and Standards of Business Practice, designed to protect *your* best interests.

Understanding the agency relationship

Real estate agents work within a legal relationship called agency, which gives them a mandate to act on their client's behalf. The agency relationship exists between you (the *principal*) and your brokerage, the company under which the individual who is representing you is licensed. The essence of the agency relationship is that the brokerage has the authority to represent you as a buyer or seller in dealings with others. Brokerages and their agents are legally obligated to protect and promote your interest as they would their own.

The rules and regulations governing agency relationships vary a bit from province to province. Ask your local real estate board or your provincial real estate council for specifics. The rules lay down what an agent can do on your behalf and how they relate to other parties to the transaction. Specifically, brokerages and their agents must do the following:

>> Show undivided loyalty by protecting your negotiating position at all times and disclosing all known facts that may affect or influence your decision with respect to the transaction.

>> Obey all lawful instructions you provide.

>> Keep your confidences.

>> Exercise reasonable care and skill in performing all assigned duties.

>> Account for all money and property entrusted to them on your behalf.

Because there are two sides to each real estate deal, the buyer's and the seller's, it's important to know how an agent serves each side. Occasionally, one agent will have dual agency, allowing her to represent both the buyer and the seller. The following sections explain these forms of agency in depth.

Seller's agent

When a real estate agent acts on behalf of a seller (a *seller's agent*), the agent owes full loyalty to the seller and must provide all relevant information and take every action to obtain a sale price and conditions of sale satisfactory to the seller. This means that a buyer won't receive insights into the seller's motivation, which could have some influence on the final sale price. The agent is legally obligated to disclose any comments the buyer may make about their motivation, such as a willingness to bid above the advertised sale price. The agent does have an obligation to potential buyers, where known issues such as a crack in the foundation or a blockage in the sewer line exist. Expect honest, complete answers to your inquiries, but remember, the agent represents the seller, so it's up to you to ask the questions if you want to get those honest, complete answers. If you don't ask direct questions, you won't necessarily get the direct answers you're looking for.

Buyer's agent

Surprise, surprise — a buyer's agent works in the best interests of buyers. Even though your buyer's agent's commission is usually paid out of the seller's proceeds from the sale, her legal and ethical duties are to you. Your buyer's agent should keep your personal and financial information confidential. If the sellers let slip that they're going through a messy divorce and want to sell the house as soon as possible, your buyer's agent will share this information with you. She'll also let you know if she finds out that the sellers are willing to accept a lower price to get the deal done (of course, because both agents receive a commission on the sale, they have a vested interest in the price not being discounted too much). Your buyer's agent will be able to look at comparable properties and advise you on how much is reasonable to offer on the homes you're considering. A buyer's agent negotiates a deal to obtain a sale price and conditions of sale satisfactory to the buyer.

TIP

If you want to purchase a home that is For Sale by Owner, you may have an agent represent you in the purchase. Just because the seller wants to go it alone doesn't mean you have to. You may be responsible for paying the agent a standard fee or a commission (if you can't get the seller to absorb the cost), but having a professional prepare the paperwork, as well as having access to info about comparable properties, may give you huge peace of mind.

Dual agency

If buyer's agent and the seller's agent work for the same broker or brokerage company, this is called dual agency. One company is brokering a deal between two parties, and it legally represents both sides. This situation can open up a number of conflict-of-interest concerns.

To head off any problems, the broker is legally obliged to tell you and the seller that she (or her company) is representing both the buyer and the seller. Ask the broker to explain clearly what the implications are for the sale negotiations. You'll be asked to accept the dual agency situation in writing. If you're unsure what to do, talk to your lawyer or contact your local real estate board for clarification. Although both agents may work out of different offices and not know each other, if they work for the same company, they must also acknowledge in writing that they're in a dual agency situation.

Sometimes, agents can act in a capacity of limited dual agency, which requires the agent to deal with both parties impartially, and prevents the agent from disclosing what either party is prepared to pay or accept or the motivation of either party. The agent is also prohibited from disclosing any personal information about the parties without their written permission.

WARNING

Many provinces have placed significant limits on dual agency because of the potential for a conflict of interest on the part of buyers. Dual agency can be expedient, but it can also leave the buyer (or seller) without a designated advocate in a transaction, which can result in a competitive disadvantage. Be sure to read up on the laws governing dual agency in your province. If in doubt, consult your lawyer.

TIP

Suppose you haven't chosen an agent and you go to an open house and absolutely love the house. What should you do? Remember that the agent holding the open house works for the seller. If you're confident that the agent can fairly represent you, you can ask her to represent you and enter into a limited dual agency agreement. However, if you aren't comfortable with the agent or the concept of a dual agency relationship, we suggest you interview agents and choose one to represent you as the buyer. You don't have to work with the agent holding the open house unless you want to.

Discovering the perfect agent

Picking the perfect real estate agent is partially luck and partially knowing what to look for. If you aren't sure who would be the right real estate agent for you, ask around. Find out who your family members, neighbours, co-workers, and friends know and trust and ask for that agent's name. If you're relocating for work, your employer or the local branch of your favourite bank may be able to recommend some candidates.

Speaking to a head broker at a major real estate company may be extremely helpful. Even if you're moving across the country, chances are the broker will have a list of contacts for agents working in particular areas, as well as agents who deal with particular types of properties. Search online too; www.realtor.ca is an excellent site that is linked to all real estate boards across Canada and can help you get a feel for local shopping, schools, transportation, and amenities offered in different neighbourhoods anywhere in the country. Through this site, you may also find an agent active in an area you want to check out, contact and interview.

If you live close to the neighbourhood that you're scouting, a casual drive may reveal the signs of agents who work in the area and are selling the type of property you're interested in buying. If you find some open houses, stop and take the opportunity to meet the agents. The same holds true if you're looking for an agent to sell your home: Look around the neighbourhood and see who is the most active. Look for agents who are familiar with the type of property you want or have. For example, if you live in a high-rise condo, see which agents are familiar with the building. Many will trumpet their latest sales with mass mailings in the hope of securing sellers just like you.

Any brokerage or agent worth their salt these days has their own web presence, such as a website and LinkedIn page, which can be a great way to find someone who specializes in the area where you hope to buy or who is familiar with the kind of property that interests you. Most agents' sites provide the agent's bio (outlining her real estate specialties), videos and images of properties she is currently representing, and information about recent sales so you can see if she has sold the types of property you want to buy. In addition to listings, these sites often feature helpful information on moving, financing, and what to look for when considering moving to a new neighbourhood in which you're interested.

After you have the names of a few agents, arrange to meet with them. Ask each of them to bring a record of all the houses they've listed and sold in the past year. This way, you can verify what kind of homes, neighbourhoods, and price ranges are most familiar to each agent. You'll also figure out quickly whether you get along with the agent. Remember that an agent with good people skills will not only be nicer to work with but also represent you well to sellers and be an effective negotiator when the time comes to make an offer.

REMEMBER

Even the coolest-looking, most impressive website shouldn't be used as a replacement for real contact with your potential agent. Meet with agents to know if they have the right personality to work with you and to make sure they understand exactly what you want. Although email and text are great ways to find out some basic information, you can find out a lot about a person through a short face-to-face interview, either in-person or via a videoconferencing app.

Sizing up the candidates

When choosing a real estate agent, look for someone who will work hard for you and who exhibits a high level of customer service and professionalism. Someone who asks questions to clarify what you need and what you want is kilometres ahead of someone who tries to *tell* you the same information. The best agent will be curious about you, your family, your finances, and your future plans. Your agent should respect your time and independence; a good agent will provide you with all the information you need and give you room to make your own decisions. The best client-agent relationship happens when both sides have similar temperaments in terms of enthusiasm, sense of humour, and energy level.

The best real estate agents score high on this list of qualities. Keep them in mind when you're asking more targeted questions during your interview. Your agent should do the following:

Be a full-time professional

Scouting properties for buyers and finding the right match takes time. A real estate agent who takes the job seriously will be more likely to do the research needed to understand market conditions and the specific needs and aspirations of their clients, whether they're scouting properties or looking to sell one.

When you sell a property, you hand over a sizeable amount of money to your real estate agent — probably anywhere between 2.5 and 6 percent of the price and up to 10 percent on small recreational properties, so you want to make sure you're getting good value for that money. A good agent earns a commission by giving you good advice, promoting and marketing your property, skillfully closing the deal, and taking care of the details.

Have a good track record

Ask the agent how many years she's been working as a real estate agent. Ask for references — get the names and numbers of at least three people whose homes she's worked with in the past year or two. Call the references the agent provides. If the people you speak to have mixed feelings about how the agent handled their purchase or sale, find out what went wrong and how, looking back, they would have prevented it. Hindsight is always 20/20.

Make selling your home a priority

Be alert to signs that the real estate agent won't have time to personally work on marketing your house. Some top-selling agents just have too many listings to take care of your property personally. Their assistants take care of the legwork, attend open houses, and schedule showings. You don't want to find out partway through the process that the agent you so carefully selected has delegated your listing to an assistant. By the same token, an agent in demand is probably a good one.

Similarly, you don't want to list your house with an agent whom you'll never see again until the listing is ready to expire and she swings by to renew the contract. If an agent is planning an extended vacation in the near future, don't use that agent. Sometimes selling your house takes longer than you think it will, even when the price is right. For all the work you're doing to keep your property looking its best, you don't want to let buyers slip through your fingers while your agent is cavorting with the locals in Bora Bora.

Be enthusiastic about the prospect of working with you

If your agent isn't excited about finding you your dream home or uncovering the right buyer for your home, you're not going to happy. You may end up coming in second if there's a bidding war or selling for less than you could have simply because your agent couldn't be bothered.

Be local

If you're looking for a starter home in the suburbs, the best real estate agent in the neighbouring city isn't the right choice for you. You want an agent who works full time in your area. When you're looking to sell, your agent's networking and connections are valuable marketing tools that can make sure you obtain widest and deepest interest in your property. The more local people your agent works with, the better the grasp of what's available in the market and the larger the pool of potential buyers for your home.

Deals in houses like yours

The agent who specializes in exclusive real estate likely won't be the most suitable agent to sell your modest home. Hire an agent who lists and *sells* lots of homes in your market segment — someone who's constantly working with people in the market for the home you want or the kind of home you're trying to sell. They'll be able to match you with properties or identify the buyers who will be most interested in a home like yours.

Have specific ideas for marketing your home

An experienced agent will likely know how she plans to market your home from the moment she pulls up. A smart agent will likely have researched the local market and be prepared to discuss how current conditions fit in with your goals. You can even request a written marketing plan from each of the real estate agents you interview. The marketing plan should include the listing price for your home, a list of comparable properties on the market, recommendations for making your home more marketable, plans to advertise and promote the property, and details on how the agent intends to manage open houses. Make sure you ask important questions about whether she plans a virtual tour, will she include professional floor plans and pictures, and does she plan to help with staging?

Charge a reasonable commission rate

When you're preparing to sell your home, find out what commission the agent charges on a sale. Is it in keeping with the range other agents have quoted? A range of commissions is charged across the country, and commissions are calculated differently in different areas and by different companies. For example, in Toronto, a seller may pay a 4 to 6 percent commission. By comparison, in Vancouver, many companies charge a 7 percent commission on the first $100,000 of a sale and 2.5 percent on the balance. Some discount companies work for a flat-fee commission ($5,000 or $10,000) or a flat percentage (as low as 1 or 2 percent).

Although the market for most recreational properties is very active, more-remote properties have traditionally been more difficult to sell than conventional, more-accessible properties, so commissions may be as high as 10 percent of the sale price for that remote cabin in the woods with water or float plane–access only.

WARNING

Be certain that you understand what you're getting in return for the commission you'll pay upon the sale of your home. If you're paying a low commission, for example, will you have to pay for the marketing activities, which can even include having to pay for the sign that goes up on your front lawn? Will you have to host your own showings and open houses? You may be required to provide all the room measurements for the listing, manage staging of the home, and other responsibilities agent's often handle on your behalf.

What you thought was going to save you money can cost you extra in out-of-pocket expenses, and you may not receive the regular feedback, contact, and advice that you'd get from a full-service agent.

Sometimes a company quotes a low commission to secure a listing, and after the house has been on the market for a month or so, recommends that you pay a higher commission for more services. Suddenly the commission looks pretty much like all the other quotes you found. Also make sure that the commission quoted allows for a commission to be paid to a buyer's agent. Make sure the total commission quoted is all you'll be paying . . . you don't want any surprises.

Inform you how she handles holdover clauses as they apply to commission

In some rare cases, you may still owe your agent the commission even if your home doesn't sell while you have it listed with her agency. Your agent can use a *holdover clause* to claim a commission even if your home's sale happens after the listing expires. An average holdover period may last 60 to 90 days from the expiration of the contract. Occasionally, a buyer who made an unacceptable offer on your house while it was listed may approach you again after the listing has expired, this time with an acceptable offer. Depending on the timing of the offer and the wording of the listing contract, you may still have to pay your agent the commission. Check the fine print of the listing contract to see if it includes a holdover period, and ask your agent if her company has ever enforced the holdover period.

If a real estate agent doesn't negotiate a fair and equitable commission for herself, will she negotiate a good price for your house when dealing with buyers? If you're looking for a good deal overall, the commission may not be the best place to cut corners. Like everything in life, you get what you pay for, so make sure you compare the value of the services offered versus the commission rate charged by the agency and you're getting a satisfactory level of service in relation to the commission structure being charged.

Quote a reasonable listing price for your home

Beware of agents who suggest a list price that significantly exceeds what other agents suggest. Is she trying to win your listing by suggesting she knows buyers willing to pay more? When you interview potential listing agents, ask them what price they think they'd assign to your house and how they determined this price. You'll quickly sense how knowledgeable the agent is about houses in your neighbourhood as well as the real estate market in your price range. Look at Chapter 14 to find out how you can get a pretty good idea of what's reasonable . . . and why pricing your home too high initially is a big mistake.

Stay in touch

Nothing is worse than feeling as if you don't matter or count, so you want to deal with an agent who responds to your calls, texts, or emails in a timely manner. Although everyone's expectations are different, be reasonable; don't expect your agent to answer your 11:30 p.m. phone call — she needs to sleep, too! Depending on the urgency of the issue, you'll want a response within a couple of hours at the most or within the day. Ideally, your agent should be responsive and stay one step ahead of you, meaning she'll call you and you won't need to call her!

INTERVIEWING THE AGENT'S CLIENTS

Some agents have a list of clients you can talk with to help you feel confident that the agent will meet your needs. Here are some questions to help guide your conversation, whether you're buying or selling:

- Did the agent show you what you were looking for? Were the choices in the right price range, with the right features, and in the right neighbourhood?

- Did the agent act with honesty and integrity when asking for or providing you with information? Were you told what information would be confidential and what the agent needed to disclose?

- Did the agent work to your schedule and have time for all your questions? Did she take time to take you to showings? Did the agent return your calls promptly with helpful answers?

- Was the agent able to explain things in simple terms for you, or did she use legal-ese and jargon that went over your head?

- Did the agent treat sellers with respect and good manners if you were present during showings?

- Do you feel the agent advised you well on writing the contract and determining time frames?

- Do you feel the agent negotiated a good deal for you?

- Will you call the agent again when you're ready to sell your home?

- Is there anything else I should know about this agent or the brokerage?

Making your agent work for you

Explain your home-buying requirements to your agent. Bring along your list of household and neighbourhood priorities (see Chapter 7). When the agent knows your needs, tastes, and budget, the fun really starts — you go on tour. Your agent will show you various homes and neighbourhoods and arrange viewings until you've found one you want. At the same time, your agent may help you remove some blinders that you don't realize you have on by expanding your horizons into other neighbourhoods or even styles of homes. When you're ready, your agent will present your offer to the sellers. Your real estate agent will help you negotiate the sale terms and conditions and then firm up the deal for you.

To facilitate the sale process, your agent should be able to provide referrals (if you need them) to other professionals, including real estate lawyers (or notaries), appraisers, financial advisers, lenders, contractors, and inspectors. (She should refer you to a couple of each, so that you have a couple of options rather than just her favourites — this avoids any real or perceived conflict of interest.) Take the opportunity to interview these professionals until you feel comfortable you have the right people in place.

A good agent will be adaptable and creative in order to meet your needs. If you can't visit a house in person, you may be able to arrange for an online tour. If you're planning a cross-country move, your agent may be able to provide a video tour of some homes that will suit your needs.

When selling your home, an agent should demonstrate a solid grasp of the local market and be familiar with the type of home you're trying to sell. An agent who's able to quote a reasonable listing price and provide the rationale for it is a good start. The agent should be well connected and comfortable with the various tools for marketing a property, including dynamic photography and virtual tours. The agent should also be responsive, not only to your needs but those of potential buyers. You don't want someone who's going to ignore incoming calls, texts, and emails (and if they're at all interested in the commission you're going to pay them, they shouldn't be ignoring those calls). Most of all, you want someone who has your interests at heart and will honestly and firmly represent you to the buyer as well as advise you on how to best position the property in a given market.

TIP

Unless you're looking in two vastly different areas, we recommend working with one agent only. Most agents have access to the Multiple Listing Service (MLS) as well as other tools, so if you're using more than one agent and both are familiar with your goals, you'll likely be referred many of the same properties by both agents. Pick the agent that you feel you can trust and has the time to work with you, as opposed to casting a wide net and using many agents. Your loyalty to the one agent will be rewarded by her faithfulness to you.

Reading the signs: Be on the lookout for poor agents

Most real estate agents are hard-working, responsible professionals who do everything they can on your behalf. If your agent doesn't fall into this category, you'll probably notice it on your own pretty quickly. Just in case, and with your interests at heart, we've compiled this handy list of warning signs that point to underperforming agents:

>> They never point out any problems with the houses they show you. In fact, they stand around playing games on their smartphones while you do all the snooping.

>> They swear up and down that the foundation isn't crumbling, even though your two-year-old has kicked in the corner.

>> They show you only houses that are being listed by their company, and when you ask to see other listings, they're uncooperative.

>> They show you only mansions when you're in the market for a semi-detached.

>> They make you feel pressured or bullied or, even worse, foolish.

>> They can't answer basic questions about construction or mechanical systems.

If your real estate agent is (a) too busy, (b) too pushy, or (c) too clueless, end the relationship!

REMEMBER

You're in the driver's seat — your agent is supposed to be guiding you into a great deal, not over the edge of a cliff. If you signed a *brochure* (an acknowledgement of the buyer–agency relationship, not a contract), it doesn't bind you to that agent. Call the local and provincial real estate boards for advice on your particular situation. Don't sign any documentation without having your real estate lawyer review it first. Remember that all documents signed have legal implications.

Most provinces require that you have a signed buyer's or seller's agreement, with the core clauses governed by provincial legislation. However, you may negotiate additional clauses if desired. If you signed a buyer's contract with the agent that stipulates you'll pay the agent a finder's fee if she finds you a house (as opposed to the usual sharing of the commission paid by the seller), make sure the contract has a termination date or a release clause if you want to terminate that agreement.

Don't commit to anything you don't feel comfortable with. Whether you're looking to buy or sell a house, you want the process to be as pleasant and as hassle-free as possible.

Choosing to Go It Alone

Whether buying or selling a home, if you decide to fly solo and do business without a real estate agent, your greatest asset is recognizing what you know and what you don't — in other words, what you can do and what you should delegate.

Realize that private real estate transactions are an extreme sport; if selling a property was as easy as slapping a For Sale sign out front and calling it a day, everyone would be his own real estate agent! Even though buying a home can sound simple, having someone advocating for you and knowing how to create a transaction that is a win-win for buyer and seller is important.

On the sale side, you'll have plenty to do between answering the phone, scheduling appointments, verifying potential buyers' identities, confirming their qualifications with financial institutions, and showing off your home, not to mention maintaining a perfectly groomed house and lawn (despite the children, pets, and general mayhem).

WARNING

Selling your home yourself is a time-intensive undertaking, especially if you're also trying to hold down a full-time job. And the stakes are high: Selling your home is a business transaction and a legal transaction — involving your largest single investment. When marketing your home, negotiating with sellers, and dealing with contracts, you have to make a lot of decisions and do a lot of work that most people rely on their agents to do.

We want you to be realistic and prepared to deal with all the complexities of making a private sale. In this section, we help you determine your limits so that you know which aspects of home selling you can handle and when an agent can step in to help.

Saving the commission

The big reason people like the idea of selling their homes privately is the anticipated cost savings. By selling privately, you don't pay a *commission* (the percentage of the sale amount that goes to the agent who made the sale). In some major urban centres in Canada, house prices have risen dramatically. This means that a typical commission is in the tens of thousands of dollars. Homeowners elect for "sale by owner" to avoid paying this large amount of money to an agent, plus the GST/HST. (For details on commissions, see Chapter 15.)

Make sure your lawyer reviews the offer and works with you through the transaction. When selling a property yourself, it's not uncommon for real estate agents to contact you to see if you'd be willing to pay them a referral fee if they find a buyer for you. However, you'd need to ensure that the buyer is aware that you're paying a referral fee to the agent facilitating the deal.

REMEMBER

If you want to sell your home yourself to save commission on the sale, it'll take hard work to ready the home for sale, to be knowledgeable about the market, and to have a comfort level with negotiating with professionals. Never sign off on a sale agreement until your lawyer has read it and advised you of any conditions or terms that you need to be aware of that could potentially cost you money — or the deal itself.

Working out the costs of selling it yourself

You're probably visualizing what you can do with all that commission money you save by selling your home yourself. Well, take those dollar signs out of your eyes! Here are the expensive and troublesome realities you face if you plan to sell your home privately:

TIP

>> **You may have to lower the asking price for your home.** If a buyer is considering two similar properties with the same asking price, one being sold by you, the owner, and the other by an agent, you may have to lower your price to offset the expertise and support provided by the agent.

>> **You incur the cost and hassle of advertising your home.** You'll have to actually sell your house before you can cash in on your saved commission. If you opt to engage a flat-rate brokerage to list your home on MLS, you're responsible for all measurements of the property and the home, and for all intents and purposes, you'll handle everything — including fielding phone calls, making appointments, taking pictures, and negotiating the sale of the property.

Some agents offer *à la carte* services; for example, you may have the agent handle phone calls and booking appointments, but you handle all showings. Similarly, an agent may now allow you to list the property via their account on the MLS. The agent charges a flat fee for the listing, but the seller handles all responsibilities in regard to the sale.

You can also choose to post your home's listing on several "For Sale by Owner" sites for a fee. The trick is to make sure you end up at the site with the most online traffic. You'll also have to try to keep track of what similar homes are selling for in your area; make sure you can keep track of selling prices on any websites you choose.

>> **You're responsible for researching and accurately determining the right price for your home.** Pricing your home is very important. If you hire an appraiser to assess the current market value of your home, expect to pay between $200 and $500 for this service.

>> **You have to make time in your schedule.** Selling your house on your own isn't going to fit neatly into a schedule. You must be very accessible — by phone (voice or text) and email — if you're going to sell your home privately. Expect prospective buyers to knock at your door at all times of the day and night . . . regardless of how large the words "By Appointment Only" appear on the For Sale sign in front of your house. You'll have to accommodate the needs of prospective buyers' schedules in order to show the home, and if you have a family, you also face juggling their schedules. When you sell privately, you don't have the luxury of a real estate agent who organizes and administrates the showings of your home.

>> **You need a clear understanding of all the legalities involved in selling a home.** You may not be aware of special legal considerations when selling your home, and you can risk the buyer holding you liable. An experienced agent is on the lookout for any possible legal issues; after all, her commission and her reputation are at stake if something goes wrong with the sale of your home. And if she by chance overlooks a legality, she has errors and omissions insurance to cover her — you don't! (See the section, "Understanding the Real Estate Agent's Role," earlier in this chapter regarding an agent's roles and responsibilities.)

>> **You need to keep a clear head.** Emotions may cloud your judgment. You need to be professional and objective during negotiations with your buyer. Your personal attachment to the property may prevent you from being an effective negotiator. If you don't have experience at a bargaining table, you're probably not the best person to haggle with a potential buyer's experienced and well-informed real estate agent.

>> **You need to be ready for real estate agents who will see your "private sale" advertisements and call you.** Like any ambitious business people, real estate agents look to expand their businesses, and they're in touch with the market. When your house appears available, agents will solicit you, hoping that you're tired of dealing with the headaches of trying to sell your home yourself and will hire them instead.

REMEMBER

Your goal is to sell your house and get on with your life. If you're determined to sell your home yourself, be honest about what you do know and what you don't know and be realistic about what you can do and what you can't do. Do your research and hire the necessary experts.

Getting some help

Selling a home is a lot of hard work, which is why many professional agents make a full-time job out of selling homes. If you're feeling a bit overwhelmed by your decision to go alone and think you may need help after all, you don't necessarily have to go for the total range of services offered by a real estate agent — and the fees that go with it. Some companies offer different packages, each with a different level of service, depending on how much help you want.

In Chapter 16, we discuss the MLS, which is a great tool for selling your home. Although only licensed agents can list properties on the website, a licensed agent will list your home on the site for a discounted price. As part of this arrangement, some agents will also provide exposure alongside their own listings and signal their involvement via lawn signs.

TIP

Don't forget about the websites made specifically for private sellers to list their properties. They may not have as many listings as MLS, but they'll help you get the word out. Several are online; just search for "private real estate sale" or "sale by owner"; you'll also get more info about advertising and other issues you may face.

Maybe you're a natural promoter and you've found a buyer all on your own. (Go on, give yourself a pat on the back!) You feel like an immense weight has been lifted, and that the hardest part is now behind you. That is, until you wake up in a cold sweat, thinking about the tonne of paperwork you'll have to take care of (and you were never very enthusiastic about numbers or contracts or those other pesky things). Some companies offer a paperwork-only option, and for a flat fee an agent will take care of the purchase agreement and be sure the transaction goes smoothly right up until closing day. Don't forget that you'll still need a lawyer (or notary) to handle your sale, and you can have the lawyer review your paperwork if you have any questions.

Valuing the Appraisal Process

An *appraisal* is an evaluation of a home's worth, giving you confidence that the price is fair and reasonable. When you pay a professional to appraise a house, you get an unbiased, informed assessment. The appraiser looks at the property and makes an assessment based on the home's size, features, amenities, and condition, as well as recent sales of comparable homes in the neighbourhood. Remember, what determines the value of a home isn't just the home itself, but also what's around it. Being next to a busy rail line close to an industrial park can negatively affect the value of a home, even if the design and finishes have won awards.

Appraisal reports must contain the purpose of the appraisal, the legal description or identification of the property examined, a listing of *encumbrances* (any financial charges owing against the property), and an analysis of the best use of the property.

The most common method of appraisal is the CMA, which is short for *comparative market analysis* (although sometimes it stands for *competitive market analysis* or *current market analysis*). To determine a property's value through a CMA, the appraiser compares the home you're considering buying to other homes in the same neighbourhood that are comparable in size, features, and amenities.

TIP

Be sure the appraiser knows why you need her services. The purpose of the appraisal may have an effect on the amount of time it will take, and therefore the final cost. Appraisals are often done when you're considering refinancing or renegotiating your mortgage, dividing property after a divorce, or for other legal purposes. A home appraisal for litigation purposes will often be more expensive, sometimes thousands of dollars, because the report is more comprehensive and includes more detailed and slightly different material as it may have to be presented in court.

The following sections examine in greater detail what an appraiser does, why you need an appraiser, and how you can find one.

Knowing what an appraiser looks for

The appraiser applies evaluation criteria to the neighbourhood and house, including:

- » **Size, age, and condition of the house:** Does the home need repairs now or in the near future? Have upgrades, refinishing, or renovation work been put into the home recently? (This part of the appraisal tends to focus on kitchens and bathrooms.)

- » **Amenities:** What kind of luxury features does the home possess, such as a pool, wine cellar, hot tub, solarium, in-floor heating, or four-car garage?

- » **Neighbourhood characteristics and immediate surroundings:** What is access to emergency and fire services, like? Are public transit services nearby? Is the home within what's considered a safe neighbourhood?

- » **Special or unique features of the home:** Is it a designated heritage home, or is it situated on a ravine lot with a stunning view?

Appraisers are required to do only a visual inspection, but they may probe further. This means the appraisal process can vary in length, from a quick walk-through to an hours-long inspection. An appraisal is an essential part of proper due diligence.

If you're looking at buying a condo, be aware that an appraiser may not be aware of the status of the condominium corporation, and so he may not take this into account (for more about condominium corporations, refer to Chapter 6). You need to be certain that in purchasing a condo you're also not liable for a significant bill to replace a leaky roof or aging infrastructure such as the elevator or piping. The appraisal process to determine market value may be a good first step in exploring the impact of these exceptional costs, which should also be flagged in a depreciation report or similar document.

REMEMBER

Depending on who orders the appraisal, results can vary. We've seen appraisals differ by tens of thousands of dollars based on the reason for the appraisal. Bank appraisals for mortgage purposes sometimes don't accurately reflect the desirability of the home; for example, they're commonly thought of to be conservative, to protect the bank's risk.

Eyeing who needs an appraiser and why

If you've enlisted the help of an agent to buy a home, you may not need an appraiser because part of your agent's job is to evaluate a property for you and advise you on the best offer to win you the property. Your agent will provide you with a market overview, and then determine where the home you're looking at is situated, price-wise, within the market. With that knowledge, you can go ahead and make an offer to the seller who is within a reasonable range for the value of the home.

On the other hand, if you're considering selling your home, you may want to consult an appraiser for one of these reasons:

>> You may want to know the property's fair market value and how certain improvements may improve it.

>> You may need to know it for tax purposes.

>> If you've purchased it with a partner (in life or business) and that partner is now your ex, you may need to decide whether to sell it or buy out your partner.

If you're buying or selling a home but not using an agent, an appraiser is an excellent resource. As someone who doesn't have an agent to help determine the property's value, but wanting confidence in what constitutes a fair price, an appraiser can size up the property and based on the criteria explain the home's market value and even the potential for adding value to it. If you're super-familiar with the market and totally confident in your ability to gauge its value, then you won't need an appraiser. Most people, however, will need the help.

In most cases, your lender will ask an appraiser to determine the value of a home so the mortgage amount is aligned with the market value of the property. These days, most residential appraisals are generated automatically by sophisticated software that assesses available sales data and the various attributes of a home to determine its value. The resulting appraisal will let the lender know it's able to secure its interest in your mortgage and recover what it loaned you in the event you default on your mortgage obligations and the property has to be sold. An appraisal can also help determine the equity in one home if you're seeking to purchase a second residence for personal or investment use.

TECHNICAL STUFF

Your mortgage lender will probably insist that its appraiser conduct the assessment of the home you're buying, even if you've commissioned your own appraisal before submitting an offer. If so, you have no say in the choice of the appraiser. Don't worry. More than likely the lender's appraiser is both qualified, accredited, and experienced. After all, a financial institution depends on the appraiser's expertise to decide whether to lend out hundreds of thousands of dollars. Bear in mind that if your lender orders the appraisal, you likely won't receive a copy. Ask to see a copy of the appraisal if possible because chances are you'll pay the fee for it. (We discuss appraisal fees in the section, "Knowing how much you can expect to pay," later in this chapter.)

Recognizing a good appraiser

Chances are good that you won't have to choose your appraiser — if you're a buyer, your lender will probably handle that for you. If the responsibility does fall to you, make your choice based on more than just the appraiser's web appeal. Consult your lender to see who it recommends. On the other hand, if you're selling your property and need an appraisal to accurately determine its market value, you may need some tips.

Certification is what you look for in an appraiser, plain and simple. An independent appraiser should have an AACI (Accredited Appraiser Canadian Institute) or CRA (Canadian Residential Appraiser) designation, both of which are trademarked and awarded by the Appraisal Institute of Canada (www.aicanada.ca). Make sure you ask to see your appraiser's credentials.

Reputation is also key. If you do need to hire an appraiser, work with someone you can trust. Ask any friends who've bought homes recently for their suggestions, or contact the Appraisal Institute of Canada for a list of professional appraisers in your area. The institute's website also has a Find an Appraiser feature that has two different search options:

>> If you need an appraiser but have no idea where to start or who to look for, never fear. Simply enter the criteria for your specific situation; for example: Canmore, Alberta, Single Family Rural, and Appraisal Review. When you submit the information, you'll be provided with a list of accredited appraisers in that area who best fit your needs. You'll also get all the necessary contact information, including phone numbers, email addresses, and websites, if they have one.

>> If you've been given the name of a top-notch appraiser (your great-aunt's neighbour's babysitter says she's fabulous) but you're not sure how to contact her, just enter the last name of the appraiser into the search box. If she's in the database, you'll get that much-sought-after contact info.

REMEMBER

An appraiser isn't a property inspector. An appraiser focuses on value, whereas a property inspector assesses the condition of a property with a view to making sure it's in good working condition and fit for occupancy. An appraiser can tell you the value of a property, but that value can change if the property inspection uncovers issues such as a cracked foundation or deteriorated piping or wiring that looks like wool the cat played with. This isn't to say an in-person inspection will be super-ficial, but the appraiser has a different objective than a property inspector. Refer to Chapter 10 where we discuss property inspectors in greater detail.

Knowing how much you can expect to pay

The price of an appraisal varies depending on how difficult a job it is for the appraiser. If there have been many recent sales in the neighbourhood and the home doesn't have scores of out-of-the-ordinary features, the assessment will be straightforward and cheaper. You can expect to pay anywhere from $200 to $500 for an appraiser's services.

TIP

If you're buying a property, you may be able to work out an agreement with your lender to pay the appraisal cost. Remember the old saying, "if you don't ask you won't receive"? Many lenders do cover the appraisal cost or have a list of approved appraisers that they frequently use and trust. After all, the lender wants to reduce its potential financial risk by being satisfied the property is worth more than the mortgage requested. Even though some lenders will waive the appraisal fee to secure a client's business, many will do so as a matter of course if you ask.

Don't forget to ask your agent to write into your offer to purchase that it's (1) subject to financing, but also (2) subject to the buyer (you) receiving a satisfactory appraisal. (See Chapter 9 for details on adding conditions to your offer.) This clause will allow you to obtain independent verification of the property's value as well as ensure that it's in line with your mortgage financing.

REMEMBER

If you're selling a property yourself, offering an appraisal as part of the documen-tation regarding the property may help you secure a better offer from a potential purchaser. It shows that you haven't just chosen a price out of thin air, but have reasons for the price you're asking. The appraisal may even show a buyer the latent value in the property.

Comprehending How a Lawyer Fits into the Picture

A good lawyer or notary is like an insurance policy. If you ever need one, you'll really be happy you got one. You'll definitely need a lawyer or notary to *close* the transaction, that is, to handle the final mortgage paperwork and title transfer (in Quebec, it's always a notary). In some cases, like if you're buying or selling a home due to divorce or separation, or if tax issues are involved, you may want your lawyer to review your documents. In these cases, you may want to make any offer subject to having your lawyer or notary review all paperwork.

Taking care of business: What your real estate lawyer does for you

Besides needing a lawyer to check all the niggling little legal bits near closing time, you may find a lawyer can be indispensable early on in the deal as well. He's there to protect your rights and to make sure every part of the contract is A-okay. In the following sections, we explain what a lawyer does for you during the home-buying experience, both before and after the closing date.

B.C. (before closing)

The *contract of purchase and sale* (sometimes called the *agreement of purchase and sale*) is the legal document you and your agent use to make an offer to purchase a home, and you need to be sure it's drawn up correctly. (It's a standard form that may vary from province to province.) If your real estate agent has many years of experience drawing up home purchase offers, you may feel confident that she can write an offer and present it to the sellers without a lawyer's scrutiny. Don't take chances. If you have any concerns, ask your agent to add a subject clause to the offer that gives your lawyer a chance to review the agreement of purchase and sale after the sellers have accepted your offer but before all the conditions of sale (the "subject to" clauses) are removed. You'll likely have to stipulate a short 24- or 48-hour time period for the legal review, or the seller may object to this condition. (See Chapter 9 for more information on the contract of purchase and sale and adding conditions or "subject to" clauses.)

REMEMBER

The agreement of purchase and sale is a legally binding contract. A lawyer may be able to give you valuable input before you sign your agreement or before you remove your conditions and commit to buying the house. If you're buying a newly built home, you'll use your builder's agreement of purchase and sale, and it will be quite different from the standard form found in your province or region. No two builders' contracts are alike; they tend to be lengthy documents and often contain details that favour the builder. Have your lawyer, notary, or agent advise you which clauses to remove before you sign and which to clarify with the builder/ seller.

When selling a property, your lawyer will ensure that the titles and documentation for any chattels that are included in the sale are in order.

Damage control is often less effective and more costly and time-consuming than prevention. Yes, everyone makes mistakes. But if it's your *lawyer's* mistake, at least your lawyer is insured, which in turn protects you.

A.D. (after the deal)

After you sign the offer, your lawyer or notary handles the final mortgage and closing paperwork. Your lawyer furnishes the following important services:

>> **Title search:** The buyer's lawyer checks that the seller is the registered owner of the property and that any claims registered against the property (any debts or liens, for example) are cleared before the title is transferred to you.

>> **Conveyancing:** The buyer's lawyer prepares and reviews all documents needed to transfer the ownership of the new home and ensures you get valid title (the deed) to the property. The seller's lawyer will ensure that the title is clear prior to transfer of ownership.

>> **Application of title insurance:** If necessary, the buyer's lawyer obtains insurance to protect the buyer and the lender in the event of problems with the title or zoning of the property.

>> **Survey review:** The buyer's lawyer confirms the survey is accurate and valid and investigates any encroachments or rights of way on the subject property. The lawyer acting on behalf of the seller should also take steps to ensure that the description of the property is consistent with the listing.

>> **Assessment of builder commitments:** If you're buying a new property, your lawyer can ensure that the builder provides everything you're entitled to receive and that your new house has a valid occupancy permit from the local city or municipality.

>> **Tax investigation:** The buyer's lawyer checks to see if any municipal taxes are owing on a resale home or determines if the buyer or builder is responsible for paying GST/HST in the purchase of a newly built home.

>> **Land transfer tax/deed transfer tax:** The buyer's lawyer calculates the amount of transfer tax that you must pay (if applicable in your province).

>> **Fees payable to seller:** The buyer's lawyer tallies the *adjustments* (the amounts you owe the seller to compensate for prepaid utility bills, property taxes, rental income [if any], and other service fees paid in advance). Every region has different issues that may need adjusting at closing. The seller's lawyer will also ensure the mortgage has been discharged properly and any taxes, charges, or refunds owing are addressed. A statement of adjustments will be drawn up for the seller indicating any outstanding amounts pending.

>> **Mortgage paperwork:** The buyer's lawyer typically draws up the mortgage documentation. In rare cases, the lender asks its own lawyer to draft the mortgage documents.

TIP

The role of the buyer's lawyer and the role of the seller's lawyer aren't set in stone. Although some tasks are commonly relegated to the buyer's or the seller's lawyer, you may be able to arrange things differently in a way that benefits both sides or makes the transaction run more smoothly.

TECHNICAL STUFF

Many of the traditional functions of a real estate lawyer, such as conveyancing, now occur online. Restrictions on meetings imposed to curb the COVID-19 pandemic in 2020 accelerated the use of technology to complete deals with signatures and other in-person tasks increasingly accepted through secure online platforms. Many of these services will simplify speed up and change how buyers and lawyers do business, reducing paperwork to a matter of pixels.

Protecting your sale

Most home sellers go to their lawyers *after* they've signed the sale contract. For simple, straightforward sales done through a real estate agent, you can safely wait to see your lawyer until you've the accepted conditional offer in hand. But if you're selling privately or if yours is a complicated sale — for example, it includes a rental suite with tenants in place — ideally your lawyer reviews the conditions of sale prior to you signing any agreement of purchase and sale.

We definitely encourage you to make the offer subject to legal review if the other side has conditions that your agent views as unconventional. It's also important to seek legal advice if the property in question has a rental unit, and all the more so if the tenants will remain after the date of sale.

IF YOU HAVE AN AGENT

If you're selling through an agent, a typical scenario might run something like this: Your agent comes over to your home at 7 p.m. with the buyer's offer. The buyer will pay the price you want with a few *conditions* (refer to Chapter 9 for a discussion of conditions). Your agent thinks the conditions are typical and shouldn't evolve into any problems, but you want a second opinion from your lawyer. You need to make up your mind quickly and accept the offer. Unfortunately, your lawyer closed at 5 p.m., so you write in a clause making the contract or agreement of purchase and sale subject to your lawyer's approval within 24 hours, and you go ahead and sign. If you have an experienced and reputable agent and reasonable buyers, you shouldn't have any problems with this strategy.

If you fear your home's sale is going to get complicated, talk to your agent to get an idea of the *likely* conditions before you see any buyers' offers. Your agent can help you compile a list of possible scenarios to present to your lawyer for an expert legal opinion. Armed with the advice of your agent and your lawyer, you're as ready as you'll ever be to evaluate an offer that comes in late on a Saturday night.

IF YOU'RE GOING IT ALONE

You risk losing hundreds of thousands of dollars if you try to sell a property yourself and get it wrong. Completing law school takes several years for a reason — laws are complex and sophisticated. If you can spare hundreds of thousands of dollars and you really want to represent yourself, you can go ahead and gamble — it's legal. But for 99 percent of home sellers, selling their homes without a lawyer's involvement simply isn't worth the risk. Remember, even lawyers use this old adage: "The lawyer who represents himself has a fool for a client."

In a private sale, the smart course of action is to review the conditions of the offer with your lawyer before signing anything. Because you don't have a real estate agent to review the conditions of the sale agreement, you take a significant risk if you accept the offer unadvised. Most buyers' offers aren't made and sealed in a slam-dunk time frame. At a minimum, the "subject to lawyer's review" clause allows you to sign the contract and still have a safety hatch in the event that your lawyer subsequently discovers problems. The buyer may have an agent who's drawn up the offer and added clauses to the contract that are to your disadvantage. However, if the property you're selling has just one mortgage and a standard contract with no unusual encumbrances or conditions, don't be afraid to go ahead and sign — that is, if you're happy with the offer.

Don't forget, a real estate lawyer has liability insurance as a safeguard in case any problems arise with transferring the title for your home. Even if you sell your home yourself, having a lawyer on your side can make sure you get it right and avoid legal hassles.

TIP

Provincial real estate associations across Canada have standard forms for their contracts of purchase and sale, which have been created by lawyers and committees of real estate professionals who review the form and content of the contracts on a regular basis. If your buyer uses one of the appropriate standard provincial forms, chances are your lawyer won't uncover any problems with the paperwork involved. However, the content of the offer may still need to be reviewed.

Finding a lawyer or notary

Look for someone who specializes in real estate law. In most of Canada, this will be a lawyer; in Quebec, you'll hire a notary. Friends, neighbours, or relatives who have recently bought or sold a home are a good source of recommendations. Your real estate agent, broker, or lender will also have contacts among local lawyers or notaries and should be able to give you the names of several real estate specialists to choose from. You can also find legal associations on the Internet.

The place to start your search for a reliable lawyer is within a self-regulated organization, whose members must be trained professionals and meet set standards. If you have a lead for a lawyer in your area, the best use of your Internet time will be spent visiting the Federation of Law Societies of Canada (www.flsc.ca). The Federation provides links to all the provincial and territorial law societies' websites. Most of these sites allow you to look up lawyers for the current members of that province's law society.

Another excellent site for verifying a lawyer's status is www.canadianlawlist. com, a searchable online database that boasts listings for 55,000 lawyers and 19,000 law offices. Simply set the location to yours and the "areas of practice" field to "real estate," and within seconds you'll be looking at a comprehensive list of lawyers in your region.

TIP

When you get the name of a lawyer you're thinking of using, you can always enter her name in your favourite search engine. For example, the lawyer may have her own website, which will give you more information, or you may find out she's nominated for "Lawyer of the Year." On the downside, your search may also bring up stories about her sordid past.

HELLO, I'M CALLING REGARDING . . .

When you're searching for a lawyer, ask the ones you interview for references. Take the names and telephone numbers of some recent clients (if possible). If you found lawyers' or notaries' names using the phone book or a professional association, asking for references is especially important. Call the lawyer's references to see what they have to say. If you feel nervous about speaking to complete strangers as you're checking references, send an email with some questions or try asking a lawyer's former clients the following:

- Were you satisfied with your lawyer's services?

- Did you find any surprises in the final bill for your lawyer's services and disbursements?

- Did you feel your lawyer adequately explained to you the implications of all the decisions you made and documents you signed?

- Is there anything else about this professional or the services provided that I should know?

REMEMBER

Just because someone's a lawyer doesn't mean that she can handle a real estate transaction for you. Chances are, your best friend's shark of a divorce lawyer is excellent — but she'd be a shark out of water when it comes to your contract of purchase and sale.

Knowing what to look for in a lawyer or notary

The most important thing in any relationship is finding someone who speaks your language. You probably don't speak legalese, so as you interview lawyers and notaries, make sure you know what they're saying, that they're open to your questions, and that they take the time to make you feel comfortable. If they make their fee structures sound complicated, they may not be able to adequately explain the ins and outs of your agreement of purchase and sale or other legal documents involved in the purchase of your home. Choose a lawyer you can understand and who has the patience to explain terms adequately.

The lawyer should be familiar with local laws and issues. Tenancy laws, title registration procedures, and local property regulations can all change periodically. A local real estate lawyer or notary is up to date on all regional laws and probably has good connections with the enforcing bodies. Finding someone who is local is important because if something crops up at the last minute that requires you to head to the lawyer's office, you don't want to drive two hours to sign a single piece of paper.

Costing out a lawyer's fees

We're sure you already know that a lawyer's fees can be positively heart-stopping. When you call a lawyer to make an appointment, ask how much it will cost, what approximate amount you'll have to bring into the lawyer's office, and the preferred method of payment. Make sure that you specifically ask for the *all in cost*, which will include all your legal fees, any applicable taxes and adjustments for property taxes, and other prorated fees. Ideally, you'd be able to sit down and chat with the lawyer about her fee structure and her level of service and expertise. But be prepared — many busy lawyers will be happy to provide a quote for their fees over the phone, but they may not be available for an interview or consultation just to explain their fee structure.

Lawyers usually charge a flat fee for the service required (the handling of the sales transaction, for example). These flat service fees are often around $300 to $500, but that amount doesn't include the total cost of their legal services. You also pay disbursements and taxes. *Disbursements* are any fees that your lawyer encounters while working for you. (Disbursement fees can include, for example, courier fees, registration fees, long distance phone calls, reproduction costs for documents, and any other costs your lawyer pays on your behalf.) And, of course, you're responsible for the tax on any goods or services provided. An average all-in cost for the straight-forward sale of a residential property with a single mortgage, which can be discharged using the proceeds of sale, may be $500 to $1,500. The cost varies, however, depending on the complexity of your case.

TIP

When contacting a real estate lawyer about flat fees or all in costs, you should also ask what the lawyer's rates are, in the event that something goes wrong and you need extra services. Most of the time, extra services can be obtained on an hourly rate basis.

REMEMBER

Don't base your final choice of lawyer or notary only on price. More experienced lawyers often charge higher rates but get more done in less time, saving you money in the long run. Also, keep in mind that you're hiring a lawyer to give you peace of mind. A competent lawyer or notary should be able to explain every step of the transaction to you in clear and simple language regardless of whether the firm occupies a flashy corporate office tower or a modest street-level suite.

PREPARING FOR THE FUTURE

When you're thinking of buying or selling a house, or engaged in the process, it's the perfect time to have a will made or revised (if neither of these things have been done recently), because

- You're acquiring or disposing of a major asset that may affect the distribution of the assets of your estate.

- At the time of *conveyance* (when ownership of the property transfers), you're already using the services of a lawyer or notary public who will necessarily be acquainted with your personal financial situation.

As you shop around for a lawyer or notary to handle your conveyance, you may be able to negotiate the extra cost of your will into the conveyance package — and you should pay less than the stand-alone cost of the drafting or review of a will. Wills and estates are different areas of law from real estate, however. Just as you wouldn't ask a family lawyer to advise you on real estate, it's wise to consult a lawyer focused on wills and estate law to advise you on those matters rather than the lawyer handling your real estate purchase.

while working for you. (Disbursement fees can include, for example, courier fees, registration fees, long distance phone calls, reproduction costs for documents, and any other costs your lawyer pays on your behalf.) And, of course, you're responsible for the tax on any goods or services provided. An average all-in cost for the straight-forward sale of a residential property with a single mortgage, which can be discharged using the proceeds of sale, may be $800 to $1,500. The cost varies, however, depending on the complexity of your case.

When contracting a real estate lawyer about flat fees or all-in costs, you should also ask what the lawyer's rates are, in the event that something goes wrong and you need extra services. Most of the time, extra services can be obtained on an hourly rate basis.

Don't base your final choice of lawyer or notary only on price. More experienced lawyers often charge higher rates but get more done in less time, saving you money in the long run. Also, keep in mind that you're hiring a lawyer to give you peace of mind. A competent lawyer or notary should be able to explain every step of the transaction to you in clear and simple language, regardless of whether the firm occupies a flashy corporate office tower or a modest street-level suite.

PREPARING FOR THE FUTURE

When selling the home or getting it leased or engaged in the process of the right time to have a few more services in matters of these things has been done essential here are:

- You're acquiring or being given a particular asset that may affect the distribution of assets of your estate

- At the time of co-ownership, when ownership of the property is unclear, you're probably using the services of a lawyer or notary public who will necessarily be acquainted with your personal, financial situation

As you shop around for a lawyer or notary to handle your conveyancing, you may be able to negotiate a flat rate or all-in cost that will include the conveyance package. If you're not able to pay less than these will not alone part of the drafting or review of a will, wills and estates are different areas of law from real estate, however, just as you wouldn't ask a family lawyer to advise you on real estate, it's wise to consider a lawyer focused on wills and estates if this is the area you really feel more comfortable than the lawyer handling your estate matters.

2

Preparing to Buy a Home

Discover whether or not buying a home is for you, and if so, whether now is the right time.

Size up your wants, your needs, and your finances to determine the kind of home you're looking for and are able to afford.

If you're ready to buy a new home, get your personal finances in order and understand the size of mortgage you can carry and the kinds of costs you'll have to cover (as well as a few extras).

Determine the kinds of financing available to you and how you can get the best deal.

Know what you want from your lender and what the lender will want to know from you.

IN THIS CHAPTER

» **Becoming a homeowner — what's in it for you?**

» **Knowing yourself**

» **Knowing your finances**

» **Deciding if you're ready to buy**

Chapter **3**

Sizing Up Home Ownership

Dorothy said it best: There's no place like home. You may be a jet-setting entrepreneur or a stay-at-home parent, but we're willing to bet where you live is your most cherished space. You need a place to wind down, to relax, and to rejuvenate. Whether you own or rent (or live in your parents' basement), the place you call home is the foundation of your life.

Like most people, you want your home to be perfect, even if your definition of perfect change over time. Maybe as a teenager, your perfect bedroom was all black with huge speakers in every corner of the room. Twenty years, three children, two dogs, and a father-in-law later, your idea of perfect is an en-suite bathroom with a rain shower head and a jetted bathtub — and a lock on the door. Everyone needs a living space that can adapt to their changing needs and wants, and, of course, what better way to have that living space than to own it?

The idea of owning a home can be scary. After all, if anything goes wrong or needs to be fixed, you're responsible. Your water pipes may freeze and break, your basement may flood, or your electrical system may need a complete overhaul. People can put thousands of dollars into their homes for renovations and thousands more for emergency repairs. And then there's daily upkeep, seasonal maintenance, taxes . . . but ask homeowners, and they'll invariably tell you that taking the plunge is worth it.

Even though owning your home can dictate how much money you have for other things and leave you constantly worrying about finances, researching and planning will help you stay in control. Part of the planning process is deciding how much home you can afford, and that's why this chapter is geared towards getting you the home you want — at a price that doesn't leave you eating peanut butter sandwiches three times a day for the next 20 years. Your home should complement your lifestyle, not crimp it. You need enough money left over to create that en-suite bathroom you've dreamed of.

Recapping the Joys of Ownership

If you're reading this book, the idea of owning obviously appeals to you. But as a helpful reminder as to why you should be enthusiastic about home ownership, the advantages of owning a home include the following reasons:

» **More stability, less stress:** Stability is a wonderful thing — it means that there will be less on your mind. Moving is widely recognized as the third most stressful experience (after the death of a loved one and divorce). Owning a home means you don't have to worry about moving from one rental apartment to the next, what rent will be next year, and what happens if the landlord decides to sell the place (or anything else to do with the landlord, for that matter). Home owning also means that you start building equity rather than paying rent to make someone else rich. Put it all together, and the result should be greater confidence when thinking about your future.

» **Your home, your style:** You can decorate to your heart's content. It's yours to do with what you want. You can change even the small things you don't like: the dripping faucets, the ugly shag rug, and the shower head that goes only as high as your belly button. And all your time, effort, and money go into your investment, not someone else's. You no longer have to deal with landlords not fixing things or going the cost-cutting route when they do. Of course, many building owners and managers take good care of their buildings and tenants, but the fact is a rental building is often an investment for them that generates cash flow. They'll give it the attention it needs to be a good business proposition, but they'll treat it differently than their own homes. And you'll give your own home more attention than you could a rental unit.

» **Deeper sense of community:** You may be more antisocial than the Grinch, but owning a home encourages you to appreciate the surrounding community. After all, protecting your property's value requires you to protect the general area, too. You may start grudgingly by organizing a neighbourhood protest against your local park being rezoned for a gravel pit (which would mean horrible things for your own property), but it's hard not to start liking at least some of your neighbours. Being part of a community can have long-term social and health benefits. We recommend that you buy a home in an area where the majority of residents own the properties they live in — homeowners tend to care more about the neighbourhood than tenants do.

>> **More self-confidence:** Home ownership speaks to a number of personality traits, such as maturity, dependability, and stability. And paying your mortgage on time every month does wonders for your credit rating.

>> **Financial benefits:** Your mortgage may seem overwhelming but think of it as a forced savings plan. The regular schedule of payments mean you can't skip a deposit or withdraw money, and each payment gives you a slightly more equity (and reduces the overall cost). Home ownership is also generally considered a good investment — one that grows over time. Better yet, if the home is your principal residence, you don't pay tax on any increase in value, or the *capital gain*. On other investments, you'd normally pay tax on these gains, but in most cases the capital gain on your principal residence is tax-exempt. (We discuss the capital gains provisions in detail in Chapter 15.)

MAKING AN INVESTMENT

Buying a house is one of the biggest financial commitments you'll make in your life, but it's not just an investment of money. It's an investment in the kind of life you want now and in the future. What and where you buy will ultimately dictate how you will live. Bought a fixer-upper with the intention of doing all the renovations yourself? Five years later, you may still be devoting all your time and money to it. Bought a home in the distant suburbs, but work in the heart of the city? You may spend more time in heavy traffic than at home. On the other hand, maybe you've become a gourmet cook because your wonderful kitchen begs to be used constantly, or that rec-room you converted into a home theatre means you can host a big Grey Cup bash every year.

You may have to make sacrifices when you buy a home — but you can make them informed sacrifices. You'll have to do some creative brainstorming to imagine the upsides and downsides of various features of the home you're considering. For instance, you may buy a house on a corner lot, knowing that you'll have a lot of snow to shovel and leaves to rake. However, you may not mind these tasks too much because you decided before you bought the house that its unobstructed south-facing kitchen windows and big garden were well worth the effort.

Many homes, particularly in major cities, come with a rental suite to help pay the mortgage or the chance to build a carriage house. You may opt to test your skills as a landlord or build a studio where you can indulge your favourite hobby or start a home business. The kind of home you buy will open doors to the kind of life you want to live.

Knowing What's Right for You

Like most people, you probably want the perfect home — white picket fence, manicured lawn, and tennis court. Or maybe your dream home has a 1,000-square-foot deck complete with hot tub, built-in barbecue, and surround-sound party speakers. If you're self-employed, maybe a suitable home office space is at the top of your list. Or maybe you're tired of mowing in July and shovelling in January, so your ideal space is an apartment in the heart of Montreal.

Whatever your current dreams, chances are your life will be different 20 years from now with new priorities. You may not need that office space as much as another parking space when your kid learns to drive. But you can't really predict 20 years down the road, so don't sweat it. Take stock of what you need now, and focus on the foreseeable future, which we discuss in the following sections.

Considering your foreseeable future

One of the first things you need to decide is how long you expect to stay. Your requirements will be very different if you plan to live out your days in your new home than if you're looking to turn around and sell it for a quick profit. But because a quick resale is a risky idea, we assume you're settling in for at least the next five years. (But if you're interested, we discuss quick resales — commonly known as *flipping* — in Chapter 8.)

In addition to what you think you need now, consider the potential for change over the next five years. If you're just married and starting out, are children part of the plan? Parenthood may seem a long way down the line, but a lot can happen in five years. That swanky one-bedroom, two-level loft may not be the smartest choice for you when a kid comes along.

If you're heading towards retirement, think about the difficulties you may face as you age. Will you still be able to climb the stairs to the third-floor master bedroom in ten years? The large back garden may be great for the grandkids, but you have to think about who is going to take care of it. Many people downsize to let them live more and worry less, so a place near a park might be wiser.

To help get your priorities straight, make two lists: one of your current priorities and another one of your future needs (the ones you can expect, anyway). Consider both lists as you look for a home.

Saving space for change

Chances are, the main reason you're thinking about a move is the potential for an expanding family. Whether your new family members are a baby (or two), a mother-in-law, or those two Irish Wolfhounds you adopted, you may need more room in the future to accommodate change.

So, if you admit that the possibility of sharing your space exists, it's a good idea to look for a home with an extra room, a basement, or an attic that can be converted when the time comes. In the meantime, of course, you can use that space as a home theatre or extra storage (shoes, anyone?).

If some flexibility — whether in the form of another bedroom or a basement full of potential — isn't built into your home, you may find yourself moving again faster than you think and certainly faster than you want.

Knowing What You Want

Many elements make up a home that deciding which ones are the most important may be difficult for you. You may take many things for granted when you have them (like an en-suite bathroom or counterspace in the kitchen), but don't forget to make a record of those (sometimes) small items that make all the difference in your satisfaction with where you live. For example, if you walk to work, living on a steep hill may be a great workout in the spring and summer but a dangerous and slippery slope in the winter.

Part of knowing what you want is knowing what you don't want. I don't want to mow grass, for example, is a good start. Or, I don't want a basement where the ceiling is so low I can't stand upright. You'll always find things you don't like about your current home and other people's homes, whether those things are a tiny backyard, drafty windows, the lack of water pressure, the windows not opening wide enough, or the lack of street parking. If a certain deficiency is going to drive you crazy, you need to avoid it so that it doesn't ultimately affect your use and enjoyment of your home. By identifying your pet peeves, you can zero in on what you're looking for.

Focusing on your needs

You probably known what you want in your ideal home. The features of your dream home provide a good starting point for your search; most people judge potential homes with their standards of perfection in mind.

YOU CAN'T ALWAYS GET WHAT YOU WANT

Prioritizing the features that you absolutely can't live without in a home alongside those features that may sound nice but you don't really need will stand you in good stead when your agent starts showing you houses. When push comes to shove, you'll be willing (and able!) to compromise. And you just may find that you get what you need, even if you can't always get what you want.

Liz was going through a divorce and needed to find a property with three bedrooms for herself and her two teenage children. A garage and adequate storage were also on her list. Co-parenting arrangements meant that she wanted to stay relatively close to her ex, who was going to stay in the matrimonial home, and near the schools that the children were attending.

Liz and her agent found a great home with loads of potential well within her budget, but she decided she didn't want the challenge of renovating it. Then her agent found her a more expensive property, all updated and in the same neighbourhood, but Liz thought the bedrooms were a bit too small and didn't like the street the home was on. On the third try, her agent showed her a fully renovated home, right on budget, with good room sizes and on a nice street, but Liz decided the home was a bit too far away from work and amenities, and the back garden was tiny and dark.

Liz's agent told her that it was time to prioritize. Each home had features that appealed to Liz, so she needed to figure out which features were the most important. Liz gave what she'd seen some thought and realized that she really liked house number three: She would just have to accept a new location and a little less sunshine.

TIP

Keep your mind focused on your home-buying needs. You shouldn't let your emotions overrule practicalities. (See Chapter 8 for the dangers of falling in love.) Even though you really want the home with the incredibly landscaped backyard, reminding yourself that the rest of the house just doesn't meet your basic needs will help you overlook the cosmetics. Face it: You're in Canada, and depending on where you live, that back garden will be unusable for six months of the year (or more!).

If you're a first-time buyer, remember you're just that — buying for the first time. You may plan to sell your home in five to ten years and trade up to a bigger one. So don't worry if you can't buy your absolute dream home in the perfect neighbourhood right now. Instead of trying to buy a home with seven bedrooms for the 12 kids you plan to raise, realize that you can live comfortably right now with a three-bedroom home with a fenced-in backyard at a reasonable price. You may not like the idea of buying a smaller starter home, but doing so puts you in a better position to buy a bigger home down the road without sacrificing to your mortgage vacations, evenings out, and hockey lessons. Nobody wants to be house poor, but being house poor is better than being cash poor. What you can afford will probably never match your ideal, but with a little bit of flexibility, you can find a home that suits you until child number eight comes along.

Making the list

Because you're probably going to be making compromises, keeping focused on your basic needs and not giving them up too quickly, while being aware of where you can be flexible, is important. Here are some of the things to consider:

>> **Location:** Perhaps the most obvious factor . . . where do you want to live? After you have been preapproved for a mortgage, you'll have a good idea of what you can afford, which may determine where you will end up living. For example, you may be able to purchase a cool two-bedroom condo in the city or a four-bedroom family home out in the suburbs, both in the same price point. Either way, you'll have lots of options.

>> **Type of home:** If the number of stairs is a concern, especially if in-laws will be spending time with you, you may want to think about buying a bungalow or a large condo. Or, perhaps you're thinking about a detached home, especially if your kid is learning to play the bagpipes. If your tastes run to modern architecture, you won't want to look at century-old Victorian-style homes. (If you're curious about what different types of homes exist out there, have a look at Chapters 4 and 5.)

>> **Exterior:** What do you need outside? Is there enough room for the Great Dane to do laps? Do you need fencing around your yard to keep the kids in? Do you need a sunny yard to garden in, or are you more of an herbicidal maniac? Do you like to throw summer parties? Then you'll probably want that sunny yard bricked in or covered with a large deck. Or maybe you need a lot of pavement on which to park your three cars, two motorcycles, and RV.

>> **Kitchen:** What do you need in a kitchen? If you have a big family, you probably want an eat-in area and an automatic dishwasher. If you're a professional cook, counter space and modern appliances may be your priority. The presence of appliances may not be the deciding factor, but room to install them is.

>> **Bathrooms:** How many do you need? If you're looking for a home with more than one storey, bathroom location is important, too. Is there one on the ground floor, or do you have to send your guests up to the one between your kids' rooms? If you like to take long, relaxing bubble baths on Sundays, you won't be interested in a home with only stand-up showers.

>> **Bedrooms:** How many bedrooms are you looking for? Do you need an extra one for a home office or frequent house guests? If you're just starting out and you may be having children in the not-so-distant future, count them in when calculating your needs. If your children are finally off to college and moving out, you may want fewer bedrooms.

>> **Renovations:** Are you willing to do them? If the home has all the bones that you're looking for — the neighbourhood works, the room sizes are great, you love the garden and the two-car garage — but it hasn't been updated since 1982 (not that there's anything wrong with a pastel colour scheme), are you willing to do the work to update it? You may find that a bit of elbow grease gets you exactly what you want.

>> **Other considerations:** How small is *too* small for your bedroom? For your kitchen? Will stairs be a problem for anyone in your household, now or in the future? Do you need a finished basement for your home office, your home theatre, or your kids' playroom?

Use Table 3-1 to organize the features you need or want in a new home. Complete the chart by considering what is absolutely essential to your needs and what you really want to have (but that you *could* live without). For some items in this table, like a dishwasher or a fireplace, it's a simple yes/no proposition. A fireplace may be "nice to have," but is it really "essential"? You decide.

TIP

Can you afford to be picky? It depends. You should be picky if you don't like where the washroom are located or how the staircase lands in the middle of the living room. For all intents and purposes, you can't change or won't want to attempt to change some things because the costs involved are prohibitive. Don't be picky if you don't like the doorknobs (you can always change them). Even central air can be installed later for less than, say, tearing down a wall or two to open up the dining room. Make concessions on small things you can fix or change yourself later on. Try to use your imagination: Sometimes fresh paint and flooring can turn drab into fab.

REMEMBER

Choosing features in a home isn't all sunshine and roses. You may think you want a corner lot with a big yard, but have you bargained for the snow shovelling, leaf raking, and lawn mowing that go with it? How about the settling foundation and structural decay of your dream Victorian mansion? We're not saying you should change your mind about what you want, but when you set your priorities, think about the drawbacks of maintenance and repair that go along with the benefits of home ownership.

TABLE 3-1 Home Priority List

	Essential Need	Nice to Have
Type of Home		
Detached, semi, and so forth		
Victorian, modern, and so forth		
Number of storeys		
Interior		
Size (m² or ft²)		
Number of rooms		
Living Room		
Size (m² or ft²)		
Open concept/separate dining room		
Fireplace		
Flooring		
Ceiling height		
Kitchen		
Size (m² or ft²)		
Condition		
Eat-in area		
Fridge		
Stove (gas or electric)		
Family Room		
Size (m² or ft²)		
Location		
Flooring		
Hallways		
Width (m or ft.)		
Linen closet		
Coat closet near main entrance		
Flooring		
Basement		
Size (m² or ft²)		
Finished		
Basement/in-law apartment		
Washer/dryer		
Freezer		
Heating (oil, gas, and so forth)		
Flooring		
Other		
CAC (central air conditioning)		

(continued)

TABLE 3-1 *(continued)*

Item	Essential Need	Nice to Have	Item	Essential Need	Nice to Have
Dishwasher			Central vacuum		
Large kitchen cupboards			Finished attic		
Accessible kitchen cupboards			Property will accommodate expansion		
Countertops			Water view		
Flooring			Security system		
Bedrooms			New windows		
Number			Sliding glass doors		
Walkout to balcony			Natural light		
Closet in each room			*Exterior*		
Flooring			Frontage (size and direction facing)		
Main Bedroom			Brick/siding/wood/stucco		
Size (m² or ft²)			Roofing material (slate, cedar shake, asphalt shingles)		
En-suite bathroom			*Parking*		
Walk-in closet, south-facing window, fireplace, or other special feature			Garage		
Flooring			Carport		
Size (m² or ft²)			Space		

	Essential Need	Nice to Have		Essential Need	Nice to Have
Location(s)			Private/shared driveway		
Shower/tub/whirlpool tub			Street parking		
Flooring			*Yard*		
Sunroom/Den/Home Office			Size of lot (m² or ft²)		
Size (m² or ft²)			Shed		
Location			Deck/patio/porches		
Flooring			Fenced enclosure		
Size (m² or ft²)			Swimming pool/hot tub		
Location(s)			Mature gardens and trees		
Shower/tub/whirlpool tub			Gardens		
Flooring					

Knowing When the Time Is Right

Although you may think researching real estate markets and waiting for the right time to buy are the only ways to get a good deal, your personal situation is what should really determine your decision to buy. Are you able to pay your mortgage, utilities, taxes, insurance, and whatever maintenance comes up, not only for the next year but also for the next 5 or even 25?

Moreover, are you willing to remain in the same place for the next five years? Considering the closing costs involved whether you're a seller or a buyer (we discuss closing costs in Chapter 2), you should be prepared to keep your home for at least a few years. Doing so isn't always possible, thanks to job changes and other factors, but we suggest you try to avoid a situation where you *have* to sell your home because chances are you'd have to accept a lower price. So even if the market is at an all-time low and interest rates are way down, buying a home could be a huge mistake if you're in the middle of a career change or planning a move to Luxembourg next year.

WARNING

Maintaining a house requires a big commitment, both in time and money. Each season presents a list of chores to maintain your home's integrity and efficiency. Overlooking the overflowing eaves or the leaky roof may lead to significant water damage; neglecting your furnace can cause hundreds of dollars in repairs. There are many situations in which a little neglect can transform into expensive repairs and sometimes irreversible damage, resulting in huge losses when it's time to sell. And don't forget that all sorts of little things that you may not have expected, such as a broken major appliance, can happen. Don't let your home nickel-and-dime you, or that may be all you have left each month. Putting away a bit of money every month in a maintenance fund will help make those occasional big-ticket (or constant low-cost) expenses a bit easier to handle.

Knowing your finances

Home buying is an investment. Although buying a home is cheaper in the long run to renting, that initial outlay of cash for buying a home is enough to send anyone's heart racing. You'll need to take a careful look at your current expenditures in order to evaluate your readiness to take on mortgage payments and home maintenance. Chapter 4 helps you determine whether you're financially ready to buy.

Knowing where your money goes now is a crucial first step. Suppose that after you've accounted for what you spend on food, clothes, transportation, and vacations, you still have a $15,000 annual surplus. You're not really sure where it went last year, but figure it should be enough to cover the new costs of being a home-owner. If your pipes freeze and you need to call in a plumber, you don't want to discover that you've already spent most of that $15,000 surplus on gifts for your friends and family or a weekly round of drinks for all your pals at your favourite craft brewery. To help you understand how much you're spending right now and to keep you on budget in the future, we provide a handy worksheet in Chapter 4.

TIP

Have a plan for the future, too. Know what you want to contribute to your retirement savings. You may have kids and want to contribute to their education; tuition is only going up. Being clear on where you want your financial life to be in five years, and then in ten years, will help you make smart decisions now about how much to put into a down payment and how much to carry in monthly mortgage payments.

Comparing renting to buying

Owning your home instead of renting almost always makes more sense in the long run, especially if you settle in one area. The biggest advantage of owning over renting is that your monthly payments are an investment (and they'll eventually cease!). The most common complaint about buying a home is having to pay the mortgage, and more specifically, the interest on the mortgage. (Of course, you can try living with your parents until you've made enough money to buy a home outright, but chances are your parents may not want to live with you for that long. And given how high house prices are in some areas, you may end up becoming their live-in caregiver before you move out.)

Renting your home instead of owning it does have advantages as well, and there are times in your life when owning isn't the best option for you. One of the biggest reasons to buy a home is for stability, but if you like a flexible lifestyle, a home may be a burden to you. Owning a home is a serious commitment, so if your priorities aren't geared to making regular mortgage payments, handling regular maintenance and upkeep, or having a permanent address, renting may be better for you. Alternatively, you may be older and wan to free up some of the equity in your home. Many seniors choose to downsize into a rental apartment and hand their equity to a wealth manager.

If you're in one of the following situations, you may want to wait a while to buy a home:

>> **Having financial woes:** Although you can leap into home ownership with as little as a 5 percent down payment, you still have to come up with that amount. You'll also have to be prepared to make regular mortgage payments for what may seem like an eternity, not to mention all the other costs of being a homeowner. And don't forget that getting a mortgage may be tricky if you've neglected other loans or have significant debts.

- **Living in transition:** You haven't decided to live in one place. Saddling yourself with a chunk of property and debt may not the best move if you're thinking about living a bohemian lifestyle island hopping around Greece for a few years. (This being said, if you've just received a massive inheritance that covers the down payment and you know a reliable tenant whose rent will cover the mortgage while you're travelling, then buying a home may be a smart investment.)

- **Living with uncertainty:** If you're part of the gig economy, your income may not be stable. If you also work remotely, you may want the flexibility of renting to keep your cost of living reasonable.

- **Facing transition:** If you're in an industry or sector that is going through change, you may have to find employment that would result in moving to a new city or province. Purchasing a home that you would have to sell in the near term may not be a wise investment.

- **Dealing with space considerations:** Although you can't predict having triplets, there's no sense buying a two-bedroom bungalow if you're pretty sure that your brother-in-law's family of seven and their three dogs will move in with you for an unspecified amount of time. Unless a small home is a way of discouraging guests, underestimating your space requirements may force you to move house sooner than you want. The same thing holds true if you're considering setting up a home office or starting a home-based business — make sure you have a spare bedroom or room in the basement to expand.

- **Buying in a seller's market:** Generally speaking, you should focus on your own situation rather than the real estate market. But there may be a time when interest rates skyrocket and homes still sell for twice as much as their listing prices; in these circumstances, it's probably better to wait until the market cools down to buy a home. If a monthly cost analysis shows that buying a home would be 20 to 30 percent more than renting a comparable home, think twice about buying. (We show you how to analyze monthly housing costs in Chapter 5.)

- **Focused on something else:** You and your friend are opening a new high-end spa in a trendy downtown neighbourhood, and you need some start-up capital. You decide to invest all your savings in the business instead of in real estate. If your spa turns out to be a successful business that you end up turning into a franchise, you may be able to buy an estate in the south of France instead of a bungalow in the suburbs. Alternatively, if the venture turns out to be a bust, you don't want to sell your swanky loft for a trailer.

- **Wanting a hassle-free lifestyle:** Renting is an ideal option if you want to avoid the hassles that come with regular maintenance of home. Often, rental apartments include the cost of utilities such as heat and hydro, reducing the need to arrange for these connections (and payment of the bills).

Considering homeowner concerns

You may be skeptical about the complications of buying a home. However, the many different kinds of homes and ownership of homes mean you don't have to let your dislike of raking leaves and mowing the lawn stop you from owning. The following are the most common reservations about home owning:

>> **Unexpected costs:** One of the main arguments in favour of renting is that you know what your monthly costs are, and they change once a year (if that). A five-year fixed mortgage locks in your basic costs, too, but you'll probably have other costs. The furnace can break down, or the roof may start leaking if you own a house. Even if you live in a condo, the condo association may ask owners to pay a special levy for maintenance in the thousands of dollars.

Being a renter does have its share of unexpected. Sure, you may be your landlord's mortgage helper, so he may guarantee some things like the furnace is fixed in a hurry, but that missing screen on your bedroom window may not be a priority. Although letting someone else worry about household mainte-nance may be nice, there's also real value in being able to take control of a situation and do what needs doing.

>> **Extra work:** Don't like doing lawn work, shovelling snow, or fixing leaks? Your partner or child refuses to do your dirty work for you? Instead of renting to avoid such chores, you may prefer to buy a condominium where someone else takes care of the outside maintenance and the repair of building systems (you'll still have in-suite maintenance to worry about). If you buy an apart-ment, you won't even have a sidewalk to worry about!

Adding up the costs of homeownership

Keep in mind that when you move into a new home, you'll have new rates for some monthly expenses, like utilities (heating, hydro, water) and municipal ser-vices like garbage disposal and recycling. You may be taking on new costs such as property taxes and home and garden maintenance. If you're a new homeowner, make sure you also prepare for the worst by ensuring you have reserve funds for emergency repairs. Ensure you have enough monthly income left over after your mortgage payments to cover these costs as well.

Here are some of the common costs a homeowner faces:

>> **Maintenance:** You may have a high-maintenance relationship or a low-maintenance relationship with the home you buy. Be sure your finances can handle the costs of regular repairs. Also, keep an emergency fund for unexpected repairs and contribute to it on a regular basis. If you dip into it

to help pay your way to Tahiti, that's your call, but be aware that if your basement is flooded when you return, you may not have the cash to pay a plumber.

» **Insurance:** You'll need proof of fire and extended insurance coverage before you can finalize the purchase of your new home, because the property itself is the only security against the loan. If your new home burns down, you'll still have to pay back the bank. Insurance costs vary, depending on your deductible, the value of your home and its contents, and the type of coverage you get (always get insurance for the full replacement cost!). The *premium*, or cost of the policy, will vary between insurers, too. Shop around for an affordable policy that covers you for the replacement of your personal property and grants you a living allowance if your home is affected by fire or water and is uninhabitable. Getting a policy with public liability insurance is also a good idea because it protects you if someone is harmed on your property. (You can find more on insurance in Chapter 11.)

» **Utilities:** When you buy a home, you assume all the heating, cooling, water, and electricity bills for the property. If you live in the colder, windier parts of this country, you already know that heat is the most important utility there is. And if you've ever rented a house and heat wasn't included, you've likely been walloped by the biggest utility bill you've ever experienced. If the house you're buying is new, you'll probably pay less for utilities because of better insulation and construction quality. If you're buying a resale home, ask the owners for copies of their utility bills so you can see these costs. In Chapter 8, we go over the costs and benefits of various heating systems commonly found in Canadian homes.

» **Taxes:** Property taxes are calculated based on your home's assessed value and the rate set by the local municipality. Property tax rates do tend to go up annually. Some real estate listings will state the amount of the previous year's taxes for the property being sold. When you're looking at homes, find out from the selling agent or the owners what the previous year's taxes were. If you need a high-ratio mortgage to buy a new home, your lender may insist that property tax installments be added to your monthly mortgage payments. (See Chapter 5 for more details on high-ratio mortgages.)

» **Condo fees:** The great thing about living in a condo is that someone else looks after all the pesky outside maintenance and landscaping stuff. The flip side is you have to pay for it in your condo fees. In some cases, condo fees can cost as much as rent.

Understanding the market

The housing market fluctuates, experiencing both strong and weak periods. History has shown, however, that the market will rise in the long run. So, don't focus too much on waiting for the right time to buy unless the evidence suggests it simply isn't the right time. Predicting how the market will go is nearly impossible, and if you wait around forever for the market to be perfect, you'll have thrown away wads of cash on rent. Generally speaking, after you buy your first home, you'll continue to own it for years to come or trade up. Your home's value will increase. So, focus on your personal situation and find housing that meets your budget, as well as your needs.

This being said, make sure you know how the market works, because there are periods when it's better to be a buyer (and conversely, times when it's better to be a seller). You can see what the current market is like by checking out the prices and sales volumes and asking your real estate agent how the current market compares to last month or 12 months ago. Your agent can tell you how quickly homes have been selling in the past year, what demand is like, and what prices are doing.

A robust economy naturally produces a stronger market where people are more willing to buy. Chances are, of course, there will be more sellers, because with more money, owners may decide to buy bigger homes. More housing is typically developed during the rising part of a cycle, which in turn feeds demand.

To understand the housing market, here are a few terms and concepts to know:

>> **Buyer's market:** Ideally, the best time to buy is during a *buyer's market*, when many sellers want to sell but few buyers are looking to buy. Homes take longer to sell, so buyers can take more time to make decisions. To sell a home in this market, sellers have to list at aggressively competitive prices, and sometimes even offer other incentives, such as secondary financing. (See Chapter 5 for a discussion of financing options.) If you have to sell your home during a buyer's market, the good news is that you're able to take advantage of these same conditions when you go to buy a home.

>> **Seller's market:** The opposite of a buyer's market is a *seller's market*. Few homes are on the market, but buyers are plentiful, which results in fast home sales at prices close to, or even above, the listing prices. Some homes sell even before they're listed. Because of the rise in sales, some owners may decide to take on selling their homes themselves. In a seller's market, buyers have less negotiating power and less time to decide and may even find themselves in a bidding war. So if you're buying in a seller's market, be prepared to make quick decisions. Have all your homework done and your financing arranged. (See Chapter 4 for details on mortgage preapproval.)

>> **Seasonal influences:** Winter in Canada is notorious for being cold and unpleasant virtually everywhere. People don't like to venture out much, unless it's for necessities like groceries, hockey games, or skiing. Besides, who wants to look for a home when they're busy buying gifts for the holiday season? Frostbite aside, the winter months also tend to be slower for the real estate market

because people with children don't like to move during the school year. A lot of properties aren't on the market simply because sellers know their homes look best in the summer with the flowers, the leaves, and the sunshine. This means there's a good possibility that the homes on the market at this inhospitable time of year must be sold, so you may find a good bargain. You just may have to deal with snowdrifts and –40-degree temperatures on moving day. In large cities, however, weather may not be an influence at all. So if you see a home you love in downtown Toronto in January, don't assume it's a fire sale.

>> **Interest rates:** If you need a mortgage to purchase your home (lucky you, if you don't), you'll find that interest rates make a big difference in how much home you can afford. When interest rates are high, fewer buyers tend to be in the market for a new home. You can see the logic: A 4.5 percent interest rate on a $200,000 mortgage loan will cost you approximately $40,845 over a five-year term, whereas the same $200,000 loan at a 7 percent interest rate will cost you $64,425 in interest. Different types of mortgages can increase or decrease your interest rate from what banks consider the current standard. We discuss mortgages in Chapter 5.

Chapter **4**

Understanding Your Finances

W hen you decide to enter the world of home ownership, it's time to take a cold, hard look at your finances. Budgeting may be something that you're well acquainted with — or it may be the area of your life where you think "ignorance is bliss." But unless you have a clear picture of your finances, both what you've got in the bank as well as your monthly income and spending, you won't have a realistic idea of how much home you can afford and what your options are.

A clear (and honest) picture of your financial situation enables you to look at just how much you have at your disposal for a down payment and what a lender will be willing to give you. You also can budget for the specific costs associated with closing the deal, making sure you have enough left over for any unexpected costs in the first months of ownership. The chapter wraps up with a look at closing-day costs, such as insurance and legal fees and land transfer taxes, so you know exactly what to anticipate before the seller hands you the keys. (Trust us, we've been there!) Just when you think you're ready to move in, you'll face a few last expenses that can really add up.

Increasing Your Down Payment

Regardless of your spending habits, you likely have some cash socked away. Chump change isn't likely to get you very far, so most people have opted for high-interest savings accounts (also called online or e-savings accounts), Tax-Free Savings Accounts (TFSAs), and other vehicles. Whatever you've been using, take a close look at your savings and add up what you have at your disposal. These savings can help you get a handle on the size of the down payment you'll be able to make, which must be at least 5 percent of your dream home's purchase price.

First, however, make sure any long-term debt you're carrying is paid off, because that debt will be a drag on your ability to save. That debt also will count against the size of mortgage a lender is willing to grant you. Here we discuss debt — how it affects your ability to save towards a down payment and your ability to qualify for a mortgage.

Dealing with debts

Reducing your long-term debts is an important step to getting your finances in shape prior to buying a home. Debt can come in many forms, but the deadliest to your prospects for a mortgage are those that take years to pay off or that saddle you with a high rate of interest because they'll be competing directly for your money with a mortgage. Mortgage lenders want to make sure you pay them first because there's so much at stake.

The most recent edition of *Personal Finance For Canadians For Dummies* by Eric Tyson and Tony Martin (John Wiley & Sons, Inc.) is a good resource that provides tips on managing your financial standing, not just in the run-up to buying a home, but overall.

Here are some dangerous debts you should pay off before you buy a house:

Student loans

Many first-time homebuyers, and even some second-time buyers, have student loans they're trying to pay off. These loans can take years to repay and usually come with strict terms because lenders consider new graduates a higher risk. But here's the good news: The steady employment that's key to paying off student loans will also make you a better risk to mortgage lenders than someone who's unemployed, so get that job, pay off that loan, and demonstrate your ability to repay debt. Doing so will set you up to repay a mortgage.

Credit card debts

This is another kind of debt you certainly want to pay off. Credit cards come with double-digit interest rates and can be extremely difficult to eliminate. Successfully managing credit card debt can demonstrate your creditworthiness; not doing so will be a strike against you. Ongoing debt also weighs on your disposable income, so clear it up! You can do this by consolidating existing debts (speak to your banker) and paring back discretionary spending so you have more cash to pay off your debts and fewer expenses adding to your burdens.

TIP

The credit limit on your credit card will count against the overall debt a lender considers you able to handle. Consider asking for a reduction in your credit limit if you don't need all that spending room. For example, if your credit card has a limit of $10,000 but you never use more than $5,000, ask for a reduction. Alternatively, if you have three credit cards with a combined credit limit of $45,000 and you only ever use $15,000, consider consolidating expenses onto one card. Simplicity is the name of the game when getting a handle on debt.

REMEMBER

Many people have ditched credit cards in favour of debit cards, which when used immediately withdraw money from an account. When saving money and building a credit rating, using only a debit card in lieu of a credit card has two dangers:

>> It may be tougher to understand where all that money you're earning is going because it never passes through your hands.

>> A debit card won't demonstrate your ability to handle debt or count towards your credit score.

Your *credit score* indicates your creditworthiness to lenders, so keeping tabs on it is important so you know what lenders know, especially if you're just emerging from a period of financial hardship. (No matter your financial situation, making sure your creditworthiness hasn't been impacted in some way, such as by identity theft, is always a smart idea.) The major agencies providing credit reports in Canada are Equifax (www.equifax.ca), which provides you with information about your own credit rating free of charge, and TransUnion Canada (www.transunion.ca). You may receive a free credit report every 12 months.

Sizing up your savings

Resolving your savings is also important when wanting to make a down payment for a home. Carefully examine how much money you have left in your bank accounts after you pay your monthly bills. Make sure to include the savings plan your uncle set up for you or the employer-funded RRSP. These are all starting points for a down payment, which must be at least 5 percent of a home's purchase price. The larger your down payment, the more willing a lender will be to grant you a mortgage, because the bank has less money at risk.

SETTLING SCORES

Many people cruise though life without the faintest idea what their credit score is. They're able to get credit, take on debt, and repay it without much trouble. Others, however, face roadblocks and need to strengthen their creditworthiness.

The credit score is the way lenders and other institutions measure people's creditworthiness. In Canada, the score maxes out at 850 or 900, depending on the company. Anything over 760 is excellent, while anything lower than 660 is considered poor. On July 1, 2020, the Canada Mortgage and Housing Corp. (CMHC) set a minimum credit score of 680 for those seeking federally insured mortgages, up from 600 previously. The move underscored the importance of a high score.

Building your credit score takes time, but doing so is relatively simple. It depends on taking out credit regularly and repaying it equally regularly. Rather than letting credit card debts accumulate, pay them down steadily. Keep up with car payments and student loans, showing that you're not only able to take on debt, but repay it.

If you don't like debt or are just starting out and trying to avoid trouble, live a little! You can't build a credit history if you don't take on debt. Miss a small credit card payment by a few days now and then, and repay the amount promptly (making sure you add enough to cover the interest charge). Within a year or so, your credit score will be looking up and lenders will be comfortable advancing you larger amounts — including a mortgage!

Here are some of the best ways to save for your down payment:

Savings accounts and term deposits

They're common forms of unregistered deposits that many people use to save money. They usually bear interest at low and unappealing rates versus other investment options, but they're great for short-term savings. Many financial institutions offer online versions that pay a higher interest rate than those designed for everyday banking for those who really do want to use them to save money. Because they have a relatively stable value, you can easily add up what you have or spend them at will.

Mutual funds

Many people also have savings in mutual funds or other instruments. Units are bought and sold daily like equities and therefore fluctuate in value daily. The value today may not be the value tomorrow, so they're generally a higher-risk savings option best suited to medium- to long-term savings. If you plan to purchase a home in the next 6 to 12 months or are concerned that market fluctuations could erode their value, shift them into a more stable investment such as a term deposit or Tax-Free Savings Account (TFSA). Your financial adviser can provide helpful advice on how to prepare for a home purchase if a significant portion of your savings are in mutual funds.

Registered savings and retirement savings plans

You also want to consider registered savings plans such as TFSAs and registered retirement savings plans (RRSPs). Both shelter your funds from taxes. TFSAs take after-tax income (currently $6,000 a year) and allow the savings to grow tax-free. RRSPs take pre-tax income and allow it to grow, but most withdrawals are subject to taxes. This generally makes TFSAs a better option if you're saving for a down payment.

However, if you're a first-time buyer (or you haven't owned a home as your principal residence in the past five years), you can take advantage of the federal government's Home Buyers' Plan (HBP), an important exception concerning RRSPs. Basically, the plan lets you borrow up to $35,000 from your RRSP towards the down payment, and a maximum of two buyers can participate. This means that if you and your partner each have an RRSP, both of you can withdraw up to $35,000, for a possible total of $70,000. And, best of all, neither of you will be penalized or be assessed taxes on the amounts withdrawn — unless you don't pay it back to the RRSP within a certain amount of time.

Of course, the following conditions do apply to borrowing from your RRSP:

>> You must sign a written agreement that you're buying or building a home in Canada.

>> You must have had the money in your RRSP for at least 90 days before the withdrawal.

>> You have to repay the amount of the withdrawal within 15 years.

>> You must repay at least $1/15$ of the amount you owe each year.

>> You plan to use the new home as your principal place of residence (in other words, you'll live in the home rather than use it as an investment property).

>> You have to be a resident of Canada.

Talk to your lender or lawyer to see if this plan is a good option for you. You can also read up on the program at the Canada Revenue Agency website at www. cra-arc.gc.ca.

Getting Up Close and Personal with Your Finances

Although stacking up your income against your expenses can be depressing, you'll be even more down in the dumps if you can't make the mortgage payments on your new home. In assessing what amount of mortgage you're eligible for, your lender looks only at the debts you have to pay, such as student loans, credit cards, lines of credit, child support, and amounts owing to government. Discretionary spending is your concern, which is why you need to get a handle on recurring expenses and your overall cashflow.

Take a look at Table 4-1, beginning with your income. Then add up your expenses (and we've given you lots of space, big spender!) and deduct these from your total monthly income. What's left over is what you can afford to pay toward your mortgage each month — and that amount should include a buffer for issues like general maintenance and emergency repairs, taxes, insurance, and other items that may crop up.

TIP

A general rule is to maintain a reserve equal to at least three to six months of expenses in case of a job loss, emergency, or other shock to your cash flow (incoming or outgoing) like a global pandemic striking. You don't necessarily have to have it all at once, but factor it into your financial plan. You may have $1,250 left over at the end of the month, for example, but stashing away some cash for a contingency fund might mean you set aside $250 a month for a year, which leaves you able to carry a mortgage of $1,000 a month. (We discuss ways to accelerate your mortgage payments in Chapter 5.)

Add up all the columns. That number is your total expenses. To calculate your maximum monthly mortgage payment, take your total income and subtract your total expenses. For example, if your monthly income is $6,000 and your monthly expenses total $3,975, you have just $2,025 to put towards a mortgage.

Several online tools exist to help you create a budget document. Many financial institutions also offer tools that help you determine your net worth. The tools they offer will often draw from your account information to figure out the difference between your assets liabilities, determining your net worth in minutes. If you have assets outside your financial institution, you may need to add these in to get an accurate calculation.

TABLE 4-1

Monthly Budget Worksheet

Monthly Income	
Net income after taxes	
Partner's net income after taxes	
Other income: investments, gifts, annuities, trust funds, pensions, and so forth	
Total Income	
Monthly Expenses	
Investments	
RRSPs	
RESP education funds	
Other	
Debts	
Credit cards	
Lines of credit	
Student loans	
Other loans/debts	
Transportation	
Auto loan or lease payments	
Auto insurance	
Auto registration	
Auto repairs/maintenance	
Fuel	
Parking	
Public transit	
Household Costs	
Groceries	
Laundry/dry cleaning	
Utilities	
Hydro	
Water	

(continued)

TABLE 4-1 *(continued)*

Monthly Income	
Gas	
Home insurance	
Electricity	
Telephone	
Cell phones/wireless devices	
Cable television	
Internet	
Health	
Medication	
Glasses/contacts	
Dental/orthodontics	
Therapist	
Special needs items	
Miscellaneous	
Life insurance	
Education/Tuition fees	
Books/supplies	
Daycare	
Entertainment	
Restaurant meals	
Vacations	
Clothing/accessories	
Recreation/sports	
Membership fees	
Equipment	
Pet expenses	
Gifts	
Other	
Total Expenses	

WARNING

Online calculators are an awful lot like, well, regular calculators. They're only as accurate as the numbers you plug in. Don't start hunting for houses based on the results if you've given only rough estimates (which can lead to rough surprises). These calculators are indications only, even with the most spot-on information.

Determining What Size Mortgage You Can Carry

After you figure out your maximum monthly mortgage payment (refer to the previous section), you may realize that you qualify for a larger mortgage than you initially considered. At this point, you're faced with two scenarios: what you can comfortably afford, and what amount you can absolutely financially stretch yourself to in order to buy your dream house. Lenders will be more than happy to give you a larger mortgage if you can afford the payments, but you should decide what monthly payment amounts comfortably fit within your budget. You don't want to be saddled with a large mortgage and not be able to afford some of the creature comforts of life.

The following sections discuss the two ways that financial institutions typically approaches determining how big a mortgage they're willing to give you and how you can make your own calculations.

Gross debt service (GDS) ratio

This ratio is calculated as the percentage of gross annual or gross monthly household income needed to cover all housing-related costs (including principal and interest payments on your mortgage, property taxes, electricity, water, and heating, and half the monthly condo fees, if applicable). It shouldn't be more than approximately 35 percent of your gross annual or gross monthly income.

You can use a calculation like this one to determine your GDS ratio (all the figures are approximate and have been rounded):

Start with you gross monthly household income (pre-tax)	$7,500
Multiply by 35 percent available for housing	$0.35 \times \$7,500 = \$2,625$
Subtract estimated monthly property taxes ($250)	$2,625 - \$250 = \$2,375$
Subtract estimated hydro, heating, and water costs (and half the monthly condo fees, if applicable)	$2,375 - \$350
Monthly income available for mortgage payments	$2,025

Total debt service (TDS) ratio

This ratio is calculated as the percentage of gross annual or monthly household income required to cover all your housing-related costs *plus any other debts* (for example, student loan, car, and credit card payments). This figure should be no more than 42 percent of your gross annual or monthly income.

Your GDS ratio can be a very misleading guide in deciding what size mortgage you can carry, however, particularly if you have a lot of other debts. This is when knowing your Total Debt Service (TDS) ratio comes in handy. You can use this method to calculate your TDS ratio:

Start with your gross monthly household income (pre-tax)	$7,500
Multiply by 42 percent available for housing and other debts	0.42 × $7,500 = $3,150
Subtract current monthly debt payments ($500 for car payment, $300 for credit cards, $200 for student loan)	$3,150 – $500 – $300 – $200 = $2,150
Subtract estimated monthly property taxes	$2,150 – $200 = $1,950
Subtract estimated hydro, heating, and water costs (and half the monthly condo fees, if applicable)	$1,950 – $250
Monthly income available for mortgage payments	$1,700

As you can see, the Total Debt Service presents a much more accurate picture of what is left over to spend on housing.

Generating your own figures

Several online calculators can also generate your GDS and TDS ratios automatically when you fill in the needed information. GDS and TDS calculations can help you determine a reasonable price range for a new home, but they factor in only the official debt you carry — not the other obligations you may prefer to forget about.

Just because the online calculators say that, according to the information you've entered, you can carry a $300,000 mortgage doesn't mean you'd have any money left over for other expenses. Remember, the calculator is just a computer program that has absolutely no need to have a social life, buy its kids' shoes, or get the car fixed. This is where it pays to complete Table 4-1.

In addition to knowing the size of mortgage you're eligible for, consider how factors like payment frequency, amortization period, and so on can affect the cost of a mortgage. We discuss these variables at greater length in Chapter 5, but the calculators available from your financial institution and sites like Ratehub (www.ratehub.ca) can help you understand what your mortgage payments would be on different payment frequencies and different mortgage plans.

Getting a Head Start with a Preapproved Mortgage

Before even thinking about looking for a new home, speak with your lender or mortgage broker about getting *preapproved* for a mortgage. The process is quick and simple, and the good thing is that it costs you nothing and can save you valuable time — as well as possible home heartbreak. You'll know exactly how much you have at your disposal because the process is exactly the same as applying for an actual mortgage.

Being preapproved is better than any estimate you may have discussed with your lender or generated from one of the many online tools, because estimates are just that — estimates. Until you provide your mortgage broker or lender with the necessary documents and go through the actual preapproval process, you aren't preapproved.

Here we take a closer look at the preapproval process by examining the advantages of getting preapproved and by explaining the process so you're armed and ready.

Understanding the advantages of preapproval

Preapproval for a mortgage has several advantages, including,

>> **You know your price limit.** Before you set your heart on the mansion up the road, know your financial limitations.

>> **Your offers are taken more seriously by sellers.** Sellers prefer to accept an offer from someone who has started to arrange financing. After all, there's a chance the buyer who hasn't yet been preapproved may not be able to get financing at all. These days, smart agents won't even take a client out to look at properties until he has his financing sorted. Getting preapproved takes the worry out of qualifying well in advance and will help your agent identify properties that are within your budget.

>> **You're protected from any rise (and can take advantage of any drop) in interest rates.** As long as you close your sale within the time period of the prearranged mortgage (typically, from 30 to 120 days), you can rest assured that your mortgage will be at the rate stated in your preapproval even if bank interest rates have risen since you initially obtained the preapproval.

Getting the lay of preapproval land

Similar to applying for an actual mortgage, when you apply for preapproval you answer questions and provide documents based on your financial position, debt load, and credit history. (We discuss details about the mortgage process in Chapter 5.) There is usually a fixed time period (from 30 to 120 days) for which lenders will offer a certain size mortgage at a specific interest rate, and they'll confirm this in writing.

TIP

With rapidly shifting lending rates and qualification requirements, you should stay in constant touch with your lender to make sure that what you were originally told two months ago still applies today. Often your lender will send weekly rate updates.

Even with preapproval, you still have to secure the mortgage after you've negotiated the buying of a home. Your final mortgage approval is subject to a full check of your finances and an appraisal of the market value of the property you want to buy. But preapproval means most of the paperwork has been done beforehand, which speeds up the process significantly.

If you're applying for a *high-ratio mortgage* (your down payment amounts to less than 20 percent of the purchase price of the home you're buying), you're also subject to the approval of the *Canada Mortgage and Housing Corporation* (CMHC), a federal Crown corporation that administers national housing programs and insures mortgages under the provisions of the National Housing Act. Your application for CMHC approval can't be processed until you have an accepted *offer to purchase contract* from your seller. (See Chapter 9 for details concerning contracts of purchase and sale.)

TIP

Just because you're preapproved for a mortgage doesn't mean you can make an unconditional offer to buy a home. Write into your offer to purchase contract a *subject to financing clause* (a very common procedure) so that you have at least a couple of days to complete your mortgage approval. A mortgage is a contract; it's a legally binding document, and you must uphold it. Make sure have a complete understanding of your financial obligations. Ask your lender questions if you're unclear on any terms.

You can also find lots of good advice online about financing sources to consider and options to bargain for when you're negotiating a mortgage.

Anticipating the Closing Costs

The last big hurdle in the home-buying process is *closing* — when you complete all the paperwork and sign off on all the documents needed to purchase your new home. At this time, you also finalize all the really boring necessary details that need to be covered when you buy a house. For example, the property has to be transferred into your name, obviously enough, but first, your lawyer must check that no one else has any claims against the house or property (also called *liens*). You may have municipal taxes to pay, land transfer taxes to pay, accounts to settle with the previous owners, mortgage details to finalize, and so on. (We walk you through closing day in Chapter 12.)

REMEMBER

Your lawyer will explain the closing costs. Be sure to make an appointment a few days prior to the closing date to review these costs so there are no surprises on closing day.

Deposit and down payment

You're generally required to pay a deposit of at least 5 percent of the purchase price of the house. (The amount is negotiable; a competitive situation may justify a larger deposit that demonstrates how committed you are to getting the deal done.) The deposit may be paid in stages or all at once. Your first offer on a house may include an initial deposit, which can be as little as $500 or $1,000, depending on real estate practices in your area.

You make the deposit with a regular or certified cheque, payable to your real estate agent's brokerage. Generally, this amount is deposited in the brokerage's trust account only after your offer has been accepted. If you aren't using an agent, your lawyer usually holds your deposit in trust. When all conditions in the agreement of purchase and sale have been settled (see Chapter 9 for information on these items), you deliver the full deposit. The remainder of the deposit is payable, like the first installment, to the real estate agent's brokerage by certified cheque or bank draft and is held with the initial portion in the brokerage's trust account.

TECHNICAL STUFF

Practices around deposits differ in every province. In some provinces, there is a one-time deposit of approximately 5 percent. This deposit may be handed over with the initial offer or may be collected when all subjects are removed. In some provinces, the more common practice is a one-time deposit held in trust by the listing agent. In other provinces, the buyer's agent holds the deposit.

The deposit forms part of the down payment — you pay off the balance of the down payment on the closing date (also known as the *completion date*). A certified cheque or bank draft payable to your lawyer or notary public is the most common way to pay the balance of your down payment. Your lawyer will advise you of the exact amount you have to bring in and the preferred method of payment.

If you make a small down payment (perhaps 5 percent on an affordable house), the amount of the deposit your real estate agent holds may also represent the total down payment. In this case, your agent's brokerage will convey the money to your lawyer or notary for you. Remember, many closing costs will be above and beyond this 5 percent down payment, so make sure you're well aware of what those costs will be.

Identifying three key closing fees

To sew up your mortgage deal, you need financing, high-ratio insurance (if applicable), and legal guidance. Of course, lining up all of these details costs money, so get ready for further costs at closing time.

Financing fees

If you use the services of a mortgage broker, the lender will probably pay the brokerage fee. However, under certain circumstances if you've had past financial difficulties, you may be required to pay this fee yourself, which could be as much as 2 percent of the total mortgage amount. Ask early in the process what to expect.

WARNING

If you're porting a mortgage, or blending a mortgage and renegotiating more favourable terms for a new mortgage, make sure you ask your lender if you will have any penalties or fees to pay. (We discuss the various types of mortgages in Chapter 5.)

Insurance fees

If you have a high-ratio mortgage, you must obtain mortgage loan insurance. Insurance costs range between 1 percent and 4.75 percent of your total mortgage amount. (This surcharge is subject to change; ask your mortgage broker or lender for the current rate.) For convenience, you can incorporate your insurance fee into your monthly mortgage payments. You may have to pay sales tax on your insurance as well, which can add up to 15 percent to the monthly premium.

An application fee may be payable on your mortgage loan insurance. The fee can range from $75 to $235, depending on whether or not an appraisal is required. You can read more about mortgage insurance in Chapter 5.

Legal fees and disbursements

You need a lawyer (or a notary, if you're buying in Quebec) to review the offer to purchase, perform a title search, draw up your mortgage documents, and tend to the closing details (you can find more information on the role of the lawyer, and how to find one, in Chapter 2). Your lawyer also takes care of any reimbursements owed the previous owner (for items such as prepaid electricity and water bills and property taxes). All other utilities, such as phone, cable, and non-prepaid electricity, are read at the time of closing and billed to the appropriate parties.

You pay only the applicable portion of the expenses from the date that you take possession of the home you're buying. (If you're buying a resale condo, and the condo fees are prepaid, they'll also be prorated.) How much all these fees will cost depends on how complicated your deal is, but you can count on about $500 to $2,000 to cover legal fees. The prorated fees for property taxes, condo fees, and any other prepaid expenses will be outlined in the statement of adjustments prepared by your lawyer. You can find more on statements of adjustments in Chapter 10.

Appraisals, surveys, inspections, and condominium certificates

Here are four more items that you may have to pay for before closing day:

>> **Appraisal:** You may need to get an appraisal for your lender. An *appraisal* is an independent confirmation that a home's purchase price is of fair market value. If you ask nicely, you can probably get your lender to pay for the appraisal. A basic appraisal fee is about $200 to $500. Appraisals are done on a comparison basis, so if there's nothing to compare with, more work is involved, hence the higher fee. (See Chapter 2 for more on appraisals.)

>> **Survey:** The Land Titles Office, or your lender, may require an up-to-date survey in order to approve your mortgage. A *survey* verifies the boundaries of your property and ensures that there are no encroachments either by you onto your neighbour's property or vice versa. The price of surveys varies widely, depending on the location and type of property. Your real estate agent can give you an idea of what to expect. (We talk more about surveys in Chapter 10.)

In some provinces, you can avoid the cost of a survey by purchasing title insurance. *Title insurance* protects property owners from survey errors or defects that would've been revealed had an up-to-date survey been done.

The cost of title insurance in most cases is less than that of a new survey, but if you're purchasing property with the idea of building, you'll want a survey regardless.

>> **Inspection:** Get a professional home inspection done on the home you're going to buy. An *inspection* is a report on the presence and apparent condition of the structural and operational systems of a home. (See Chapter 10 for details.) The cost of an inspection ranges from $300 to $800. If your property is very large or unusual in its construction, count on a higher fee. If you're moving to a rural area where wells or septic tanks are involved, get separate inspections for the septic tank and/or field and the system itself. Also, have the well tested for water potability (basically, is it drinkable?), supply, and pressure. These separate inspections can be pricey, but to pass on them can be expensive and cause future inconveniences (unless you don't mind using an outhouse in the winter or waiting for a water truck to deliver to you every two weeks).

>> **Condominium certificate:** If you're buying a condo, you'll need a document confirming the seller has fulfilled all obligations to the condominium corporation. This information is contained in a document variously known as the *condominium certificate, estoppel certificate, information certificate, Form F,* or *status certificate,* to name a few of its incarnations. Ask your real estate agent what the local alias is. This certificate and its supporting documents will cost you from $50 to $100, although if you're buying in Quebec, you don't need it (*C'est bon, non?*).

Taxes

Your new home-owning adventure wouldn't be complete without taxes. Get ready for these additions to your closing costs, too:

>> **Property tax:** If the previous owners of your new home paid any property taxes in advance, the tax paid is prorated to the closing date and you have to reimburse the sellers. The reimbursement you make is called an *adjustment.* (See Chapter 10 for more information on adjustments.) When you take possession of your new home, all bill payments become your responsibility.

>> **Land transfer tax/deed transfer tax:** Depending on where you live, you may also have to pay a transfer tax. The calculation and applicability of this tax varies across Canada. The provinces with a transfer tax are British Columbia, Manitoba, Ontario, Quebec, New Brunswick, Newfoundland and Labrador, Prince Edward Island, and Nova Scotia (though rural Nova Scotia is exempt, as is all of Alberta and Saskatchewan).

Your real estate agent or lawyer can tell you what to expect. Generally, the amount of the transfer tax works out to between 1 and 5 percent of the purchase price of your home, sometimes calculated on a sliding scale. Some provinces waive part or all of the provincial transfer tax for first-time buyers.

>> **Goods and Services Tax/Harmonized Sales Tax:** If you're buying a newly built house (that is, you're the first one to live in it — no prior owners), you may pay 5 percent GST on the price, or, if you live in Ontario, Quebec, Nova Scotia, Newfoundland and Labrador, or Prince Edward Island, you'll be subject to the *Harmonized Sales Tax*. HST (or QST in Quebec) combines the provincial and federal sales taxes into a single tax. For instance, in Ontario, the HST is 13 percent. These taxes also apply if you purchase a house that has been substantially renovated.

Depending on the province and the price point of the home you're purchasing (among other things), you may be entitled to a tax rebate. Don't forget to find out how and when to apply for any rebates before you purchase. Every province's rules are different, so speak to your agent or lawyer for details.

REMEMBER

Don't forget that you will pay GST or HST on all services provided by your lawyer, your listing agent, your inspector, your appraiser, and so on.

Remembering Little Extras You May Not Have Considered

Each province has its own way of doing things. If you're moving from one province to another, keep the following points in mind:

>> **Local oddities:** Ranging from the obvious to the unexpected, there are probably as many obscure local costs in each part of Canada as there are regional accents. Your real estate agent and/or lawyer can advise you what your statement of adjustments will include. Any of the following may apply to your purchase: garbage/recycling charges, diking fee (if the area is below sea level), meter hookup, tree planting, education development fees — the list goes on. If you're buying a resale house, the fees are prorated to your closing date to ensure continuity between the previous owner and you, the lucky new owner.

>> **Moving costs:** Do some research to arrive at a reasonable budget for your move. Of course, the exact amount will vary depending on how much stuff you have to move, how far you have to move it, and how much you're willing to move on your own. Expect moving rates to be higher at the end of a month

or during the summer, because these are high-traffic times for moving companies. Try to plan ahead. Make some calls to request moving cost estimates. A higher moving estimate with a guarantee may end up being the better way. Often moving companies will charge considerably more than the original quote they supplied to get your business. Ask others for referrals. If you decide to rent a van or truck, reserve it in advance.

» **Utility charges:** Be prepared to pay connection fees for hooking up your telephone, cable, and electricity, and don't forget to ask the post office to redirect your mail to your new address (this currently costs $85 for 12 months within a province, or about $107 if you're relocating across the country).

» **Keeping interest payments low**

» **Deciding which type of mortgage you need**

» **Insuring your mortgage and yourself**

» **Choosing a mortgage broker or lender**

» **Getting information from your lender**

» **Understanding what information you must provide**

Chapter **5**

Knowing Your Mortgage Options

I f a home is the single biggest purchase someone ever makes, the mortgage that makes it possible is the biggest debt someone ever takes on. The typical mortgage required to purchase a home in an urban centre or even a desirable suburb is often in the hundreds of thousands of dollars. The good news for purchasers is that the range of mortgage options today are a lot more flexible than they once were. A fixed-rate mortgage on a five-year term used to be the norm. Now, you can get fixed-rate, variable-rate, or a mortgage that combines the two. The terms can vary (within reason), and a mortgage is often portable, which means you can take it with you when you go (to your next house, anyway).

This chapter introduces you to some of the key options so that you can tailor your mortgage to your needs. We explain the various kinds of mortgages available, including the main features and benefits (and possible drawbacks). Being able to access the right kind of financing is critical to being able to buy the right kind of home and ending up a little better off financially for having done so, too.

Of course, when you know what kind of mortgage you want, there's the small matter of actually getting it. We provide tips that can make for smooth sailing through the qualification process: who to talk to, what questions to ask, and what you'll need to tell them about yourself. Being prepared for the process can help you protect your interests and money.

Defining Your Financing Goals

Getting the best deal on a mortgage may seem like Mission Impossible, but it doesn't have to be if you know your priorities and have clear objectives. Your mission, if you choose to accept it, is to get the best mortgage for your personal situation while paying the least interest possible. Just like other aspects of the home-buying experience, the best mortgage isn't necessarily the one with the lowest rate, but one that gives you the home you want at a price you can afford. Knowing how to structure your mortgage, and the strategy you'll use to pay it off, can help you make financing work to your advantage.

Knowing the potential scenarios

Buyers face many scenarios that require different types of mortgages, which include the following:

>> A down payment of a minimum of 20 percent with the balance of the home's purchase price arranged through a mortgage.

>> A down payment of less than 20 percent with the balance of the home's purchase price arranged through a mortgage and high-ratio mortgage insurance.

>> A down payment of 15 percent for the first nine months until additional funds become available, allowing for a closed mortgage for the majority of the amount required and an open mortgage (which can be repaid anytime) for the remainder.

>> A down payment of 5 percent for a specified period of time (say, six months or a year) until sufficient funds become available and the high-ratio mortgage can be converted to conventional financing.

>> Low interest rates may make an open, variable-rate option more attractive for a portion of the mortgage, reducing short-term costs while the fixed-rate portion provides a hedge against the possibility of interest rates increasing.

>> A term shorter than five years allows you to accommodate changes in your personal circumstances that may allow you to avoid charges for early discharge of the mortgage.

Keeping interest payments in check

One of the advantages of being a homeowner is building equity, not making someone else rich (and that includes your lender, not just a landlord). Because interest costs can easily equal half the value of the mortgage over the cost of its life, they're not pocket change. Use these strategies to keep your interest payments low:

>> **Make as large a down payment as you comfortably can.** The larger your down payment, the less you'll need to borrow to buy the home and the less interest you'll pay. First-time homebuyers can use funds from their Registered Retirement Savings Plan (RRSPs) to help boost their down payments; refer to Chapter 4 for more information.

>> **Arrange to pay back the loan as quickly as possible.** The longer the *amortization period*, or the life of the loan, the more interest you'll pay.

>> **Commit to making weekly or biweekly payments.** The more frequent your payment schedule, the faster you'll pay off the *principal* (the amount owed on the mortgage), resulting in lower interest charges.

>> **Make extra payments whenever you can.** Many mortgages allow an anniversary (or annual) payment equivalent to 10 to 20 percent of the outstanding balance. Others let borrowers top up their regular payments on a regular basis. This means that when you receive a bonus at work or win the lottery or inherit billions, you're able to put money towards paying down your mortgage and saving interest.

>> **Ensure your mortgage allows you to prepay principal.** Some mortgages allow you to not only make extra payments, but to pay off the mortgage before the term is up. These mortgages are typically more expensive, either because the mortgage rate is higher or pre-payment penalties are applied.

After you define what you want your mortgage to do for you and how fast you think you'll be able to pay it down, you'll be in a good position to choose the type of mortgage that's right for you.

BANKING ON FAMILY

With the high cost of housing mean you may wonder if you'll ever be able to afford a place of your own. Many people have thrown tens of thousands of dollars away on rent while trying to save up for a down payment. And many look enviously at their parents, who were able to scrimp and save and buy a home — and eventually burn the mortgage. Billions of dollars of equity are locked up in residential real estate in Canada, and for many people the Bank of Mom and Dad has been an option when pulling together a down payment.

If your parents — or aunt or grandparent — are willing to support you in purchasing your first home, congratulations! Do them proud, and make sure you pay them back handsomely for their trust. Being able to work with family has a few benefits when buying a home:

- The debt isn't counted against your capacity to borrow (but make sure you protect your family's interests by putting your commitment to them in writing).

- In some cases, if a family member advances you cash, he may be able to also serve as a guarantor of your commitments (but again, make sure you have the arrangement in writing, because he'll be on the hook for your debts, which means both of your savings could be in jeopardy, so talk to your lawyers!).

- Funds from family may serve as a kind of short-term bridge financing while you wait for other sources of cash to become available. For example, if your purchase closes before you've sold your existing home, you may save thousands of dollars in interest if you can borrow from family; private lenders can be a temporary solution, but they'll often charge twice the going rate banks and other financial institutions charge.

They key point is, when you're trying to figure out how you're going to manage a mortgage, don't forget to ask what your family can bring to the table.

Mastering the Lingo: Mortgage Jargon 101

One cool thing about getting a mortgage is that every element has a clear purpose. When you start crunching the numbers, everything starts to make sense really, really quickly. Every mortgage has four chief elements, which we explore here.

Mortgage principal

The total amount of the loan you get is called the principal. If you need to borrow $350,000 to buy a house, then the principal is $350,000. The principal will become smaller and smaller as you pay off the loan.

Interest

Interest is the money you pay a lender in addition to the money you pay to pay off the principal of your loan — a sort of compensation so your lender profits from giving you a loan. The *interest rate*, calculated as a percentage of the principal, determines how much interest you pay the lender in each scheduled payment — the cost of borrowing the money. Most interest rates are set in some relation to the prime rate set by the Bank of Canada (www.bankofcanada.ca), which sets monetary policy in Canada. By paying attention to the rate set by the Bank of Canada and any proposed rate moves, you can often stay ahead of what your own lender is going to do. The two don't always move in sync, but the Bank of Canada isn't a bad star to steer by.

People like to buy property when interest rates are low because they can either buy a more expensive house than if the rates were higher or pay off the mortgage more quickly. For example, borrowing $200,000 at a 5 percent interest rate would cost you approximately $47,000 in the first five-year term. But at a 7 percent interest rate, you'd pay approximately $66,000 extra. Borrowing at the lower rate lets you put that extra $19,000 towards the principal, effectively paying yourself rather than the bank.

REMEMBER

The way your lender adds up the interest you owe has a big impact on the amount of interest you pay over the life of the mortgage. If interest is *compounded*, or charged on the balance owing every day, you'll pay more over the lifetime of the mortgage than if interest is compounded semi-annually. Most mortgages are compounded semi-annually, but your lender may offer you other options.

Amortization period

The *amortization period* of your mortgage is the length of time in which the calculation of your monthly payments is based. The advantage of a longer amortization period is that the monthly payments are smaller and therefore more manageable. The disadvantage is that the longer the amortization period, the longer you carry a principal and, therefore, the more you pay in interest. And interest really adds up. Currently, the longest amortization period available in Canada is 30 years; however, the standard period — and the longest allowed for insured mortgages — is 25 years. You can see in Table 5-1 that the total interest on a 25-year amortization is almost double what you'd pay for a 15-year amortization.

TABLE 5-1

Amortization Payment Comparison

Amortization	Monthly Payments	Total Paid	Total Interest
15 years	$1,186	$214,000	$64,000
20 years	$990	$238,000	$88,000
25 years	$877	$263,000	$113,000

Note: Calculations for a $150,000 mortgage at 5 percent interest, compounded semi-annually.

Mortgage term

A *mortgage term* is the specific length of time you and your lender agree your mortgage will be subject to certain negotiated conditions, such as the interest rate. Terms usually range from six months to ten years, but occasionally a lender will offer a 15- or 25-year term.

At the end of the term, you generally have the option to pay off your mortgage in full or to renegotiate its terms and conditions. If interest rates are ridiculously high, you'll probably want to negotiate a shorter term and then arrange a longer term when rates are more favourable. If rates are on their way down or very low, a *variable rate* — which allows you to lock in when you want — may be the way to go. At the end of your mortgage term (or before, if you're refinancing), you can transfer your mortgage to another lender. Refer to the next section for more information on the types of mortgages.

REMEMBER

If you're *refinancing*, or renegotiating, the terms of your mortgage before the end of your mortgage term, you'll very likely incur penalties. However, if the rate you'll receive after renegotiating is much more competitive, those one-time costs may well be worth it.

Understanding the Types of Mortgages

Mortgages break down into two types — conventional and high-ratio — based on the amount of the down payment and, therefore, the amount of risk the lender is assuming by advancing you the money. These can be further broken down according to the type of interest rate charged — fixed rate or variable rate — and how the interest is collected — either separately from the principal, or (most commonly) together in the form of a blended payment. This section drills down into the details of each.

Conventional mortgages

A *conventional mortgage* covers up to 80 percent of a property's purchase price or appraised value, whichever is lower. So if you want to buy a $300,000 house, you need a $60,000 down payment (20 percent of the purchase price) if you're applying for a conventional mortgage.

High-ratio mortgages

High-ratio mortgages account for between 80 and 95 percent of a property's purchase price or appraised value, whichever is lower. If you purchase a property with a down payment of less than 20 percent, your mortgage will need to be insured by one of the following:

>> Canada Mortgage and Housing Corp. (www.cmhc.ca)

>> Genworth Financial Mortgage Insurance Co. of Canada (www.genworth.ca)

>> Canada Guaranty Mortgage Insurance (www.canadaguaranty.ca)

The insurance protects the lender if you default on your mortgage. An insurance premium ranging from 2.4 to 4.5 percent of the mortgage amount, predetermined by a sliding scale, will be added to your mortgage and incorporated into your payment schedule. You may also have to pay an extra premium if you take out a variable rate mortgage. We talk more about mortgage insurance in the section "Playing it Safe: High-Ratio Mortgage Insurance," and of course, your lender or mortgage broker can answer all your questions, too.

Fixed-rate mortgage

Because interest rates rise and fall, some times are better than others for taking out a mortgage. To give yourself some stability, you can choose a *fixed-rate mortgage* that allows you to lock in at a specific interest rate for a certain period of time (known as the *mortgage term*). If interest rates are rising, you may want to lock in at a fixed rate so you know what your monthly costs will be over the term of your mortgage. When a mortgage term expires, you can renegotiate your interest rate, regular payment amount, and the term.

As you shop for mortgages, you'll see that each lender specifies a certain interest rate for a certain term. Under most market conditions, the lower the fixed interest rate, the shorter the time period you can lock in to pay that rate. However, a longer-term, fixed-rate mortgage allows you to put a dent in your principal before facing the possibility of an increase in your monthly payments. You can easily compare rates from various lenders using online services such as Ratehub (www.ratehub.ca), which also provides calculators that let you adjust variables such as down payment, payment term, and payment frequency to figure out which option is best for you.

REMEMBER

Fixed-rate mortgages have a variety of options, such as different prepayment rules and weekly, biweekly, or monthly payment schedules, so make sure to talk to several lenders (or a mortgage broker) to see who offers the most competitive interest rate and terms.

Variable-rate mortgage

A *variable-rate* mortgage is usually set up for a one- to six-year term. The interest rate fluctuates with the market. If you, the borrower, see that interest rates are starting to rise, you may be able to lock into a fixed rate for the balance of the term. There's plenty of variation among variable-rate mortgages, however. Similar to fixed-rate mortgages, make sure the terms suit your particular needs and the market conditions.

The interest rates of variable-rate mortgages vary from lender to lender, but most are offered in some relation to the *prime rate*, which is the interest rate that financial institutions charge their most creditworthy borrowers (that is, the big corporate clients). Rates for variable mortgages usually vary from half a percentage point below prime to half a percentage point above prime. Borrowers should also make sure that they're comparing the same prime rate; some lenders will list a variable rate mortgage at half a percentage point above the well-recognized and respected Bank of Canada prime rate, while another lender will offer a rate one-quarter of a percentage point below prime. This figure may be an elevated prime rate, too, which of course means the lender's supposed lower rate is no bargain at all.

Variable rates aren't for everyone because you'll need to keep track of interest rates to make sure you lock in your mortgage rate before interest rates rise. You may benefit from lower overall interest charges if you're prepared to monitor interest rates and know when to lock them in.

TIP

The choice between a variable- and a fixed-rate mortgage is also a lifestyle decision. With a variable rate, you can usually buy more of your home with a smaller payment and save interest costs, but if you worry about rising rates and want peace of mind, go for a fixed-rate mortgage. There's more to life than worrying about interest rates.

TIP

If you use a mortgage broker or have a good relationship with your lender, you may get a heads-up that a jump in interest rates is looming. If you get that call, you can then decide if you want to lock in the balance of your variable mortgage or float with the fluctuations in interest rates. Any rise in rates may be temporary, of course, so you'll have to decide (with the input of your lender) whether or not to lock in your rate. You'll soon determine how well you handle stress, uncertainty, and risk. This is where it also pays to know your prepayment options: For example, if you pay out the mortgage before the third anniversary, what penalty will be charged?

Blended payments

When you make a mortgage payment, it consists of two parts. One portion of the payment is applied towards paying down the principal, and another is applied towards paying the interest. That's what's known as a *blended payment*. A non-blended payment would see a fixed amount paid to the principal, and the interest charge added on, resulting in two separate payments. Because some principal is being paid down, subsequent payments are a bit less every time. Blended payments are far more efficient, giving the borrower certainty over how much is to be paid each week and accelerating the reduction in principal and interest.

Here's an example: If your mortgage is $300,000 with a 5 percent interest rate compounded semi-annually with an amortization of 25 years, the basic monthly payments will be approximately $1,745. Table 5-2 shows how, as you pay down the principal, the distribution of your payments changes. Gradually you begin paying more money towards the principal than towards the interest you owe to your lender.

TABLE 5-2

Breakdown of Blended Payments

Timeline	Your Monthly Payment of $1,745		
	Principal	Interest	Balance Principal
1 month	$508	$1,237	$299,492
6 months	$518	$1,227	$296,923
1 year	$531	$1,214	$293,768
5 years	$647	$1,098	$265,522
10 years	$829	$916	$221,388
20 years	$1,358	$387	$92,572

TIP

The more frequently you make mortgage payments, the faster you pay down your principal — which means that the more quickly you eliminate your mortgage, the less interest you pay. Payment schedules can be arranged monthly, semi-monthly, biweekly (every two weeks), or weekly. You can also opt to pay more than the minimum required; you can increase the basic payment in Table 5-2 to $1,800 or more, for example, allowing the principal to be paid faster. Of course, after you commit to a certain payment, you have to maintain it for the life of the mortgage; you can't reduce it without paying a penalty. Arrange with your lender to make payments as often as you can reasonably manage. If you can make weekly payments rather than monthly ones, you'll save thousands of dollars over the lifetime of the loan. Table 5-3 illustrates how making more frequent payments can really whittle down the time it takes to repay a mortgage.

TABLE 5-3

Mortgage Payment Frequency Comparison

Payment Options	Monthly Payments	Years to Repay Mortgage
Monthly	$1,745	25
Biweekly	$872	22
Weekly	$436	22

Note: Calculations for a 25-year $300,000 mortgage at 5 percent interest, compounded semi-annually.

Mortgage-a-rama: All the Nifty Options

How much of a down payment you can make will determine your eligibility for either a conventional or high-ratio mortgage. If you have money on hand that allows you to pay at least 20 percent of the purchase price, then you'll be able to obtain a conventional mortgage. If you have less than 20 percent of the purchase price as a down payment, you'll require a high-ratio mortgage.

Since 2018, federal rules have also required that lenders assess all new borrowers — both those that require insurance and those that don't — to ensure they have the means to continue making mortgage payments if faced with "a sudden change to their circumstances (income loss, increased interest rates, additional expenses, etc.)." Set by the Office of the Superintendent of Financial Institutions and known as the *B-20 stress test*, the qualifying rate is defined as, "the greater of the contractual mortgage rate plus two percentage points, or the five-year benchmark rate published by the Bank of Canada." This rate was being reviewed in spring 2020, but the process was cut short by the COVID-19 pandemic.

Regardless of the financial position you find yourself in, you have several types of mortgages to choose from. Some financial institutions even try to match your financial personalities with a specific mortgage type. You may even want to consider not getting a mortgage at all and going with a line of credit instead. In this section, we consider each option.

Payment options: Open, closed, or in between?

Choosing the right mortgage means understanding your mortgage payment options: open mortgages, closed mortgages, or mortgages that offer something in between. The option you choose will affect how much money you pay over the lifetime of the loan and the flexibility of the terms. Some mortgages allow you to pay off your principal in lump sums as you wish and prepay your principal without any penalties. Other mortgages allow you to prepay only once a year on the anniversary date of the mortgage. Some permit no prepayment at all.

Different financial institutions offer a range of mortgages involving different degrees of flexibility for prepayment. Even most closed mortgages have some prepayment options. You can make specified maximum prepayments, usually between 10 and 20 percent of the outstanding principal, once a year either on any payment date or on the anniversary date of the mortgage, and in some cases you can increase each payment. You're charged a penalty if you pay down more.

Open mortgage

If you have an *open mortgage*, you can pay it off in full or in part at any time with no penalty. By chipping away at your principal early, you can save crazy amounts of money in interest. Of course, every penny you save in interest is a penny that doesn't get into your lender's hot little hands — which is why the average fixed interest rate quoted for an open mortgage is 0.4 to 0.6 percent higher than a closed mortgage for the same term.

The majority of open mortgages with a fixed interest rate are available only for a short term. Most variable-rate mortgages have a fixed five-year term without an opportunity to pay them off at will (they're closed), but they may open up after three years. Variable-rate mortgages are usually offered at a lower rate when they're closed, whereas open variable rate mortgages come at a higher cost for the convenience of leaving them early.

REMEMBER

An open mortgage is a good choice if you're going to move again soon, if interest rates are expected to fall, or if you're expecting a bonus or inheritance to apply against the mortgage. This kind of mortgage is good for the short term when rates are high, and it can usually be converted to a closed mortgage at any time.

TIP

Prepayment options differ between lenders. However, many will give you a discount on the posted rates if and when you convert your mortgage to a longer, fixed rate option. Research your options before you commit to a mortgage to make sure you're getting the best deal.

Closed mortgage

The advantage of signing on to a *closed mortgage* is that you'll typically get lower interest rates and you'll be able to budget for fixed, regular payments. The downside is that if you need to move before your term is up, or if you have extra cash, such as an income tax refund, that you'd like to put toward paying off a large portion of your principal, you may pay a penalty for this privilege.

Most closed mortgages give the borrower the ability to prepay 10 to 20 percent of the outstanding balance without penalty at least once during the year, often on the anniversary date of the mortgage.

Some cases may have restrictive conditions that make getting out of your closed mortgage an expensive proposition. You may face a prepayment penalty (Chapter 13 has more information about paying off your mortgage early and the possible penalties) or rate differential fee if you want to discharge the mortgage before the end of the term. Read the fine print, and ask lots of questions.

Portable mortgage

If your mortgage is *portable,* you can take it with you to your new house. When you get ready to move, you'll be glad you asked about this option, especially if you negotiated great terms or if interest rates have gone up since you locked in to your current mortgage. Even if you're buying a more expensive house, having a portable mortgage is still to your advantage.

For example, if you have a $300,000 mortgage at 4 percent interest and you're in the third year of a five-year term, you can take the mortgage with you to the $425,000 house you want to buy. You may need an additional $75,000 loan added to your principal to make it work, though. If the going rate on new loans is 3 percent interest for a three-year mortgage to match the remaining three years of your five-year term, you'll need to negotiate a rate on the new amount. The new mortgage payment will be composed of two parts: your initial payment toward your $300,000 mortgage plus the second payment toward the additional $75,000 mortgage. Remember that your payment will reflect the two mortgage rates, and of course, your monthly payment itself will consist of interest and principal components.

WARNING

Although many mortgages now include a clause allowing them to be applied to a new property, there's typically a window in which this can be done. If you're planning to exercise the portability clause, make sure the closing date for the new property allows your existing mortgage to be applied to finance the purchase.

Assumable mortgage

When you're buying a house, in addition to contacting financial institutions about mortgages, you may want to ask the sellers if they would allow you to take over their mortgage as part of the price you pay for the house. This option may save you some of the costs usually associated with setting up a mortgage, such as legal, appraisal, and survey fees.

You may also save money in interest payments if the seller's mortgage rate is lower than what is currently available on the market. Check the remaining term on the mortgage, and then discuss this option with your real estate agent or your real estate lawyer.

Having an assumable mortgage on your home means that when you want to sell it, you can have a qualified buyer assume the mortgage. This option is a great incentive if you have good terms and conditions, and it saves the buyer time finding financing and money setting it up. Most mortgages are assumable as long as the buyer can qualify for the mortgage amount.

Buyers can still expect some financial scrutiny even if they're assuming the seller's mortgage. The lender will want to ensure the buyer meets its mortgage qualification requirements. See the section, "Helping Your Lender Help You: Prepare Your Information," later in this chapter for more on the kinds of personal and financial information lenders want.

Vendor (seller) take-back mortgage

A less common type of mortgage, especially in strong housing markets, is the *vendor take-back mortgage*. This type of mortgage is sometimes used if a seller is anxious to move, for example, or if the market is really sluggish, or if a seller wants to retain the mortgage as an investment. Not only does the seller take the equity from the house, but holds the mortgage for the new buyer and earns interest on the loan amount. In each case, the seller may offer to lend you the money for your mortgage. Sellers may offer you lower rates than big financial institutions will, and they won't require the appraisals, inspections, survey fees, and financing fees you expect to pay a traditional lender.

WARNING

A vendor take-back mortgage can get very complicated, however, so you'll want to have your lawyer draw up the papers to guarantee that everything is in order. Some sellers will sell buyers a mortgage and then pass it on to a mortgage broker to handle instead of dealing with it personally.

Builder/developer interest rate buy-down

If you're in the market for a new home, you may find builders and developers willing to offer mortgages with an interest rate buy-down. This arrangement may take the form of a vendor take-back mortgage where the builder/developer will lend you the money, or more commonly, the builder may buy down the interest rate of the mortgage you're getting from a bank. This mortgage option explains those newspaper ads for projects and subdivisions for sale with 3 percent mortgages.

The goal of the interest rate buy-down is to sell real estate. Buy-downs help buyers who are having trouble qualifying for a mortgage at current rates, or allow buyers to qualify for larger mortgages and therefore buy more expensive properties in the development. Keep in mind, however, that these mortgages typically aren't renewable, meaning that after the term is up, your mortgage rate, and therefore your monthly payment, is likely to climb.

WARNING

After your first mortgage term with an *interest rate buy-down* is up, you need to negotiate new terms, and if you've borrowed the money from the builder or developer, you need to find a new lender — usually a bank. Naturally, your lender will do an appraisal of your property. You're expecting this. What you're perhaps not expecting is that your new lender may appraise your one- or two-year-old house at several thousand dollars less than the price you paid for it. Here's why this happens: Builders want to offer reduced interest rates as an incentive to buyers. However, they're still protecting their bottom lines, so to compensate for offering lower interest, they incorporate the cost of the buy-down into the price of the house itself. This practice means you pay a larger principal on the builder's inflated price of the house.

The solution? Don't borrow the money from the builder or developer in the first place. Arrange a mortgage with a financial institution, and ask the builder or developer to buy down the interest with your lender. This way, you can take advantage of the deal on the interest rate and you still have the option to renew your mortgage with your lender at the end of the term. Another option is to take your mortgage at market rates and ask the builder to lower the selling price accordingly.

WARNING

"Can I have a mortgage with that, please?" Like car dealers, sellers can really sweeten the deal by helping you put the financing in place with assumable mortgages, vendor take-back mortgages, and builder/developer interest rate buy-downs — options that can save you a lot of money. But buyer beware: Read the fine print. Consult with your agent and lawyer before accepting any seller's mortgage offer; it may be a great deal for you, but an even better one for the seller.

Self-directed mortgage

Tapping your RRSP for a down payment is something we discuss in Chapter 4. Many mutual funds include mortgages as part of their holdings. So, what if you can hold your own mortgage within your RRSP? Some financial institutions allow this clever option, which not only allows you to build equity in your home, but also pays yourself interest as the lender.

A *self-directed mortgage* functions just like any other mortgage and comes with the same risks and obligations, but it's held within your RRSP. It must be set up through a licensed lender, and the rate can't undercut the bank's posted rates. You'll also have to demonstrate that you can pass the B-20 stress test, so unless you have a rocking income, you won't be able to charge a usurious interest rate in the hope of building a sizeable retirement nest egg. The mortgage must also be insured in order to protect your RRSP in the event you default on payments to yourself.

Line of credit

Buying a property using a line of credit instead of a conventional mortgage is increasingly common, and it works a bit like a credit card. You'll need to make a minimum monthly payment, but that payment covers only the interest — it won't pay down the principal. Anything else you pay beyond that monthly payment is up to you. To reduce the outstanding balance of the line of credit, however, you must pay more than the minimum monthly payment, or the principal won't be reduced.

The benefits of the line of credit are

>> Lower monthly payments (should you choose to pay just the minimum)

>> Total flexibility paying off the outstanding balance of the loan — with a regular mortgage, you can't change your monthly payments at will

The downsides of buying with a line of credit are

>> At the minimum payment, no reduction in the outstanding balance

>> Rate fluctuates with prime, meaning that it's not fixed (for example, at the prime rate or 0.25 percent or 0.50 percent over prime)

If you're someone whose income fluctuates with occasional high-income months, this option may be right for you. To qualify, you need to have a higher down payment (at least 25 percent) and a very good credit rating (ideally, at least 750). Determining if a line of credit is something that will work well for you, as opposed to a conventional mortgage, will take some time and analysis with your bank or mortgage broker.

Playing It Safe: High-Ratio Mortgage Insurance

If you have a down payment of less than 20 percent (but more than 5 percent) of the purchase price of your house, then you're eligible for a high-ratio mortgage. However, lenders will require you to have mortgage insurance so that their risk is protected. The lender arranges high-ratio insurance.

Qualifying for high-ratio mortgage insurance

Many buyers have high-ratio mortgage insurance coverage through the Canada Mortgage and Housing Corp., owned by the federal government. There are also two private high-ratio mortgage insurers, the largest of which is Genworth Financial Mortgage Insurance Co. of Canada and Canada Guaranty Mortgage Insurance. However, CMHC is the granddaddy of the group and does the vast majority of the business. All institutions have four standard eligibility requirements:

>> The home you're buying will be your principal residence.

>> The home you're buying is in Canada.

>> Your *gross debt service* (*GDS*) *ratio* isn't more than approximately 35 percent. In other words, the total you spend on housing (including principal and interest, property taxes, heating, and 50 percent of condo fees) isn't more than

approximately 35 percent of your gross (pre-tax) household income. (See Chapter 4 for help in determining your GDS ratio.)

>> Your *total debt service* (*TDS*) *ratio*, including any car loans, student loans, and credit card debt, isn't more than 42 percent of your gross (pre-tax) household income. (See Chapter 4 for details on calculating your TDS ratio.)

Determining the cost of high-ratio mortgage insurance

The premium for high-ratio mortgage insurance is currently 2.4 to 4.5 percent of the mortgage amount, determined by a sliding scale. Changes in recent years regarding high-ratio mortgage insurance have been frequent. Make sure you discuss the implications with your mortgage broker or lender. (Insurance premiums are also different for those who are refinancing.) You may also expect a surcharge for amortizations greater than 25 years.

TIP

Be sure to ask about incentives for you, the borrower, if you buy an energy-efficient home or borrow money to make more energy-saving renovations to an existing home. You may qualify for as much as a 10 percent refund on your mortgage loan insurance premium.

Covering Your Bases: Life and Illness

Sometimes life throws curveballs that no one can expect that make you unable to pay your mortgage. These types of insurance can help:

>> **Mortgage life insurance:** It guarantees your mortgage will be paid in full if you die. Some lenders offer this insurance and will add the premium to your mortgage payments. Shopping around through an insurance broker for the best rate is still a good idea, though. You may want to get insurance coverage for all parties responsible for the mortgage (for example, if your home is in your name and your spouse's, both of you should be insured).

>> **Declining balance insurance:** With this insurance, the lender may offer insurance where it will pay off the balance of your mortgage upon your death. However, you may also want to consider regular term insurance. The premiums are comparable to declining balance insurance, but this policy covers you for the full amount of your mortgage should you pass away — not just the outstanding balance.

>> **Critical illness insurance:** In addition to mortgage life insurance, some lenders offer this type. This insurance usually covers certain serious illnesses only — the main three being cancer, heart attack, and stroke — but many people want the security of knowing their mortgage will be paid off, or close to it, not only in a case of death but also if they get really sick. This type of coverage is an add-on, so you can't get it independently of life insurance. Whether this option is right for you depends solely on you and your insurance preferences, but make sure you ask the right questions before deciding. Find out exactly what illnesses are covered, if you need to take a medical exam, and exactly what the extent of your coverage would be.

TIP

Knowing your mortgage will be paid if you fall ill or die is definitely a peace of mind for some people, be sure to consider other options. One of the reasons you should have a six-month contingency fund socked away is in the event of illness. Ideally, the fund will be in both your name and that of your spouse or partner, giving them access to the funds they need to pay the mortgage not only if you're sick, but if you die (joint ownership can be a wonderful thing). On the other hand, you can also purchase personal term life insurance to cover not only the immediate expenses your survivors will face, but the bigger ones, such as a mortgage. (Of course, we hope you outlive your mortgage.)

Going Mortgage Hunting: What You Need to Do to Get a Mortgage

For the longest time in Canada, if you wanted a mortgage, you went down to the local bank, spoke to the manager or loans officer, filled out the forms, and waited patiently. Eventually you'd be told whether you qualified or not and what interest rate you would pay. In most cases, the rate that was posted in the window was the rate you would get. But with the surge in real estate transactions in recent years and the advent of the Internet, things have changed.

When you go looking for a mortgage today, you'll find the process is much more transparent. Major banks and lenders often post their rates; they're happy to discuss discounts to be competitive with other lenders. Mortgage brokers also post rates from the lenders that they deal with. The wealth of information available online has also given purchasers some leverage with lenders, ensuring everyone is able to access the best rates available fully aware of all the available options.

You may find the sheer amount of information overwhelming. It may even drive you to seek professional help (no, not *that* kind). What you need is a mortgage broker to help in your search. We discuss just what they do and how to find one that meets your needs. If you want to go it alone, we have you covered, too.

Enlisting a mortgage broker's help

These days, more and more Canadians are using a mortgage broker to help them organize the financing of their home purchase. A *mortgage broker* is a licensed lending professional who represents several different lenders and usually offers more loan options than a commercial bank.

Mortgage brokers can work independently, or they can work for the lending arm of a major bank. In the latter case, those brokers represent the lending products of their bank alone, but don't be deterred — they may well be able to get you superior rates and terms. Independent mortgage brokers often use many different lenders, including banks with in-house mortgage brokers. Independent brokers also have access to some innovative broker-only lenders that may even offer more attractive rates and features.

Understanding how a mortgage broker works

A mortgage broker is your representative with lenders and works to find the right mortgage at the right price for your needs. All you to do is provide the broker with the information required to qualify for a mortgage (that's a little further on in this chapter, in the section, "Helping Your Lender Help You: Prepare Your Information"), and your broker takes care of the rest.

A broker helps you navigate the bumps you may encounter in qualifying for a mortgage. If you have any little glitches on your credit history, your broker can help fix them. For example, you may think that the store credit card with a $25 balance you forgot to pay three years ago is no big deal, but it may have become a very big deal on your credit report. Your broker can help you clean up that spill.

TIP

When you work with a mortgage broker, your credit history is pulled only once. Why is this important? Consider this: Say you decide you're going to be hands-on, and you go to five major Canadian banks to apply for a mortgage. At every bank you approach, you fill out an application and the bank pulls your credit report. Every time your report is requested, your credit score is negatively affected. In the eyes of the credit bureau, every request for your credit information is an application for money, and it affects your overall score. Of course, you aren't really applying for five separate mortgages, or car loans, or credit cards, but the process is such that it recognizes each application.

After your broker helps you sort through any credit issues, she can preapprove you for a mortgage, helping you set your budget for the property you want to purchase. You can also talk to your mortgage broker about amortization rates and payment frequency, determining the best options for you. (Refer to "Mastering the Lingo: Mortgage Jargon 101" earlier in this chapter for more on these terms.)

Finally, armed with your information and your needs, your broker can find you the rates, terms, and conditions that will work best for you. Generally, mortgage brokers aren't tied to just one lender (unless you're using a bank's in-house mortgage specialist), so they can provide options from many lenders. Another plus? They'll represent your interests and advise you objectively on your options.

Finding a mortgage broker

The best way to find a good mortgage broker can often be by asking family members and friends who have recently purchased a home or by asking your agent. After all, your agent wants to sell you a home, and a good mortgage broker helps to do just that. Your agent will probably have several mortgage brokers to recommend who will work hard for you. If you're determined to remain with the financial institution that you've been with for your other accounts and loans, you may want to deal directly with their in-house mortgage specialists.

Seeking out mortgage brokers online

Although the rules governing mortgage brokers differ from province to province, all mortgage brokers in Canada must be licensed. In addition, many brokers hold the Accredited Mortgage Professional designation, introduced by Mortgage Professionals Canada (https://mortgageproscan.ca) in 2004. Mortgage Professionals Canada members handle 90 percent of mortgages in Canada, making it the leading organization for this aspect of the real estate business.

Any brokerage worth doing business with should be a registered member of Mortgage Professionals Canada. The company's website should offer a company profile with a clear and thorough explanation of the brokering process. The site should also feature a list of preferred lenders. The longer this list, and the more major banks whose names you recognize, the better — this information shows that the broker has a good business relationship with many clients and can cast a wide net to find you the best deal.

Many mortgage brokers also work out of local offices of national companies, so you may have to go through a national site to find a local mortgage specialist. You may be asked to fill out an online form with contact information such as your email address, street address, and phone number. At this stage, give only the information that is necessary to get in contact with the mortgage broker — you don't need to give private information to anyone over the Internet.

WARNING

If the website you're visiting starts asking for private information (such as account numbers and credit information), leave the site immediately — you may have stumbled across a bogus and fraudulent company pretending to be a helpful lender.

Searching on your own

Of course, you can always apply for a mortgage the old fashioned way: by yourself. Many trust companies, credit unions, and *caisses populaires* (cooperative financial institutions similar to credit unions) don't deal directly with mortgage brokers, so you may want to approach them individually, if they're who you want to do business with. Don't be afraid to negotiate!

If you've decided that DIY is the way you want to go, in many cases you can contact the lender directly (if it's a major bank or credit union). Other lenders may be accessible only through mortgage brokers. Don't be afraid to network. Ask friends who have recently bought or sold a home where and how they got their financing and if they were satisfied.

Ratehub (www.ratehub.ca) is one of the top sites for quickly comparing current mortgage rates from lenders across Canada. Rates are constantly changing, however, so be sure to inquire directly with any institution whose rate catches your eye to see if it's still valid or if there's a better rate to be had.

Getting an online mortgage preapproval

Ready to go for that mortgage preapproval? Well, most banks provide an online preapproval application. Here are a few reasons we mention it:

» No one is on the other side of the desk or the phone helping you through. This means that you're your own financial adviser and must have a very good idea of your financial capabilities and the type of mortgage you want and can afford.

» About one-third of the way through your online application, after you've plugged in all the relevant numbers and the whirring central bank computer is happy enough with your down payment to proceed, you'll get a proposed preapproval amount. You may be tempted to jump up from your computer and yell "Whoopee!" But this isn't your final answer. This amount is a conditional preapproval, based on the truth of the numbers you've provided, pending a credit check, and so on. The online application will walk you through all of those conditions in the steps to come, you can be sure.

TIP

Keep in mind that when your virtual bank offers you these numbers, you haven't even given your name yet! What kind of lender would give you money at this stage? No one. Take a deep breath, and keep typing and clicking through right to the bitter end. And, as we mention in Chapter 4, even if you have a preapproved mortgage, you should still make any offer "subject to financing" because your lender will usually require at least an appraisal before granting you a mortgage.

To get an absolutely firm preapproval, you'll have to provide detailed income and debt verification. Without this verification, your online preapproval is only an indication of what you may be able to afford; it isn't a guarantee that you'll be able to get the mortgage amount that you determined through your online preapproval process.

REMEMBER

At some point in the online preapproval, your bank will put a disclaimer screen in front of you. Read it. Print it out. Keep it. Read it again. You get the picture. . .

Questioning Your Lender

Just because you're the one requesting money doesn't mean should be timid about asking. Lenders profit from your business, so don't be afraid to bring up your concerns. You should expect to be answered directly, in a courteous manner, and you should reply to your lender's questions in kind. Prepare a list of questions and be prepared to take notes.

Stay cool and calm as you chat with prospective lenders. Remember, you're shopping for a mortgage, not begging for one. Keep this list handy to be sure you ask the right questions:

>> **What is your name, title, and phone number?** Start with the basics.

>> **Do you comply with all the provisions of Canada's privacy legislation?** In case you're wondering if your information will be kept confidential, don't worry. In Canada, the *Privacy Act* and the *Personal Information Protection and Electronic Documents Act (PIPEDA)* are two federal laws that forbid lending institutions (and other businesses) from disclosing your private information. For more details about privacy legislation, visit the Office of the Privacy Commissioner of Canada (www.priv.gc.ca).

>> **What mortgage types and terms do you have available?** Do you have any that are specifically designed for my situation? Many major banks have special offers for first-time homebuyers, for example.

>> **What are your current mortgage rates?** Compare the rate offered for closed mortgages to the rate offered for open mortgages. An open mortgage gives you more flexibility and can save you money, but usually has a higher interest rate than a closed mortgage, as we explain in the section, "Open mortgage," earlier in this chapter.

>> **How are you making your mortgages competitive with other lending institutions? Are any discounts or cash-back options available?** Some lenders lower their interest rate a bit if you ask nicely or show them lower

rates from the competition; other lenders offer you a percentage off your mortgage up front — usually between 1 and 3 percent as a cash-back program — to help you with your closing costs.

» **What mortgage fees do you charge? Is there a mortgage application fee?** Make sure you know what kind of costs your lender expects you to cover.

» **Do you preapprove mortgages? Is there a fee for this?** Most institutions don't charge a preapproval application fee.

» **How long will it take to process my loan request? After it's approved, how long should I allow before I close the deal?** When you set your closing dates for the purchase of a new home, the schedule for your transfer of funds is crucial. Know what to expect.

» **How is the interest compounded?** Most lenders compound interest semi-annually (every six months). Ask if your lender offers any other compounding options that may save you money.

» **Can I convert from a variable-rate to a fixed-rate mortgage?** As we explain in the "Understanding the Types of Mortgages" section earlier in this chapter, if you choose a variable-rate mortgage, you're vulnerable to fluctuations in the current interest rate. When interest rates rise, you must make higher mortgage payments; when rates fall, you pay less. You'll want to have the option to convert your variable-rate mortgage to a fixed-rate mortgage if interest rates begin to climb significantly.

» **Is the mortgage portable?** You may want this option if you do end up moving in the future. Refer to the earlier section, "Portable mortgage," where we discuss portable mortgages.

» **What are my payment options?** To save yourself a lot of money in the long run, you should make payments as often as you can — weekly is best. (Refer to the "Blended payments" section earlier in this chapter.)

» **Can I pay off the mortgage early? Is there a penalty for this? Can I pay down some of the principal without penalty? How much a year?** You'll probably want the option to make an extra lump-sum payment toward your mortgage principal at least once or twice a year to help you save on the interest.

» **Is mortgage life and critical illness insurance available with your mortgages? Will they cover both my partner and me?** You'll want to protect your family members in case a serious illness prevents you from working. But check the cost. A separate insurer may offer lower insurance premiums for the same coverage.

» **If my credit rating isn't acceptable at this point, what can I do to improve it? Or what options do I have?** Be prepared. Any lender who offers mortgages will check your credit rating.

Helping Your Lender Help You: Prepare Your Information

No matter who you use to secure your mortgage, mortgage lenders always ask for a lot of information. Just like you need to ask a lot of questions about the lender, the lender will want to know all about you, too. Here are some pieces of information you should share.

Sharing about yourself

The starting point for any mortgage request is the application. It will ask for details about your financial status and employment, as well as your personal information and history. Expect questions like these:

>> **What is your age, marital status, and number of dependents? Where do you work? What is your position? How long have you been with the company? What is your employment history?** Unless you're self-employed, you'll probably need a letter from your employer confirming your position with the company. If you're self-employed, bring your notice of assessment (not your tax return) for each of the past two years to confirm your income.

>> **What is your gross (pre-tax) family income?** You may need proof of income, like a T4 slip or, if you're self-employed, personal income tax returns. You'll also be asked to show proof of other sources of income, such as from pensions or rental property.

>> **What do you currently spend on housing? If you're a homeowner, what is the current market value of your house?** You may have to provide copies of your rental lease agreement for the apartment or suite you're renting or a copy of your current mortgage.

>> **Do you have funds for a down payment?** The lender wants to ensure that your down payment will be available when you need the money to close on your purchase. The lender will want to see where your down payment is coming from — is it sitting in the bank, or will it be coming from your beloved Aunt Bibi in the near future?

>> **What assets do you have, and what is the value of each one?** You can include vehicles, properties, and investments.

>> **What liabilities do you have?** As we discuss in Chapter 4, lenders are focused on the debts you're required to pay, such as credit card balances, car loans, student loans, and lines of credit. You may have other types of

debt that aren't necessarily a concern of the lender, such as loans made on a handshake with your best friend, or non-repayable loans from family, but if you're carrying too much debt you're obliged to repay, it may affect your ability to carry the cost of owning a house over the long term.

TIP

Your mortgage broker or lender will also ask for your consent to do a credit check. A credit check may reveal a good or bad credit rating, depending on your financial history. We recommend you contact a credit-reporting agency, such as Equifax Canada or your local credit bureau, to obtain a copy of your credit report. Examine it in detail. If you find inaccurate or outdated information in the report, you can have those items corrected or removed to make your credit rating as glowing as it can possibly be.

Getting it in writing: The paperwork

Banks or mortgage brokers will generally preapprove your mortgage over the phone. You may have to email them the required paperwork, and in return, they'll provide written confirmation outlining the terms of your mortgage preapproval. Meeting your lender face-to-face isn't always possible until you receive the sellers' acceptance of your offer to purchase their home and you're ready to seal the deal by finalizing all the financing.

Getting a head start on documentation to get a preapproval is a good thing. As the process of purchasing a home gets closer to the finish line, here is a list of documents you'll need for the lender:

>> Copy of a recent appraisal for the home you're buying (if requested — the lender may already have ordered it for you)

>> Copy of the property listing

>> Copy of the agreement of purchase and sale (for a resale house)

>> Plans and cost estimates if you're buying a new house (construction loans only)

>> Certificate for well water and septic system (if applicable)

>> Condominium financial statements (if applicable)

>> Survey certificate

>> Property disclosure statement (signed by both parties) or condominium certificate (if applicable)

>> Copy of title

3

Discovering Your Perfect Home

Choose between detached homes, condos, and co-ops, and whether having a mortgage helper could be just the thing to help you pay the bills. Figure out what kind of home you want to live in. Not all homes are created equal, and not all homes fit all lifestyles.

Zero in on your ideal neighbourhood by assessing your own needs, pounding the pavement, and diving into the world of online listings.

Weed out the problem homes by knowing which ones have good operating systems and which ones may be beyond repair.

Identify what's awesome, what's worth changing, what you can't, and what kinds of drawbacks you're willing to accept.

IN THIS CHAPTER

» **Discovering a home that meets your needs**

» **Considering condominiums**

» **Weighing your condo options**

» **Drilling into the details of condos**

» **Joining a co-op**

» **Contemplating a residential investment**

Chapter **6**

Finding a Home That's Right for You

The home that you choose to live in is a reflection of your lifestyle and personality. You may think you have only a few basic housing options to choose from, but a little digging will uncover a variety that may fit your budget. Knowing what you want and matching it with what's available is part of the fun (and sometimes, the frustration) of finding the home that's right for you.

This chapter describes some of the common home types and outlines the common advantages and disadvantages of each. Sometimes location or price determine the kind of property you choose, but this chapter helps you know what to expect and choose the best possible option from a given set of choices.

Looking Closer at Your Housing Options: Determining the Best Fit

Most people know from the outset whether they're looking for a house or an apartment (often called a condo). But if you've decided you want a house to call home, you have additional considerations. Do you want a detached house or a townhome? Do you want to build it yourself, and if so, will you start from scratch or opt for a prefab unit? On the other hand, location may determine what you can afford. A semi-detached house in the best part of town may be what you can afford, but an older detached home in a less appealing part of town can give you more home for your money.

Don't forget to ask yourself what's most important to you when it comes to your living space. Determine the kind of home you want to live in before you start looking seriously. (Chapter 7 can help you sort out your priorities.) Share your priorities with the agent you're working with to make ensure you're presented with options that suit your needs and tastes. The following sections discuss the important factors to consider.

Discovering a home that meets your personal tastes and needs is important. For instance, some people like to hop in the shower at 6 a.m. and sing at the top of their lungs, a habit best-suited to a detached house rather than anything with shared walls or venting. But if yard work isn't a high priority for you, a condo is probably the right fit. But some houses come with minimal yard space, so know your options. These include the following:

>> **Single-family detached:** *A single-family detached* house sits by itself on its own lot. Ownership includes the entire structure and the lot. You, as the owner, are responsible for all repairs and maintenance, property taxes, and associated costs.

>> **Semi-detached:** Semi-detached houses are joined by a shared wall, but the structure as a whole (that is, both units) is independent of other houses on the street. Ownership includes your half of the structure and land, and you're responsible for all the costs and work associated with that half.

>> **Carriage houses:** *Carriage houses,* also referred to as *laneway houses,* are an increasingly popular option in many urban centres. Designed as a kind of in-fill housing to gently add density (more units) to residential neighbourhoods, they've grown in number over the past decade. Many were required to be part of the main property, meaning they were best suited for additional family members or tenants, but a growing number are available to purchase in their own right. Ownership and responsibilities are similar to those for detached or semi-detached houses, depending on whether or not they sit on their own lot.

- >> **Rowhouses or townhouses:** *Rowhouses* or *townhouses* share a common wall on one or both sides. You may have full ownership of a townhouse, although in some cases, townhouses are condominiums. Often, a group of independently owned townhouses has a housing association that collects dues and handles some of the maintenance for the whole row.

- >> **Apartments:** *Apartments*, or multifamily units, are built in low-rise (typically five storeys or less) or high-rise buildings (six storeys or greater) that usually offer a secure entrance, elevators, and shared common areas — and lots of neighbours.

REMEMBER

Condominium refers *only* to a type of ownership, *not* to a type of architecture. Condo owners have sole ownership of their individual units, which could be an apartment, townhouse, carriage house or building lot. They share the title and right to common areas with other unit owners.

Obviously, the closer your house is to your neighbours, the more exposed you are to potential noise and disturbances. Attached homes also tend to require less yardwork, but the maintenance considerations, including the impacts of neglect, can be greater. Renovating a detached property is easier than attached properties, but if you're in the market for a ready-made community, a condo may be right for you.

FREEHOLD AND LEASEHOLD: TREAD VERY CAREFULLY

Most properties are offered to buyers on a *freehold basis* — that is, the buyer has full rights to the property under the law and doesn't owe anyone anything (the title deed will outline any encumbrances, such as rights of way or the like). Sometimes, however, a home sits on *leasehold* land, and the buyer owns only the building and not the land it sits on. The land is typically leased by the owner or developer from a government or a First Nation, and enjoyment (or use) of the land is subject to the terms of the lease agreement.

The terms and conditions of any leasehold arrangement demand careful attention. You need to be are if any elements of the lease impact you. The last thing you want is to purchase a home built on leased land only to face a massive increase in the rent five or ten years down the road. The good news is that most leases are for the long term, typically 99 years or longer. The leases won't be up for renewal until long after the useful life of the building has ended.

(continued)

(continued)

This isn't always the case, though. During the late 1990s, about 75 leaseholders saw their annual rent to the Musqueam First Nation on the south side of Vancouver jump from $375 to $23,000. Ultimately, they took their dispute to the Supreme Court of Canada and won a settlement that reduced their average annual rent to $10,500. More recently, owners along the south shore of False Creek – also in Vancouver – have fought against potential rent increases. The original rents were very low as an inducement designed to establish a community in the former industrial area. Now the neighbourhood is so desirable that increasing rents to market rates for the next term of the land lease threatens to put occupancy out of reach of the current tenants.

The controversies and disruption such situations cause mean most developers now enter a *prepaid lease* arrangement in which rents are incorporated into the development costs. This lets buyers pay for their homes without ever having to worry about the details of the lease. However, knowing that you're on leased land is important, just in case. For example, if the lease is coming up for renewal at the time you want to sell your house, you may find it difficult to sell if the new lease rate isn't set. Any potential purchaser will want confirmation of the cost.

Because of the uncertainties related to leasehold properties, homes built in such situations are typically cheaper than those on freehold property. The lease often makes them harder to sell and finance than freehold properties.

Buying into a Fresh Start

Most people see a new home as a chance for a new start, which often means buying into a newly built property. This section discusses your three options.

Buying new

People buy a newly built home because it's all theirs and never has been anyone else's. The structural components, operational systems, or appliances (assuming they're included) won't have any wear and tear. The home will also be under a mandatory warranty, offered by one of the provincial new home warranty programs that cover defects in materials and construction and may also cover building code violations and major structural defects (check the details of the program offered in your province). You can find more information on the NHWP in Chapter 12.

Purchasers of a new home buy a pristine home built to the latest building code requirements. The home has current technology and building techniques, and the latest standards in safety and energy efficiency making it a healthier structure and one that should save you money in the long run. A new home will also reflect today's design preferences (no orange countertops). Indeed, many builders give buyers a chance to see the builder's specs and even choose the finishes and other details so that the house truly reflects what they want.

However, buying a new home isn't for everyone. Unless the home is built and ready to move in, you can't be sure of what you're getting or when you'll get it. The building trades also are notorious for taking longer than expected to finish a job, meaning you may not move in when you think. The fact that you're the first occupant means you'll also be the one discovering and working out the kinks (commonly known as *deficiencies*).

REMEMBER

Although most builders will address deficiencies in a reasonable amount of time and you have recourse to the home's warranty in the event of a major failure on the builder's part, the location of the property may make the prospect of buying new unattractive. Potential issues include

>> **Lack of services:** The area may not be serviced by public transit, schools, grocery stores, shopping, and other amenities that are found in established areas.

>> **Undeveloped landscape:** You may move into your home and find that you're surrounded by mud fields and a giant dirt heap with no sidewalks or lawn anywhere in sight. With time you can, of course, add your own landscaping, but lush greenery will take a while to create.

>> **Construction inconvenience:** You may have to put up with noise and dust created by the continual construction in the area.

>> **Distance to work:** New subdivisions and lots are often located outside of densely populated regions, so you may not be able to build or buy a new house in the urban area of your choice.

>> **Distance from your family doctor, friends and family:** These are important relationships that might be affected by opting to buy in a new housing development.

>> **Uncertainty about your neighbours:** You won't know in advance what the neighbours are like. Will they be organizing all-night street dances every time there's a full moon? This uncertainty may be particularly true in an apartment-style condo if a number of the suites are sold to investors who will rent them out.

You also have financial drawbacks to consider when buying a new home, such as

>> **Selling price:** The price may be high than for similar, older properties because of all the advantages that come from buying new.

>> **Property taxes:** Property taxes may be higher, because it's assessed at current market value for a prime property. (On the plus side, a new home should retain its value for several years, because of all the advantages we outlined earlier.)

>> **GST/HST:** A new home is also subject to GST/HST, something others properties are not. However, in many cases you may be eligible for a rebate. Refer to Chapter 2 for more information regarding GST/HST on new houses.

Building a home of your own

Rather than let an experienced developer sell you a house that it has built, maybe you're keen to buy a lot and build your own. Being glued to every home-building, home-fixing, home-staging, and home-arranging show on the airwaves does wonders for the imagination and self-confidence. But we have a reality check for you: These shows are heavily edited. The more likely scenario will have you working with a builder with your part limited to specifying the materials you want for your dream home.

Nevertheless, you can be involved significantly in building your dream home. The opportunities and responsibilities include the following:

>> **Making it exactly what you want:** You get to choose and/or design the actual structure and components of your home — the building materials, the appliances, the position on the lot, and so many other features. In a nutshell, you get what you want. However, if you're in a position to buy land in a new subdivision, be aware that many have *building schemes* attached, meaning that the homes built within that area must meet certain sizes and architectural standards.

So, if you think that you're going to build a mini replica of the Taj Mahal, think again. Even exterior paint colours can be part of that building scheme. Infill housing in established urban neighbourhoods may also face design restrictions. Check zoning bylaws first for size allowed, setbacks to property lines, and so forth. Be prepared for unhappy neighbours if you do something very different from surrounding homes.

>> **Scheduling and planning risks:** Delays and extra expenses are practically guaranteed. Building a new home almost always costs more and takes longer than you think it will.

TIP

Work with a qualified contractor and get everything in writing. Because you're ultimately make the final decisions, you deserve the best, and you also want to make sure that you have recourse in case anything goes wrong. Your lender will also want to know that the home is eligible for a new home warranty as well as homeowner insurance.

You can minimize the stress of added costs during the construction process by doing your research. Be sure to fully understand all the costs associated with building. Get a detailed breakdown of all estimated costs from your builder so you know exactly what's covered and what's optional or extra. The contract to build a house includes a lengthy specification list that can run 10 to 15 pages. Make sure that everything down to the towel racks is outlined.

REMEMBER

Be prepared for delays for your new home not to be complete on time — whether you're building it yourself or you've waiting on a developer to deliver — because they're bound to happen. You can minimize surprises by keeping on top of your contractor (who should also be keeping in touch with you).

TIP

Have a contingency plan in the event that the home you're hoping to move into isn't ready on time. These suggestions can help:

>> **Develop a reserve fund of money you can access should the need arise.** You don't want to create delays by not having the money to complete the building after it's begun. We suggest padding your building budget by an extra 10 to 15 percent, just in case.

>> **Plan ahead with your current accommodations.** If you're still living in your home you're selling, you may be able to insert a clause into the sale agreement that makes the occupancy date for the buyer of your existing home contingent on the occupancy date of your new home. You may even choose to rent your existing home for a few months after you take occupancy of your new residence, providing you with a little extra income until it's time to sell (there may be tax implications, however, so consult your accountant to determine the best plan).

TIP

If you're moving out of a rental, you may be able to extend your lease a bit or continue month to month in case of a delay. Check with friends or relatives just in case you need a temporary place to stay.

>> **Budget some extra cash for any temporary living expenses.** This extra money can cover rent or a few nights in a hotel.

>> **Make a list of storage companies where you can keep your stuff until the suite is ready.** Be sure that you make arrangements not only for yourself, but also your stuff. You want everything taken care of when you move.

Not being able to move into your new home isn't the ideal situation, but having a plan B (or even C) helps make things a lot easier.

Building a home yourself brings the possibility of savings. Many provinces levy a land transfer tax or a deed transfer tax when you purchase a home. The calculation and applicability of this tax varies across the country, and in some cases people building their own homes receive a break: You may pay the transfer or deed tax on the value of the land only and not the finished value of the home.

REMEMBER

When your new home is finished, the builder will tour you through the property before you take possession, allowing you to see that everything you asked the builder to do has been done properly. But keep in mind that this tour in no way replaces a professional inspection. A building inspector will need to make sure that the house complies with the current building code, and a fire and safety inspection will be required, too. See Chapter 12 for more information on inspections.

Country living in a new home

The idea of building a home on a remote acreage is romantic to many people, but doing so also has some harsh realities. The same holds true if you plan to renovate a remote property, thinking it will be easy to renovate and outfit with the latest technology.

GOING GREEN: PASSIVE HOUSES

Protecting the environment and reducing costs continues to be an emerging area of interest among both builders and homeowners. *Passive houses* are one manifestation of the trend. These houses aim to consume little energy, employing construction materials as well as sophisticated building systems that allow the structure to maintain a stable temperature and avoid wasting energy. Although they're more costly to build, the payback comes in reduced energy and maintenance costs. They're also tipped as being healthier for the occupants.

The key requirements for certification as a passive house according to the Passive House Institute, based in Germany, include

- A maximum heating load of 10 W/m2

- A maximum pressurization test result of 50 Pa and 0.6 air changes per hour (ACH);

- A total primary energy demand not exceeding 120 kWh/m2a

Groups such as the Canadian Passive House Institute (www.passivehouse.ca) serve as key resources to the growing number of firms and homeowners embracing this form of building. Some projects are being marketed to buyers on the basis of their being passive buildings, and more are likely to follow. If you choose to build your own, it's an option worth considering both for your own comfort, overall resilience, and future marketability.

Keep these extra considerations in mind:

>> **Electricity:** Bringing in power lines may cost you extra. Nowadays, alternative energy sources can minimize your demand on the grid, but if you need the connection, you may need to pay.

>> **Water:** Water quality may be an issue, and you may have to install a filtration system. If you have to drill a new well, and if that well is particularly deep, you may be looking at some big costs.

>> **Sewage and plumbing:** Building a septic system or hooking up to a sewage line can be extremely expensive and may require substantial preliminary work to understand local aquifers and other limiting factors. (We discuss septic systems in Chapter 8.)

>> **Extra taxes:** If you're in a relatively isolated and unincorporated area, services such as road maintenance and schools may be supported by a small population base, requiring a higher per capita tax burden to maintain even a minimal level of services.

>> **Fire and flood considerations:** The increase in wildfires means that a new home may face restrictions on where it's located or the amount of space needed between it and adjacent forested land. You'll also want to make sure that it's within reach of the local fire department. If not, insuring it could be tough, or you'll face higher premiums because of its remote location. Similar restrictions exist with respect to overland flooding, for which insurance coverage is unavailable or prohibitively costly in many parts of Canada.

>> **Garbage:** As with any home in the boondocks, new or resale, garbage and recycling pickup may be unavailable.

>> **Snow removal:** You may need to organize and pay for snow removal or with others who share your road.

ABSOLUTELY PREFABULOUS

Prefab homes, also called *manufactured homes,* have come a long way from your cousin Lurleen's double-wide trailer. The term prefab means the home is prefabricated in a factory, delivered, and then set up on your property, very often on its own foundations. It's prefabricated, not mobile, and measures up to all relevant building codes.

(continued)

(continued)

Prefab homes have several advantages.

- **Construction timelines are shorter.** That means you can take occupancy faster.

- **The finished structure isn't weather worn.** Because the components are made in a factory, they're not exposed to the elements during construction.

- **Most are indistinguishable from any other home.** Gone are the days when prefab homes had a stigma about them. Many people think of trailers when they think prefab, but these days even high-end hotel builders are using prefab construction. Your home will stand up next to the best-looking home on the block. (In fact, it might even be the best-looking home on the block!)

- **They're eco-friendly.** No matter what prefabs are used for — a main home, a vacation home, or an addition on an existing house — they're better for the environment. Off-site assembly means the manufacturers use only the amounts of material needed, significantly reducing the amount of construction waste. Some prefabs are made with renewable materials like bamboo flooring and earth-friendly products like nontoxic paint and built-in water-saving fixtures. Many models are created to make the most of natural light, with lots of windows to reduce electricity costs.

Prefabs do have some downsides:

- **They're smaller and limiting.** If your dream house has an indoor pool, prefab probably isn't for you (not yet, anyway, though some prefab hotels are being built to accommodate these features). Many prefab homes tend to be about the size of a one-bedroom apartment, but the largest ones can have several rooms and two storeys.

- **They aren't necessarily cheaper.** When you factor in the costs of construction, assembly, installation, and delivery, a prefab costs per square foot about the same as a house constructed the old-fashioned way.

When you buy a prefab, you do need land on which to plunk down your house. Because the shipping costs are quite high, you may not be able to park a prefab on a mountain peak, but it can be delivered by truck, train, or even helicopter. When the house arrives, the site has already been prepared for the home's installation with hookups for power, water, sewer, and phone/cable. And the prefab home already includes systems for plumbing, heating, and electricity that will be connected to the services at the site. You choose any extra features, like ceiling fans and light fixtures, cabinets, and, in some cases, furnishings.

Following a Lead: Resale Houses

If purchasing a resale home is a viable option for you, within any established urban centre there is usually lots of housing choices across a range of prices. Here we examine the pros and cons with purchasing a resale house and the important considerations when purchasing one.

Eyeing the pros and cons with resale houses

You can expect some of the following perks from buying one of these pre-existing beauties:

>> **Convenience:** More than likely, the existing neighbourhood amenities, like public transportation, schools, parks, shopping, groceries, and so on, will already be established.

>> **Luxuries:** Extras that would put a serious strain on your wallet to build or buy new (such as a swimming pool, hot tub, custom cabinetry, or a finished basement) may come with the house.

>> **Character:** Older homes may have unique or antique-quality features that give them character and add to the potential resale value.

>> **Tax savings:** You don't pay GST/HST on the purchase of a resale home (unless substantial renovations were done, typically more than 90 percent, making the house a new home).

>> **Landscaping:** The lawns, gardens, and trees are probably mature.

>> **Immediate possession:** Unless something occurs in leading up to the closing date, you expect to move in on the date that is stipulated in the purchase agreement.

Every rose has its thorn, too — sometimes more than one. You may have to deal with some of the following difficulties:

>> **Less energy efficiency:** Older houses are often (but not necessarily) less energy efficient, utilities may cost more, or upgrades may be needed in the not-too-distant future.

>> **Repairs needed:** Previous wear and tear on the house may make maintenance more expensive.

>> **Decor challenges:** A used home may not feel like your own until you redecorate.

>> **Space constraints:** Room sizes in older homes are often smaller than room sizes in newer homes. Some bedrooms may not have closets. Basement ceiling height may also be an issue.

>> **Modern updates needed:** Minor renovations or repairs may be necessary to accommodate your lifestyle or to meet new safety or building codes.

>> **Structural concerns:** You have no say in the layout or what building materials are used, so you may not be entirely satisfied with the structure of the home.

>> **You're not covered by your province's New Home Warranty Program.** The program applies to new homes only — it doesn't apply to properties already built, although the balance of the warranty will transfer to second owners if they buy the unit in the warranty period.

Choosing the right resale home

Although many resale homes are well kept, some clearly have that lived-in look. The answer to whether or not buying a resale home is a good idea will depend on how much effort you're willing to put into it. Most people want a home that's move-in ready so that they have time to figure out what, if anything, they want to change. Other homes need some work to get into tip-top shape, but they come at an attractive discount, making them a bargain. A portion, however, will need some TLC (usually "tender loving care," but possibly "truckloads of cash"). We examine these three instances in greater detail here.

Ready to move in

Houses in move-in condition are exactly that — ready for you to drag the furniture up the front steps and then settle in. A house in move-in condition may have been repaired or renovated to bring it up to tip-top shape. Buyers pay more for a premium house — but many prefer a lower price and the chance to do upgrades their way, rather than a higher price and lots of sparkling new designer cabinetry that's totally at odds with their taste. Nothing is worse than a house with a new $20,000 custom kitchen tiled from floor to ceiling in colours you can't stand. With a move-in-ready home, chances are you won't have the ability to build any new equity (meaning you may find it difficult to add value to the property).

Room for improvement

Most resale houses fall into the category of adequate condition — houses that are in good condition structurally and are certainly livable, but need to be recarpeted, repainted, or redecorated to become *your* home. Don't be afraid to tackle cosmetic changes — in fact, expect it.

Although having to make structural, plumbing, or electrical repairs to your new home is cause for worry, basic finishing changes are par for the course — especially to make it feel like home. Putting a fresh coat of paint here and there or refinishing the hardwood floors is most often a worthwhile expense. If you're uncertain what everything will cost, make your offer subject to receiving and approving a contractor's or architect's estimate before committing to the purchase.

Time for some TLC

A handyman special is a house that is below market value because it needs some work, which may include structural, plumbing, HVAC, and electric improvements and upgrades.

WARNING

A handyman special is potentially a bargain if and only if the defects are fixable — and fixable within a reasonable budget. For instance, if the defects include structural damage resulting from the dwelling's past use — say, for an illegal *grow-op* (unlicensed cannabis production) or a meth lab, don't even consider purchasing it. The moisture and chemicals for those activities can lead to wood warping and harmful mould growth. Many municipalities require such properties be inspected before they're declared fit for humans again. Additionally, insurance companies won't touch these properties with a 10-foot pole unless this inspection has been done, so you may not be able to get a mortgage on a home that has been used for the mass production of illegal drugs. Check with your municipality, your insurance company, and your lender before you proceed with a purchase of a home that has this scarlet letter attached!

Assuming that the problems are fixable and the property's value can be increased, if you're an electrician, plumber, or carpenter, for example, involving yourself in this sort of venture may be worthwhile — *if* you have the time. But, whatever tasks you don't have the skill, expertise, or time to manage yourself, you'll have to pay someone else to handle. You'll be financially responsible for materials, labour, tax, and other expenses, which can get very expensive, very quickly.

For first-time homebuyers, who generally have enough trouble finding money for the down payment, investing in a house that needs a lot of work may be a bit of a stretch. But don't be discouraged from buying one of the cheaper houses on the block — that's *always* a smart move, because the value will be affected positively by the more expensive neighbouring houses. Remember, not everything in the home has to be done all at once: A lot can be accomplished cosmetically with a bit of paint and some elbow grease.

WARNING

Many people buy houses that badly need renovation to fix them up and then sell them for a profit. But remember, don't renovate your house beyond the property value your neighbourhood can support. A two-storey Georgian-style home would be out of place and look overvalued in a trailer park, for example.

If you plan to sell your house in the future, get detailed estimates of how much your intended renovations will cost and compare the money you'll put into your home (purchase costs + renovation costs) to neighbouring home values. You'll want the purchase, renovation, and carrying costs to align with local market values. You may not be able to recover excessive costs.

Work with your agent or an appraiser to determine the extent of upgrades you should undertake based on the condition and value of other properties in your area. Know the limit and build within it.

Rising Ambitions: Investigating Condos

To lots of people, the word *condominium* is associated with living in the equivalent of a beehive: Your unit is just one of hundreds of cramped, cookie-cutter living spaces far above the madding crowd. But a condominium is a kind of ownership rather than a type of property, including townhomes, row housing, and even office and industrial space (but that's for another book).

Even though the standard urban condo puts you at the heart of city life where amenities are at your doorstep and the building may even have a concierge to accept deliveries and screen visitors, not all condos are created equal. It pays to know what you're buying into and what buyers will be scrutinizing when your time to sell comes. This section gives you the basics, with an emphasis on these units that now make up close to 15 percent of Canada's housing stock.

Weighing the ups and downs of condo living

Whether you buy into a *new condominium corporation* (the organization responsible for the condominium's upkeep) or an established one, there are several advantages to condo living:

>> **Greater security:** Some condominium residences have a 24-hour concierge to screen visitors to the building. In a modern condominium complex, you can expect security cameras and coded passes for access to the building, elevators, garage, and amenities.

CONDOS IN BC — YOU MEAN STRATA UNITS

In British Columbia, condominiums are often called strata units, especially in listings and legal documents. This name traces back to 1967 and comes from all the way Down Under. Before 1966, B.C. lacked condominium legislation, so, seeing a need for one, the province simply adopted the legislation, The Strata Titles Act of New South Wales, Australia. In 1980, B.C. changed the name to the Condominium Act, but the term condominium wasn't used once within the Act itself. Then, in 2000, the act governing condominiums in B.C. was changed to the Strata Property Act. So if you're looking for a condo on the West Coast, you'll hear "strata title" and "strata unit" an awful lot.

» **Low maintenance:** You have less outside maintenance to do — no house painting in the blistering summer sun for you! Never again will you muck out an eavestrough (or argue with your partner over who will do it). In most cases, yard work is also a thing of the past for a new condo owner.

» **Amenities:** Much like a university residence, a condominium complex may feature on-site amenities such as a gym, laundry and dry-cleaning facilities, swimming pool, and sometimes even a putting green! (Just remember that the more amenities there are, the higher your monthly condo fees will be!)

» **Sense of community:** Ideally, you'll find that a condominium is an engaged community that looks out for its members. Although you may not get along with everyone at the condo meetings, you'll likely discover a supportive group of residents.

Before you start rubbing your hands together anticipating your carefree lifestyle as a condominium owner, let us bring to light a few of the downsides as well:

» **Less autonomy:** You can't always do exactly what you like — you may not be able to hang bright curtains in your windows, blast the radio on your balcony, or accept the little kitten your friend gives you for your birthday.

» **Unpleasant restrictions:** You may have to accept inflexible rules or disagreeable decisions made democratically by your condo corporation. You may be forced to compromise on rules governing the conduct of condo owners, or issues regarding the building structure or facilities (for example, if everyone in the condo complex but you votes in favour of erecting a 20-foot-tall gold statue in the lobby, you're stuck paying for your share of the cost regardless).

- **» Proximity to neighbours:** Your home will be very close to your neighbours, and you may not get along with them — but you'll still share a business and managerial role with them in the condominium corporation.

- **» Maintenance concerns:** You depend on the condominium corporation (and the management company they hire, in most cases) to handle building repairs and to be financially responsible with your maintenance fees. For example, you may feel your building needs a new roof and that putting it off will be more costly in the long run. The condo corp may feel otherwise. Your neighbours will need to agree with you in order for that new roof to proceed.

- **» Financial risk:** You share responsibility for large, unexpected repair bills — for example, if your condo springs an ominous leak.

TIP

The condo development you buy into, whether it's a high-rise, low-rise, or townhome development will become your own neighbourhood. This isn't just because you're all neighbours, but because the condominium corporation sets the bylaws that govern residents' lives as well as the fees owners pay for maintenance, landscaping, and other initiatives and amenities. Owners who live in their condos tend to be much more hands-on as neighbours and concerned with the upkeep of the property, including the common areas. Many buildings also allow owners to lease their units to tenants, which may increase wear and tear and overall maintenance cost. (Just think of the first place you rented: the stained carpet, the scrapes in the wall from where you propped your bike, and other things you didn't pay much attention to because maintenance wasn't your job.) Ask the property manager or your real estate agent for the renter/owner ratio before you buy.

Understanding condo ownership

When you buy a condo, you're buying an interest in the condominium corporation and the common, shared property of the condominium complex. As a unit owner, you have some say in how the condominium corporation (or *strata corporation* in B.C.; see the nearby sidebar), conducts itself. The corporation has an elected board of directors, each of whom must be owners in the development. Although the board of directors is composed of unit owners, the board will often hire professional property managers to act under the board's supervision.

The corporation has a legal obligation to hold regular meetings that all unit owners can attend and discuss the business of the building corporation. Ownership of one unit usually equals one vote at these meetings. Having information about how the corporation operates is your right, but taking an active role in this process is your responsibility also.

Knowing your responsibilities

When you own a home, you're responsible for all improvements and repairs to your property. Things are less straightforward with a condominium, so a document is needed to clear up who's on the hook for what. The *condominium certificate* lays out exactly what expenses are the responsibility of the condo corporation, which fall to individual owners, and which all the unit owners will share. The condominium certificate also outlines the financial status of the condominium corporation.

The condominium certificate will tell you the following:

>> What the code of conduct for residents is, including how many units can be rented, and whether pets are allowed, among other things (refer to the section, "Living by the rules: condos and condon'ts," later in this chapter)

>> What your monthly condo fees will be for shared expenses

>> What your individual unit costs will be

>> What the financial status of the corporation is, especially regarding the reserve fund

REMEMBER

A *reserve fund* is money put away by the corporation for any repairs or upgrades that become necessary. Usually, a portion of your monthly condo fee goes into this fund. Having a well-maintained reserve fund is crucial.

>> Whether the condo corporation is involved in any legal proceedings and may outline how many units in the building are rented and how many are owner-occupied

>> Whether the seller has paid all the fees

WARNING

If the seller hasn't paid the condo fees, provisions exist for any unpaid fees to be paid upon the sale of the unit. Your real estate agent or lawyer can advise you on how to proceed with your purchase, but make sure you don't get stuck with any of the seller's liabilities.

REMEMBER

Before buying into an existing building, review a current condominium certificate prepared by the condominium corporation or the property manager acting on behalf of the building. If you're buying into a new building, in lieu of an existing condominium certificate, you have the right to ask the developer for a copy of the proposed condominium certificate (if one is available) or a *full disclosure statement* or *prospectus*. This document should contain a proposed budget and outline a number of features for the new development. (If no proposed budget exists, get out as fast as you can!) Have a lawyer review this document before agreeing to purchase a unit.

Others documents to consult, and which should be provided, included the latest two years of meeting minutes as well as a depreciation report (if available). A qualified professional, usually an engineering firm, prepares the depreciation report, which outlines the condition of various elements in the development. It will provide any major expenses that are pending or recommended in the coming years.

Living by the rules: condos and condon'ts

In addition to the financial details of ownership, the condominium certificate lays out the bylaws that are the code of conduct for residents. By purchasing a unit in the condominium, you agree to be bound by these rules. One advantage of purchasing in a new development is that you get a say in what those rules will be; in an older building, changing the established rules can be more difficult.

BYLAWS FOR NEW CONDOS

For a new development, the new owners will establish a new set of bylaws and regulations when the building has transferred from the developer to the individual owners. Your province's legislation regarding condominiums should form the basis of the bylaws. The advantage of buying a unit in a new building is that you can have a say in the formation of the new bylaws and rules and regulations.

You have to assume that the proposed rules will be enforced. But as with any rules, the bylaws are good only insofar as they are enforced. When you decide to buy a new condominium, you have no way of knowing who will buy in that complex and how the rules will change in accordance with the other residents' tastes and demands. On the other hand, the proposed bylaws may not change after you move in, but the corporation or, more important, by the other residents may not be enforce them.

If a big selling point with you is the proposed bylaw stating that there will be "quiet hours" after 10 p.m., for example, you have no guarantee that this rule will be enforced. If some residents ignore the rule and other residents don't seem to care (or are kind of hard of hearing), you may simply have to put up with noise all night long. Even if residents get up in arms over the ill conduct of a few, complaints may fall on deaf ears — you can't be sure the governing body will be receptive. In all provinces getting rid of a problem tenant is possible, but removing a problem owner is very difficult.

BYLAWS FOR WELL-ESTABLISHED CONDOS

In a well-established complex, current residents may be happy to speak with you about how well the condominium is run. It pays to make several visits to any new home you're considering buying. Go at different times of the day and night to get a real feel for the atmosphere. An agent may have you drop by at the best time for showcasing the unit, so you may end up with an overly positive opinion.

You can also call the building's property manager for insights into the building and the running of the complex in general. Find out how any complaints about bylaw violations have been received and are handled, what rules are enforced, how often or drastically the bylaws have been changed, and so on. Doing your due diligence gives you a better understanding of the social life of the complex and how many compromises you may have to make while living there. Often, you can glean a lot of this information by reading the minutes of the board meetings. You can see what issues have been brought up and how they were addressed. Knowing how quickly owners' concerns were dealt with can give you an idea of how proactive the building is when it comes to solving problems.

Closing the deal

Because the form of condominium ownership brings you together with others, buying a condo is necessarily more complex than buying a detached home or even a townhome that's not part of a condominium corporation. On the plus side, you have a chance to work with others to define the culture of the development and be a contributing member of a community. But you must also face several factors that make purchasing a condo different from other types of properties and some specific questions you'll want to ask as you size up a condo unit, which we discuss here.

Collective uncertainties

In many respects, buying a new condo is similar to buying any other new home (we discuss the pros and cons of buying a new home in the section, "Buying new," earlier in this chapter). But unlike other forms of ownership, where you're the only person responsible for managing the property, a new condo may not have the board in place or the bylaws or the management fees. Even though the developer will typically get the ball rolling, establishing a competent board of directors and choosing a property manager that makes everyone (or at least a majority) of owners happy takes time.

WARNING

If a new building is mismanaged or, worse, the inexperience of the directors leads to insufficient funds being set aside for repairs, renovations, or upgrades, you and the fellow owners can be responsible for the additional costs. Although a new building shouldn't require major attention in the first few years, the warranty every new building must have may not cover some deficiencies. As a result, you (with the other condo owners) may face a sharp and sudden rise in condo fees or a special assessment in the thousands of dollars. This increase could result in a sharp (but hopefully temporary) decrease in the resale value of units.

TIP

When you buy into an established condo project, you're buying into a corporation with a track record. It can provide assurance that the property managers have unit owners' best interests at heart (and if they don't, you can decide not to buy). You have access to minutes of the building meetings to see how the corporation has responded in the past when repairs were necessary or emergencies arose. You can find out how well the reserve fund has been maintained, how well the governing body has responded to owners' requests for upgrades, and whether condo fees have increased or are about to increase because of planned renovations.

The listing agent will provide most of this information about a condo's history if you show serious interest in the condo, usually after making an offer. You should always make your offer subject to your approving the building's records and other documentation (for more regarding conditions and subject to clauses, see Chapter 9). Having all this information ahead of time provides peace of mind, knowing that you're making a sound investment.

Delayed move-in dates

One of the risks of buying any newly built home is the chance that it may not be ready when you are. This risk is a particular hazard of newly built condos and can affect not just your plans but also those of hundreds of new buyers. And it's all perfectly legal, so long as the developer has alerted buyers to the possibility in the agreement of purchase and sale and provided adequate notice.

REMEMBER

The developer is required to give you sufficient notice if your date of occupancy needs to be extended. Each province has homeowner legislation to protect you in the case where no clause exists in your contract to delay your move-in date or you haven't received proper notice that your condo won't be ready when the time comes. Knowing your rights is always important.

The clause in the agreement of purchase and sale that deals with move-in dates usually says something like this:

"If the condominium unit is not ready for occupancy on the specified completion date, the developer may, by written notice to the buyer or the buyer's solicitor, extend the completion date at any time and from time to time as required to any date determined by the developer, by which time the developer expects the condominium unit will be ready for occupancy and a separate title for the condominium unit issued."

When you initially visit a condo development or speak with the developer (or its representative), find out what the anticipated date of occupancy is and then consider how any delays might impact you. Sometimes, depending on the type of development you're interested in, the occupancy date can be years away. Something else to keep in mind: If the condo won't be ready for occupancy for two years, will your life still fit that condo? If you're in your 20s, a lot can happen in two years. You may be single when you sign the purchase contract, but married with a baby on the way when the condo is finished!

You may rely on your real estate agent for advice, as your search for a condo will have taken into consideration your lifestyle needs and timing. Your agent can keep you up-to-date on construction progress.

Moving into your new condo unit can only happen when the developer receives an *occupancy permit* for the entire building from the local town, municipal, or city government. Even if your own suite is ready and finished, you can't move into the building until an occupancy permit indicates that the entire building is safe, and the elevators, sprinklers, and emergency systems are all working. The one variation from this rule may occur in a phased townhouse development, where a *partial occupancy permit* may be issued to cover different phases of a project as they're finished.

We discuss how to prepare for a delayed move-in date in the section, "Buying new," earlier in this chapter.

Condo assignment sales

Sometimes the developer's plans change, and sometimes it's your plans that do. Many presale agreements for condos (and other properties, too), include a clause allowing you to assign the contract of purchase and sale to someone else. Assignment sales may also allow you to purchase a unit in a project you thoughts was sold out. Assignment sales usually involve three major players:

>> The developer

>> The original buyer (*the assignor*)

>> A second buyer (*the assignee*) who buys the unit from the original buyer

An assignment sale occurs when the assignor transfers the contract and all its terms to the person (you) who wants to buy the unit and become the new owner. The original owner remains on the hook for obligations until the time the building completes. When it does, you receive title to the property and become the registered owner.

REMEMBER

Given the concern in many hot markets over the use of assignment clauses as a tool for speculators to flip properties and make a fast buck, some provinces and developers limit the use of assignment clauses. For example, the contract may contain a clause between the original buyer and the developer denying the buyer permission to assign the contract to a subsequent buyer during the construction period.

Permission from the developer (in writing, of course) is always required for an assignment to take place. The assignee is buying the contract to purchase the condo and involves both legal paperwork and an exchange of money (just like any other purchase arrangement), so you'll definitely need a lawyer and an experienced real estate agent to make sure you get everything right.

WARNING

The assignor isn't off the hook for the sale until the assignee closes on the purchase of the condo as specified in the original contract. If the assignee doesn't complete the sale as specified in the original contract, the assignor is, in most cases, still liable for any damages suffered by the developer.

TECHNICAL
STUFF

Assignment listings are seldom listed as such on the Multiple Listing Service (MLS) system because the assignor doesn't own the unit (the developer still owns it) and real estate boards across Canada usually require the owner to sign a listing form. An assignment listing can be listed on MLS only if the developer consents, but many developers don't want an already-sold property to be re-listed, because it may be in competition with units that the developer has not yet sold. (For more on MLS listings, see Chapter 8.)

Converting condos

Condominium conversion projects are an opportunity to buy into a building that conforms to current building standards, but with all the character of its former incarnation. Some are former apartments that switched over to condo status, some used to be workaday office buildings. Still others boast interesting past lives as schools, churches, warehouses, or factories, and may be perfect for you if you're looking for a cool and unusual home.

You may also like a conversion because in some cases the building exists in an area that offers an amount of space that would normally be out of your price range. A converted warehouse in a gritty industrial area is a case in point. The transition of commercial and industrial areas into residential neighbourhoods have offered plenty of opportunities for young professionals seeking live-work space to buy a home studio that would cost significantly more (and face more restrictions) in a staid residential area. These new neighbourhoods may not be for everyone, but if you're overcome by the pioneering spirit, a funky conversion in a nonresidential area may offer you more bang for your buck.

Although you may love the idea of living in a building with history, you need to think about the practical impact that old exterior will have on your unit. All the internal parts of the building will be new (the developer usually has to gut the old building and create the new units within its shell), but the outside may not offer you everything you want in a home, especially if the building is older. If it's an old church that's been converted, you may not get as many windows and balconies as you would in a new building.

If you're keen to buy this kind of condo, have the building inspected to make sure major renovations won't be needed shortly after you move in (see Chapter 10 for information on inspections). A qualified home inspection can check that the quality of the construction and design are good and functional and won't lead to major problems down the road.

WARNING

Even though condo units may be new homes, the building itself may be an existing structure in the eyes of your province's New Home Warranty Program. Be sure to check with the warranty program in your province before you buy. Of course, if the project was converted years ago, you'll be able to check the condo corporation minutes to see if there are any issues and how these are being handled.

Asking the tough questions

When buying a condo, asking questions is particularly important because of the type of ownership involved and the fact that many are marketed before they're even built. Some questions to ask when considering condos specifically include

>> **How big is my condo, really?** Do the floor plan measurements include both inside and outside walls, or do they represent the actual floor space? A foot or so can make a big difference when you're trying to fit that L-shaped couch into your new place.

>> **How's my view?** You won't be able to see the view from a new condo before construction is completed, but you will know which way your unit will face, which floor you'll be on, and what'll be outside your window. You may experience a virtual reality view of the unit and view as part of the developer's marketing strategy. Ask what other developments are planned for the area. The stunning view you're being pitched on or which exists now could vanish if another shiny new tower goes up in front of yours blocking your mountain view. If you're looking at a lower-floor unit, ask where the garbage cans are going; you don't want to be admiring the smelly dumpsters from your living room.

>> **What's in it for me?** Does the purchase price include a parking spot? Will there be a pool or a rooftop garden? Do you have to pay extra for a storage locker? Find out exactly what you're getting, and confirm everything in writing so you're not surprised later on.

>> **What options do I have?** Can you choose light fixtures, countertops, or cupboard hardware specifically for your unit? What appliances are included, and do you have any choice as to what kinds?

>> **Where will the heating vent, air-conditioning vent, and electrical boxes be placed?** You don't want a vent smack dab in the middle of the living room wall. Systems located in odd places can seriously affect the functionality of your space.

>> **Will my walls be soundproof or paper-thin?** Because you'll be living so close to your neighbours, finding out about the quality of the building materials and if any provisions have been made to ensure privacy is important.

Living Co-operatively

Two different kinds of co-ops exist: *market co-ops* and *non-market (subsidized) co-ops*. Although the units in a market co-op are for sale, those in a non-market co-op are for rent only and cannot be sold. In this book, because we're all about buying and selling, we focus on market co-ops. Co-operative housing is often thought of as synonymous with low-income housing, but this simply isn't the case.

Co-operative living is something of a compromise between house living and condo living. Co-ops retain the community feel of a condo complex but with greater control over living space. In a market co-operative, owners don't own a unit itself; rather, they jointly own, with the other members of the co-op, the *co-operative corporation*, which is the corporation that owns the structures and land that form the co-op. Owners are assigned shares in the company based on the size of their unit — and these shares are the owner's "equity" in their unit. As a shareholder in a co-op corporation, you're entitled to occupy one of its units. The lease you have on the unit is different from a rental lease — it gives you the legal and exclusive right to occupy that unit (so long as all the stated obligations to the co-op corporation are met), and it gives you the right to participate in governance of the co-op. Take note: Whereas in a condo complex you have the option to participate, in a co-op you're *expected* to put in the time and effort required to take your share of responsibility for the governance of the community. In fact, in a market co-op you must be approved by the board of directors (made up of other elected owners) before buying in. When you buy in to a condo, you approve the building. When you buy in to a co-op, the building approves you.

Finding a bank that will finance the purchase of a co-op unit may be tricky, but not impossible. The equity in the suite is the assigned shares in the corporation, and many banks won't accept these shares as collateral for a mortgage. Therefore, co-ops are both harder to buy and harder to sell. Co-ops will generally appreciate as the market moves up (or depreciate as it slides down), but because any potential buyer may have difficulty securing a mortgage, co-ops tend to have lower market values than equivalent freehold condos.

Considering the co-op's pros

You may be inclined towards buying a co-op rather than a condominium for several reasons:

>> **More bang for your buck:** The price will be lower, so you should get a larger unit for your money than you would get in a conventional, freehold condominium.

>> **You're not just buying, you're joining:** In contrast to condominium corporations, many non-market co-ops are nonprofit organizations.

>> **You have lower costs:** Monthly fees are typically less in a co-op compared to those of a condo (and monthly fees are set by a vote of the co-op members).

>> **You perform less maintenance than with a house:** As with a condo, some of the maintenance and yard work won't be your responsibility.

>> **Your opinion counts:** Your views will probably have greater weight in a smaller co-operative community than in a larger one.

>> **You have some influence over who lives there:** As a co-op member, you have a say in who is allowed to purchase shares in the co-op corporation (and, therefore, who your neighbours will be) if you sit on the board of directors.

Weighing the co-op's cons

Some serious disadvantages to co-operative living should also be considered:

>> **Member approval controls the community:** Selling the right to your unit requires that your buyer be approved by the co-op community.

>> **Limited choice of location:** You may not be able to find a co-op in the neighbourhood you want.

>> **Financial arrangements:** Getting financial backing for the purchase of a co-op is often more difficult than with a condo, and mortgage rates are often higher.

>> **Community commitments:** Being a participating member of the co-op community takes time and effort.

>> **Participation in the upkeep of the co-op:** Some maintenance and yard work *will* be your responsibility.

>> **Regulations:** Often, the codes of conduct for members of a co-op are similar to those of condo owners, and these codes may be restrictive.

>> **Group finances:** Member accountability to maintain a level of liquidity, which is usually mandated by a government authority.

Home Owning as an Investment

Many people buy residential real estate as an investment. An even greater number secure a tenant — commonly known as a *mortgage helper* — for the suite in the basement. Buying a home with a view to the investment or income potential isn't a bad idea. It can make excellent short-term sense *and* help you pay down your mortgage that much faster. Though your return on your real estate investment isn't as exciting as the stock market can be during exuberant times, it's proven to offer a stable return.

This section just touches on this topic; if you're really interested in becoming a real estate mogul, check out Doug and Peter's other book, *Real Estate Investing For Canadians For Dummies* (John Wiley & Sons, Inc.).

Doing your due diligence

Before purchasing a residential investment property, do the necessary research to avoid future problems. Do the following:

>> **Consult your financial planner to make sure it fits into your long-term investment strategy.** Are you buying this property for cash flow, or are you planning to hold and sell it after a set period of time? How soon do you expect to need the money you're investing? What are the tax implications. These are all questions you'll want to discuss with your financial planner prior to becoming involved in an investment property.

>> **Consider the amount of time you have to manage the property.** Real estate isn't a passive investment, any more than owning a home is carefree!

>> **Make sure you handle all financing considerations if the home isn't your principal residence.** Most secondary or income properties don't qualify for Canadian Mortgage and Housing Corp. (CMHC) financing, which means you'll need a down payment of at least 20 percent to get the deal going. Because

lenders take property taxes, maintenance fees, and insurance into account in deciding how much to lend you, don't forget to factor these into the budget (fortunately, you can claim some of these costs as business expenses related to your investment property).

>> **Pay attention to tax implications.** Canada Revenue Agency investigators are also closely scrutinizing residential sales to make sure that all applicable taxes are being paid, especially if they've been used as rental properties. British Columbia and Vancouver both have special taxes designed to limit speculation and encourage the renting out of properties. Second homes may face special taxes designed to address the use of residential real estate as an investment.

Helping your mortgage

Many homeowners get by with a little help from their tenants. But when it comes to secondary suites and mortgage helpers, local bylaws vary across Canada. Check with the local authorities before buying a house with a secondary suite.

On the plus side, buying a house with a secondary suite may boost the amount of mortgage a lender will give you. Most lenders will consider rent from a secondary suite as income, factoring in approximately 50 percent of the expected annual revenue towards your mortgage limit. Rental income can give you access to a larger mortgage, allowing you to look in a higher price range. However, if the basement suite is illegal or nonconforming, you may be denied extra financing. Banks want you to stay on the right side of the law and don't want to be seen to be funding illegal activities.

A primary residence with a rental unit that generates cash flow can be a good long-term investment because the resale value of the residence is typically higher. However, the potential profit from renting will depend on location. Before you buy any kind of rental property, find out what demand is like and average rents for the area. This information is available from the Canada Mortgage and Housing Corp. (www.cmhc.ca), which produces an annual survey of rental markets across Canada each fall.

REMEMBER

Talk to a lawyer about the legalities of buying a rental property or a home with a mortgage helper. If the rental suite currently has tenants, you need to know where you stand. Confirm your rights under the tenancy legislation in your province (the tenancy branch in your province will be able to assist). Also, make sure the property conforms to local bylaws and zoning. Just because the previous owner rented out the basement doesn't mean it was allowed.

Buying a property that will have tenants doesn't often go as smoothly as planned. Most people don't realize how much work, or how expensive, it is to be a landlord. Don't take the responsibility lightly. If your tenant's toilet springs a leak, you have to look after it, or if they're late with the rent, you have to deal with the financial strain.

Your financial adviser can tell you how owning a rental property will affect your income taxes — both now and when you sell. If you claim part of a home's rental income as personal income and write off part of your home expenses, this may affect your claim to principal residence tax exemption should you realize a profit when you sell the house. (See Chapter 15 for details on the tax benefits of the principal residence exemption.)

IN THIS CHAPTER

» Discovering homes for sale

» Considering foreclosures

» Looking at overall style and resale value

» Reviewing your priorities

» Understanding exactly what you're getting in a new home

» Comparing the homes you see and picking a winner

Chapter 7

Shopping for a Home: The Nitty-Gritty

When you start looking for a home, you have to replace the visions in your mind with the one you can realistically afford to buy. (Unless, of course, you've won the lottery or just inherited a fortune, in which case buy exactly what you like.) But how do you find the right home to fit your budget and your basic needs? You can choose to sit back and leave the legwork to your agent, but most people want to be more involved in the process. In this chapter, we give you home-hunting tips and suggest ways for you to evaluate the advertised listings and homes you tour so that you can zero in on the best possible property faster.

Finding the Right Home for You

When looking for your dream home, you need to make a list that describes all the key features you want. The list will clearly outline the features you need to have and those that would be nice to have but aren't deal-breakers. These features will include not what's inside the house has to offer, but what's in the immediate neighbourhood and where it is in relation to everything else.

Making the list

A list is an important exercise that can help you narrow down the most important features you want your home to have. It sharpens your vision and also keeps you on track when having to make compromises (and believe us, everyone makes compromises). You want to make sure your basic needs are met while being aware of where you can be flexible. Here are some of the things you'll need to consider:

>> **Location:** Perhaps the most obvious factor . . . where do you want to live? After you have been preapproved for a mortgage, you'll have a good idea of what you can afford, which may determine where you will end up living. For example, you may be able to purchase a cool two-bedroom condo in the city or a four-bedroom family home out in the suburbs for the same amount of money. Knowing whether location trumps space is important.

>> **Type of home:** Figure out what type of home suits your needs. Look at your list and then look at the different types of homes that are on the market. Young professionals may opt for a downtown condo. A bungalow may be the preference of people considering retirement. Or, perhaps you're thinking about a detached home, what with your talented family of violinists and all. (We discuss the types of homes in Chapter 6.) If your tastes run to modern architecture, you won't want to look at Victorian-style homes.

>> **Exterior:** List the features of the property you need. What do you need outside? Is there enough room for the Great Dane to do laps? Do you need fencing around your yard to keep the kids in? Do you need a sunny yard for a garden or one suitable for summer parties? Maybe you need a lot of pavement on which to park your three cars, two motorcycles, and RV.

>> **Kitchen:** If you have a big family, you probably want an eat-in area and built-in dishwasher. If you're a professional cook, counter space and large appliances may be your priority. The presence of appliances may not be the deciding factor, but room to install them is.

>> **Bathrooms:** If you're looking for anything with more than one storey, bathroom location as well as the number of bathrooms is important.

>> **Bedrooms:** How many bedrooms are you looking for? Do you need an extra one for a home office or frequent house guests? If you're just starting out and hoping to have children in the not-so-distant future, count them in when calculating your needs. If your children are finally off to college and moving out, you may want fewer bedrooms.

>> **Renovations:** Are you willing to do them? If the home has everything you're looking for — the neighbourhood works, the room sizes are great, and you love the garden and the two-car garage — but it hasn't been updated since 1982 (hey, who doesn't love an entire house finished in a dusky pink colour scheme?), are you willing to do the work? You may find that a bit of elbow grease gets you exactly what you want.

>> **Other considerations:** How small is *too* small for your bedroom? For your kitchen? Will stairs be a problem for anyone in your household, now or in the future? Do you need a finished basement for your home office, your home theatre, or your kids' playroom?

Use Table 7-1 to organize the features you need or want in a new home. Complete the chart by considering what is absolutely essential to your needs, and what you'd really like to have (but that you *could* live without). For some items in the chart, like a dishwasher or a fireplace, it's a simple yes/no proposition. A fireplace may be "nice to have," but is it really "essential"? You decide.

TABLE 7-1   ## Home Priority List

Feature	Essential Need	Nice to Have	Feature	Essential Need	Nice to Have
Type of Home			Location		
Detached, semi-detached, or so forth			Flooring		
Victorian, modern, or so on			*Hallways*		
Number of storeys			Width (m or ft.)		
Interior			Linen closet		
Size (m² or ft²)			Coat closet near main entrance		
Number of rooms			Flooring		

(continued)

TABLE 7-1 *(continued)*

Feature	Essential Need	Nice to Have	Feature	Essential Need	Nice to Have
Living Room			*Basement*		
Size (m² or ft²)			Size (m² or ft²)		
Open concept/ separate dining room			Finished/ Partially finished		
Fireplace			Basement/ in-law apartment		
Flooring			Washer/dryer		
Ceiling height			Freezer		
Kitchen			Heating (oil, gas, etc.)		
Size (m² or ft²)			Flooring		
Condition			*Other*		
Eat-in area			Central air conditioning		
Fridge (age, stainless steel, capacity)			Central vacuum		
Stove (electric or gas, convection)			Finished attic		
Dishwasher (age, capacity)			Property will accommodate expansion		
Kitchen cupboards (age, size, style, accessibility)			Water view		
Countertops (material, age)			New windows		
Flooring			Sliding glass doors		
Bedrooms			Natural light		
Number			*Exterior*		

Feature	Essential Need	Nice to Have	Feature	Essential Need	Nice to Have
Walkout to balcony			Frontage (size and direction facing)		
Closet in each room			Brick/siding/wood/stucco		
Flooring			Roofing material (slate, cedar shake, asphalt shingles; age)		
Master Bedroom			***Parking***		
Size (m² or ft²)			Garage		
En-suite bathroom			Carport		
Walk-in closet, south-facing window, fireplace, or other special feature			Space		
Flooring			Private/shared driveway		
Bathrooms			Street parking		
Number of bathrooms			***Yard***		
Size (m² or ft²)			Size of lot (m² or ft²)		
Location(s)			Shed		
Shower/tub/whirlpool tub			Deck/patio/porches		
Flooring			Fenced enclosure		
Sunroom/Den/Home Office			Swimming pool		
Size (m² or ft²)			Established landscaping		

(continued)

TABLE 7-1 *(continued)*

Feature	Essential Need	Nice to Have	Feature	Essential Need	Nice to Have
Location			Landscaping/ garden space		
Flooring			Sunlight		
Family Room					
Size (m² or ft²)					

REMEMBER

Choosing features in a home isn't all sunshine and roses. You may think you want a corner lot with a big yard, but have you bargained for the snow shovelling, leaf raking, and lawn mowing that go with it? How about the settling foundation and structural decay of your dream Victorian mansion? We're not saying you should change your mind about what you want, but when you set your priorities, think about the drawbacks of maintenance and repair that go along with the benefits of the home you want to own.

Checking what's on your doorstep

When identifying your home needs, focus on both the home's interior and exterior elements. However, the neighbourhood where your home is located is also a consideration. You may be able to renovate a bathroom in your house, but you can't just move the bus stop in front of your white picket fence or force the fire department to move several blocks away. Your location can affect the way your home value appreciates or depreciates — the old saying, "Location, location, location," isn't an exaggeration.

Consider the specific location of your desired home, as well as the general area. Living three streets away from train tracks may be fine for you, but being across the street from them is absolutely unthinkable. Or maybe you like a certain neighbourhood, but don't want to live on the busy main drag.

What about local amenities — is it important to be close to shops, parks, or community hubs like a school, library, or place of worship? If you drive everywhere, then perhaps you don't need amenities close by. On the other hand, if you don't have a car, having some of these places within walking distance may be important. Access to public transportation is also a consideration.

A neighbourhood isn't only a particular location; it's a type of environment. Look at the characteristics of the areas you like best. Do you like a dense community with people and activity? Or does a secluded location appeal to you? Do you like to see Christmas decorations up in the middle of November, or would you rather not see any at all? Do you want plenty of trees, playgrounds, and parks? Or are sleek high-rise condominium towers near the theatre district more your style?

Think about your family's needs. If your family is athletic, you may want to be near a community centre or a soccer field. If you have children, check out the local schools and find the boundaries (if any) for the catchment areas. A *catchment area* is the geographical area that outlines the boundaries of the neighbourhood that qualifies for admission to a certain school. Maps of school catchment areas are available from local school boards. If you want Junior to go to that special French immersion academy, you'd better make sure the location of the house you're considering allows him to attend that school.

Staying connected

Home is where the heart is, but many people spend a lot of time outside the home: the office for you, and schools for the little ones. How far away are you willing to live from where you work? Don't forget there's added expenses the farther away you live (more gas, more wear and tear on your vehicle), as well as more stress (longer travel time, more traffic). Having said that, what you need and where you want to live may not always fit in the same budget. That four-bedroom detached home close to work may be two or three times more expensive than the home that's a 45-minute train ride away.

TIP

Try to do a test drive or transit ride from your potential neighbourhood to your workplace during rush hour. How long does it take? How is the traffic on the new route, or the transit service? Your initial reaction to the commute will tell you whether you're making a good move.

If you're a parent, think about transportation challenges for the kids too. Can you let the little ones walk to school, or will they need to take a bus or get a drive from you? Is there a nursery or daycare conveniently near to your commuting route?

Of course, location is all about work. Jobs and schools will change, but what brings you joy when you're not at work is also important. You want a place you're happy to come home to (even if it does take an hour). Consider where you want to be when you are *not* at work and then how far you're willing to travel to be there.

Checking Out the 'Hood

If you get a deal on a home because of the train tracks through the backyard, chances are you'll have to list it at a lower price when the time comes to sell. You may also have to wait longer to sell because you'll need to find someone else who is willing to accept not just a bargain price, but the train tracks.

Defining neighbourhood character

You may find that your community is relatively quiet during the day, but the park across the street becomes a hive of activity on evenings and weekends, potentially clogging streets and is just plain noisy. Make sure your potential neighbourhood suits your needs during the day, in the evenings, and on weekends. Find out what you can't see just by looking. Word of mouth can also be a huge factor in your decision.

>> **Safety:** Consult the local police stations and community papers for statistics on neighbourhood crime. Police statistics are increasingly available online, often broken down by neighbourhood.

>> **Emergency services:** Check for the proximity of fire stations, police, and hospitals. Not only will these services make you feel safer if they're close by, but they can also help reduce your insurance costs by reducing the risk of burglaries or total destruction in a fire.

>> **Local information:** Check community newspapers and websites to assess how much of a community the neighbourhood really is. Consult the local planning department to discover plans for major infrastructure projects, housing or commercial developments.

>> **Owner statistics:** Consult the Canada Mortgage and Housing Corp.'s Housing Market Information Portal (accessed via www.cmhc-schl.gc.ca/en/data-and-research) to discover the ratio of owners to renters in the neighbourhood. A greater proportion of owners generally means a greater commitment among residents to keeping the neighbourhood clean, safe, and happy.

>> **Education facilities:** Visit the local schools. Find out if most of the children in the area attend the local schools, and if not, why. Conversely, if many students attending school in the area come from other neighbourhoods, then you can be confident it's well-respected.

The Fraser Institute publishes annual reports that rate secondary schools in British Columbia, Alberta, Ontario, New Brunswick, and Quebec. If you're considering buying a home in these provinces, you can visit `www.fraser institute.ca` and click the "School Rankings" tab for the latest report.

>> **Commercial activity:** Visit local eateries and businesses. If new ones are moving in and businesses are thriving, it's a sign that the community is growing and that property values may go up by the time you get around to reselling your home. Lots of For Sale or Lease signs in a nearby commercial area can be a signal of change. The type of businesses in an area also indicates the demographics of the community. Retailers do a lot of market research before choosing a location.

>> **Major construction:** Keep your eyes open for street construction, transportation expansion, or shopping malls and community centres being built — all are signs of a growing community.

>> **Public transit services:** Find out how accessible public transportation is in your area. Easy access increases the value of homes for resale, even if you don't need to use it yourself.

>> **Community affairs:** Attend a neighbourhood meeting to get an idea of how involved residents are in local affairs, as well as what their local concerns are.

>> **Overall contentment:** Talk to the people in the area to find out how happy (or unhappy) they are. You will most likely feel the same way after you move in. Alternatively, you may find your potential neighbours cramp your style.

Improving the prospects

What if you find that perfect neighbourhood, but a few quick inquiries tell you that it's out of your price range? Well, you'll probably have to start neighbourhood hunting again, but now that you know what you're looking for, it should be an easier process. Check out the fringes of your dream area for gems that are close to, but not smack in the middle of, your preferred community. You may be able to find a home in the path of that community's expansion. Or, find yourself a neighbourhood that seems to be up-and-coming. Here are some things to look for when trying to find that diamond in the rough:

>> **Home improvements:** Look at houses in the fringe areas for signs of renovations or improvements. When homeowners spend money to improve their homes, it shows that they're happy enough with the neighbourhood to invest in it. What was once down and out may soon be up-and-coming: Large packs of hip young professionals roaming the streets are often a good sign.

>> **Real estate activity:** Look for "sold" signs on homes, which means that many buyers want to live in the area, or a number of sellers who want to leave. Your

agent should also be able to tell you how quickly local homes are selling and point you to areas where activity is strong rather than sluggish.

>> **Commercial postings:** Look for signs that shops and restaurants are moving in. A healthy area attracts the investment of new business owners. A new coffee shop can be seen as a good sign; a pawn shop . . . not so much.

>> **Major public developments:** New transportation sites can be a stimulus for business and development, and new zonings can indicate the government's interest in investing in the area. New parks and schools can indicate the growth of families in the area.

>> **Attractive exteriors:** Look for well-maintained homes and well-groomed gardens and yards. A neighbourhood where residents care about their homes is a place to be.

You can also keep an eye open for *flipped homes,* one of those homes that someone has purchased, renovated, and hopes to sell for a quick, healthy profit. You can usually spot a flipped home with the help of your agent: It was purchased recently and renovated by the seller, often within the space of several months. Your agent has the ability to track the home's history in most cases, so you'll most likely be able to determine what the seller paid for the property and the state the home was in when it was purchased. Expect to see a lot of cosmetic upgrades, like new kitchens and bathrooms, flooring, and paint. Changes to the exterior, like paint and possibly even a new roof, as well as alluring landscaping, gives the property the street appeal to pull in buyers.

Up-and-coming neighbourhoods are often key targets for home flippers because these areas will be attracting many buyers, and because homes in their original condition will be less expensive than their counterparts in more established areas. Flippers also tend to target the type of buyer who wants everything already done — and for many buyers, an essentially all redone home in a neighbourhood that's moving up on the food chain can be an attractive option.

TIP

Nothing's wrong with purchasing a flipped home; however, do make sure that the seller has pulled all the appropriate permits necessary and has made all upgrades to code. Just because the home looks all new and shiny doesn't mean you don't need to do an inspection. We discuss flipped homes in greater detail in Chapter 8.

Your neighbourhood priorities

What's going on outside your home is as important as what's going on inside. Use Table 7-2 to help you form an idea of what qualities in a neighbourhood and a community matter to you, just as you did for a home using Table 7-1.

TABLE 7-2   ## Neighbourhood and Location Priorities List

	Essential	Nice	Not Applicable
Close To			
Work			
Partner's work			
Schools			
Place of worship			
Family			
Parks, playground			
Daycare			
Shopping			
Public transportation			
Major roads, highways			
Fire station			
Police			
Hospital			
Doctor/dentist			
Public library			
Cultural centres (theatre, museums)			
Restaurants			
Recreation/health centre			
Public swimming pool			
Ice rink, baseball diamond			
Airport			
Other			
Away From			
Noise			
Traffic, major roads			
Train tracks			

(continued)

TABLE 7-2 *(continued)*

	Essential	Nice	Not Applicable
Hydro corridors			
Airport/flight paths			
Family			
Other			
General Location Features			
Established neighbourhood			
High property values			
Neighbourhood Watch/Neighbours concerned about neighbourhood issues			
Good snow removal			
Good garbage/ recycling pickup			
Quiet street			
Picturesque view			
Other			

Drilling into Opportunities

You also need to focus your attention on what's actually available in the market. Your agent can help you identify possible opportunities, but don't forget to keep your eyes open, too. While your agent works the listings, you can do your part by checking online, cruise the streets of your target neighbourhood and keep your ear to the ground. You never know when you'll hear about someone preparing to sell, or discover a gem your agent might not have noticed.

Working with your agent

Be open to the expert guidance your real estate agent has to offer (refer to Chapter 2 for advice on finding an agent). Agents spend hours scouring listings and often bring years of real estate experience to the table. A good agent who's in touch with the market may even know about purchase opportunities before they're officially put on the market.

Give your agent as much information as you can about what you're looking for, but be open to her advice about the kinds of homes that might fit your budget or neighbourhoods that might have what you want. Be sure not to limit your search too much; you want your agent to cast a wide net at first so you can see what's available, and then you can narrow down the choices to what's realistic. For example, if your budget is $300,000, see what's available for that amount in your region; you may discover that you should be looking in a specific area or for a specific kind of home (say, a two-bedroom home rather than one with five bedrooms, home theatre, and heated pool).

Many real estate agents have access to a home tracker tool, where the agent enters in the vital statistics of your dream home (including price range) and you're sent notifications when a home goes on the market fitting that description. In many cases your agent can target specific streets and even blocks. You can narrow down the style of home you're looking for and set minimum values for the number of bedrooms, bathrooms, and interior dimensions — you name it. These alerts will keep you on top of any new listings that meet your criteria and can save you hours of scrolling through listings or visiting random properties.

If you want to live only on one particular block or in one specific building, your agent will be able to send a letter to people living there to see if they're considering moving. This is another way to find a property before it hits the market.

REMEMBER

If you feel your agent isn't listening to you or isn't providing you with good service, talk about the situation. If you're not able to clear up the problem, you may need to find a different agent.

Working online

Going online is a vital tool for home buyers looking to do their own groundwork. One of the best tools, and one that will let you match wits with your agent, is the Multiple Listing Service (MLS) site with listings from agents at real estate boards across Canada (www.realtor.ca). A typical MLS listing gives you a great deal of detail about a given home, including the number and size of rooms, lot size, interior dimensions (square metres or square feet), approximate property taxes, and additional information — details such as "renovated kitchen" or "professionally landscaped."

Professional integrity requires that agents write listings that are neutral in tone and in no way prejudicial. However, keep your eyes open for clues in the description such as "reduced" or "motivated seller" that may tip you off to potential bargains. Terms like "with a little TLC," "fixer-upper," or "handyman special" signal properties that may take more work than you're ready to put in.

Using MLS is a good way to start your search and get familiarized with various neighbourhoods and price points. You can even map the opportunities, allowing you to identify neighbourhoods where you may have more luck finding a home. For example, a friend of Peter's realized that if she ever hoped to buy a home, she would have to accept a 45-minute commute. Although she gave up on her dream of being close to downtown, by watching the MLS she was able to narrow down her target market and find a home in an affordable neighbourhood — and finally become a homeowner.

Plenty of properties aren't listed on the MLS, however. Homes for sale by owner have separate sites, and many brokerages and agents maintain their own database of listings. You can dig into this data by becoming familiar with what's available. Your agent can help you discover more information about any listings you uncover.

REMEMBER

Even though newspapers and other print resources carry real estate ads, most of the listings are also available online. Although we don't discourage you from leafing through newspapers and magazines looking for listings, we do believe the most efficient way to search for properties is via the MLS system and other online tools.

Working the neighbourhood

Despite all the tools that help you search for a home without ever leaving where you live now, you can still pound the pavement. While you're scouting a potential neighbourhood to get a feel for the area, keep your eyes open for new developments and "For Sale" signs. Agents will tell you that a home that doesn't seem like a winner online can be a real gem in actuality. If you see something that grabs your eye at street level, do more research.

Working your network

The more people who know you're buying, the more people who will suggest properties to you. Friends may have friends in the area who are thinking of selling. Talking with people in the neighbourhood you're considering may also turn up leads. Neighbours may know who's outgrowing their home or who's retiring to Florida next winter. Don't underestimate the value of word-of-mouth networking.

Thanks to social media, you also have a chance to tell people that you're in the market. Social media may also help you sell your existing home (we discuss marketing your home in Chapter 15). But remember to play it safe! Although you can let people know that you're in the market, hold your cards close to your chest and keep conversations of specifics private; you don't want to give other people a head start on your offer or make yourself a target for identity theft.

WARNING

Don't get so caught up in getting a bargain that you lose sight of what you're buying. If your cousin's neighbour's daughter-in-law's brother is trying to sell you a home, make sure you actually want it. You're trying to buy a home, not make a deal or keep the extended family happy. Never ever engage in oral agreements, even if the price seems right (see Chapter 9). You need a written agreement and the opportunity to do some in-depth investigation before you negotiate the price and terms of sale. An objective assessment of the property's value, a professional home inspection and the proper legal paperwork need to be carried out to make sure everything's on the level (including the house's foundation).

Attending open houses

Often sellers have open houses when they first put their homes on the market, giving you a great opportunity to check them out. You can talk to the seller's agent in person. Find out (if you can) why the sellers want to sell, and how motivated they are to sell. If you don't like the idea of having other people looking at the home at the same time as you, remember you can always make an appointment to see the home again privately. Pay attention to what other potential buyers have to say; they may notice something about the home that you've missed, or have done some productive snooping where you were too shy to look. Listen to their potential plans for the home; they may give you some good ideas.

WARNING

Be sure to tell the agent at an open house that you are working with an agent. It avoids any expectation on the agent's behalf that you need assistance in your house search.

In a hot real estate market, you'll find that many properties sell without ever hosting an open house. A home may be listed on MLS and then a few days later the selling agent holds an open house to give other agents an opportunity to view the home, but a public open house just isn't necessary. If you're working with an agent, you may well be able to attend that agents' open house in her company — and get a jump on the competition.

Getting Up Close with Foreclosures

Although we don't go too deep into the foreclosure process from the homeowner's point of view, suffice it to say that purchasing a foreclosed property takes a certain amount of doggedness and a special type of buyer.

REMEMBER

A *foreclosure* is a legal proceeding that bars or terminates the mortgagor's right of redeeming a mortgaged property. It typically happens when mortgages are in arrears for at least three months, but many lenders — unless they're very concerned, based on the borrower's history or the amount of debt that's accumulated — will try to find a compromise before calling the loan and triggering the sale process.

Two types of home foreclosures exist, and the process of purchasing a home in foreclosure really depends on which province you live in:

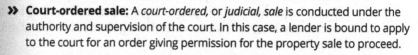

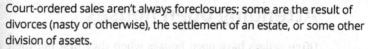

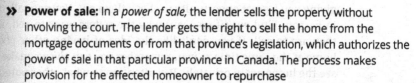

TECHNICAL STUFF

>> **Court-ordered sale:** A *court-ordered*, or *judicial, sale* is conducted under the authority and supervision of the court. In this case, a lender is bound to apply to the court for an order giving permission for the property sale to proceed.

Court-ordered sales aren't always foreclosures; some are the result of divorces (nasty or otherwise), the settlement of an estate, or some other division of assets.

>> **Power of sale:** In a *power of sale,* the lender sells the property without involving the court. The lender gets the right to sell the home from the mortgage documents or from that province's legislation, which authorizes the power of sale in that particular province in Canada. The process makes provision for the affected homeowner to repurchase

In Prince Edward Island, Newfoundland and Labrador, New Brunswick and Ontario, the power of sale is the primary recovery method for the lender. On the other hand, judicial sales are the way to go in Alberta, Quebec, British Columbia, Manitoba, and Saskatchewan. In Nova Scotia, the main recovery process is known as *mortgage foreclosure and sale* or *mortgage foreclosure,* but it is regarded as a judicial sale because the court is still involved.

When you're buying a foreclosure, either you're buying a home directly from the lender (and its bureaucracy) or the lender has to receive court approval of the offer that you present. Either way, the purchase isn't going to be as simple as dealing with a living, breathing homeowner. Finding out if your offer is accepted can take weeks, and if you have to set a court date, nothing's stopping other interested parties from presenting offers that may be better than the one you submitted originally.

WARNING

If you're buying a foreclosed home, the previous owners may have been just a wee bit grumpy about losing the roof over their heads. So, you may find damaged walls and floors, or missing appliances . . . heck, you may even find that the toilets are gone. Chances are good that if the former owners have been in financial difficulty, they may not have been doing regular maintenance, either.

Be aware that the court or lender provides no warranties on the property you're looking to purchase. The purchase is basically on an "as is, where is" basis. You can't say to the lender that you'll take the home if they fix the foundation crack: They're not going to. Lenders will proceed only with *clean* or *unconditional* offers — offers without conditions or subjects (we discuss subject clauses in Chapter 9). A prospective purchaser must do all due diligence in advance and make an offer without being guaranteed of getting the property or what condition it will actually be in when the deal closes.

Although there is no single database listing home foreclosures, you can find good deals out there by being attuned to the wording used in listings ("motivated seller" is a common one). Be prepared to do lots of homework if you're looking for foreclosures and wait.

Taking a Closer Look at Properties

No two properties are alike, but telling the difference between your ideal home and the one that's almost ideal can be tough. Some people know at a glance that they've found "the one," but most are prone to making mistakes. A gut feeling isn't the best way to decide which home to buy. This section guides you through the process of drawing up a short list and honing in on the best prospects.

Stacking up the properties

After you identify a few homes you like, you need to examine them closer to make sure they meet your needs and wants. Keep an eye open for the following:

>> **Curb appeal:** The first thing you think about when you view a home is what it looks like from the outside. Even if the property may look a bit run down right now, will a coat of paint and some sprucing up of the landscaping make a difference?

>> **Architectural style:** You may find it difficult to choose what you like from the many styles of home architecture available. Conversely, you may want to steer clear of certain types of homes that just don't float your boat. Perhaps you'll "just know" your favourite when you see it. Your gut instincts play a big part in choosing a home.

>> **Investment potential:** Consider buying a home the same as making an investment, because it's probably the biggest purchase you'll ever make. Think about the resale value of the home you're buying and what kind of profit you'll make on your investment. Someday, for some reason, you'll want to sell your

home and hopefully receive more than you paid. Buy with a long-term outlook and look for features that will stand the test of time. You'll reduce hassles for yourself and make it a better option for the next owner.

Scrutinizing more than one house

The more homes you see, the greater your focus will become. You'll know what you like and what you dislike. But we hope you don't have to view a hundred houses! If you can, stick to the ten-house rule: Visit at least ten homes, including public open houses as well as private viewings set up through your agent, before you decide to make an offer. You may think this is extreme, but the first set of homes will probably wow you with their cosmetic charms; after ten wows, you'll have become more critical than "I really like the colour of that bathroom."

Keep in mind that if you're focused on a specific neighbourhood, it may take years for ten houses to come on the market. To hone your critical skills, visit others in the surrounding area and perhaps draw up a short list of three in the area you want instead.

However, sometimes when you know, you know. You may fall in love with the first condominium you see, knowing full well that the place has everything that you need and want. If that's the case, you may want to pounce. Think about it: If you found the perfect partner, would you keep dating others? (We're hoping you'll say no.) Try not to talk yourself out of a good fit. You'll ultimately drive yourself (and your agent) crazy.

When looking at homes, it makes sense for you or your agent to book appointments one after the other. This approach is efficient, and comparing homes is easier when they're fresh in your mind. But try to look at only three or four homes in a day, and take careful note of each home's features. Seeing ten homes in one day will result in nothing but confusion: Was house number two the one with the great kitchen or was that number four? (Refer to the section, "Stacking Them Up — How the Homes Compare," later in this chapter to help you compare the properties you see.) Many homes also have *feature sheets* that present detailed information and include a picture. Remember to pick up feature sheets wherever you can to help your recall when you're trying to make decisions later. Your agent should be able to provide you with detailed information sheets as well (often from agent-only information sites).

Look at homes more than once; don't feel you have to make a decision about a home as soon as you've seen it. Unless you're looking in an incredibly strong seller's market and squaring off against other buyers making aggressive offers, make more than one visit to a home you're seriously interested in, preferably during different times of the day and of the week. And, if do feel pressure to make a decision, either from the seller or other buyers, discretion may be the better part of valour: If it's not love at first sight, it may not be the right fit.

REMEMBER

Avoid buying the most expensive home in the neighbourhood. Because home values are influenced by the values of the other surrounding residences, the most expensive homes on the block will have a smaller appreciation than others. After all, if most homes on the street are selling for $225,000, people will probably think twice before making an offer on the home that's listed at $450,000, regardless of how nice it is. Consider buying the lowest-priced house in the best neighbourhood to maximize the potential appreciation in value (especially if you plan to make upgrades).

Coming to Grips with Coming up Empty

If you've looked at what seems like a million homes and you haven't seen any you like, discuss your concerns with your agent. Possibly there has been some miscommunication somewhere, and the two of you are working at cross-purposes. Review your priority list (see Table 7-1) together, and talk about why you haven't liked any of the homes you've seen so far.

The problem may be that you have too fixed an idea of what is essential and you need to be more flexible. We can't help but say it again: The home of your dreams may not exist. What you're looking for is a home that's as close as you can get to your ideal, but you're going to have to compromise. The home that may be the right fit may not make your heart race right away, but in the cold light of day it ticks a lot of boxes. Your agent will probably let you know if you're being too picky and may redirect your attention to some homes you've already seen. After you've rethought your priorities, you may have a new appreciation for some homes' advantages. Your agent should also keep you informed if one of the houses you found somewhat interesting has had a price reduction. Suddenly, the house that wasn't quite right can become much more appealing given a $25,000 price reduction.

If you sense your agent doesn't understand what you really want, now may be the time to part ways. Do try to explain to your agent why you feel a change is necessary. Sometimes an agent and a buyer are just not a good fit, and there's no point continuing with a relationship that isn't working. If, however, you have very, very specific criteria, be prepared to wait a long time to find your home. Agents don't have a magic wand that'll be able to make your dream home appear (though we're sure they'd love one). You may have to relax your requirements a little bit, and find a patient agent who understands the importance of your specifications.

Getting Fired Up: Recognizing What Powers the House

Although you definitely need a professional home inspector to tell you if all the systems in your potential home, such as heating and electricity, are in good condition (refer to Chapter 9), you may be wondering what all these different systems are about, anyway. Knowing the kinds of systems you're buying will help determine what your future home expenses will be, as well as warn you about potentially costly problems you may not notice. Besides, what is a GFCI outlet, anyway, and why is it recommended? You should understand what the difference is between 60-amp service and 100-amp service before you get an inspector involved. This section clarifies the differences.

Heating systems

Although you get an estimate of what your heating costs will be from your seller's previous bills, knowing what kind of system — electricity, gas, oil, solar — you're getting makes sense. A poorly maintained furnace with overused filters and clogged ducts will be more expensive to run than a serviced one, regardless of its heating source.

To conserve energy, many homes now have heat pumps or mini-splits that are more efficient and allow for zoned heating and cooling. Ask whether this option is in place or can be installed. In many parts of the Canada, the cost savings can be significant at the same time as improving a home's comfort.

This following sections discuss the various options available in terms of systems and the fuels they use.

Forced air

A forced air furnace is the most common type of furnace. Fuelled by *natural gas* or *oil* to heat the air, the furnace then pushes warm air up through the house. A properly maintained forced air furnace can be very efficient and economical, but there are different levels of efficiency. Older, conventional furnaces rely on the "hot air rises naturally" idea, which can result in cold basements and warm third floors. This heating system may necessitate ceiling fans on the third floor to circulate the heated air.

Newer, high-efficiency furnaces are, as the name suggests, more efficient than older forced-air models and cheaper to run, but they can be relatively expensive to install. In the long run, you can recoup the installation expense through savings on heating bills. High-efficiency furnaces are also very compact; they take up much less space than the older-style forced-air furnaces. Many homes can be heated with a high-efficiency furnace that's no bigger than a hot water tank. Any home that already has a high-efficiency furnace installed has at least one solid feature going for it. A forced-air furnace can last between 10 and 25 years and can cost about $2,500 to as much as $10,000 to install, depending on the level of efficiency you want and the size of the home you are heating.

Hot water

Hot water heating uses radiators, baseboards, or in-floor radiant grids to heat a house or condominium. A hot water system heats very well and is controlled through thermostats that control zone valves throughout the system. In older systems, it may be impossible to control the temperature of individual rooms because one thermostat controls the whole house. Also, the valve on above-floor hot water radiators has a tendency to rust.

The hot water is heated in a boiler. A standard gas boiler for a hot water heating system may cost around $3,000 and should last between 15 to 50 years, depending on the type. The benefit of hot water heat is there's no dust blown around by a forced-air furnace, a great benefit for people with allergies. The hot water system is quieter than forced air and provides a more consistent heat.

WARNING

If you want to install central air-conditioning in a home that has a hot water heating system, you may find it very expensive. That's because you'll probably have to either install new ductwork or install a higher-efficiency system.

REMEMBER

Many people rent or lease the hot water tank in their home instead of owning it outright. Ask the seller (or seller's agent) what the status of the hot water tank is; if it's a rental, it may cost you about $10 to $20 a month to continue renting. Furthermore, ask how the hot water is heated. You'll find it more costly if the water tank is heated by electricity, which will probably be the case if your heating system also runs on electricity. (Electric heat takes much longer to warm a tank of water than gas- or oil-fired heating does.) One final thing: Check the water tank's capacity. You don't want to run out of hot water every time you shower. A rented hot water tank can easily be exchanged for one with a larger capacity, and if it breaks, it'll be replaced at no cost to you.

Baseboard heaters

Using baseboard heaters means that there is no ductwork to fill your walls, and each heating unit has its own thermostat, so different rooms of the home can be kept at different temperatures. Hot water baseboards can usually be controlled by a valve on the baseboard, and electric baseboards are controlled by a thermostat dedicated to that baseboard. These heaters can get hot to the touch, so be careful where you place furnishings. This might also be a consideration for parents of young children with curious fingers.

Fuelling up

Several kinds of energy are available to power your heating system. Here are the choices a home may have.

Electricity

Rising energy costs in some parts of Canada have made electric heating a very expensive option. However, it may be cheaper than oil or gas in many other areas and remains the default heating choice in many homes.

Heating your home with electricity can be done two ways: through baseboards or using a forced-air furnace or hot water boiler. Although some people complain that electric systems don't heat as well as forced-air systems or radiant heat, electric heat tends to be more efficient, thanks in part to the ability to target it to specific rooms or zones.

If your property (a new condominium, for example) was designed for electric heat and it's well insulated, you may find electric heating to be economical and efficient. However, if you're converting a drafty old house to electric heat, your heating bills will be sky-high. Be wary when buying any property where electric heat has been installed if the structure wasn't designed with this kind of system in mind. On the plus side, many organizations, including power companies and the government, offer incentives to improve the energy efficiency of your home.

Oil

Oil furnaces were commonplace before the 1970s, but have declined in popularity because they're more expensive than natural gas and require an oil tank that sits in your backyard or takes up room in your already overcrowded basement. Complaints about oil heating include having stinky oil odours in your home if the system isn't working properly and dirty walls near the tank. Despite the move toward natural gas forced-air heating systems, many homes still have oil-fired forced-air systems, which suggests that they're remarkably reliable.

Supporters of oil heating argue that modern oil furnaces can be the best and cheapest way to heat your home, especially if natural gas lines aren't available in your area. With proper maintenance (you should have it serviced every year), an oil furnace can be quite efficient, though oil has to be delivered by truck to your home. Oil can be used to fire a forced air or hot water heating system. An oil-fired furnace can be replaced with a natural gas furnace if gas lines are available in your neighbourhood. Converting from oil to gas may require relining your chimney and installing a better ventilation system.

In many parts of the country, incentive plans exist to convert from oil-fired heating to a more economical natural-gas-fired furnace.

WARNING

If you find a home with an outside oil tank, have the tank inspected thoroughly before you complete the purchase. Oil is great for heating, but a leaky tank will cost you thousands in terms of environmental clean-up (see the nearby sidebar for more information).

OIL'S WELL THAT ENDS WELL

When underground or *in-ground* heating oil tanks are abandoned, they pose a major environmental hazard if they aren't decommissioned properly. But that's not the only reason why it's important to investigate before you buy a property. If you find out after you've bought a home that your property includes an abandoned oil tank, you'll most likely incur the cost of removing the tank — which could be substantial. The seller of the home may not know whether a tank is present or not, especially if the home has changed hands many times since the conversion to natural gas (most likely in the 1960s or 1970s).

Most municipalities or utility companies will keep records of when a property converted from oil to natural gas heating and whether the oil tank was removed at the time of conversion. If there is no record of an oil tank being removed, look for a vent pipe running up the side of the house for no apparent reason. The pipe is a telltale sign that there may be a tank present — vent pipes were required to ensure the oil flowed smoothly from the tank to the furnace. If there's no vent pipe, you can contact a specialized company that searches for in-ground oil tanks. The cost for the initial search is usually $100 to $200.

If the presence of leaking oil is determined, the abandoned tank and any contaminated soil *must* be removed. If the tank hasn't leaked and it's readily accessible (like in the middle of the front yard), the cost to remove it can be in the $1,500 to $3,000 range.

The absolute worst-case scenario is a real nightmare: The tank had oil left in it when the house converted to natural gas usage, and the tank has since rusted out and has slowly leaked oil into the ground, trickling undetected into the neighbours' yards. At this point, the cost to remove all contaminated soil can be as much as $100,000 or more if the oil has entered the groundwater and adjacent properties.

Natural gas

Natural gas is generally more economical than other types of fuel. The catch: You can have it installed only where there are pipelines. The beautiful thing about natural gas is that other appliances that require heat can be bought to run on natural gas, and they tend to be cheaper to run. Many people swear by gas stoves; others love the economical benefits of gas dryers or the option of having a direct line to a barbecue or patio heater.

In very rare cases, homes with natural gas heating may have a problem with carbon monoxide, but with proper maintenance (you should have your furnace serviced every year) and carbon monoxide detectors in your home (required by law in some provinces), this shouldn't be an issue. Natural gas can fire a forced air furnace or a hot water heating system.

Natural gas also tends to be a stable source of energy. A pipeline explosion in British Columbia in early 2019 disrupted supplies in that province, but such occurrences are rare — far less common, at any rate, than power outages, which can disrupt heating that runs on electricity.

Propane

Propane isn't just for barbecues any more. Many homeowners consider propane to be the most convenient and versatile fuel for home heating, and the benefits of using propane are numerous, including the following:

>> **Propane goes everywhere.** Pressure is used to turn propane gas into liquid, making it very easy to transport, and it's cheaper too. As an easily portable fuel, it can be used beyond the end of the natural gas mains, and Canada's extensive road and rail network means it can be delivered almost anywhere it is needed — making it an especially smart choice for off-the-beaten-track recreational properties.

>> **Propane is as Canadian as maple sugar.** Close to 90 percent of the propane used is produced in Canada.

>> **Unlike with electricity, you don't need to worry about power outages.** A home served by an individual storage tank, which is constantly topped up, means propane can run virtually uninterrupted.

Heat pumps

Heat pumps work like air conditioners, but as the name suggests, they provide heat as well as cool air. Like a refrigerator, a heat pump compresses and decompresses gases to create or use heat through electricity. Because a heat pump can use more energy than it will produce if the outside temperature is less than 10 degrees Celsius, it works best in conjunction with a central furnace. Heat pumps have various degrees of efficiency, so check what the rating of the one in the home you're considering is. If you're scouting options to install in the future, be aware that they often require larger ductwork.

Heat pumps have traditionally been very expensive to install, sometimes running three times the price of a gas or oil furnace. Recent years have seen the advent of new ductless units that can be mounted on ceilings or outside walls. These so-called *mini-split units* may also be pricey, but they're highly efficient and have a faster payback window. They're also expensive to maintain and benefit from regular service. However, with a heat pump in your home, you don't have to worry about installing a separate cooling system. For more information, contact an independent air conditioning expert.

Renewable energies

A number of renewable heat sources are available, depending on the region. Solar power is among the best known, and a small array can largely or even entirely offset the standard energy needs of a small house.

Many high-rise apartment complexes rely on geothermal heat. Although these systems are often expensive for single-family homes, they're ideal for larger complexes where the costs — and benefits are shared among a large number of owners.

Some mixed-use complexes with retail or office space on the lower levels will capture and recycle energy in a way that benefits the residential portion. For example, cooling operations may remove energy from the commercial portion during the day. It can be captured and released to warm the residential portion at night, maintaining a constant and comfortable temperature at a significantly lower cost to occupants.

Considering electricity

From lighting to cooking, electricity runs most of the important household services you use on a daily basis. You need a reliable and safe electrical system in your home. Be aware of service amps and GFCI — they're two important aspects of a home's electrical system. Don't forget to make sure that the actual wiring is up to snuff, too — it only takes a spark to get a fire going.

Service amps

Electricity comes in three common sizes: 60 amp, 100 amp, and 200 amp. Sixty-amp service is an older electrical standard, usually found in homes built before 1970. While there isn't anything inherently wrong with 60-amp service for a smaller home, 60-amp service poses two big problems: First, you may be hard-pressed to find an insurer willing to cover the property, and second, if you ever had dreams of central air conditioning, a dishwasher, or an electric hot water heater, forget them.

Sixty-amp service can't usually handle the demands of anything beyond small appliances, and pushing those limits can increase the risk of fire (which explains our first point). Remember, too, that 60-amp homes were often wired before the advent of the power-hungry electric dryer and microwave. Think twice before buying a home with 60-amp service, because sooner or later you'll likely have to upgrade to a minimum 100-amp service. If you want to proceed, be aware that it can cost $750 to $1,500 to bring a house up to 100-amp service, and adjust your offer accordingly.

WARNING

Older homes may have knob-and-tube wiring, a technique that fell out of favour in the 1930s. If you're installing 100-amp service or more, replace it. This upgrade will, however, require rewiring most of the house, another expensive proposition depending on the size of the house.

Aluminum wiring

If your home or condominium was built in the 1970s, it may have aluminum wiring that isn't reliable. With aluminum wires, electricity actually flows away from the screws used to hold the wiring in place at the back of an electrical outlet. Air pockets form between the wires and the screws, letting electricity arc between them, ultimately burning the wire away and deadening the outlet. This obviously poses a significant fire hazard, and such wiring should be replaced.

GFCI

GFCI stands for *ground fault circuit interrupter*. You've probably seen them in a hotel bathroom: You know, the outlet with the little red button and the little black button. GFCI is designed for places where water (a very good conductor of electricity) may cause an electric shock and possibly seriously injure a person. GFCI receptacles should be placed in all wet environments, including kitchens, bathrooms, wet bars, laundry rooms, and outdoors. Inexpensive safety measures, GFCI outlets should be installed if the home you buy doesn't already have them.

UFFI

No, we're not talking about Martians; insulation is the alien creature in question. *UFFI*, or *urea formaldehyde foam insulation*, was a popular insulation in the mid-1970s. Unfortunately, when the UFFI foam ingredients weren't mixed properly, the resulting insulation released quantities of formaldehyde gas in homes, causing breathing problems and other adverse health effects for some people. UFFI was banned in Canada in 1980. However, UFFI may still be in some homes today. The government gave out three times more grants for manufacturing UFFI insulation than the number of rebates that have been applied for to replace it.

If the UFFI in a home was installed properly, it shouldn't break down or pose a risk to you. The Canada Mortgage and Housing Corp. (CMHC) will now insure UFFI-equipped homes. As a safeguard, you may still want to include a clause in your offer to purchase contract, stating that the seller warrants that the home isn't insulated with UFFI (in some provinces the clause is preprinted in the paperwork). Most sellers will be able to disclose that, to the best of their knowledge, they are or aren't aware of any UFFI in their home.

Asbestos time, the worst of times

The amazing insulating and fire-resistant properties of asbestos made it a popular material for home builders through the mid-20th century. Demand boomed, and a town in Quebec even named itself after the mineral. But a connection with mesothelioma, a deadly cancer of the lungs and abdomen, eventually saw it outlawed.

A lingering source of asbestos in buildings today is *zonolite* (also known as vermiculite), a grey popcorn-like insulation material that was blown into the attics and walls of homes for years. The insulation was made from asbestos-contaminated vermiculite ore mined from the 1920s until 1990. Although the mine that was the likely source was closed in 1990, the insulation remains in thousands of homes across Canada.

Owners of older homes may encounter asbestos panels or insulation during renovations. Special precautions are needed to prevent exposure to the material's lethal fibres during removal and disposal. Health Canada says that the best way to prevent asbestos exposure is to leave the insulation undisturbed, but if it's a concern, it can cost thousands of dollars to have the asbestos-contaminated insulation removed.

Septic tanks

Many rural areas aren't connected to the local municipality's waste management system. Even some urban properties rely on private septic systems to dispose of wastewater. Rather than flowing through a city sewer system to a treatment site, wastewater from these properties flows into a septic tank with a leaching bed (also known as *weeping tiles* or a *tile bed*) that treats the water before it goes back into the soil. The average septic tank requires a space of about 1 square metre (10 square feet). Your septic tank should be at least 1½ metres (5 feet) from your home and 16½ metres (55 feet) from sources of water. The leaching bed should be 30½ metres (100 feet) from sources of water. Sludge collected in the tank should be pumped out every four years. According to the Canada Mortgage and Housing Corp., minimum tank volumes range from 1,800 litres to 3,600 litres, depending on the province or territory.

Unfortunately, Canada doesn't have a uniform standard for septic systems. At best, provincial regulations govern them. The result is no one standard that manufacturers need to meet. You can get a certificate for the septic system from the home's municipality, but it verifies only the location of the tank and the leaching bed, not its condition.

Don't assume that every rural home has a septic system; ask the seller exactly what kind of waste system is in place. The house can possibly have a holding tank instead. Unlike a septic system, which processes sewage on-site and needs pumping every few years, a holding tank must be pumped every few months. If the home has a holding tank, speak with the seller about the cost of maintaining it.

If you buy a home with a septic system, you should get a plan (either from the owner or the municipality) that shows where the septic tank and leaching bed are located in relation to the house and water sources. Ask about the tank's capacity and when the tank was pumped out last. To ensure the tank was indeed emptied when the seller claims, ask for a receipt of the cleaning, which will confirm the date.

WARNING

The *drainfield* is the area in the yard directly over the septic system. The drainfield should consist of at least 1¼ metres (4 feet) of native soil between the system and the surface of the yard. When looking at this area, watch for the following problems:

>> **Trees or shrubs on the drainfield, rather than grass:** The root systems of trees and shrubs can interfere with the septic system.

>> **Pavement, a parked car, a patio, or a building of any kind, such as a garden shed:** These items put undue downward pressure on the septic system, which can crush pipes and prevent the system from working properly.

>> **Patches of lush growth, or overly moist soil over the drainfield:** This may be a sign that sewage isn't being processed properly.

>> **A bad smell around the yard:** Odour may be a sign that sewage is surfacing, which can pose a major health hazard.

Don't expect a home with a septic system to switch over to a sewer system in the near future, unless there are firm plans for the municipality to do so. Sewer systems are expensive to install, and the local government will usually decide it's not worthwhile. A septic system, however, should last about 30 years, depending on maintenance.

Well water

Similar to septic systems, a private source of water is used in a home where there are no municipal water lines to supply the residence. The minimum water storage tank you should consider is 40 litres. The main problems with well water are that it can become contaminated and therefore undrinkable. If the well goes dry, you may have to do some serious digging.

If you buy a home that draws water from a well, ensure that you get a certificate from the seller that guarantees the water to be drinkable. You can determine the quantity of water available as well — you should be able to get a certificate outlining the quantity of available water and the possible lifespan of the well. Water is generally tested for bacteria, hardness, and other harmful chemicals. For instance, you may find that there is arsenic in the water. In small amounts this isn't an issue, but if it's above acceptable limits you may need to install an expensive filtration system. The well water should be tested annually.

If water becomes contaminated, the municipality sometimes has no choice but to extend a water line up to the area. Your property taxes may increase if water services are extended to your property, however.

Stacking Them Up — How the Homes Compare

To help you organize your thoughts as you look at various homes, use Table 7-3 to record information about the homes you see. Make a copy of the table, and take it with you when you go to an open house or on a private home tour. Recording all the details makes keeping track of the potential benefits or drawbacks you observe about each home easier.

TABLE 7-3   **Home Comparisons**

	Home 1	Home 2	Home 3	Home 4
General Info				
Address				
Type/style of home				
Dimensions (m² or ft²)				
Age of home				
Size of lot (m² or ft²)				
Facilities (applicable to condominiums)				
Asking price				
Property taxes				
Fees (applicable to condominiums)				
Financial reserve fund (applicable to condominiums)				
Overall condition				
Exterior				
Frontage				
Siding				
Condition				
Eaves				
Roof				
Material				
Age				
Parking				
Driveway				
Garage				
Number of parking spots (applicable to condominiums)				
Yard				
Condition				
Size				
Landscaping				

	Home 1	Home 2	Home 3	Home 4
Porch				
Deck/patio				
Shed				
Fencing				
Swimming pool				
Special features				
Utilities				
Heating				
Type				
Average annual cost				
Electrical service				
Amps				
Type/age of wiring				
Water				
Municipal/well				
Hot water tank				
Utilities				
Sewers/septic				
Central air conditioning				
Living Room				
Size				
Condition				
Flooring				
Windows				
Dining Room				
Size				
Condition				
Flooring				

(continued)

TABLE 7-3 *(continued)*

	Home 1	Home 2	Home 3	Home 4
Windows				
Kitchen				
Size				
Condition				
Eat-in area				
Flooring				
Windows				
Appliances				
Stove/oven (electric/gas)				
Fridge				
Freezer				
Washer				
Dryer				
Dishwasher				
Freezer				
Microwave				
Attic				
Condition				
Insulated				
Bathrooms				
Number of bathrooms				
Size				
Ground-floor bathroom				
Basement				
Finished				
Size				
Flooring				
Windows				

	Home 1	Home 2	Home 3	Home 4
Separate entrance				
Bedrooms				
Number of bedrooms				
Main bedroom				
Size				
Condition				
Flooring				
Bedrooms				
Closet				
En-suite bathroom				
Other features				
Bedroom 2				
Size				
Condition				
Closet				
Bedroom 3				
Size				
Condition				
Closet				
Family Room				
Size				
Condition				
Sun Room/Office/Den				
Size				
Condition				
Other Features				
Central vacuum				
Light fixtures				

TABLE 7-3 *(continued)*

	Home 1	Home 2	Home 3	Home 4
Fireplace				
Coat closet				
Linen closet				
Security system				
Soundproofing (applicable to condominiums or townhouses)				
Balcony				
High ceilings				
Kitchen pantry				
Jacuzzi/hot tub				
Sliding glass doors				
Neighbourhood				
Overall				
Police/fire station nearby				
Public transportation available				
Parks				
Schools				
Shopping				
Distance from workplace				
Traffic				
Nuisances				
Other comments				

Chapter **8**

This Home Is Great! (Except for . . .)

hile home hunting, you'll find that many houses match some of your requirements but not all of them. A house might have everything you want inside, but there won't be any parking, or it won't be in the ideal neighbourhood. Don't be too narrow in your requirements; remember the difference between what you absolutely need and what you just want to have. The art of buying real estate is making as few compromises as possible while being realistic in your expectations.

Each home is different, and each will have its pros and cons. The home you want may not be in the price range you can presently afford. You may simply not be able to afford Montreal's Westmount area, though you're dying to live there . . . or you may sacrifice your dream home to live in your dream neighbourhood. Theoretically, you can always change your home if it isn't perfect, but there isn't much you can do about the neighbourhood. Keep an open mind when searching for a new home, and make comparisons to help you narrow your list of priorities.

But even a dream home can become a nightmare if you don't do your homework and make sure it's in (at least) acceptable condition. Sometimes the flashy, staged home that makes your pulse race is, in reality, in worse condition than it appears, whereas the one that needs a bit of elbow grease is a winner. Some things can be remedied for a minimal amount of expense (think: replacing the stove) while others can cost thousands of dollars (think: replacing the roof). Knowing the difference can save you time, money, and stress.

In this chapter, we discuss what is fixable, what may be a deal breaker, and the importance of digging deeper when things may not be all they seem to be.

Putting Your Emotions Aside

Most people find home buying a very emotional experience. After all, you're not just making a purchase; you're also choosing a new lifestyle and environment, for at least a few years. Although you must like the home you purchase, you can easily fall in love with a place for the wrong reasons. Don't overlook or underestimate a home's faults or its problems simply because the kitchen has been updated with new appliances or the view from the master bedroom is spectacular. By the same token, don't dismiss a home because you detest the neon-pink paint job in the bathroom. A wonderful home may spring to life with a new paint job.

MINOR DETAILS CAN TURN INTO MAJOR HEADACHES

Mike and Monique had been searching for the perfect character home in an established neighbourhood. Though they had hoped to find a home with a double garage, their dream home had only a single garage and a driveway so narrow that in order to get one of their vehicles out of the garage, the second one would need to be moved out of the driveway.

Mike and Monique were undeterred — they figured that they could always leave one vehicle on the street if they had to and went ahead with the purchase. What they didn't realize was that parking in the neighbourhood is restricted to the south side of the street only. Consequently, when either Mike or Monique arrives home, all the street parking is invariably taken. What was supposed to be just a minor nuisance has become an ongoing annoyance because one or the other constantly has to move one's car to get the other car out of the garage, which is particularly annoying in the long and snowy winter. Adding to the inconvenience is the fact that friends don't like dropping by because they have to park blocks away.

A combination of location and practicality is essential when you're looking for a home that fits your needs. If a house appeals to you, view it and the area more than once. Every neighbourhood has its own activity periods. Visit the area at different times (evening, during the day, weekends) to assess the amount of traffic and noise. Take a walk around. If it's nice weather, are people enjoying the outdoors? Are children playing outside? Are there yappy dogs? If you don't like the 'hood, it's not any good.

Reality Check: Can You Fix the Home's Problems?

Part of the evaluation process when looking at homes involves trying to convince yourself, "I can always fix that after I move in." In many cases, that may be true. If you're lucky enough to be a professional contractor with time on your hands, more power to you. But if you're an average Joe or Joanna, you may be biting off more than you can chew.

Some issues are simple to fix: painting over an ugly wall or stripping off 20-year-old wallpaper, for example. Others are just too big to take on, especially if they require immediate attention after you've already sunk your life savings into the property. And remember the sad truth about home renovations: They'll almost always require more time and money than you anticipate. To be on the safe side, add 10 to 20 percent to your renovation cost estimate to cover unexpected difficulties. Expect timelines to run long as well. All it takes is a subcontractor to experience a delay or that new tile you ordered to ship late and you can find weeks added to the renovation timeline.

Other issues aren't so simple. Cosmetic changes can work wonders, but deeper changes may not be worth your time, effort or money. The following sections guide you through the various scenarios.

Household cosmetics

Your personal style may look like you stepped out of the pages of a French fashion magazine, but Mrs. Olafson, whose 75-year-old bungalow is up for sale, may not share your highbrow tastes. Making cosmetic changes to personalize your home isn't a big deal, and you can undertake the expense gradually. Living in a salmon-pink stucco-clad home for a few months until you can afford to repaint the exterior won't kill you.

The good news is that many sellers paint their homes in neutral colours to make it easier for potential buyers to visualize the home as they would want it (we can't stand salmon-pink stucco, either). Of course, not everyone is fond of beige or taupe, so you may encounter a home that requires you to look beyond the shiny turquoise lacquer on its kitchen walls. Then again, if all the appliances, cupboards, and countertops are in shades you find horrifying, you may have a problem, depending on your budget.

Curb appeal may be important to you, and small changes can make a huge difference. You can add some new plants, tear out a few bushes, and add some mulch to define the flowerbeds. Oftentimes just weeding the beds can work wonders. You can also add a new splash of colour to the front door. A home's front yard can always be landscaped in ways that reduce the area you have to mow. Squeaky planks can usually be fixed with a nail or two.

If you're a handy person, you probably won't worry about the sticky closet door. If you're really a do-it-yourselfer, you can rip out that ugly '70s shag carpet and refinish the hardwood underneath. Just make sure that there *is* hardwood underneath, and that it's in good condition. Remember that if the hardwood has been refinished once, refinishing it a second time may not be possible and you may need to replace the floor.

Things you can't change

Accept that you can't change some things about a home, no matter how much you may want to do so. If there's no room for parking, you can't make space that isn't there. You can't make a semidetached home as soundproof as a fully detached home. You can solve some floor-plan problems through renovations, but if you need to tear down walls or relocate your staircase (likely putting you out of the house during renovations and ransacking your child's college fund), you may want to find a home that requires less work.

REMEMBER

A home's location is largely out of your control. Unless you put up a mural or demolish the home next door, the large bay window in your dining room is always going to be flush with the neighbour's brick wall. You can erect a fence to separate your backyard from the path where the local teens gather after school and local dog walkers don't stoop to scoop, but the locals are still going to gather there. Or perhaps you'd rather not be next to the local cemetery. It isn't likely to move any time soon (and you really wouldn't want its residents to get up and leave, would you?).

When it's not worth it

Some problems aren't worth changing, even if you can. Although major renovations such as a bathroom makeover or adding a second floor to a bungalow are up to you, some problems do require immediate attention — things that take a lot of time and cost a lot of money, usually more than your original estimates.

Our friends Radek and Maya found a wonderful, spacious, completely renovated home with a legal second suite that gave them a bit of extra income. The price was great. There was only one catch: The foundation was sinking, a condition the inspector discovered. The happy couple loved the home so much that they thought they could just have it repaired and take the cost out of the price they'd pay for the home. But because the home was hedged in by the house next door, the estimated cost to fix it — including jacking up the house to do the work, disconnecting and reconnecting the utilities, and re-drywalling the basement — was $200,000. Moreover, neither the tenants nor owner would be able to live in the home during the work. The cost of the repair, plus the cost of finding somewhere else to live while it was being done (in addition to putting up the tenants somewhere else), outweighed the good things about the home, so Radek and Maya abandoned the idea of buying it.

TIP

If you decide to purchase a *fixer-upper* of a home, which is a home that can be upgraded with a reasonable budget, check out your financing options. Most banks will extend lines of credit to ambitious types like yourself. Talk to your mortgage lender.

Even if you're an accomplished do-it-yourselfer, you have to be realistic about projects you can start and complete yourself. Relocating a bathroom, stairway, or kitchen takes professional skills because the renovation may involve relocating pipes, rewiring, and perhaps changing the roofline. Ultimately, the price you pay for renovations may not be recouped when you go to sell in the future.

In case you've never done any major renovations to a home, Figure 8-1 gives you a rough idea of how much they can cost. As you can see, renovations are expensive, so take care when deciding how much you can spend to achieve the results you want.

Item	Approximate Cost	Recovery on resale
Bathroom renovation	$5,000 and up (depending on the quality of fixtures and amount of plumbing and electrical work required)	75%-100%
Kitchen renovation	$10,000-$75,000 (or more, depending on the scope of work and quality of materials and appliances)	75%-100%
Furnace — gas, forced air (mid efficiency)	$3,000-$7,000	50%-80%
Central air conditioning, with existing ducts	$2,500-$6,000	50%-75%
Aluminum storm door	$400 and up	50%-75%
Metal insulated door	$700-$800	50%-75%
New roof	$3,000-$50,000 (or more, depending on the roof materials and your home's architecture)	50%-80%
Home rewiring (complete)	$2,500 and up	100% *
Hardwood flooring	$6-$12 per square foot	50%-75%
Replace galvanized plumbing	$500-$3,500 (or more, depending on the size of your home and the number of storeys)	100% *
Exterior basement door	$6,500-$10,500 (including cutting through concrete foundation and new exterior stairs)	50%-75%

FIGURE 8-1:
Rough estimates for home repairs and renovations.

* Rewiring or repiping a house is often considered routine maintenance. However, it will repay the full value you invest because it will avoid giving the buyer a reason to seek a discount, often one in excess of the job itself.

© *John Wiley & Sons, Inc.*

Catching a Flipped Home

Technically, a home that's flipped is one that's purchased by an investor (sometimes referred to as a *speculator*) at below-market value and fixed up and sold, usually within a few months. A broader definition includes any home that's purchased, is upgraded to add value to it, and then resold at a profit. The buyer is one who wants a move-in ready home in a desirable area with nice finishes. The investor usually has a team who can do the work well and keep costs within reason. The name of the game is to make a profit, but there are risks for the investor who wants to flip houses.

Though many flipped homes have been renovated properly and to code, just as many have not. House flippers expect a healthy return on their investment: Not only do they have to cover the costs of the purchase and renovations, but they have to cover the carrying and closing costs, too. If expensive work is required that the investor didn't budget for, a flip can go sideways very quickly.

Purchasing a house that has been renovated but the work has been done without oversight is risky. In other words, the contractor or investor did the work without getting the necessary building permits not to mention permits for electrical, plumbing, and gas connections. The work might be subpar and lead to electrical or water issues. As the new owner, you inherit these challenges, and the municipal authorities may require you to bring the renovations up to code, which could be costly. Your ability to insure the property may be affected. You may have trouble selling the house because you are obligated to disclose material problems with the house.

Don't be fooled by a cleverly staged home! Someone who's trying to flip a home will often pay close attention to jazzing up the most obvious things, and distracting your attention from the less obvious, lower-return elements of the home. Did the seller invest in the latest kitchen gadgets and finishes but go cheap on things like light fixtures and switches? You need to know if everything is as it seems. As with all properties, if you suspect that you're missing critical information, make sure to ask questions and have a certified home inspector evaluate it.

Your agent will have a listing history for the property, which will indicate if the house is being flipped. Your agent can request confirmation that the necessary permits were acquired and the necessary inspections done. The home inspector can advise you if work meets minimum standards.

Even if the list price accurately reflects the work done, it may be out of line with those for comparable properties in the same neighbourhood. You may have a decision to make about paying above market value for the upgrades versus buying a less expensive house and investing in renovations.

Check It Out: Investigating Your Prospective New Home

After you tour a few homes and the surrounding neighbourhood, you can narrow down your prospects to your top choice. You then have to look more closely at a few considerations. Book an appointment for a good second look. Although we recommend you check the interior and exterior of any home you're buying, remember that your own once-over is no replacement for a professional home inspection done by a certified building inspector (professional inspections are covered in Chapter 10).

TIP

If you're flexible about timing, you may want to consider buying a home in the winter. Not only do the homes in some areas tend to be cheaper in winter, but you can also get a better sense of how the home copes with the cold. Is the furnace capable of keeping the home sufficiently warm? At what cost? Check the home for drafts: Are some areas of the home much colder than others? One common place for drafts is electrical outlets that haven't been sufficiently insulated. Is there snow on the roof of the home? If all the other homes have snow, and the one you're looking at doesn't, the attic probably isn't properly insulated, and escaping heat is melting the snow. How well do the eaves work? If there are huge icicles hanging at one point in the eaves, they probably need work because water's been leaking from them.

Other great times to check out a home are in spring or after a big rainstorm. You may be able to see whether the roof or foundation has leaks that need repair. Basement leaks are difficult to detect during the winter because the ground may be frozen and homes are dry from heating.

Moving beyond appearances

Consider all the following items when you make your initial serious inspection. And then, if you're really interested in the home, hire a qualified building inspector and attend the inspection.

>> **Foundation:** Check for trees, especially willows, near the foundation. Roots can get into sewer lines and damage your pipes. Inspect cement cracks blocks for cracks, which is a sign of water infiltration. Also, see how far the foundation walls come up — the higher the cement walls for the foundation are, the better protected your foundation is from water damage. The land should slope away from the house to provide proper water runoff.

WARNING

Seeing poured cement sloping between detached houses can be an indication that the residents attempted to prevent water from seeping in. Sometimes this cement helps, but sometimes it doesn't. Have a careful look at the foundation and basement inside. A good home inspector can determine how successful any past repairs were.

>> **Eaves and eavestroughs:** Visually check the condition of the eavestrough. Note any rust-through and other damage. Ensure the runoff from the downspouts is directed away from the foundation. The home inspector will inspect the eaves and eavestrough at roof level and advise you of their condition.

TIP

Nobody likes to stand outside in stormy weather, but this may be the best time to examine the eaves of a house and to judge their capacity to handle heavy rain or snow. Focus on the areas where the eaves overflow. Does rain build up in a particular area? Building inspectors may be the only people who like heavy rain — every house looks good on a sunny day. When it rains, though, you can see problems with a home that may not otherwise be evident.

>> **Basement:** Inspect a finished ceiling and floor corners for water damage. Use your nose: Does the basement smell musty? Tap any exposed wood foundation; if it's soft or damp, you have a problem. A dehumidifier in the basement may point to a water problem, and you should check it out. In areas where cold is definitely a problem in winter (say, Ottawa), follow the exposed water pipes as much as possible. Are they all insulated? Are there drafts around where you know the pipes run? Ask if the owners have had problems with freezing pipes.

>> **Electricity and wiring:** Make sure the property has at least 100-amp service, and ideally 200-amp service. Older homes were built with 60-amp service which can't handle the demands of most households today (refer to Chapter 7 for more on electricity). Nobody wants to plug in the toaster and have the house go dark. Insurance companies may not even be willing to insure you until you improve the electrical service, which can cost $500–$2,000 or more to upgrade. Count the number of electrical outlets in each room. Are there enough to service appliances and lamps? Watch out for lots of extension cords too; their presence probably means there aren't enough electrical outlets in the home. In older homes, be on the lookout for irregular wiring or unusual phone or cable lines that suggest the house was a former rental property. Are there enough phone jacks for your five teenagers? Check the dryer and stove outlets, if possible, and flick all the light switches on and off; sometimes light switches are also attached to outlets, rather than to lights. If switch plates and outlet covers have been replaced, don't assume that the wiring behind them has been upgraded or grounded.

>> **Water pressure:** Turn on the shower. How is the water pressure? Does it make you feel like you've been through a car wash or just skipping under a lawn sprinkler? Run water in the tub and sink — is it a trickle or a steady, solid flow? Now, do both and flush the toilet — is the pressure the same? You don't want to be surprised by a sudden loss of hot or cold water while you're taking a shower! (And don't forget to check the shower head: you don't want to have to take a shower on your knees.)

>> **Water quality:** Taste the water; even though most homes on municipal water systems will probably have decent water, it may be different if you're dependent on a well. Drilling a new well or having to rely on bottled water because

the local water tastes or smells bad will be an added expense. Don't forget to fill the tub or sinks, pull the plugs, and watch the drainage speed.

>> **Signs of water damage:** Stains on the ceiling can be evidence of a leak in the roof. Look at closet ceilings as well. A flashlight or light from your phone can come in handy. If repairs have been made to a roof, get confirmation from the seller of the specific work that was done.

>> **Evidence of pests:** Look for ant traps, mouse traps, roach motels, or other signs of infestations of any kind. Brown stripes in the corners of kitchen cabinets also indicate treatment for cockroaches. These may be temporary or one-time-only problems, but they may not. Silverfish, termites, and other pests are all worth asking about. If the property has mature trees, be careful that you're not sharing the home with carpenter ants or squirrels.

>> **Windows:** Check the screens, the window locks, and the glass. Are they single- or double-paned? How secure are the basement windows? If they're an older style, they may not be as energy efficient or as safe as you'd like.

>> **Attic:** Check the level of insulation in the attic. Proper insulation can make both cooling and heating your home more efficient.

Make full use of your senses when looking at homes — they can tell you a lot about the atmosphere, and alert you to potential problems. What do you smell, hear, and feel when you approach the house? When you enter different floors and rooms?

TIP

Some of the issues you discover during the inspection may be easily fixed, and you may be able to take advantage of government incentives or grants to upgrade the property. When you've made a list of the issues and problems with a building, know what some of the solutions are. (By the time you've scouted two or three properties, you should be familiar with some of these, allowing you to move quickly when you find a property whose faults don't scare you.)

Don't be afraid to snoop

Remember not to ignore nooks and crannies when you're inspecting a home. Look inside closets and cupboards for signs of water damage or drafts or cracks. Many new homeowners run into problems later that they didn't notice — but should have — when they inspected the home. A common complaint is that the closets are considerably smaller than they remember, or there are no medicine cabinets in the bathrooms or linen closets in the hallway.

Out of shyness or courtesy, you may skip over some details when you're touring a new home. We're Canadian, after all, and intrusiveness isn't our style (we'd like to think so, anyway). It's important to know what you're getting into, however, so don't be afraid to look through everything! The sellers should be prepared for a thorough inspection, so you probably won't encounter mounds of dirty laundry or an avalanche of sports equipment when you open the closets. Open the fridge, and see how cool it is; look under the carpet if you're thinking of pulling it up and exposing the hardwood underneath.

TIP

Measure the doorways: Can you get your washer and dryer down to the basement? Will your great-grandmother's armoire fit through the door? Also, you may want to consider measuring the sizes of the existing furniture in the home. The measurements will give you a good idea, beyond the actual room sizes themselves, of the scale of furniture the room can handle.

Ask questions

If the seller's agent is at the home when you make your inspection visit, don't hesitate to ask lots of questions. Prepare a list, and write down the answers. You don't want to rack your brain later trying to remember what the agent said the average hydro bill was. Ask for a *seller's property information statement* (SPIS), also called the *property disclosure statement* (PDS), which provides a seller's disclosure of the home's condition. If the seller isn't forthcoming with a copy of the SPIS/PDS, make sure your offer is subject to your receiving, reading, and approving it. Has the home been pre-inspected by a building inspector? Ask about the current owners, the reason why they're selling, what's new about the home, what the neighbours are like, what problems the owners are aware of — the list is endless. Check the zoning department for the municipalities to see if there are any projects proposed that could negatively impact the neighbourhood.

Even if the selling agent can't answer your questions on the spot, you can expect the agent to get back to you. The more you know about the home, the better position you're in when you go to the bargaining table — and the fewer surprises you'll have when you move in.

Determine whether the home has been maintained

Like a car, a home requires preventive maintenance. You want a home that has been taken care of by its previous owners, because past neglect can translate into huge problems later. This concept applies to condominium buildings as well as detached houses. If you can, try to find out about the owners and whether they looked after their home. An absentee owner could be a red flag, especially if a management company rented the property was rented. Owners who don't live in a home full-time may not have paid the same attention to it as if they were living there every day. Here are some indications that the present owners are maintaining the home properly:

>> **Appliances:** Major appliances like the fridge and stove are well maintained and in good working order.

>> **Bathrooms:** Caulking is in good condition and areas around the fixtures have no signs of water damage or mould.

>> **Electrical system:** Ground fault connection interrupter (GFCI) outlets are installed in all the necessary areas.

>> **Exterior:** The landscaping and yard(s) are in good condition.

>> **Fire safety:** Working smoke detectors and carbon monoxide detectors are in the necessary spots in the home, and sprinklers are in good condition (if present).

>> **Foundation:** No cracks exist in the foundation.

>> **Furnace:** The seller can provide proof that the furnace has been regularly cleaned and maintained.

>> **Overall appearance:** Pride of ownership will always show through, even in a house that lacks all the latest upgrades.

>> **Porches, decks, patios, external stairs, and railings:** These features are well maintained. The wood isn't rotting, and the cement is even and without cracks.

>> **Roofing:** The roof is no more than 10 years old — although some roofs are steel or long-wearing duroid/asphalt that can be good for 50 years or more. Ask about the type of roof the home has, and see if any warranties are in place.

>> **Windows:** The windows are well sealed.

TIP

A property inspector can help identify any issues with the building that may need attention after you buy or prompt you to cancel the purchase altogether. We discuss property inspections at length in Chapter 10. Condominiums that are proactive in property management may have a depreciation report that can fill you in on the status of the common property, such as parkades, pools, the elevator, and roof. If a depreciation report hasn't been prepared, carefully review the building council's minutes and speak with the property manager for additional insights.

4
Getting the House You Want

Develop an offer that's sure to please, and if it doesn't, know how to negotiate one that will. Have your financing ready to go, and be prepared to fend off competitors.

Understand the paperwork required to seal the deal, know what to look for in an inspection, and realise how a survey can confirm you're buying what you think you're buying.

Be sure you have insurance ready to cover your big purchase and, if you're buying new, make sure there's a warranty in place to cover deficiencies.

Pack up and get ready to move, making sure that closing, possession and occupancy flow as smoothly as possible to make the transition to home ownership hassle-free.

Chapter 9

Making a Deal on Your New Home

After a lot of hard work and pounding the pavement — not to mention all the time spent researching homes and neighbourhoods — you've found the home that works for you. This chapter tells you what you need to know in order to complete the purchase and become a proud home owner. You can find advice on making an offer to purchase a home and writing the best possible terms into your sale contract. We explain what the conditions (*subject to clauses*) in your agreement mean — and why you want them in the first place.

Preparing to Make an Offer

As you know from all the time you've spent searching, a home is no impulse buy, so a lot is involved even before you make the offer. We recommend a few steps to take before you put your cards on the table. Waiting another moment when you've finally found that perfect home can be painful, we know, but the time you take on these steps up front can save you a lot more time and hassle later on.

Get your mortgage preapproved

If you haven't spoken to your mortgage broker or lender and had yourself preapproved for financing, put this book down and pick up the phone to get the process started. Whether you handle everything over the phone, online with a mortgage broker, or walk into your local bank, this step is crucial. Your real estate agent should encourage you to take this step before you begin shopping for a home. You don't want to waste your agent's time and your time by looking at homes outside your price range. Remember that getting preapproval doesn't guarantee mortgage financing. You want to take this step with your lender.

REMEMBER

Preapproval is a great tactic in the hunt for your dream home — it shows the sellers how serious you are, and more important, it shows you can pay them (refer to Chapter 4 for more information on mortgage preapprovals). Indicate to the sellers that you have a preapproved mortgage. If five offers come in for the home you want after an open house, those that come from people with preapproved mortgages will move to the top of the pile.

Get to know the local market

Make sure your offer falls in the right price range. Check out comparable properties to compare prices. Know what to expect. Just as you know you shouldn't have to pay $5 for an orange, you should also know the approximate value of the homes that interest you. You'll also want to be savvy to what other buyers might be offering. You want your offer to be reasonable, but also competitive if you're keen to come out the winner.

Prior to preparing your offer, your real estate agent should provide you with the area's sale statistics, including a list of selling prices versus asking prices of homes recently sold in the neighbourhood. Contrast the original asking prices and the selling prices. The length of time homes spend on the market indicates how much demand there is for homes in the area. If the market is slow for selling, then you may be able to offer a price slightly under the market value. (Slow sales in the neighbourhood can also indicate that local homes were overpriced.) On the flip side, if the market is full of eager buyers, you need to be able to compete. Cyclical factors also apply; for example, the market is usually much slower in the winter months because fewer people move when the weather's cold and miserable.

Your goal in making an offer is to identify the lowest reasonable offering price without possibly insulting the seller, which is no small feat. You need to know your stuff. Your offer carries more weight if it matches average selling prices for similar homes and is confirmed by an appraiser's assessment (if you aren't using a real estate agent) or your agent's evaluation of the market. This objective approach shows you're serious about making a deal work, but also supports what's in your interests, too. Develop a strategy with your agent for presenting your offer to sellers. Be prepared to show how your offer is a fair and attractive one by referring to current sales data. (Ideally, the listing agent will have worked with the current owner to set a price and explained that offers might come in above or below asking, depending on local market conditions.)

REMEMBER

Keep in mind when preparing to make an offer that statistics are only a starting point; homes aren't all created equally, nor have they aged equally well. The property next door, even if it looks similar from the outside, won't be an exact match in terms of value with the one you want. In the end, only you know what you're willing to pay, and only the seller can say whether or not that's a value that reflects the home's worth.

Get to know the seller's motivation

Your agent may be able to obtain information about the seller's decision to sell, but it depends on what the listing agent is willing to share. There are privacy laws to be abided by. However, if you do find out that the home is being sold due to a break-up or other pressing financial matters, you may be able to help the situation with a quick closing and a reasonable offer.

TIP

Time can sometimes be as good as money! Besides using the excellent manners your mother taught you, you can sweeten your offer by accommodating the seller's time frame if he's in a rush to move or if he needs some leeway while finding a new home. You may also agree that he can take all the appliances and the drapes.

Get to know your limits

To get to the happy stage of a binding contract, you have to know what you really want and what methods of negotiation will help you get your new home. Do your research and establish your priorities. To help you put things in perspective, take a look at Chapter 7 where you rate the features you need and want in a new home. Remember, your home-buying needs are nonnegotiable. List your wants in order of importance. Beside each want, indicate the price limit you're willing to pay. Make a list of your "I can't live without this" items and your "I can take it or leave it" items.

After you make your lists, put them aside and take a moment for quiet contemplation to think things over. That way, you can come back to your initial impulses with a fresh perspective. You may find that certain things you think you can't live without may actually become easy sacrifices if you really fall in love with a home. Besides, maybe you'll find that when you listed a humongous kitchen as a must-have it was only because you'd just been watching the Food Network and were feeling really hungry.

REMEMBER

Expect to have at least one round of negotiations. Your agent will explain the process, but be prepared to receive a counter-offer from the seller. Advise your agent when you're *firm* on the price, meaning it's your financial limit and final offer.

Ready to Purchase: Making an Offer

Before you can call any home yours, you have to make an offer to purchase it from the seller, and he must agree to accept your offer. The offer must be made in writing. Just saying, "Hey, I'll give you millions of dollars for your house" won't hold up in court, even if the other side does believe you. An offer is meaningless unless you put pen to paper. Your agent will have all the necessary paperwork required to make an offer. If you don't have an agent, your lawyer can draft the contract for you. Known as a *contract of purchase and sale* or an *agreement of purchase and sale* in some provinces, the contract includes basic terms and phrases that protect both the buyer and the seller.

Although your agent completes the entire contract form, the contract of purchase and sale is considered an offer to purchase a home only up until you and the seller come to full agreement on the contract's terms and conditions, and you both meet those conditions acceptably. In some cases, you and the seller will go back and forth several times before you decide on conditions and terms you can both live with. Because much of the contract's legalese can be daunting, in this section we describe the main parts of the contract in plain language. Also, your lawyer or agent will be more than happy to go through it with you and answer any questions you may have.

WARNING

Go through any contract you sign very carefully. Determine your needs and wants for each item. Write them down if it helps. The common advice for every decision also applies here: Be realistic. If you don't want to go above your offer price, be flexible on the other terms.

The following sections explain the various elements of the contract and how to use them to your advantage.

Figuring out who's who and what's what in your contract

The exact terminology and organization of contracts may vary from region to region, but five elements are basic to every contract of purchase and sale:

- **Seller:** The seller's full legal name, exactly as it's shown on the current title deed to the house, is written into the contract.

- **Buyer:** Write in your legal name, exactly as it's shown on your personal identification documents and exactly as it should be shown on the deed. If you and a partner are making a joint purchase, add both full names. Joint purchases can take two forms:

  - *Joint tenancy* allows for the *right of survivorship* from one owner to the other when one dies.

  - *Tenancy in common* means an owner's interest in the property goes to their heirs, not the other partner(s). Unless *joint tenancy* is specifically chosen, all co-ownership situations (whether spouses, family, or friends) are deemed to be *tenancy in common*. Tenants in common can have unequal interest in a property (for example, two-thirds versus one-third) and can specify who will inherit their interest in the property on their death.

- **Subject property:** *Subject property* refers to the street address and an exact legal description of the property you're buying. This description may include the lot size, a general description of the home (semi-detached, single-family dwelling with a mutual drive, or other), the specific lot and plan number, and any *easements*. If the contract mentions an easement, the body of the contract will provide further details. An easement or right-of-way is a specified area of a property held by another party. For example, your neighbour's driveway may cross the corner of your property. Because it's her driveway, even though it's technically on your property, she has the right to use that part of your property to park her car. The more common rights-of-way are those held by a government or utility. This right is registered on your title and will be acknowledged in the contract.

- **Purchase price:** The *purchase price* is the price you're initially willing to pay. This price will probably change throughout the negotiation. When setting your offer price, keep in mind the additional expenses you'll be incurring, such as land or deed transfer tax, realty taxes, fuel and water rates, legal fees, and insurance costs (these expenses, known as *closing costs,* are described in Chapter 4).

TIP

Allow yourself room to negotiate up. If it's a seller's market (more people looking to buy than homes for sale), you may want to make a higher initial offer right off. If it's a buyer's market, you may offer slightly lower than you're willing to pay so that you give yourself room to concede a higher bid when the seller rejects your initial offer. We discuss price negotiations in the section "Competing with multiple offers."

REMEMBER

The purchase price may list the approximate value of any *chattels* — that is, movable items, such as appliances, furnishings, or fixtures such as chandeliers and antique doorknobs — that are to remain in the house and be part of the purchase. Assigning a separate value to the chattels is important in establishing the price of the real estate, potentially reducing taxes owing on the sale. Specifying what other items you're purchasing can also help hold the seller to account, and make clear what you expect to receive on taking possession of the property. Every chattel should be in writing so that you have recourse if an appliance or light fixture is taken out of the property. A garage, tool shed, landscaping equipment, or the back 40 may be worth itemizing as a separate expense. Be aware of the tax implications in doing so.

>> **Deposit:** Your *deposit* is not only part of your down payment but also an indication to the seller of your interest in the house and a sign that you're negotiating in good faith. The initial deposit may be relatively low, but the total deposit may be much substantial. In some provinces, paying the full deposit upon final subject removal, meaning after the deal is firm, is normal. At least 3 to 10 percent of the purchase price is often considered a fair amount for a total deposit, but no hard and fast rules exist. Your real estate agent can advise you what is standard practice regarding deposits in your area. Refer to Chapter 4 for a full discussion regarding deposits.

TIP

List the amount of the deposit that is accompanying your offer, and specify that it will be applied to the purchase price of the house on the closing (or completion) of the sale. Normally, your agent holds the deposit in a trust account until the completion of the sale. In some provinces, the standard procedure is for the deposit to be held in the listing agent's trust account. You may want to write in that any interest that accrues while the funds are in trust will form part of the down payment at the time of completion.

TECHNICAL STUFF

Deposits aren't always repaid with interest. Regulations in British Columbia, for example, require interest on deposits be paid to the Real Estate Foundation of BC, which then uses the funds to support a variety of community-related projects and initiatives.

TIP

Consider inserting an *assignment clause* in your offer if you anticipate a need to change course after the deal has gone firm (or even beforehand). (An *assignment clause* allows you to assign the contract to a third party prior to the closing of the sale.) If you want the right and flexibility to assign the purchase agreement to a third party, consult a real estate lawyer and obtain the correct wording in advance to avoid any nasty surprises for yourself, or the seller.

WARNING

If you back out of an offer after it has been accepted and all the terms and conditions have been met (that is, the subjects have been removed), and have neither an assignment clause or any other exit option, you'll most likely forfeit your deposit to the vendor. You may also expose yourself to other expensive legal action and possible damages.

Comprehending the terms and conditions (subject to clauses)

Most contracts have a blank space where you can write in the specific terms and conditions of your offer. This space is where you build as much safety into your offer as you need. You can make your offer *unconditional,* meaning that you don't require the seller to do anything except agree to the purchase price, deposit, and other terms of the contract. However, we advise that you make your offer subject to some conditions — these conditions will give you some protection from making a bad purchase. As we mention in the next section, if you're pursuing a property that's going to receive multiple offers, you may have to try to satisfy your concerns before making your offer instead of making them conditions.

Conditions are typically worded as *conditional upon* or *subject to* clauses ("I will buy the house, *subject to* financing, *conditional upon* inspection, *subject to* selling my current house," or some other condition). What you're saying in legal terms is, "I will buy your house if particular conditions are met (within a set time frame)," such as the following:

>> **Subject to financing:** You have a specified time frame to work with your lender to be approved for the mortgage. You have been preapproved, but now it's time to firm up the financing.

>> **Subject to selling my present home:** You'll buy the seller's home if you can sell the home you currently own (within a set period of time, such as 30 to 60 days). This usually has an *escape clause* allowing the sellers to continue to market their home and in the event they obtain a second offer satisfactory to them, they agree to give the buyer first right to firm up or release them from the original deal.

>> **Subject to the home's repair:** You'll purchase the home if the seller fixes the leaky roof or some other substandard feature. Your option is to negotiate a lower purchase price and get the work done yourself.

>> **Subject to legal review:** You'll purchase the home provided that your lawyer reviews and approves the contract (usually within a specified amount of time, such as 24 to 48 hours).

>> **Subject to inspection:** You'll buy the home if it passes an inspection carried out by a certified home inspector.

The home inspection is a chance to review the home before you commit to buying the property. In general, you need to have a reasonable reason not to proceed with your purchase. Therefore, in many provinces the property inspection clause includes a maximum price for repairs that the buyer is prepared to accept before deciding not to proceed with the purchase. This clause prevents the buyer from walking away from a house because a light bulb is burnt out. Also, if the buyer simply changes his mind and no longer wants to buy the property, he won't be able to use the inspection clause to get out of the purchase.

A typical inspection clause with a cost consideration could read like this:

- *This offer is subject to the buyer on or before* [insert date], *at the buyer's expense, receiving and approving an inspection report against any defects whose total cost of repair exceeds $____* [this amount can be negotiated, but it may be $500 or more] *and which adversely affect the property's use or value.*

This condition is for the sole benefit of the buyer.

>> **Subject to survey:** You'll purchase the home if a land survey is conducted or a legal, up-to-date land survey is provided, showing that the home doesn't violate any easements or rights-of-way, and showing the location of any buildings, such as a garage, on the property that also don't violate any easements or rights-of-way.

>> **Subject to appraisal:** Although your financing is preapproved, the house is in your price range, and you know you can get a mortgage, you may want to confirm that your offer is reasonable and at fair market value. If you have any doubts, you can make the offer subject to your receiving and approving an appraisal of the subject property.

>> **Subject to approving a property disclosure statement:** A *property disclosure statement* is a form that is filled out by the homeowner that asks standard questions regarding the condition of the home and neighbourhood factors that may influence value. If incorporated into the contract, the statement may establish a case against the seller if it can be proven that she knowingly misrepresented the property in question.

>> **Subject to bylaw approval:** When purchasing a condominium or townhouse, this condition may be one of several you include. This condition means that your purchase is contingent on agreeing to any and all bylaws affecting the unit in question, which may include rental or pet restrictions.

GET IT IN WRITING!

Just like during every other step of the process, don't engage in oral agreements when it comes to the various conditions of your contract. Always put them in writing. If an oral agreement comes up in conversation — "Hey, those are great drapes, would you consider leaving them?" — remember to write it into the contract. Then, and only then, can that portion of the contract become binding. Your offer to purchase a home becomes a binding contract when the seller signs the contract of purchase and sale that contains all your terms and conditions.

Specific requirements can also be written in the same area as your conditions, such as the stated requirement that the seller agrees to remove the abandoned car from the garage prior to the completion date. If you don't have enough space on the contract to add all your terms and conditions, your agent can write them on *schedule forms*, which are attached to the main body of the contract. Schedule forms (or addenda, or appendices in some provinces) are extra forms that allow you to write as many terms and conditions as are necessary on additional pages that form part of the contract. Make sure that all the schedules you attach are listed on the contract. Keep in mind that when you start negotiating, you may end up adding or removing conditions, and so may the seller. For example, if the seller won't fix the roof, you may agree to remove that condition, but try to deduct the estimated cost of that repair from your offered price.

TIP

Don't overdo the conditions. Write a thorough, detailed offer, but make sure you keep your conditions from piling up. Be reasonable. Don't write into your offer that you have the right to inspect the property five times before the closing date — one or two times should suffice.

After you and the seller sign off on all the terms and conditions of your purchase offer, your conditions will (hopefully!) be met. You can then add the paperwork (amendments of waivers or notices of fulfillment, if necessary) to confirm, for example, that the roof has been repaired, that you have secured a mortgage, that you have sold your current house, and so on. After all the conditions are removed, you enter into a binding agreement to purchase and, here's the best part — you've bought your new home.

Competing with multiple offers

In a sellers' market, buyers frequently find themselves in competition to purchase a home. Though this news is obviously great if you happen to be a seller, it can leave prospective property purchasers with a raging ulcer. Generally in these circumstances, a property will sell for above asking. Just how far above asking depends on a number of factors.

In a sellers' market, homeowners and their agents sometimes strategize to under-price a property in order to generate a lot of interest, which may lead to a number of competitive bids. Certain types of homes are more likely to benefit from this tactic: in particular, single-family homes in desirable neighbourhoods. For example, if you happen to fall in love with a home in your target area that's completely renovated — with a new roof and furnace, and new landscaping and fencing — impeccably presented, and priced 5 to 7 percent below any comparable home in the area, you may find that you've fallen for a home that's positioned to get multiple offers. Chances are, the seller isn't going to consider offers until a certain date. A typical strategy is to list the property, hold an open house on the weekend so that many prospective buyers can see the home, and then deal with offers several days later.

In multiple-offer situations, logic can go out the window to a certain degree. You need to be prepared to make your best offer and walk away when logic tells you to. Don't let emotions rule.

TIP

Price isn't everything. If you offer a lower price than other buyers but include no subject to clauses (essentially saying that you're willing to enter a contract immediately), you can still end up a winner. The competition may have to sell another property first (an offer subject to the sale of), or perhaps they need to secure financing and want to do an inspection. The seller may be willing to forgo a bit of money in order to accept your offer, which is quick and guaranteed.

Doing your homework

If offers are being withheld until a certain date, you need to get cracking:

>> Make sure that your home financing is secure. You can still include a financing clause in your offer, but if you can avoid it, you'll move up the competition ladder in the eyes of the seller.

>> Ensure that the property title won't offer you any nasty surprises. Do the research needed to find out if there are easements or rights-of-way that may affect the property's use or value. These problems may affect the offer that you plan to present.

>> If possible, do an inspection in advance. You may sweeten your offer by not including a subject to inspection clause if you manage to do an inspection ahead of time and determine that you're happy with the home as is. (Refer to the previous section for more about conditions.)

>> With your agent, look at other homes in the area that sold for more than the asking price. Make some calls to determine how many offers were presented. The same thing applies to the property you're interested in: Are you competing against two other offers, or ten?

>> Figure out the price you're willing to pay. If this is truly your dream home and you've been in this type of bidding war before, you may decide that you're willing to pay a premium to get the home that you want (especially if you've lost out on five others). You'll want to write an offer that you can feel good about; if you lose the home over a mere $1,000, you don't want to be kicking yourself later. You have to find the balance between a higher offer (the premium you're paying) but one that is still affordable and not stress-inducing.

Considering bully offers

A *bully offer* is an offer presented in anticipation of multiple offers. Basically, you're bullying your way to the front of the pack by presenting your offer first, in the hopes that the seller will consider your offer without seeing any other offers that may come forward on the set presentation date. If you're a buyer set on writing a bully offer, try to present as clean an offer as possible, with very few — if any — conditions and a price that will entice the seller to accept.

WARNING

Bully offers can be risky. First of all, what if it ends up that you had no competition in the first place? You may have paid an unnecessary premium for the property. That question is one that you'll never know the answer to. You may also risk alienating the seller, who may be put off by such an aggressive strategy. Or, you may be turned away altogether and told to submit your offer on the day that the seller originally selected.

IN THIS CHAPTER

» **Finalizing details with your home-buying team**

» **Understanding important parts of the contract**

» **Getting what you pay for: Professional home inspections**

» **Staking out your territory: Land surveys**

Chapter **10**

Signing On to a New Life

A fter a lot of work, you and the seller agree on the conditions of the contract of purchase and sale, and then the seller accepts your offer. But just because the offer's signed doesn't mean you can sit back and relax just yet. You have a home inspection to arrange, an insurance company to call, a mortgage to finalize . . . you name it. All this official stuff may not seem that glamorous, but it's vital to your purchase of a home.

This chapter deals with the fine print your lawyer sifts through when closing your deal (don't worry, you'll find no legalese here) and then takes you through the process of getting a mortgage signed off. To finish, we give you the rundown on professional inspections and surveys so that you can be confident you're actually buying what you think you're buying.

Taking Care of the Paperwork

Don't be fooled — there's always *more* paperwork, even after you feel you have carpal tunnel syndrome from signing and initialing so many forms and documents. While a growing number documents can be digitally signed using Docu-Sign and other tools, there's still a virtual mountain of paperwork to tackle. To climb it, you'll need help from your carefully selected team of home-buying professionals. So make those calls, schedule appointments, and get things rolling.

GIVE IT DUE PROCESS

The time frame for your lawyer's duties will vary, depending on how many days you have until closing. One little piece of advice: Trust in the process. You may have a lot of questions and concerns, but don't panic if your lawyer advises he'll take care of the legal aspects and will see you again in a month and a half.

He'll let you know when he needs anything from you, whether it's a signature, the survey, or your agent's number. Waiting for the day that home is yours isn't easy — especially if you're waiting 90 days to move out of that tiny basement bedroom in your parents' home — but you have many more things to do before you close. Stop worrying that something may go wrong because you haven't talked to your lawyer in a couple of days. Make sure that things are getting done; it's just as important not to interrupt your lawyer while she's doing what you asked her to do and trust the process.

Removing conditions

The main reason why you have to see so many people after you've finalized the contract of purchase and sale is to take care of the conditions you've written into your offer. In order for the contract to be binding, every condition — every *subject to clause* that you wrote into the contract of purchase and sale — must be met. If your offer to purchase is subject to financing, subject to approval by lawyer, or subject to roof repair, these conditions must be fulfilled. (For more on conditions, or "subject to" clauses, refer to Chapter 9.)

In most provinces, you sign waivers to confirm that you and the seller have met each of the necessary conditions. Be sure that every condition the seller is responsible for, like fixing the roof, is done — and done properly — before you sign off. Make sure all conditions have been met by the prescribed subject removal date. After all the conditions have been removed, the contract or agreement of purchase and sale is binding, so make sure all of the conditions have been met; for example, that any defect that required fixing was addressed properly. Usually, the remediation of any deficiencies will require an inspection prior to the removal of subject conditions. You will acknowledge the removal of conditions by signing a waiver prepared by your agent or lawyer.

Paying your lawyer a visit

We recommend you choose a lawyer early in the game if you're undertaking a complex sale or you're not using a real estate agent, so that when you're ready to sign the deal you know exactly who's going to review the paperwork. (Chapter 2 includes tips on how to choose your legal counsel.) Take the contract of purchase and sale to her when the seller accepts your offer.

Ask your lawyer to do the following:

» Review your contract of purchase and sale with you.

» Examine the conditions of sale and the subject to clauses.

» Discuss the completion (closing) date and the anticipated subject (conditions) removals.

» Answer any questions or concerns you may have.

The contract of purchase and sale will note the names of the purchaser and indicate the type of ownership. This information will also tell your lawyer how you and your partner (if you have one) have agreed to hold title. If you're buying a house alone, then you'll have, of course, *sole ownership*. With co-ownership, however, you have two options:

» *Joint tenancy* (with right of survivorship, in which the untimely death of your co-owner sees ownership pass to you without interruption)

» *Tenancy in common,* in which the deceased owner's rights pass to his or her heirs

We discuss forms of ownership in Chapter 9.

REMEMBER

Your lawyer not only acts as a legal guide for your contract but also oversees the entire process of transferring the property from the seller to you. Your lawyer will interact with many of the professionals you're seeing, so make sure she has all their contact info. Your lawyer will

» Arrange with your lender to transfer money from your mortgage to the seller. In most cases, your lawyer also drafts your mortgage document, double-checking that all the terms and conditions of your mortgage are properly met.

» Contact your insurance agent to verify for the lender that your home insurance is in place on the closing date. (Most lenders won't finalize your mortgage until you have home insurance.)

» Calculate the amount of money you owe the seller because of prepaid rents (if applicable), utilities, and taxes (these are known as *adjustments*). Often, your lawyer will also transfer the utilities to your name. (More on adjustments later in this section.)

>> Check out the background of the property to ensure that it's legally owned by the seller (called a *title search*) and that there are no debts or claims against it (called *liens*).

>> Arrange with the seller's lawyer to transfer the deed from the seller to you on the closing date. The balance of the purchase price — the agreed price, minus the deposit, plus any adjustments — and the keys will also be exchanged. Review the condominium certificate with your lawyer, if you're buying a condo. We discuss condominium certificates in Chapter 6.

TECHNICAL STUFF

Because condominiums are regulated provincially, each province has its own documents, regulations, and procedures. What we refer to generally as the condominium certificate may comprise more than one document and may go by a variety of names depending on the location, including (but not limited to): estoppel certificate, status certificate, information certificate, declaration document, and Form B. Ask your real estate agent which documentation applies in your situation.

At the end of all this, your lawyer draws up a *statement of adjustments*, a summary of the financial transactions among you, your lawyer, your lender, and the seller. A statement of adjustments lists the following dollar amounts:

>> Purchase price of the home (owed to the seller)

>> Adjustments owed to the seller, such as the pro-rata portion of paid or owed property taxes, condo fees if applicable, plus electricity, water, and gas charges

>> Buyer's deposit

>> Mortgage money from the lender

>> Taxes, including GST/HST and land transfer tax, if applicable (to be paid through the lawyer)

>> Lawyer's fees, including disbursements (costs the lawyer has taken for the buyer; for example, couriers and photocopying) and GST/HST

You then get a final tally of the money you owe, which should essentially be your down payment (minus deposit) plus your lawyer's total fees and applicable taxes. You must give this money to your lawyer by the closing date.

Getting that mortgage

Most mortgages won't be finalized until after the seller has accepted your offer. Hopefully, you got your mortgage preapproved before you started home hunting (refer to Chapter 4). After your offer is accepted, all you have to do is go back to your lender with the details about the home and sign lots of paperwork. Taking the MLS listing or feature sheet with you is a good idea because it should have all the information about your home that your lender will need. Many lenders will also require an appraisal; they may have their own appraisers do the job (often, the valuations are now generated automatically), but the appraiser or the listing agent may make an appointment with the seller (refer to Chapter 2 for more information about appraisals). If you're buying in a rural area, you also have to present certificates from the provincial government that verify the location of your well and septic tank.

Some mortgages are more flexible than others in terms of missing payments, making extra payments, and the like. Review your requirements with your lender and make the necessary adjustments prior to completing the paperwork (refer to Chapter 5 for information on the various options).

You may be short on cash after you've bought the home, paid the lawyer, redecorated, and purchased that antique armoire for the master bedroom. Many mortgages include a line of credit secured by the property to give you some extra breathing room. Known as a *home equity line of credit* (*HELOC*), you build up borrowing room in sync with the amount of equity you're building in your home. Beware, however, the interest rate may be higher than on the mortgage itself.

After your lender finalizes and approves your mortgage, your lawyer will receive payment in trust to be given to the seller's lawyer on closing day for the purchase price, pursuant to the statement of adjustments. Even though this was traditionally a certified cheque or bank draft, the transaction (like many other aspects of the transaction) is now paperless and is transferred electronically as part of the mortgage process. Before the lender transfers payment, however, you have to verify that you have home insurance covering the home from the day of possession.

The Ins and Outs of Inspections

We can't stress this enough: Make sure your offer is subject to an inspection. You may think everything looks like it's in tip-top condition, certified or licensed property inspector is trained to detect issues you won't notice. Although no one has X-ray vision, you can look for clues to underlying issues that could be red flags for future problems. Every real estate agent and home inspector has stories of the unexpected results that come from a seemingly straightforward home inspection.

We include a couple of stories here to show you just how important an inspection is. Some sellers commission inspections before they put their homes on the market (a pre-sale inspection), but as a buyer you should have your own professional home inspection done. Occasionally lenders require an inspection before approving a mortgage, so unless you're Mr. or Mrs. Moneybuckets and have the cash in your back pocket, getting financing may require you to carry out a property inspection. The same goes for condominiums, notwithstanding the growing number of properties with depreciation reports. Even though a depreciation report will flag issues with the building as a whole, a property inspection will focus on your particular unit.

This section helps you understand the inspection process, how to select an inspector, and the kinds of issues they're trained to catch.

Getting an inspection, no matter what

After the seller accepts your offer, have the house inspected as soon as possible. If the inspector spots any problems, you'll want as much time as possible to resolve them and make some decisions. You may be able to renegotiate the price of the property in question if some serious deficiencies are discovered — or you may decide to walk away. Even if the home is sound, the inspector can share a lot of good information about your new house and tip you off to anything you'll want to keep an eye on.

Even if you're planning to radically renovate or tear down the home in question, you still need to do an inspection. For instance, the inspection may uncover asbestos on the premises or urea formaldehyde foam insulation (UFFI; see Chapter 7 for more information on these hazards). Removal is expensive, and if you're not willing to deal with the cost, a property inspection can help you avoid the hassle.

If you aren't able to do an inspection before submitting your offer (for example, if multiple offers are required on a pre-set date), include a *subject to inspection clause* in your contract of purchase and sale. (Refer to Chapter 9 for more information on these types of clauses.) In effect, a subject to inspection clause acts as a safety mechanism: It releases a buyer from the obligation to purchase a home if an inspector finds major faults in the building.

Understanding what your inspector does

A professional inspector knows what to look for to ensure that a home is up to snuff — that it meets current building code requirements and has a sound structure. An average inspection takes at least two or three hours, depending on the size of the home. A good inspector will have you accompany her and will encourage lots of questions. Sometimes the inspector will start when you're not in the home — you won't have much to do when the inspector is poking through the attic. You should definitely be present for the last hour or two of the inspection so that the inspector can go over the good, the bad, and the ugly with you.

An inspection is a visual walk-through to report on the elements of the home. It's not meant to be a picky this-doorknob-won't-turn-fully kind of examination, but an overall report of whether the home is sound. Of course, you don't get any guarantees, because a home may have problems even the inspector can't find. For example, a property inspector is limited to issues with the building, not the property itself; if your house is built on unstable ground and a sink hole is a hazard, you'll need the assessment and advice of a geotechnical expert rather than a property inspector.

REMEMBER

A good inspector won't offer to do home repairs for you — it would be a huge conflict of interest. Your inspector also shouldn't recommend contractors to do the repairs unless they're very specialized repairs that require highly skilled trades. Your inspector's role is to investigate your home, not to give work to his buddies in the building trades.

Choosing a good inspector

To find an inspector with a good reputation and a membership in the Canadian Association of Home and Property Inspectors, look at www.cahpi.ca. The inspector should hold be able to demonstrate some form of accreditation or certification. CAHPI maintains minimum standards for home inspectors regarding education and professional conduct, and its members may be National Certificate Holders (NCH) or have the Registered Home Inspector (RHI) designation. Some designations are specific to the province of practice.

CAHPI's site features a directory that can be searched by location, including proximity to where you live (or hope to live). Your local CAHPI office can provide the names of home inspectors in good standing who work in your neighbourhood.

If you know any people who have recently bought or sold their home, see if they're willing to recommend their inspector (and if they were happy with the service). If not, you can try a number of resources. For example, ask your real estate agent. If any friends or relatives have recently purchased a home, ask them for a referral. You may also call your provincial or regional association of home inspectors.

WARNING

Home inspectors may not be regulated in your province, so if they aren't members of CAHPI, make sure they have the training, background, experience, liability insurance, and continuing education that members of CAHPI have as a condition of membership. Training is available through community colleges and private companies.

Knowing what to expect when you're inspecting

Building inspectors look at the structural elements of a home, including the basement, the roof, and the heating, plumbing, and electrical systems. An inspector usually goes through the home systematically and gives you a full, written report when finished. A good inspector also makes recommendations on what should be improved (for example, installing GFCI outlets and a vent in the bathroom, or adding a handrail to the basement stairs).

If any problems are uncovered — and these problems can be anything from a leaky gutter to a leaky basement — it's decision time. You have a couple options:

>> **Write a new term into the contract (if the seller agrees) that requires the seller to fix the leaky basement and any other problem areas.** You're now renegotiating the contract, and adding new terms requires consent from both the seller and the buyer (refer to Chapter 9 for more on the negotiating process).

   If the seller refuses to accept a new conditional clause or an added term, your next option is to propose a price reduction to cover the costs you'll incur to fix the problem.

>> *Collapse* **(cancel) your offer, because the condition of a positive inspection wasn't met.** If you and the seller can't reach an agreement, you can collapse the offer and look for another house.

REMEMBER

Keep in mind that the seller is under no obligation to renegotiate. In fact, she may have priced the house acknowledging there was work to be done, and in her mind she has already discounted the price to cover the repairs.

Inspection costs can vary greatly if you're buying a very large or unusual property. In most cases, however, you'll find inspectors charge a fee in the range of $250 to $1,000. There's no set price because some inspectors charge based on the complexity of the property, whereas others charge using a sliding scale based on the size of the property. A typical building inspection takes at least two or three hours. On completion, you'll receive a full, written inspection report that's signed and dated by the inspector.

TIP

In the event you're buying a larger, custom-built house (lucky you!) or a multi-family property, you may want to have a more comprehensive inspection conducted to inspect and analyze complex systems within the house. In this case, you may want to pay extra for a comprehensive inspection that will produce a technical audit report. This type of inspection typically takes 20 hours or more to perform and includes the disassembly and disruption of the home's systems and components. You'll need to get the owner's permission before conducting a technical audit, because the inspector will be dismantling key components of the owner's home. If you're interested in a technical audit, check to make sure your inspector is capable of performing this type of inspection and be sure to get a price estimate before proceeding.

WHAT YOU SEE ISN'T ALWAYS WHAT YOU GET

You can remedy a few unpleasant surprises that an inspector may discover, but the problems still need to be uncovered in order to address them. Say you make an offer on a beautiful detached two-storey house in Toronto's Little Italy. Elsie and Peter, the older couple who've lived there for 45 years, have lovingly maintained the home. You arrange an inspection as a condition of the sale. You and your partner are both present when the inspector does a routine check behind a three-prong electrical outlet, and she discovers that it still has the old two-wire, ungrounded system. Local building code requires that every three-prong outlet be connected to a grounded system. When you look behind an electrical outlet, you should see three conductor wires: a black hot wire, a white neutral wire, and a green ground wire. Elsie and Peter's outlets have only a hot wire and a neutral wire. The outlets weren't grounded at all.

Peter and Elsie are devastated. They had paid thousands of dollars to have the house rewired with a grounded system. It turns out that the contractor had only changed the two-prong outlets to three-prong outlets, nothing more. Behind the walls, the original, ungrounded system remains. When you go back to the negotiating table, you can ask for a significant price cut to cover the costs of getting the house properly rewired. But Peter and Elsie are still horrified that the contractor has duped them, and they can't bring themselves to cut the price on their house, which represents the bulk of their retirement fund.

At this point, you can break off negotiations by choosing not to remove the subject-to inspection clause, thereby collapsing your offer. Alternatively, Peter and Elsie can follow your agent's suggestion to keep the deal alive by contacting the electrician and requiring him to deliver the grounded electrical system he was hired to install.

Inspecting a Newly Built Home

A newly built home will require a building inspection prior to occupancy. However, it's not a bad idea to commission your own inspection so you know exactly what you're getting into. Although a municipal building inspector will ensure everything is up to code and the property has no deficiencies that could create life-safety issues, your own inspection may be able to alert you to inconsistencies between what you commission and what you're receiving.

You can make an inspection part of your pre-completion inspection, before the completion of the sale. In new construction contracts, you can usually find a provision for a pre-completion deficiency inspection of the property. You can write into your contract that a professional building inspector will accompany you when you're doing your *deficiency inspection*. Before you agree to the terms of the sale contract, talk to your agent or lawyer to ensure that you're entitled to a deficiency inspection. As with all inspections, a professional home inspector has the training and experience needed to pick up on clues to underlying issues that you may not recognize. Don't think you can manage a property inspection on your own!

Following the visual inspection, you'll be asked to sign a *certificate of completion* (sometimes also referred to as a *certificate of completion and possession*), stating that everything you paid for is complete. You can have the certificate drawn up by your lawyer and a representative of the builder, although many New Home Warranty Program–registered builders will already have professionally prepared documents for this purpose. Any apparent omissions or defects discovered during your inspection should be noted on the certificate of completion, because this certificate is registered at your local NHWP office. Filing the certificate is necessary for your warranty coverage to commence (we discuss New Home Warranty Programs in the section of this chapter, "Finding Out Whether the Property Comes with a Warranty").

TIP

Most home inspectors, especially if they're affiliated with CAHPI or its provincial counterpart, are honest and pride themselves on thorough work. If, however, you've had a home inspection and you feel dissatisfied with the results, you have the right to have a second inspection performed (like a second doctor's opinion). If you feel the original inspector was incompetent, file a report with the local professional association. If the inspector isn't a member of an association and lacks certification, then you have little recourse except to file a complaint with the Better Business Bureau.

Sizing Up an Inspection Report

The inspector completes most of the inspection report while touring the property, so the report is usually organized into locations starting with the site itself, and then working through the exterior and interior of the house. Your inspection report should cover all categories of concern relevant to each part of the house and property, including structural, exterior, interior, plumbing, electrical, and heating and ventilation components. Here we break what the inspector looks at into two sections.

Home exterior

A building inspector examines the following exterior components of the house:

» **Roof surface:** The roof should be in at least *visibly* good condition. Although severe deterioration of the roof surface will be obvious, the early signs may be subtle and invisible to the untrained eye. A roof surface that's in poor condition can point to poor insulation and can facilitate water ingress (leakage), and in extreme cases it can lead to roof collapse.

» **Eaves:** The eaves should be in good condition, with no holes and minimal rust. Eaves in poor condition mean rain and snow won't drain appropriately. Poor drainage can cause serious problems if water backs up and accumulates on your roof or overflows and pools around your home's foundation.

» **Chimney(s):** The chimney(s) should be free from cracks or loose sections in the masonry, and should have a chimney cap. Chimneys in poor shape can cause ventilation problems.

» **Chimney flue(s):** The chimney flue is the exhaust vent over the fireplace. An unused fireplace can have its flue blocked by debris or even a bird nest or two, which is a fire hazard. Flues that aren't in good condition may signal a malfunctioning or improperly maintained chimney.

» **Windows:** The windows shouldn't show any signs of wood or water damage. Damaged windows are sure indications of water and air penetration into the interior of the home. Double-paned windows shouldn't be fogged; if they are, it's a sign that the vapour seal has failed.

» **Siding/exterior walls:** Whether brick or siding, the house's exterior walls should be free of cracks, gaps, or signs of water damage. These are possible indications of damage to *interior materials,* rot, or molds inside walls. Watch out! Also, look for possible rot on window trim and shutters, as well as any wooden decks and patios or external stairs.

>> **Gradient:** The gradient, or slope of the ground, should be angled away from the home. An incorrect gradient will allow water to pool around the foundation and possibly even drainage into the basement. This can result not only in water damage but also rot and even fungus growth.

>> **Foundation:** The house's foundation should be free of cracks, bulges, or deformities. These abnormalities can indicate an extremely serious structural problem. Also, termite tubes or other signs of infestation may manifest themselves in this area.

>> **Septic system/cesspool:** Septic tanks and cesspools should be tested for possible leaching. You can request a dye test if the inspector doesn't plan to run one.

Home interior

You can expect your inspector to check for these problems on the house's interior:

>> **Flooding/leaks:** The inspector notes these and other visible signs of water damage inside the home. The inspector is also able to tell you if any water-proofing measures, such as a sump pump or other additions, have been installed. A *sump pump* is an electric pump installed in a recess in the basement (or occasionally outside the house) that will kick into action if the level of water in the drainage system starts to rise. The pump will mechanically aid the gravitational flow of the water away from the house. Waterproofing a home is extremely expensive, and this makes it important for buyers to be aware of measures already in place.

>> **Insulation/ventilation:** Insulation and the ventilation system become problematic if the home leaks or doesn't allow moisture to evaporate, putting pretty much all of the major structural components at risk. Excessive moisture can cause rotting, rust, electrical shorts, and fungal growth. Furthermore, good insulation and ventilation will keep heating and cooling costs to a minimum.

>> **Radon seepage:** Radon is a colourless, odourless gas that occurs naturally in many parts of Canada. It has also radioactive and is linked to cancer. It is a particular concern in the Maritimes and the Prairies. The gas accumulates in enclosed spaces, particularly basements. Testing is the only way to determine whether levels are sufficient to pose a concern. The solution typically involves improving basement ventilation to reduce the air pressure and prevent the gas from entering the space in the first place.

>> **Other unsafe components:** The other problems inspectors watch out for are largely dependent on the age of the house. For example, paint may be old

enough to contain lead, some railings on staircases may be missing, or urea formaldehyde foam insulation (UFFI) or asbestos-laced Zonolite/vermiculite insulation may be throughout the home (refer to Chapter 7 for information on these hazards). Building materials change over the years, as do safety standards. A qualified inspector has up-to-date information and can recognize potentially dangerous components in the interior systems/mechanics.

A FIRE SALE (LITERALLY)

Zack and Caroline's offer on a 65-year-old home that seemed to be in good shape was accepted. Zack had owned five or six houses before, but because the couple was recently married, this home was their first big purchase together. At first, Zack didn't feel a home inspection was necessary. He's a fairly handy guy who's comfortable handling lots of small repairs around the house. Caroline was concerned about the mixture of old and new wiring, however, so they decided to make their offer subject to inspection.

A proper home inspection was a good call. They were stunned to find out that not only was the wiring not up to code, but it was also an extreme fire hazard. A previous owner (not the current seller) rewired an extension to the family room and mixed two different types of wiring that were twisted together with electrical tape that had since fallen off. The home inspector couldn't figure out why a light was flickering in the family room, and he couldn't figure out how the newer wiring was routed through the wall cavity. With the owner's permission, the inspector removed one piece of wall panelling. Burn marks were on the back of the panelling where the wires were connected, and it was still very hot — a disaster waiting to happen.

When the seller had bought the house three years before, she didn't do a home inspection. Therefore, she was completely unaware of the danger in the family room where her two small children always played. After Zack and Caroline's inspection, she immediately called an electrician. Zack and Caroline bought the house, with the written understanding that the seller would pay for the professional rewiring as necessary to bring it up to code and pass inspection from the city inspector.

The home inspection not only saved Zack and Caroline the cost of rewiring, but it also may have saved their lives. When you get an inspector's full report, you're able to evaluate whether the home in question is as good as it looks. The inspection report should list any substandard or failing elements, and the inspector should make suggestions regarding necessary repairs and how those jobs should be prioritized. Your inspector may also be able to furnish some rough estimates of the repair costs.

Your inspector will also examine building systems, including:

>> **Plumbing:** Plumbing systems and pipes may no longer be up to scratch. The inspector is on the lookout for rust and leaking or water stains that warrant deeper examination. Checking water pressure and the condition of drains and pipes is also part of the job.

>> **Heating:** Heating systems may be outdated or inefficient. For example, the valve that controls the flow of hot water into radiators can rust away, leaving you with no way to turn down the heat in that individual unit. Other problems may be unsafe exhaust venting or chimneys that are blocked. The inspector looks for all these problems, as well as for indications that the furnace, including the motor and burners, is functioning properly. An inspection should also note the presence of safety devices such as smoke and carbon monoxide detectors to protect you against failures in these systems.

>> **Electrical:** Electrical systems may be potential fire hazards or simply not dependable. Wiring always warrants extra attention. Your inspector checks for signs of unreliable wiring, and closely inspects the condition of any exposed wiring. Reverse polarity outlets and two-prong convenience outlets present issues, as do older electrical systems (we discuss these in Chapter 7).

Checking Out Condo Inspections

If you're buying a condominium, you may think you don't need an inspection. You've read the council minutes and all the other documentation you've received and have confidence the management company is on top of issues and that residents take pride in the premises. Or perhaps it's relatively new, and the warranty hasn't yet run out. How can there be anything wrong with it?

Our point is, home inspections don't apply strictly to detached homes; condominiums — and apartments in particular — should get inspected, too! Because condominium refers to the type of ownership, check out the property you're buying just like with any other purchase. This section gives you the overview to condo inspections.

Outside the building

The inspector usually starts with the outside of the development. He'll check to make sure all exterior components are well designed, well maintained, and functioning properly. He'll examine the caulking and sealing around the windows, doors, and building details to be sure they're in good shape. If the building has a brick facade, the inspector will check the brickwork for loose bricks and to see if the mortar is holding the bricks properly and not deteriorating and leaking. If the building has a stucco exterior, the inspector will check to make sure there are no hints of water ingress and staining. (This was a particular issue in British Columbia during the late 1990s, but building codes have changed and resulted in the mitigation of risks. However, a good inspector should always be on the lookout for water issues.) The inspector also walks through the parking garage and checks for any leaks or water ingress into the underground parkade.

The inspector checks out the building's roof to make sure the roof and drainage system are being well maintained and serviced. He may also check out any vents and skylights and ensure they were properly installed and are being maintained. If the building has a central boiler supplying hot water (as opposed to individual in-suite hot water tanks), most inspectors look in the boiler room to make sure the system is up to date and working properly. As for balconies or patios, the inspector also checks to verify they have adequate drains and that no water is pooling on them, which can lead to rot in balconies that have a membrane over a wood frame.

B.C.'S LEAKY CONDO CRISIS WASN'T JUST ABOUT CONDOS

One of the first things they teach budding architects is, "Water is your worst enemy." Home-owners in coastal British Columbia learned this lesson the hard way. The building boom that took place from the mid-1980s to the late 1990s soon resulted in a problem no one saw coming. Buildings began leaking all over the Lower Mainland and Vancouver Island, and protective tarps became a common sight. Multifamily condo projects were singled out as the problem at first but it quickly became clear that building envelope problems, structural flaws that permit water to penetrate a building, don't affect condos exclusively.

In 1998 the B.C. government passed the Homeowner Protection Act and opened the Homeowner Protection Office (HPO), a provincial Crown corporation, to license builders and conduct research and education programs for the construction industry and the public.

Home builders in B.C. and contractors who repair leaky condos must be licensed through the HPO, and the HPO sets the terms of the warranty coverage for new construction and condo repairs. When buying or selling a new home or a rebuilt condominium in B.C., determine the warranty coverage of the construction and find out exactly what's covered by the warranty and when the warranty terminates. You'll also want to make sure the builder/contractor is registered with the HPO by checking the HPO website (www.hpo.bc.ca), which has plenty of helpful information regarding water ingress and what's been done to make the leaky condo crisis — for the most part — history.

A RIVER RUNS THROUGH IT

Yvonne finally paid off her student loans, got a great job, and was going to be a home-owner. With a little help from her parents, she could buy her first apartment. Having been around the block a few times, her parents placed one condition on their financial assistance: that Yvonne have a full inspection done before she bought anything.

After looking for a couple of months, Yvonne found a nice top-floor, one-bedroom suite in a very nice and seemingly well-maintained building, just one block off the bus route that took her to work. The building was recently painted and looked great. Best of all, it was within her price range. The minutes of the building's meetings looked clean, if somewhat short on details. The building had just 12 suites, too small for most manage-ment companies to handle, and so it was self-managed. The 12 owners did their best to maintain the building, manage the finances, and take notes during their condominium meetings. The small number of owners also meant that they hadn't invested in a depre-ciation report. Because the owners seemed highly engaged, Yvonne was confident that all would be well. But it wasn't.

The property inspector identified several issues that a depreciation report would have flagged. Her unit's balcony had substantial dry rot under the membrane, for example, and needed immediate repair. The inspector poked around on a couple of other balco-nies and found that they all needed repair or replacement. The minutes of the condo meetings didn't indicate that the roof had actually been patched continually during the last couple of years. The inspector deemed the roof to be near the end of its lifespan and in need of replacement very shortly. The inspector also identified numerous sub-stantial water leaks in the parkade.

The inspector estimated the repairs could cost a minimum of $500,000 to $600,000, including the cost of resealing the parkade and the foundation. Because the building had so few residents and a very small reserve fund, Yvonne estimated that her portion of the future repairs would be at least $50,000 (her unit was slightly larger than average, saddling her with a greater share of the common expenses). Although Yvonne loved the unit, she passed and bought another, slightly more expensive suite in a professionally managed building that her inspector said was one of the best she'd ever seen.

Inside the building

A condominium development has two parts to the inside: the unit and the com-mon areas. Both will typically warrant inspection, though circumstances may prevent as thorough an inspection as in other kinds of housing.

Within the unit being purchased, the inspector will check the wiring and electrical panel as well as the electrical outlets. Just as with other forms of housing, these outlets need to be grounded and working properly. The inspector also checks all plumbing fixtures. The suite will be examined for signs of leaks. Most inspectors also check the appliances that are included in the sale, but some focus more on the structure of the building and the condition of the systems within the suite.

He'll also inspect common areas, including the owner's designated storage area (if assigned). Some areas may be off limits or accessible only with the help of a building representative.

TIP

Before booking an inspection for a condominium, the inspector may ask you to arrange access to the roof, the boiler room, or any other common areas. Sometimes the inspector will arrange access personally. These places are usually locked, so the property manager, the caretaker, or a building council member may need to provide the inspector access. In some cases, access may be denied.

You Are the Owner of All You Survey

Once upon a time, kings and queens built their castles on hills because they could rule over all they could see. In today's smaller kingdoms, your home may still be your castle, but you need to make sure you don't just survey it, but survey it properly. These days, homebuyers have a choice: You can you can purchase title insurance, which is increasingly common, or you can request an updated survey from the seller. We discuss both options here.

Considering title insurance

Title insurance provides protection against problems you may encounter with the title of your property. For example, if you buy a residence on five acres, you'll want to make sure the boundaries are accurately surveyed so you know you actually have five acres of land rather than four (on the plus side, and we've seen it happen, you may find that you actually have five and a half or six acres). On the other hand, you want to protect yourself against title fraud, whereby someone robs you of title to the property you thought was lawfully yours.

Title insurance covers expenses associated with repairing the title and provides compensation if your property's title comes under dispute. Lenders require either a survey or title insurance in order to finance your purchase, and your lawyer will incorporate it into your title documents so that they know you own the property; having title insurance protects not only your interest, but theirs, too. However, many reasons exist for getting an up-to-date survey as well as title insurance (though you don't need a survey when buying a condominium).

Figuring out why you need a survey

A *land survey* is a legal map of a property's boundaries. Surveys are also known as *building location certificates, mortgage certificates, surveyor's certificates, real property reports, plot plans,* and *certificates of non-encroachment.* In the best-case scenario, the seller will provide you with an up-to-date survey that's perfectly legal — in other words, one that's copyrighted and valid only if the original is signed and sealed. If the survey the seller hands you is old, unsealed, or otherwise fishy in any way, get your own done. When it's performed by a professional who is familiar with your region, a land survey

>> Gives you certified, accurate measurements of the property and the exact location of the house, garden shed, garage, and any other buildings on it

>> Lets you know of environmental issues or contamination on your site, such as whether your runoff from a nearby major road seeps into your well water or whether the site is in an area proven to contain dangerous levels of lead in the soil

>> States who may review the survey (because a land survey, contrary to popular belief, isn't a public document)

If no up-to-date survey is available, you may want to write "subject to survey" into your offer — doing this will give you time to commission a proper and thorough survey. A slipshod, cheap, or hurried survey won't do you any good if a boundary dispute comes up, or if you decide to subdivide, build an addition, or remortgage. But again, you may find that title insurance for the type of property you're purchasing is adequate. Every jurisdiction is different, so consult your agent.

Finding a professional surveyor

Like finding a good doctor or mechanic, the first step in the hunt for a professional surveyor is to ask around. Query the previous homeowners for the company they used. Or, if your lender has requested a survey, it can often recommend one. Your lender may provide you with an excellent surveyor who is familiar with your locality — and all the environmental, archaeological, and regulatory quirks that may go along with it. Your agent, banker, or lawyer may also be able to recommend a surveyor.

Many provincial land surveyors' associations maintain a publicly accessible registry of members, complete with contact information. The umbrella organization for these associations is the Association of Canada Lands Surveyors (www.acls-aatc.ca). When sizing up potential surveyors, look for long-established companies. Call three of them, describing the job you need done, and be ready to supply them with a legal description of the property as well as the civic address. Record how each company proposes to do the job and approximately how much they would charge to do it. Finally, ask to see samples of their work. Compare the companies' methods, estimates, and samples, and you can find a surveyor right for you.

SURVEY SAYS . . .

Brian and Evan were first-time homebuyers who decided they couldn't afford the cost of any of the homes on offer in Vancouver. Because they both had good jobs that allowed them to work from home, they decided to move to Vancouver Island, where real estate prices were cheaper. They found a small acreage just outside Courtenay that came with a small house and room for the family they hoped to have. The ten-acre property looked perfect, and the survey provided didn't raise any questions — besides, the property was cheaper than a Vancouver townhouse.

When they began walking the property and making plans for improvements, however, they noticed that the drainage channel that served as the boundary on the survey seemed closer than described. Their neighbor, of course, treated the opposite side of the ditch as all his. The back of the property abutted a railway right of way, and stakes marking the corners had been covered by brush not to mention gravel from the track bed. Brian suggested having a survey done to determine what they had purchased, so they could plan where to locate a small studio.

The survey revealed that the property was actually not as deep as expected, and that the planned studio would need to be set back from the tracks farther than anticipated. It also found that the drainage ditch that everyone believed to be the property boundary had actually been re-excavated since the original survey was done. The actual property line was several feet beyond the existing ditch, meaning that the ten-acre property they bought was still ten acres — but included more than they expected. This didn't make their neighbour very happy, but it gave Brian and Evan peace of mind and the ability to enjoy all that they surveyed.

IN THIS CHAPTER

» Safeguarding your investment with insurance

» Insuring a newly built home: New home warranties

» Walking through your home

Chapter **11**

Protecting Your Interests: Insurance and Warranties

A home is the single biggest purchase of your life, so naturally, you want to protect it. This chapter discusses the different types of home insurance available to safeguard your new investment, including warranties provided on new homes. We also discuss the final walk-through before closing, an important exercise that confirms the state of the home that's about to come into your possession.

Insuring Your Home

Mortgage is just a fancy term for a whopping big loan. Because your collateral for this loan is your home, it needs to be protected from anything or anyone that may cause damage (this includes *you*). Suppose you forget to close a window or didn't get around to reinsulating your basement before a nasty freeze hit and the pipes freeze and burst, causing a flood. The damage could be in the thousands of dollars and lead to mould issues. You'll wish you had insurance. (Don't confuse this with *mortgage life insurance*, which we discuss in Chapter 5.) Because you can choose from different items to protect and different ways to protect your home, talk to your insurance broker to make sure you get the coverage you need.

The following sections familiarize you with what to protect, how to protect it, and most important — how to make sure you're getting the best deal for the kind of protection you're seeking.

Knowing what to protect

Home insurance has two parts: *property coverage* and *liability coverage*. Property coverage protects both your dwelling and its contents; liability coverage protects *you*. Although most policies cover all three aspects (your dwelling, your dwelling's contents, and you), you can tailor your insurance to fit the coverage you need. For example, if you're renting your home, you may simply need your dwelling protected and not its contents. (The policy will also need to use of the premises as a rental property.)

Protecting your dwelling

A *dwelling* is considered to be the home's structure and all permanent attached components. This definition can include different elements depending on the specific policy you have, so confirm what's covered with your insurance provider, especially if you get a different type of insurance for your contents than for your dwelling. The insurance provider will most likely insure you for the amount of money it will take to rebuild your house, rather than the price you paid for it.

WARNING

Your policy likely covers the replacement cost of your home *exactly as it was*. Suppose a horrible fire burned your 75-year-old house to the ground. When building codes and regulations are changed, they generally exempt existing homes. Now suppose that current building regulations don't allow houses to be built in the same way, with the same materials, or even in the same place on your lot (current regulations may no longer allow waterfront homes to be so close to the shoreline, for example). If new building standards require an upgrade when you rebuild, the extra cost will most likely *not* be covered by your insurance policy. Ask your insurance agent about a *rider* (an add-on policy that lets you specify additional items to be covered) or extended coverage, if you have any concerns.

TIP

When insuring your home or renewing your insurance policy, getting bylaw insurance is a good idea. *Bylaw insurance* (also known as *compliance insurance*) ensures that any repairs your house may require will comply with the current building code and any extra cost to bring your home repairs/restoration up to the current building code will be the responsibility of your insurer. Many insurance policies include bylaw insurance in their standard policy, but check to make sure.

Otherwise, your insurance company will rebuild your home only to the way it was before a fire, not to the extra, updated current standards for wiring, plumbing, and fire protection (sprinkler systems are expensive!) that are now required by the building code in some Canadian provinces.

REMEMBER

Coverage above and beyond the basic coverage will come at an extra cost. Be sure to weigh the value of the added insurance against the potential risk. For example, earthquake coverage might be something to consider in coastal British Columbia, but it may be less of a consideration on the Prairies.

Protecting your contents

Homeowners need to insure not only the permanent structure (the dwelling) of their properties *but also the* contents. The two forms of contents insurance that exist are as follows:

>> **Actual cash value:** When you make a claim (assuming it's approved), you receive cash for the current value of the item. This value is *not* the value of buying the same item new, but rather the cost of buying the item minus the depreciation in value due to age, wear, or obsolescence.

>> **Replacement cost:** The lost or damaged item is covered for the cost of replacing the item with one of comparable quality. Obviously, because a replacement cost policy costs your insurance provider more than a depreciated-value cash payout, this kind of coverage comes with a heftier price tag.

Because condo buildings are generally insured by the condominium corporation, most condo owners need only worry about insuring the contents of their homes. If you're a condo owner, you need to find out exactly what the condo corporation's insurance covers and what yours will need to address. Sometimes the corporation's policy will cover only the bare walls, leaving you to provide coverage for fixtures like kitchen cabinets, for example. A common consideration is water damage; because this type of claim is common, especially in high-rise buildings, the deductible is often high, and to protect themselves a homeowner's insurance needs to make up the difference. For example, if your building has a deductible of $50,000, your policy should specify this amount of coverage for your unit.

Protecting yourself

Liability insurance protects you in the event that you, or a tree on your property, damage either someone else's property or someone else's person. This type of coverage covers you anywhere in the world. You may be super-tired after a day of hiking in the Welsh countryside and knock over a lamp, causing a fire that burns down your B&B. But if you have liability insurance, it will cover any damage, medical, or legal fees that become your responsibility. This insurance also covers you if a flowerpot on your railing flies through the air and hits your mail carrier on the head during a windstorm. How much coverage you require is up to you. If you buy a new home with a swimming pool at the edge of a cliff and you know the neighbours' kids will be hanging around your place, you may want more liability coverage than if you buy a basic bungalow (of course, you'll also want a high fence to reduce the risk of anything happening to the kids, too).

Understanding how you're protected

You can be covered by insurance in two general ways. Both policies work on an *exclusion principle*: Either the insurance provider will cover an event only if it's specifically named in your policy (standard), or the provider will cover all events *with the exception* of those specifically named in your policy (all-risks). Because an all-risks approach covers many more situations (such as your dog causing significant water damage by knocking over your 400-litre fish tank), all-risks policies are more expensive.

>> **Standard (or basic):** *Standard* policies generally cover most "acts of God" damage, such as fire, lightning, wind or hail, as well as theft, vandalism, and other incidents that are inherently beyond your control. Standard policies work on a *named perils* basis. A *peril* is what insurance companies call potentially damaging events, like the ones just mentioned. To work on a named-peril basis means that an event is covered only if it's specifically named in your policy.

>> **All-risks:** *All-risks* coverage typically involves some *exclusions* — specific events named in the policy contract that will *not* be covered under the policy. Exclusions may include faulty workmanship, wear due to regular use, or damage that would have been prevented with proper maintenance. Any event not specifically listed in your policy is covered, so if unfortunate things seem to just happen to you, consider getting an all-risks policy.

Although the term standard is also applied to dwelling and content coverage at a standard level, insurers usually use the term comprehensive to describe insurance that protects both your dwelling and your contents in an all-risks policy. (Be aware that even under a comprehensive policy, limits will be imposed on the value of your claims for some items of personal property; you may wish to consider extended coverage or a rider to protect these items. We discuss these in the next section, "Extending your coverage.") Homeowners wanting to protect both their dwelling and their contents don't necessarily have to protect both parts with the same kind of policy. They can also get protection known as broad coverage.

Broad coverage works partly on an all-risks basis and partly on a named-perils basis. A broad policy covers "all risks," meaning anything that may cause loss or damage to your dwelling. A broad policy covers named perils when it comes to the contents of your home.

WARNING

Read your home insurance policy carefully! Make sure you understand exactly what is covered and what is not. Insurance providers can differ greatly on their coverage of certain types of damage — coverage for water damage, in particular, ranges all across the board. Note the deductibles for various categories.

We can't offer any ballpark figures here on what home insurance costs. Your premiums (annual fees) depend on a large number of individual factors. For example, home size, modernity, and features, as well as neighbourhood, proximity to fire stations and hydrants, type of coverage, coverage provider, and your track record can all play a part in determining your premiums. The value of your home will also come into play, but that isn't necessarily the same as its sticker price. The important price for an insurance provider isn't how much you paid for your home or what its current market value is, but how much it would cost to rebuild it. This amount may not be equivalent to what you paid for your house.

ARE YOU COVERED?

If you take nothing else away from this sidebar, take this single piece of advice — assume nothing; question everything. Make sure you ask at least the following questions when you investigate different insurance providers:

- Whom does the policy cover?

- Exactly what property is covered? (For example, does the policy include the backyard shed?)

- What perils/items are included, and what perils/items are excluded?

- What discounts do you offer?

- What are my responsibilities as a policyholder? Under what conditions are you allowed to terminate my coverage?

- Are riders or endorsements available? How will they affect my premiums? How will they affect my responsibilities as a policyholder?

- What is the procedure for making a claim?

- How and when can I contact a representative with questions about my policy or a claim? (For example, is there a 24-hour toll-free hotline for policyholders?)

- How long does it usually take to process claims? What is the maximum time limit, upon your approval of my claim, for providing me with due compensation?

Extending your coverage

If you want particular items covered or you're worried about particular events, you can introduce *riders* to your insurance. *Riders* are add-on policies that allow you to customize (as much as possible) your policy by specifying that particular additional items or perils are covered. However, your insurance provider has to agree to provide coverage for these items or events, which isn't a given, and your provider will adjust your premiums — upwards! — to pay for the extended coverage. You can also choose *endorsements*, which are similar in purpose to riders but are simply add-on statements or amendments to your current policy, as opposed to whole additional policies.

Again, the more you ask to be covered, the more expensive your premiums typically will be, but if you want your $10,000 painting fully protected, your peace of mind will be worth a rider or endorsement. Ask your insurer about the various extended coverage packages offered.

TIP

Even though extending your coverage can cost you money, not having any claims can save you money. Be sure to inquire whether your premiums reflect all applicable discounts based on upgrades, proximity to emergency services, and a history of few or no claims. The less risk your property presents to an insurer, the more likely it is you'll receive a favourable rate. We discuss options for negotiating lower insurance premiums in the next section.

HOME OFFICE OWNERS BEWARE

Home insurance isn't business insurance. If you run a small business out of your home, have a home office, or have property in your home that you use for business purposes, chances are this property is *not* covered by your home insurance policy. Furthermore, if a client is injured while visiting your home office, your liability insurance may not cover the accident. Many insurance providers offer home business packages as either riders or endorsements. If you use your home for business purposes at all, ask specifically what is covered and what is not under your home insurance policy.

In this information age, your home office's data may be more valuable than the computer you use to access it. Although you may be reimbursed for hardware, and perhaps software under some policies, you won't be reimbursed for lost data. Similarly, if your website triggers a liability claim against you, your insurance may not protect you. Find out before you upload that sensitive classified document! Ask your insurance provider exactly what is and isn't covered.

Getting the best deal

After you know what sort of policy you want and which particular riders and endorsements suit your needs, you can start comparing prices. Here are some things you can do to make sure you're getting the best deal:

>> **Shop around.** Different insurance providers offer a variety of packages and prices. The cheapest isn't always your best option — ensure that the insurance you're buying meets your requirements as closely as possible.

>> **Ask all the providers you investigate about special discounts.** For example, some insurance providers may give discounts to nonsmokers or for houses that have good safety and security systems.

>> **Find out what the reduction in your premiums will be if you increase your deductible.** The *deductible* is the amount that you, the policyholder, have to pay toward replacement costs. For example, if your $2,000 camera is stolen, you pay the $500 deductible and your insurance company pays the remaining replacement cost. You can usually save a lot of money in the long run by increasing your deductible. Standard minimum deductibles are anywhere from $200 to $500, but if you increase it to $1,000, you should be able to reduce your premiums significantly.

TIP

Picking up the tab on less expensive accidents or damages, even if they're covered by your home insurance policy, can save you money over the long haul. The fewer claims you make, the less your premiums increase. If you make numerous small claims, you may even be branded a potential risk, and not only will your premiums increase, but you'll also run the risk of other insurance providers rejecting you in the future.

Make sure your home insurance kicks in on the very same day you take legal ownership of the property — whether or not you actually move in on that day. But, if you're building your home you should be aware that damage or loss during the building process is often not covered by home insurance policies. Once again, and we can't repeat it enough, ask providers exactly what is covered and what is not and takes steps to protect yourself.

Finding Out Whether the Property Comes with a Warranty

A $30 blender comes with a warranty, but what about your house? If you're buying a newly built home, more than likely your province's New Home Warranty Program (NHWP) covers it. But this warranty is nothing like the piece of paper that came with your new laptop. It's actually a type of third-party insurance, and it may or may not come with your home, depending on whether or not your builder has bought into a plan. (All members of the Canadian Home Builders' Association are required to provide a warranty as a condition of membership.) These sections help you wade through the different facets of a new home warranty.

Understanding the new home warranty

Basically, a *new home warranty* is insurance for your builder while the home is being built. Then, after the certificate of completion is transferred over to you, it becomes a kind of consumer warranty. Unlike homeowner's insurance (which you'll also need, as we discuss in the first section in this chapter), the builder rather than the homebuyer buys the policy. Of course, just because you don't buy it doesn't mean you won't end up paying for it: The builder will likely tack the cost of the warranty on to the purchase price.

Legislation concerning new home warranties varies across the country, and not all provinces require them. (Saskatchewan, Atlantic Canada, and three territories were the only regions that didn't require new home warranties at the time of writing.) Moreover, not all homes are covered in the same way. You'll have to ask your builder whether your home is protected by one, and what exactly is covered. Your builder should be able to provide you with a registration, enrollment, or membership number for the warranty plan. That way, you can check with the issuer of the warranty to ensure that everything is in order.

TIP

If you do have a warranty for your house, keep it. Keep all documentation and policy information, registration confirmation, and contact numbers somewhere safe, where you can access them if you ever need to.

REMEMBER

In order to be covered under a province's NHWP, you may have to pay a registration fee, although generally the builder pays all associated fees. Pay attention to the timing and schedule of the warranty. Some coverage is good for only one year after you take possession of the house, and coverage of different problems may expire at different times. If you do have any problems or questions, call your provincial NHWP office for answers to your questions and a list of builders that are registered as members of the NHWP. Some provincial NHWP offices provide ratings of the local registered builders based on their track record for both creating and solving problems. Others supply you with a list of criteria that builders have to meet in order to be registered members. Either way, you get the security of knowing you're choosing a builder that has been evaluated on a regular basis and meets high standards for quality and service.

Knowing what's covered

So what does your new home warranty cover? The details vary across the country. Most include protection for some (but not necessarily all) of the following:

» Defects in workmanship and materials

» Down payment protection

» Settling cracks in drywall (usually for the first year or two)

» Structural defects

» Violations of building and safety codes

» Water penetration

Timelines on the coverage vary by policy, and some may be governed by provincial legislation. Check your specific policy for the details. As with all insurance policies, you need to know what you're covered for as well as what you're *not* covered for.

With a warranty, you're in the driver's seat

A warranty can come in handy when things go wrong. If you see your unobstructed view of the lake through a gaping hole in the wall, you'll want to have that certificate to turn to. In the best of worlds, you let your builder know of the problem and then he builds you a new bay window where you can relax and enjoy the vista. In the worst of worlds, he may argue that the hole isn't really a hole but a great alternative to a cat door. Without another person there to arbitrate — except for the courts — things can get ugly pretty quickly.

In the event that you and your builder disagree over needed repairs or what exactly qualifies as a defect, a new home warranty can come in handy. Because a new home warranty is backed up by a third party, someone else can step in to settle disputes, keeping both your interests and the builder's interests in mind.

WARNING

You may want to think twice about your purchase if your builder isn't offering a warranty. If you're buying a condo, make sure you get a warranty for the unit and that the condominium board has a separate warranty that covers the common elements.

Putting it in writing

Verbal agreements don't usually hold much clout. If you notice any defects and want to make a claim, you *must* put the complaint in writing to your builder and keep a copy for your records. You should also send a copy to the issuer of the warranty to keep on file in case of a dispute. Taking photographs is also a good way to document problems.

Many builders will give you a form to fill out; otherwise, organize your concerns room by room and include as much detail as possible about the nature of the problem. These documents should always include the plan number, lot number, and address of the residence in question. Oh, and of course, you have to file before the end of the warranty period.

Handling things if they go awry

Your warranty should outline a reasonable time frame in which builders must fix any problems that have been brought to their attention. *Reasonable*, unfortunately, can mean a lot of things. One plan, for instance, gives builders up to a year to rectify defects. So, if the light fixture in your bathroom doesn't work, you may be sitting in the dark for a long, long time. Getting your brother to rewire may not be a good idea. Most plans won't automatically reimburse you if you go ahead and get someone else to do the work, and some repairs may void the warranty altogether.

WARNING

If you're considering buying a converted condominium, you may not qualify for the NHWP, because although the individual units are new, the outside of the building isn't. Check with what provincial regulations require as well as individual policies to see if the unit you're considering qualifies, and always get the details of the developer's warranty in writing.

Preparing for the Preclosing Walk-Through

Taking a preclosing walk-through is more common in some parts of Canada than in others. In some provinces, this *walk-through* is a term of the contract that allows you to inspect the property and to be sure that the seller hasn't neglected any contractual obligations before handing over the home. Your agent will arrange a time that is suitable for you and the seller, and will accompany you on the walk-through; an hour should be sufficient.

TIP

Try to schedule your final walk-through a day or two before your scheduled closing date. Leaving little time between your final check and the actual closing ensures that you'll definitely take possession of the home in exactly the condition you want. Hopefully, the home will be empty of all the seller's possessions, so you'll find it easier to imagine where you'll put the grand piano, but chances are the home will be waiting for a final packing. This is a perfect time to take measurements for curtains and blinds, carpets, and large pieces of furniture. You may also want to bring in paint chips or wallpaper samples — or your decorator — if you plan to change the decor.

WARNING

When you take your final preclosing walk-through, check that all the *chattels* are in place — that all items the sellers agreed to leave with the house are still present. Items like the fridge and stove are commonly indicated as chattels in a contract of purchase and sale. Besides confirming that the home contains all the chattels agreed on contractually, your preclosing walk-through gives you a chance to check that everything you *expected* would stay with the house is still there. Some people, for reasons yet to be determined, take fixtures with them. They cut off phone jacks and remove light switch panels, towel racks, cupboard doors, toilet roll dispensers, and sometimes fridges. If you find out early, you can discuss the issues with your lawyer before your final exchange with the seller.

The walk-through can also be a good opportunity to talk to the seller, if she happens to be home. You may be able to find out the neighbourhood gossip and helpful tidbits like which neighbourhood kids can mow lawns and shovel snow, are reliable and responsible babysitters, and other pieces of information that can help you adjust to life in your new home.

Chapter **12**

Closing Time: Closing Events and Moving Day

When finalizing your home purchase and making the property your own, three critical dates are the closing date, the date of possession or occupancy, and moving day.

Stripped to its bare bones, on the *closing day*, sometimes called *completion day*, you'll sign papers (actually, your lawyer will review the paperwork with you and get your signature a day or two prior to closing day), pay for your new home, and receive title. What happens on closing day depends on what you do before closing day. If your real estate team is well organized, you may be able to simply wait for your lawyer or agent to call and congratulate you that your home is now registered in your name and the keys are yours.

The date the keys are handed over to you is known as the *possession date.* It may be the same as the closing date, or as long as a month afterwards, depending on the circumstances. You can plan your move and make the necessary arrangements for your great leap forward into home ownership with this extra time. Occasionally, the possession date is also moving day — the day on which you get the keys and take physical possession of the property, and the moving company delivers your personal possessions to the property so you can make it your own. However, it's often wise — because of everything moving involves — to leave a few days between taking possession and moving in, just in case you want to make any improvements.

This chapter walks you through what's involved from closing day to move-in.

Identifying What You Sign

All the professionals on your team — your real estate agent, your lawyer, and your lender — will be able to give you an idea of what remains to be done on the closing day and your degree of involvement, as in what you're required to do. You probably don't need us to remind you to read all documents and raise any concerns you have *before* you sign.

How does closing work? First of all, you have to read, clarify, and sign the following:

» **Mortgage:** Also called a *deed of trust,* this includes all the details of the mortgage agreement and, typically, allows that the lender can take possession of your property if you default on the loan.

» **Mortgage note:** Also known as a *commitment letter,* this guarantees you'll pay your mortgage and lays out the terms of the loan, when and how it must be paid, any penalties that may apply, and so on.

» **Affidavits:** Depending on the laws of your province or the requirements of your lender, you may sign several of these. Your lawyer can explain the implications of each. For example, often buyers are asked to confirm that the property will be their primary residence (in other words, that the property hasn't been purchased as a secondary residence or investment property).

» **Down payment cheque:** To seal the deal, you have to hand over 5, 10, 15, or 20 percent of the purchase price (less the deposit) — whatever you've promised to pay to start making the house your home. Payment is often via a certified cheque, but your bank may directly debit the amount from your account.

» **Title:** The transfer of title (registration of change of ownership) is done at the land titles office. The seller must sign a warranty deed stating that no new loans have been taken out against the title and it's clear for the new owners. A lawyer or notary must notarize this deed, and it should be registered at the land titles office. If the land titles office happens to be busy on the date you planned to close, the title may be transferred on the next business day (if it's a

Friday, this would be a Monday — unless the Monday falls on a provincial or federal holiday, in which case it would be the next business day). The good news is that in this world of computers, your lawyer can do many title transfers online. However, glitches can happen, even here!

Recognizing What You Pay

We explain closing costs in Chapter 4, but here is an overview of the costs you're expected to pay on closing day:

- **Down payment:** You pay the portion not covered by the deposit that accompanied the offer.

- **Mortgage costs:** You may pay some or all of the following:
  - Application fee (usually waived)
  - Assumption fee
  - Processing fee
  - Prepaid interest
  - Mortgage insurance
  - CMHC insurance
  - GST/HST on the insurance premiums

- **Insurance:** You pay for insurance on your property. Purchasing this insurance before closing is necessary.

- **Lawyer's fee:** You usually pay between $300 and $800, not including disbursements. Discuss this fee with your lawyer early in the process. Your lawyer's fees are subject to GST or HST, depending on the province.

- **Lawyer's disbursements:** You usually pay between $250 and $600 in addition to the lawyer's fee. This amount not only covers the cost of more complicated procedures your lawyer performs on your behalf, such as the title search, but also covers miscellaneous everyday tasks like courier fees and photocopies.

- **Adjustments:** You pay money due to the seller for prepaid taxes and utilities.

- **Land transfer taxes:** You pay provincial tax on a home purchase, ranging from 0.5 to 4 percent and beyond. Some provinces grant first-time home buyers an exemption. Toronto also charges a municipal land transfer tax in addition to the provincial tax. Check with your agent, lender, or lawyer to see which taxes are charged in your city and province.

>> **GST/HST:** You pay GST or HST (depending on which province you live in) on a newly built home as well as on a home that has been substantially renovated. You may be eligible for a rebate depending on the purchase price of the property.

REMEMBER

Lawyers offer packages that include all disbursements, which means you know all the costs from the get-go. When you're collecting quotes from different lawyers, make sure you ask whether disbursements can be included in the prices quoted.

TIP

Most people pay closing costs with a certified cheque or bank draft. This means having sufficient funds available to cover the costs. Be sure to give yourself enough time have these funds available in one account. If you're wiring substantial amounts of money from investments or from a partner's account, you may need a couple of days to process the transfers. Most lawyers will let you know well in advance of the closing date how much money you'll need, but make a point of double-checking the closing charges with your lawyer at least one business day before closing. Be sure to have extra funds (or a spare credit card) on hand in case the total is more than you expected.

Taking Possession on the Possession Date

In some cases, the *possession date,* the day you get the keys, is the same as the completion or closing date. If so, the seller's lawyer or agent gives your lawyer or agent the keys when the title is transferred, and she'll bring them back to you.

When you have the keys in your hand, at the open door of your new home — now you can celebrate! The drapes, appliances, and any other chattels that were specified in the contract should be right where you last saw them. But really, this is the fun part: The home is legally, officially, and absolutely yours, so do what you will. Enjoy.

You've been in decision mode for so long that you may just be in shock now that you're sitting comfortably in your living room with no more people to meet or papers to sign. So your mind starts to wander, and you start to think that maybe you should have tried harder for that house with the brand new turquoise and orange kitchen . . . it was kind of funky, after all . . .

Instead of wondering "What if?" concentrate on the "What now?" Nothing's stopping you from painting your kitchen turquoise and orange. It's your home now — and you can personalize it the way you want. Congratulations!

Making Your Moving Experience One to Remember

Hopefully you had a good party when you got possession — because your life is about to turn upside down. Moving ranks as one of the ten most stressful events in a person's life. Why? Well, technically, moving means transporting all your worldly possessions from one place to another. What it really means is moving your life. From finding a new school for your children to figuring out where the best place is to get pizza in the middle of the night, moving involves more than packing tape and a loaded van. Moving your stuff may take as little as a few hours. Moving your life will take a lot longer.

Even though moving may be the furthest thing from your mind as you run around making arrangements for your grand purchase, the more organized you are about moving, the less stress you'll have as the closing date approaches (besides, you want to save all that worrying for real problems that may arise). The best way to tackle the workload is to create a list of tasks that need to get done and a calendar that sets deadlines for accomplishing them. The lists in some of the following sections give you a head start, but keep in mind that every situation is unique. We suggest jotting down extra to-dos as you think of them in your phone or in a notebook.

TIP

A wealth of relocation resources is just a few clicks of the mouse away. The power company in your province and the local chamber of commerce in the new town you're moving to are all ready to help with checklists. Canada Post offers a helpful guide, because they'll be the ones handling deliveries to your new door. See www. canadapost.ca/makeyourmove for more details.

Moving day versus the day of possession

You actually may not take possession on moving day. There's a good chance you'll have plenty else to do before moving in, including making sure that everything in your new house is in good order and ready for your arrival. You may have some extra time — or plan on some extra time — to undertake minor renovations, such as painting or other tasks that are ideally done when the house is empty of furniture, children, and pets.

Regardless of how long after the date you take possession you move in, the real work of becoming a homeowner is about to begin.

Timing is everything

When you move can have as much of an impact on your wallet as what you move and how you move it. You can sometimes save a lot of money by choosing your moving date strategically.

Keep in mind that, like hotels, rental and moving companies often have off-season rates geared to times when demand is at its lowest. Pricing rates generally revolve around renters' patterns. For instance, a truck rental company may charge you less if you're not moving within the first or last week of a month.

People want to move when it's most convenient. Generally, this means that rates get hiked from Thursday to Sunday, because most people want to move sometime around the weekend. Consumer demand also drops dramatically during snow season. After all, who would want to move in the middle of a snowstorm? (Answer: someone who wants to save money!) Accordingly, May to September is high time for moving, while October to April can land you a deal. You should be able to negotiate a discount if you

>> Move during an off-peak time (October to April).

>> Choose a day that falls early in the week (Monday to Wednesday) rather than a weekend.

>> Pick a date that falls outside of the roving-renter period (first and last week of each month).

LESS IS MORE

One big way to save on moving costs — and hassle — is to move only what you'd really like to keep. Not only will you save the cost of moving these articles, you'll also save the chore of packing and unpacking them. If you're moving across the country rather than across town, consider selling the furniture instead of taking it with you: The cost of moving it may be greater than purchasing new furniture when you arrive at your destination. You can make some money by holding a garage sale and selling what you don't want to take along. Or you can do a good deed and give what you don't want to local charities like a local women's shelter, refugee relocation agency, or charity-run thrift shop.

WARNING

Whatever you do, try your very best to avoid moving from June 30 to July 2. In most provinces, and overwhelmingly so in Montreal where many leases have traditionally ended on June 30, Canada Day is the busiest moving day of the year. But even if a lease isn't involved, it's the end of school and the beginning of summer holidays — an ideal time to pick up stakes and get used to a new neighbourhood before another school year begins. Unfortunately, movers will book up sooner and many will charge higher rates. We've even heard of people being forced by dishonest movers to pay more money than the amount in the contract, just because those villains know that all other movers are fully booked and their victims have no choice after their boxes, furniture, and assorted bottle cap collections are in the truck.

Moving your life

Be prepared for the long haul. When you start trying to take care of all the little details, you'll realize that your life is a lot more complicated than you thought it was. If you're moving to a new city, for instance, medical, dental, and even veterinary records for every member of your household will have to be sent on. You'll also want to track down a qualified provider for each of these services. A simple task like redirecting your magazine subscriptions can require a month's notice or more, even if you're just moving down the block. Your lawyer may take care of some of these details, like water and property taxes, but the rest is up to you.

TIP

If you're being relocated, and you're moving at least 40 kilometres closer to your new school or job, your expenses incurred by the relocation (such as meals, travel costs, real estate fees, the works) are tax deductible. These expenses include the cost of shipping and storing your belongings and up to 15 days' temporary accommodation near either your current or future home. Visit the Canada Revenue Agency website (www.cra-arc.gc.ca) for details, including eligibility requirements and the necessary claim forms.

Moving your stuff

Before you begin sorting out what you want to take with you to your new home, consider that one person's trash is another's treasure. If you can, have everyone in your household participate in the weeding process. That way, you won't end up accidentally discarding a beloved object. Children need to be part of this process so that they'll understand why old favourite sweaters have suddenly disappeared. You may want to encourage small children to keep a memento, like a prized teddy bear. Soon they'll have to adjust to a strange new environment and may find themselves hankering for an old friend.

Decluttering your home takes time, especially if you've been in it for any length of time. Take a serious look at your attic, basement, closets, and other storage spaces. You may be surprised (or scared) by what you find there. Don't forget the garden shed and garage. These places are chockfull of items you can't take with you, including flammable, explosive, and other hazardous materials. To make the job a little easier, as you go through your belongings, keep the following tips in mind:

>> **Get rid of anything you've outgrown.** This especially includes bulky items like that old pair of skis with size-five boots and bindings.

>> **Get rid of duplicates.** You don't need five kitchen spatulas, 12 guest towels, or four sets of dishes. Take just what you need, donating items in good shape or tossing those that are at or nearing the end of their useful lives.

>> **Use the two-year rule.** Unless it's a vintage piece, part with anything you haven't worn in the past two years or gadgets that have outlived their usefulness. There's no time like the present to be ruthless. If your sweater shaver hasn't seen the light of day in over five years, it's time to get rid of it — no matter what you paid for it originally. Same goes for the carrot juicer that's gone untouched ever since you moved on from your macrobiotic diet.

>> **Look at your new home's floor plans to evaluate what will fit in and what won't.** You may discover that you're not truly wedded to the loveseat Sparky the cat has been using as a scratching post for the past five years. Or that your grandmother's kitchen table doesn't look good in your new stainless steel kitchen.

>> **Work your way up.** Instead of doing a bit in every room in the house, approach the job one room at a time. Start in the basement, then move on to the main floor and keep going (or start on the top floor and work your way down — whatever works best for you). You'll have a better sense of accomplishment if you see the house getting organized step by step.

>> **Scrap it, but not literally.** Some things you'll want to keep — just keep them organized. Put photographs, important newspaper clippings, or your children's artwork in albums, or create a scrapbook.

>> **Recycle all that paper.** Even in the age of the Internet, paper clutter is almost inevitable. Put old newspapers and flyers in the recycling box, donate your paperback mystery novels to charity, and invest in a small filing cabinet to store what you absolutely need.

>> **Clear off surfaces.** Colognes, sunscreens, and cosmetics on the bathroom counter make it look small and crowded. In the kitchen, decide whether or not the mixer, the blender, and jars of multicoloured pasta need to be on display, or if they can be stored in the cupboard.

>> **Put your toys away.** Sure, your knick-knacks and collectibles are *trés* cool, but they also take up a lot of space. Pack them in advance, and rent a cheap storage space to keep nonessential stuff until moving day.

>> **Keep it up.** Unfortunately, you can't just do this once and then be done with it. Your hard work will be wasted if you don't make an effort to keep your house clutter-free. Try spending 15 minutes a day putting things where they belong. It's not a fun 15 minutes, but it's well worth it.

You may also want to start thinking about your storehouse of food. Generally, transporting food isn't worth the hassle, especially perishables like cheese and meat that can spoil en route. If you have hundreds of dollars' worth of ham hocks in a deep-freezer, you'll want to be sure to eat them before moving day. You may well find that you have two months' worth of food in the home — and it all has to disappear by the time the last box is loaded into the van. In fact, planning on eating takeout the night before moving day is a good idea — or better yet, go to a restaurant and celebrate.

Packing it all in

Packing is a loathsome chore. It always takes longer than you think it will, and you'll always need more packing supplies than you planned on. That said, we know some ways to make packing — and unpacking — a lot less painful.

If you can, give yourself plenty of time to pack. Otherwise, you'll end up throwing things haphazardly into boxes or, worse, not packing them at all. Count on packing being a big job, not a last-minute chore. Trust us: You're sure to find that you have more stuff than you thought you did.

Here are some essential supplies:

>> **Boxes:** Big boxes, little boxes, picture boxes, and bike boxes. Boxes are far easier to pack into a van than irregular shapes and will save you and your movers space and time. Use new materials, even though you may be tempted to pick up some discards at your local grocer. Used boxes may not be clean or sturdy enough for the job.

>> **Tissue paper or old newsprint and bubble wrap:** Lots of it. Tissue paper is ideal for wrapping small objects, like coffee mugs, to prevent breakage. Although newspaper may seem like a good, cheap, and environmentally friendly alternative, it blackens whatever's wrapped inside. Fortunately, you can get ink-free options from your favourite packing or home improvement store or online.

>> **Packing tape with a tape dispenser and extra rolls:** This puts the final seal on every box. Jake, who works in the shipping department at a local bookstore, recommends a crisscross pattern around the box for added strength.

>> **Big markers:** Indicate the destination and an abbreviated list of the contents of each box.

Before the packing begins, photocopy the floor plans of your new home, clearly marking each room with labels like Bedroom A, Bedroom B, Bathroom A, Bathroom B, and so on. Give everyone a copy, and arm your crew with markers. Then, pack the boxes by room, labelling each box appropriately when it's full. You may also want to micro-label, indicating which kitchen cupboard or dresser drawer the contents belong to. The movers will (or at least, they should) use these labels as directions, putting each box in its rightful place. If you keep a running list of the boxes and what's inside, you'll have a full inventory by the time the job is complete. When it comes time to unpack, everything will magically end up where it belongs. You won't have to move heavy boxes from room to room, nor will you have to guess what's in each one. This is a simple trick that will save you a lot of headaches.

TIP

Pack with care. After you're all packed, you'll have very little control over what happens to your boxes en route: They may get jostled around in the truck, stacked one on top of the other, or (worse still!) accidentally dropped. Packing in bubble wrap or tissue paper cradles your belongings. Towels and other linens can also double as padding. Large appliances, like refrigerators, often require special handling before and after a move.

Beware the random packer: If your partner or children are helping you, make sure they understand your system. Deciding you need to redo their work will probably create tension you'd all be better off without!

TIP

After everything's packed, resist the urge to flee the scene without one last walk-through. Check every closet, shelf, and cupboard to make sure you've left nothing behind. Kids are natural snoops and are great at this sort of thing. Pretend it's a treasure hunt, and they'll most certainly find the antique ornaments you hid away five years ago and forgot about.

Moving it yourself versus hiring professional movers

Figuring out the best way to move into your new place depends on a few things:

>> How much stuff you have

>> The size of your budget

>> The time you have to spend

>> The distance you're moving

>> The number of large friends with strong backs who enjoy heavy lifting that you have at your disposal

If you're moving from a one-bedroom apartment to a house or if you're a minimalist, you may be able to save a few bucks and move it all yourself. Well, not completely by yourself — unless you're a professional wrestler — but with the help of a few strong, not clumsy, friends and family members. Get on the phone and start calling in those favours. (Keep in mind, if you call on your friends for help moving, be prepared to return the favour.) If you decide to take this route, understand that it's a big responsibility and you'll be in charge of the packing, loading, driving, and unloading, not to mention making sure that any valuables arrive unbroken. Depending on the load, you can rent a small trailer or a large truck (which you'll pay for either by the hour or by the day), but if you're nervous about manoeuvring a beast of a vehicle, some companies will provide a driver. We can't emphasize physical safety enough. Weigh your well-being and that of your friends against hiring professionals to do the heavy lifting.

TIP

Be good to your friends, family, and movers. Make sure you have a cooler stocked with plenty of cold drinks for when you arrive at the new house. If someone starts to get cranky from all the heavy lifting, tell him to take a break and send him out to pick up the pizza.

Convenience and less stress are good reasons to hire a team of professional movers. Also, if you're relocating from Dartmouth to Iqaluit and you don't have time to drive the truck cross-country, then your only choice is professional movers. Moving costs more this way, but if your budget permits, you may be happy to leave it to the pros. They're experienced and know where to place your antiques in the truck so they don't break. And because you won't have to spend all your time saying "One, two, three, lift!" you can focus on other things, like making sure you haven't forgotten one of your kids or your dog. Some companies charge on an hourly basis if the move is small, and others charge based on a combination of things, like how many movers you need, the type of furniture you have (a piano and a marble-topped dining table will up the price), and the number of boxes you've packed. The travel time and distance are always factored into the cost as well. Call or email a couple of different moving companies for quotes, and ask your real estate agent for recommendations.

Keep in mind that you can really move in style by having the moving company do all the packing for you too! Though this will add significantly to your costs, you will be able to take advantage of insurance if anything they have packed breaks during transport. Make sure the insurance terms are clearly stated in the contract. There are usually time limits on making a claim for a damaged item.

The Canadian Association of Movers (www.mover.net) has a searchable online directory of its members. The goal of this group is to help the buying public access credible, professional moving services. The association expects its members to adhere to its system of professional ethics and standards — so check the database for members that are approved. While you're online, check with the Better Business Bureau (BBB) for any complaints that may have been filed against the movers on your short list. Do a BBB search by typing "Better Business Bureau" plus your city into your search engine.

Although some moving companies are small operations, you'll find some online with fairly sophisticated websites that let you plug in your information (how far you're moving, how many rooms' worth of stuff you have, whether or not you have a baby grand piano) and receive a price quote by email. These online tools are great for budgeting for the big day, but we recommend that you also talk to someone from the moving company so that you can get the closest estimation of the cost before you sign anything.

Again, as with most things associated with a real estate transaction, asking satisfied friends for recommendations is often extremely helpful. Ask questions. The national moving chain you decide on may have a sterling reputation in general, but the local franchisee may give disappointing service.

TIP

When dealing with movers (well, heck, when dealing with any professional), your level of confidence in getting good service will grow if you've used referrals, interviewed the moving company, and have a written contract that has been clearly explained to you. Some movers may offer you a terrific deal, such as a very low price, as long as you agree to forgo a written contract and you pay in cash. Agree to this deal, and you'll be open to serious risks when the work begins. You may encounter poor service quality, no warranties, and extra costs that keep piling on. Without a contract, you won't have any course of action to deal with those cheaters.

REMEMBER

Moving companies range from small and local — one-person operations run with a small truck and a cell phone — to huge operations with fleets of vehicles. But before booking any movers, always ask questions. Find out how BBB, and if they're fully bonded and insured. Working with a reputable, experienced company may cost a couple of extra bucks per hour, but you'll gain peace of mind. Moving is stressful enough without worrying about damage to your valuables, or your stuff ending up in Chicoutimi instead of Chibougamau.

Being Organized: The Moving Timeline

Trust us, organization is so important as you work toward your move. Use this moving timeline as a reference while you pack, make calls, wrangle with your movers, and generally tear your hair out.

Two months and counting

Hey, it's never too early to get things rolling! Did we mention now is a good time to start packing?

» **Start saving!** Moving is a huge expense. If you start budgeting in advance for movers, insurance, supplies, utility transfers, child (and pet) care, and the bevy of incidental costs, your wallet won't be so surprised when the bills start rolling in. Remember, too, to factor in the costs after you arrive: Painting, housekeeping, and carpentry work should all be taken into account.

» **Begin the pick-and-choose process.** Decide what you want to take with you and what you want to leave behind. Plan to sell any discards — at a garage sale, for instance, or through online services such as Kijiji, Craigslist, or Facebook Marketplace — at least a month and a half in advance.

» **Start scouting out your new neighbourhood.** Speak to the principal of your children's new school to take care of transfer details and find out about important dates. While you're there, find a neighbourhood restaurant where you can feast after the big move. You won't be in any mood to cook.

» **Book the movers, van, or truck.** You don't want to get stuck with your things all packed up and no way to move them. We suggest making your reservation as soon as you have a firm purchase agreement on your new home, especially if you're moving around the first of the month, when the rest of the world is doing the same thing.

One month to moving day

The number of people who apparently care that you're moving is amazing. Here's what to do to keep them in the know. Oh yeah, and keep filling those boxes.

» **If you rent your current premises, make sure to give your landlord written notice of your intention to move if you haven't already done so.** You'll typically need to give at least one month's notice to avoid penalties, so giving notice will mark the final countdown to your move.

>> **Ask your doctor, dentist, and veterinarian for referrals and arrange for the transfer of records.** While you're giving notice to everyone else, don't forget the health professionals who look after you and your loved ones, including your pets. Ask them for referrals to practitioners in your new neighbourhood, if needed.

>> **Contact providers of utilities and Internet service.** While you'll technically some leeway in hooking up your phone service — it usually takes only a few days — getting in touch with the power company, Internet provider, and phone company (if you still have a landline) in advance is a good idea. Thanks to mobile service, many people take their phone numbers with them when they move, but you'll want to make sure people know where to reach you the days and weeks after your move. You don't want to be disconnected from people or power when you move.

>> **Order mail forwarding service from Canada Post at least two weeks in advance of your move.** For a period of four months, any mail that is sent to you at your old residence will be redirected to your new address, and you'll pay only about $55 for the convenience. A year's worth of forwarded mail costs $85 (at current rates) and should give you plenty of time to make sure all items are transferred over. Alternatively, this may be a great time to go paperless, if you haven't already.

>> **Transfer subscriptions.** Contact the subscription office of any magazines or newspapers you subscribe to and inform them of your new address, letting them know when to begin delivering to your new location. Alternatively, you may wish to wait till after you move, updating your address as issues are forwarded to your new address.

>> **Start packing nonessential items.** This can include trinkets and knick-knacks, off-season sports equipment, and books. This really eases the packing load as the big day gets nearer.

One week before

Now the countdown's really begun. Take deep breaths. Keep packing.

>> **Pick up any dry cleaning, shoe repairs, or other items left with local businesses.** Return any outstanding library books (and that glue gun you borrowed from your neighbour three months ago).

>> **Call a locksmith to arrange to have your locks changed after you have possession of the house.** While you might have possession of the home, you want to make sure you're the only one with access. Even though the sale might have completed on good terms, there may be keys with neighbours, old

tenants and who knows who else. Securing access by changing the locks will make sure you have full possession.

» **Get boxes if you need more, and keep packing.** You'll find tips to make the process easier in the section "Packing it all in" earlier in this chapter.

» **Get rid of your kids and pets!** Having children and pets underfoot can slow down movers and increase the chances of an accident. If possible, make arrangements to send young children to a best friend's for a sleepover on the evening before moving day. You should also board pets for the few days around the move. (The last thing you want to do is hold up the moving process because Sparky the cat escaped and is nowhere to be found.)

The day before

Look at all those boxes! Did you know you had so much stuff?

» **Stock up on snack food and bottled water to keep you going through moving day.** Consider preparing some sandwiches, too.

» **Buy paper plates and plastic cutlery and cups.** You can use them until you can unearth the real things.

» **Deliver Sparky to the kennel or to a generous friend so that the fur doesn't fly on moving day.** At the same time, drive the kids over to a best friend's house for their sleepover.

» **Confirm your movers.** You may have full confidence in your movers, but mistakes happen. It pays to confirm that they know where they're supposed to be at what time and on what day. Your moving experience will be memorable for all the wrong reasons if you're left waiting for movers at 14 West 15th Street and they've gone to 15 West 14th Avenue.

» **Designate a box or bag for essentials.** This box includes just what you need at the last minute, including bedding and pillows, medication, and toiletries.

The big day

This is it — the day you've been working toward for the past two months. You probably wish you could just go away somewhere and leave it to the movers. Bad idea. We suggest you stick it out until the bitter end.

» **Be there when the trucks arrive.** You want to be able to give instructions to the movers and to point out any items that need special handling.

>> **Stay out of the way.** A good moving team works like clockwork: They have a coordinated way of moving as a group and an efficient method for packing a truck. Although you may think carrying boxes out to the truck will speed things up and save you money, lending a hand may actually impede progress.

>> **Count the boxes as they're loaded onto the truck to make sure everything makes it on board.** Because you've left the heavy lifting to others, you can supervise to make sure they're doing it right! You know what has to be loaded, meaning you can keep track and make sure that it gets done. (And if the weather's hot, don't forget to have some water or other refreshment on hand to make sure the movers stay fresh.)

>> **Do a final check around the house after everything is loaded.** Look inside cupboards, closets, and the garage. If you're leaving rental premises, you may need to do a final cleaning and have the landlord or property agent check the condition of the premises so that you can receive your security deposit (if it hasn't been applied to the final month's rent).

>> **Collect your children and pets after the move is complete.** Your new home won't be the same without them!

After the move

That is, after you've slept. You should consider the following:

>> **Tell the government you've moved.** Different provinces have different regulations regarding change of address notifications. In Ontario, for instance, you're obliged to change your driver's licence and health card within ten days of moving. Most provinces enable you to make the change yourself online for some if not all provincial agencies and services. Be sure to let the Canada Revenue Agency know you've moved, too, especially if you operate a home-based business. A list of common government agencies you might want to contact are here: www.canada.ca/en/government/change-address.html.

>> **If you're a first-time homeowner, stock up on some of the basics.** These basics can include items such as a mop, stepladder, drill, hammer, screwdriver set, wrench, snow shovel, rake, hedge clippers, garden hose, outdoor broom, light bulbs . . . . You get the idea. Otherwise, you'll end up going to the local hardware shop every other day for a month. If you're planning a housewarming party, make the most of your friends' generosity and ask them to bring an item on your "stuff needed" list. If you're planning a painting party, make sure your friends bring brushes, sandpaper, and paint. When Marcus first moved into his new home, his friends put together a cooler full of stuff they thought he would need, including duct tape, bandages, a flashlight, and slippers.

Try not to second-guess yourself. Chances are, after you've bought your home you'll start seeing For Sale signs on all sorts of other dream homes. You'll begin to wonder, should we have waited longer to buy? Did we make a hasty decision? Was this the right choice for us? Doing so is normal. Don't regret your choice. Lots of hard work, careful consideration, and late-night debate went into your purchase. Remember what you discovered throughout your search: The outside of a house gives no reliable indication of its interior.

Accept that every new place you move to will cause you to feel a bit unsettled at first. The rooms may seem smaller (empty homes often do, with no furniture to give them a sense of scale), or the room colours may seem different than you remembered. Often this feeling will pass as you start to put up your own pictures, get your furniture where you want it, and put your favourite sheets on your bed. You'll need some adjustment time before you can move about the house in the dark without bumping into anything.

5

Preparing to Sell Your Home

Determine whether the time is right to sell or whether you should buy, then sell, or vice versa. Figure out whether you can afford to move and whether you can find something better or more suitable than what you have. If you decide you don't want to sell, your options include refinancing and reverse mortgages if your goal is to free up equity.

Understand the market value for your home and the tax implications of any proceeds from the sale and then discover how to reduce your exposure to taxes.

Prepare your home for sale through home improvements and an appealing listing in order to maximize exposure to the market and buyer interest.

Know the importance and value of inspections and appraisals when selling your home and how to use them to your advantage.

IN THIS CHAPTER

» **Determining your wants and needs**

» **Identifying good reasons to stay put**

» **Identifying good reasons to sell**

» **Timing the sale**

Chapter **13**

Deciding To Sell (or Stay)

hange is the only constant. There comes a time when everyone has to move on, no matter how good or happy the circumstances are. When it comes to the house or apartment you live in, family size, economic factors, and meeting your needs and wants all influence your living space. A starter home may give way to one with room for kids or a granny suite for aging relatives. You might finally get a windfall that makes your dream home possible. Or, you might stay in your home till you can't take care of it any longer and the task of selling it falls to someone else. Ultimately, however, you can't stay where you are forever.

A major change is scary, but you may also decide, after seriously considering the alternatives, that you don't really need to move — you simply need to reorganize your current home. This chapter explains how to sort out your priorities so you can be sure that you really do want to sell your home and know how the sale will make a positive difference to your life. Taking the time to consider how selling your home affects your life helps you avoid costly and unnecessary mistakes, and ensures that you'll be satisfied with your choices. Thinking it through and deciding what you really need gives you incredible peace of mind.

Making the Big Decision

You may choose a house that fits your lifestyle, but don't forget that where you live will also influence your lifestyle. The amount you spend on housing determines how much money you can save for things like vacations, your retirement, or your kids' education. The location of your home dictates how much time you spend getting to work, school, and shopping — and how much money you spend on transportation, utilities, taxes, and maintenance. Your home also affects your social life and leisure time. The following sections identify some of the key factors to take into account when you're considering selling, including the personal, financial and logistical reasons for making a move or staying put.

Identifying the reasons why people sell

Even if you love your home, your life will change in unpredictable ways. Recognizing that you can't always build what you need or change the neighbourhood to fit the new you, finding a new place to call home is often your only option. If any of the following conditions describe your situation, then you're probably ready to sell:

>> **The location of your home is unsuitable.** If you have a job offer in a great location with long-term employment potential or if you're ready to retire and look forward to the security and low maintenance of a retirement community, selling your house makes a lot of sense. (And if you're relocating for professional reasons, you may get a tax break on all your moving expenses — refer to Chapter 14 for more details.)

>> **Your house is too small or too big.** If you and your family need more space and you don't want to renovate or you can't get a building permit to put an extension on the back of the house, moving is probably your best bet. On the flip side, if the last of your six kids has finally moved out of your seven-bedroom home, it may be time to downsize — before any of them decide to move back!

>> **Life throws you a curveball.** A traumatic event like a divorce or the death of a family member may force you to sell or prompt you to make a fresh start. Take time to review your financial situation and personal goals so that you can be sure that you really want to move.

>> **Life is fine, but the neighbourhood isn't.** Maybe your life hasn't changed a bit, but somehow the neighbourhood has. If the unremarkable home you bought 20 years ago is now the best house on the street, it's probably a good time to move.

Recognizing reasons to stay put

Most people hope things will change for the better, but that's not always the case. Sometimes it's best to work with what you have, working inside the ticky-tacky box of your suburban row home than trying to find someplace new. Sometimes, the financial consequences of moving mean you should wait until the financial impact is in your favour. If the following two points apply to you, consider waiting to sell.

REMEMBER

>> **Renovating is a viable option.** If you're after more space, a new look, modernization, or greater efficiency, renovating your home may be the wisest course of action. If you live in a great neighbourhood, consider building an addition. Renovations may be a steal compared to the transaction costs of selling, and they may also add to the resale value of your house. See Chapter 8 for more details on which home renovation projects add the most value when you do decide to sell your house.

If you want to move because your house needs some costly repairs, investigate your options carefully. You may end up paying for the repairs anyway because the next buyer's offer will require you to cover them. Buyers often overestimate repair costs in order to protect themselves from the worst-case scenario, so it's better to keep your house in good order unless you don't need the proceeds from the sale.

>> **Your finances are shaky.** If you're already having trouble living within your means, then delaying the purchase of your dream home probably makes sense. Instead, consider refinancing your existing home to try to get your financial house in order. Even if you're thinking about moving to a less expensive house, keep in mind that you'll incur plenty of one-time expenses when you sell your house, buy a new one, and then move. Factoring in these expenses may mean you have to look for accommodation in a range several thousand dollars below what you initially thought you could afford. If you can possibly get your debts under control while staying in your current home, it will relieve your financial and emotional stress. Speak to a financial advisor for guidance.

Taking stock of wants and needs

If you're thinking of moving, take stock of what you have and what you need. Don't try to keep track of all the reasons you want to sell in your head. Put together lists of your likes, dislikes, needs, wants, and priorities (we provide guidelines for such a list in Chapter 7). Pay particular attention to the physical features you want or need in a home and your financial status and goals. Both of these considerations may be reasons for you to stay in your current home.

REMEMBER

Not all of your reasons to move carry equal weight. After you've made your list of likes, dislikes, needs, and wants, start thinking about what your priorities are and which factors are most important. When you feel you've got a handle on the issues, organize your list according to your priorities.

Organize your likes and dislikes for your current home, as well as your needs and wants for your future home, into three categories: property, location, and finances. In this section, we explore each of these categories in discussing your decision to stay or sell.

Home sweet home: Your property

What makes your house a great place to live? Consider aesthetics like style, decor, and view, as well as practicalities like an eat-in kitchen, a two-car garage, room sizes and total area, and plenty of natural light. What's lacking in your living space? Do you find yourself coveting your neighbour's stunning stone fireplace, landscaped backyard, and sunny solarium?

Often, people change homes because their needs change. Room for a patio and garden may be an absolute must when you're retiring and finally have daylight time to spend outside. Perhaps your home office has to expand beyond the corner under the stairs.

Make a list with two columns: one for all the benefits of your current home, and the other for all your dislikes concerning your living situation. Then make a second two-column list of the items that you and your family may need now or in the future, and all the things you don't absolutely *need* but would still give an arm and a leg for.

How significant a change do you need to make? Look at your lists, and think about whether your home can grow with your needs. If you build the sunroom that you've always wanted or finish the attic to add an extra bedroom, keeping the home you have makes sense. But adding one extra bedroom may not be sufficient if you're planning to have three more children. Be realistic about how much renovation your home can accommodate.

Location, location, location: Your neighbourhood

Look at the logistics: Is your home located in a good area that suits your needs and tastes? The location of your current home was probably the single biggest factor when you made your last move. Consider what sets the neighbourhood apart now. Are the streets nice, safe, and quiet? Are good schools, public transit, and shopping in the area? Are there job opportunities for you and your family members? Is your extended family nearby?

Just as your housing needs may change over the years, your priorities concerning location may change. You may not want to live near your favourite bar anymore, but you do want to be close to good schools for your kids. In addition to the basic physical features of your location, don't forget the intangibles. The personality of your neighbourhood may be a big factor in your happiness or dissatisfaction with where you live. Over the years, communities change as people move in and out of neighbourhoods.

Remember why you moved to your neighbourhood in the first place. Ask yourself if those reasons are still valid. Are the people still as friendly as when you first moved in? Is the crime rate still low? Are the surrounding woodlands still unspoiled? Is the air quality good? Do your neighbours still show incredible enthusiasm for Hallowe'en festivities? Make sure your list of likes and dislikes concerning your current home includes mention of the surroundings. Chapter 7 helps you size up your existing one against the others that are on offer.

TIP

Don't overlook commuting time when you consider the merits of your location. Although you may stand to earn a lot of money by selling your house in a premium location and moving farther out, it may not be worth it when the new 90-minute commute takes its toll on you and your family. The extra 45 minutes on the road may end up costing a mint in gas and vehicle costs, too. On the flip side, you may decide that the driving time is worth having more space and a large garden. You have to weigh the various benefits to make the right decision.

You may want to sell your home because you want to make a big change in location. From the big city to the suburbs, from the West Coast to the East — even though the grass may be greener or the salmon tastier on the other side, you may find the climate really isn't for you.

Looking At Your Budget: Your Finances

Think about your budget when selling. In addition to paying the mortgage on your home, you also pay for utilities, insurance, taxes, repairs, and basic maintenance (refer to Chapter 4 to help you examine your current financial picture). When you add up your current expenses versus what you'll pay for the same costs in a new home, does a move make sense? Consider doing the math, taking into account refinancing options on your current home.

Doing the math

If you're looking to reduce your expenses, then downsizing to a smaller, less expensive home or area may be the smartest thing to do. However, if you're a prosperous business owner who was once a struggling entrepreneur, you may be ready to leave the cramped starter home behind and spend some money to get yourself a big house with a two-car garage and heated indoor swimming pool.

Your financial position should factor into the pros and cons of your current home. Is it too costly? Or is it very affordable but simply not big enough for you, your spouse, and growing family?

WARNING

Don't forget that selling your house costs time and money. The transaction costs of selling a house can easily total 3 to 6 percent of the price at which you sell your property. In addition, be aware that unless you have paid off your mortgage or it's portable and can be applied to your new property, interest payments and discharge fees can take up an even larger percentage of the money you have invested in your home. (Fortunately, we discuss mortgages in the next section.)

Get a good idea of what the market offers in your price range. If you're considering selling your $400,000 townhouse to invest in a $700,000 detached house, go to open houses and compare whether the houses in that price range have all the features that you expect. You may discover that the benefits of buying a house in that price range aren't as great as you think.

The money you have tied up in your house is the money you don't have for other financial goals. Determine the minimum you'd like to have to set aside for holidays, your retirement, and your children's education. Then decide how much you have to spend on your next home.

Contemplating refinancing

If the main reason you're thinking of moving is the result of budget issues, you may want to look into refinancing your current home. Currently, you can refinance a principal residence and take up to 90 percent of the equity. But remember, after the 80 percent mark, you'll need high-ratio mortgage insurance (refer to Chapter 3), most often provided by the Canadian Mortgage and Housing Corp. (CMHC).

Refinancing can substantially reduce your monthly payments for credit cards, vehicle costs, and other expenses that may have become more than you can manage. By taking the equity in your home, paying off debt, and perhaps even getting a more favourable interest rate, you may find that you don't have to move after all.

A complete refinance may not have to be the answer, though. Your mortgage broker or lender may be able to provide you with a line of credit secured by your current home, also known as a *home equity line of credit (HELOC)*. You can use that money any way you want, and in many cases just pay the minimum interest on the line of credit each month. So, if you have a big-ticket item that won't wait, such as roof repairs, you can use your line of credit to pay for it and not have to worry about the roof over your head (literally).

SAVING YOUR HOME AND YOUR SANITY

James and Jenny bought their home eight years ago, right after they got married. The home was perfect for them then, and it's still great for them now — even though they now have two small children. But, as with any growing family, the cost of living grows with them, and with car payments, day care costs, and the fact that Jenny has gone back to school to get her MBA and won't be working for a year, those monthly payments are creating stress for the family.

James thinks they should sell the place and move somewhere more affordable — maybe even consider renting — but Jenny is dead set against moving from the neighbourhood they live in and love. Luckily, they also have 70 percent equity in their home and a good mortgage broker.

By refinancing their home, they were able to pay off the minivan, pay Jenny's tuition, get rid of their credit card balances, and even top up their RRSPs. The good news is they still have 45 percent equity in their home and a better interest rate, and aren't being nickel-and-dimed by all their bill payments. In fact, they're saving $1,200 a month!

WARNING

Refinancing your home can have fees or penalties associated with it. Be sure your banker or mortgage broker fully describes these fees to you before you proceed. Whatever you decide, make sure that you discuss all your financial options with your mortgage broker or lender. You may be surprised by the options that you have.

Considering Your Mortgage When Moving

You may want to move, but will your mortgage allow you? Although some people regularly reflect on where they want to be in five years' time, that reflection isn't on the top of most people's mind when renewing a mortgage. A lucky few can plan for a move, but most people will find ourselves faced with an opportunity or a need to relocate. You usually have three choices:

>> Pay off your mortgage.

>> Let your buyer take over your mortgage along with your home.

>> Take your mortgage with you to your new home.

The following sections take a closer look at these three choices.

Paying off your mortgage early

If you've owned your home for a long time, you may have built up substantial equity. *Equity* is the difference between the value of your property and the outstanding debts against it — for example, if your home is worth $550,000 and you have paid off all but $55,500 of your mortgage, you have accumulated $495,000 worth of equity in your home. If you have only a small portion of your mortgage to pay off, you may want to consider *discharging it* (paying it off early).

Most lenders offer financing plans to help you pay off your mortgage faster while avoiding penalty fees. The terms of your mortgage may allow you to

» Increase the amount of your mortgage payments.

» Make mortgage payments more often.

» Exercise prepayment options. (You can pay a certain amount of the principal each month or each year in addition to your regular payments, or a percentage of the principal can be paid down each time you renew your mortgage terms.)

Using any of these three options decreases the length of time required to pay off your mortgage. (We discuss mortgages in detail in Chapter 5.)

TIP

If you're a long-range planner and you're considering selling your home in the next five years, talk to your lender to see about renegotiating your terms. You may be able to modify your payment schedule or negotiate a mortgage renewal that permits you to discharge your mortgage as soon as possible without paying a penalty fee (you pay this fee to your lender as compensation for paying off your mortgage early).

WARNING

If you want to pay off your mortgage all at once, you'll likely pay a penalty fee. The amount of the penalty will depend on the original mortgage terms and interest rate that you negotiated. Make sure to read the fine print. Ask your mortgage broker or lender to explain the ramifications of paying off your mortgage early.

Some financial institutions may reduce the penalty fees you pay if your buyer also takes out a mortgage with the same institution, or if you use the same lender for your next mortgage, but don't hold your breath. Whatever arrangement you make with your lender, get a copy in writing.

Letting your buyer take over your mortgage

If you're trying to sweeten the deal for a potential buyer and your mortgage rate is lower than the current rate, consider taking advantage of the *assumability* option. This strategy isn't common, but it's one that can work in a tough market when the seller needs to give a buyer an incentive. Basically, you allow your buyer to assume your mortgage at its existing rate when purchasing your home. Assumability is often restricted to fixed-rate mortgages. (Refer to Chapter 5 for a discussion of fixed-rate and other types of mortgages.)

However, if you have a mortgage with a low and competitive interest rate, you may consider lowering the selling price rather than allowing a buyer to assume the mortgage. For example, a $25,000 reduction in the asking price might be enough to draw in a buyer, allowing you to port your mortgage and save twice as much in the interest owing on a new mortgage in just the first term. (Because the price of the home, your mortgage requirements and interest charges will vary, always be sure to run your own calculations.)

TECHNICAL STUFF

A mortgage that's assumed by the buyer isn't the same thing as a vendor *take-back mortgage*, in which the seller finances the buyer's purchase. The original lender continues to have an interest in the assumed mortgage, and the buyer takes on, or assumes, the former owner's obligations.

Here's how the assumability option works: The buyer must meet your lender's credit requirements before your lender approves the mortgage transfer from you to your buyer. Fees (which can be hefty) for the legal work and paper shuffling may be incurred. Fortunately, because most lenders now require your buyer to meet their credit and income standards, you no longer risk taking financial responsibility if the buyer defaults on the mortgage in the future as was the case in the past in some provinces.

If the buyer assumes your mortgage, you may benefit in three ways:

>> An assumable mortgage is a marketing tool; the lure of a lower interest rate may be just the enticement a buyer needs to close the deal.

>> Because your lender is already familiar with your home, the appraisal requirement may be waived, saving the buyer a few hundred dollars and making your property more attractive.

>> If the buyer assumes your mortgage, you're no longer responsible for the discharge penalty fees, which saves you even more money.

WARNING

When letting the buyer assume your mortgage, don't take it for granted that you'll be absolved of all responsibility if the new owner defaults on mortgage payments! Make absolutely sure to indemnify yourself — get it in writing — that you have no further financial obligations with regard to the mortgage after your buyer assumes it, and that you are *fully discharged* from the mortgage.

Taking your mortgage with you to your new home

Most mortgage agreements have a portability option that allows you to apply your current mortgage to a new home if you decide to sell. *Porting* your mortgage may be your best alternative if there's too much still owing on your mortgage for you to consider paying it off immediately and if your existing mortgage rate is lower than the current rate.

TIP

Often, only fixed-rate mortgages are portable. If your new home requires extra financing, you can usually borrow additional funds at the current rate — your new mortgage rate will be a blend of your mortgage's existing interest rate and the current interest rate. For example, if you have three years left on a five-year mortgage term, you may be able to borrow the extra money at the current three-year rate. (The additional $20,000 you borrow to finance your new home will fit into your existing mortgage at the current three-year rate.) The additional mortgage you just took out to finance your new home has the same expiry date as your original mortgage. When the time comes to renew them, you renew them as one mortgage.

Porting mortgages has become quite common due to the low interest rates of recent years, but choosing what's best for you always depends on your unique financial situation and how much risk you're willing to take. If you've taken to following the rise and fall of mortgage rates religiously in the past few years, you may feel confident in allowing your buyer to assume your current mortgage so that you can take out a new variable-rate or short-term open mortgage on your new home. (Refer to Chapter 5 for details on variable rates and open and closed mortgages.) If you can stand the headache of renegotiating your mortgage every six months, you'll probably end up saving money in the long run.

If you're not a risk-taker and can't be bothered to scour the financial news every morning for the latest trends in mortgage rates, the bit of extra money you may pay to port your fixed-rate mortgage is worth it, just for the peace of mind.

Scouting incentives

When your parents were buying their first house, securing a mortgage was a nail-biting experience and the cost much, much higher than it is today. Times have changed and the mortgage market is buyer-driven. Banks want to keep their customers and are happy to listen and find the right solution. When you're getting ready to sell one property and buy another, a lender may offer one of the following perks:

SHOULD YOU KEEP THE MORTGAGE YOU ALREADY HAVE?

If you're wondering about the benefits of porting your existing mortgage to a new home, you can check out the financial consequences online. Sites like Ratehub (www.ratehub.ca) offer an overview of current rates as well as calculators that help you work out the advantages (and pitfalls) of various scenarios. The calculator can determine the new blended interest rate for your ported mortgage and tell you what your payments will be.

Use the mortgage calculator to figure out the total amount you would pay on a new mortgage at whatever the current interest rate happens to be. If the total amount payable for a new mortgage is less than you would pay by keeping your current mortgage with a new blended interest rate, then you stand to save if you pay off the current mortgage rather than porting it to your new home. Just be sure that the savings you'll make with the new mortgage are greater than the penalty fee you'll be charged for paying off your current mortgage early.

>> **A discount off the current posted interest rate if you're looking for a new first mortgage on a property:** The number of mortgages you've had in the past on other properties doesn't matter — only the home you're looking to buy now is in question here.

>> **A legal package that allows you to use the lender's lawyers, at a discount, for the conveyance of the title and preparation of the mortgage documents:** The conveyance of title is the transfer of ownership, the registration of the new owners, and the registration of the mortgage at the appropriate land titles office. (See Chapter 17 for more information on conveyancing.)

>> **A free appraisal:** This can save you several hundred dollars if your lender absorbs this cost.

Knowing the Ups And Downs Of Financing

When you're ready to trade, you should ask yourself whether you want to trade up or down. We describe assessing your needs and wants in the section, "Making the Big Decision," earlier in this chapter. After doing the self-assessment, you can know whether you need a larger home or a smaller one and what's most important to you in each scenario. The following sections serve up a bit more food for thought related specifically to financing.

Trading up: Your options

When your plans for the future involve investing in a home bigger and better than the one-bedroom condo you currently own, you're trading up. It's probably going to be a more expensive home, so the most economical financing option depend on the state of the mortgage market. Here are a few scenarios:

>> **If the current interest rate is equal to or lower than the rate on your existing mortgage:** You may want to discharge your current mortgage and take out a new one with the same lender. Because lenders usually offer a discount on the current mortgage rate to keep your business, you're guaranteed to get a lower rate. But bear in mind the fact that discharging your mortgage early may result in penalties.

When considering whether to discharge your mortgage, don't sacrifice important options for a discount on your mortgage rate. For example, if your current mortgage allows you to prepay as much as you want every six months, you may end up saving *more* by sticking with your current mortgage and paying it off faster — even though it has a higher interest rate.

REMEMBER

The mortgage market is highly competitive these days, and it's likely to remain so in a low interest-rate environment. Lenders want your business, and they'll bend over backwards to get it. The posted rate and the rate you can negotiate are often very different — you may be able to get a rate one point or more below what is published.

>> **If the current mortgage interest rate is higher than your existing rate:** You may want to port your mortgage and borrow a little extra at the higher rate — your new rate will then be a blend of the two rates. As a previous mortgagor (someone who's taken out a mortgage), you may have some extra bargaining power. Your existing mortgage lender may offer you a new mortgage with attractive terms. Or a new lender may sweeten the pot by offering you better terms to lure your business away from your existing lender.

TIP

If you're thinking about porting your mortgage, talk to your mortgage broker or lender about any fees or restrictions that may apply to your case. If you know you're going to be taking out a new mortgage, shop around for the best deal and get preapproval. Most major lenders now offer online preapproval services, as we discuss in Chapter 5.

Trading down: Your options

The kids have all moved out, it's too quiet, and you have more space than you need. Besides, you can always use some extra money for those approaching

TRADING-DOWN DILEMMA: TO BUY OR RENT YOUR NEXT HOME?

Renting does allow greater flexibility than simply trading down. If you think that it won't be long after selling your home that you may need to move to a long-term care facility, you may want to rent for that short time. If you're in perfect health, renting may allow you to spend your retirement years living a few months here and a few months there — experiencing life in all those little towns you wanted to visit but didn't have the time to explore while you were working.

If you're no longer interested in or capable of dealing with the responsibilities of home ownership and you don't mind letting a landlord call some of the shots, renting may be a viable option. Keep in mind, however, that many of the freedoms afforded by renting are also available to condo owners. Condo upkeep is a shared responsibility, plus you have a smaller likelihood of break-ins if you decide to spend a few winter months somewhere sunny.

Renting involves three big pitfalls you should be aware of:

- You'll be vulnerable to rent inflation.

- You'll have to deal with a landlord (who may decide to sell your home, leaving you with nowhere to live).

- Each time you move there is a chance that your new landlord won't be compassionate and fair.

If you have many years of independent living ahead of you and would prefer to settle in one place, buying a condo may be the safest course.

retirement years. Turning Sally's bedroom into the other half of your home office may be nice — but maybe now is the time to trade in your home to recoup some equity and buy a smaller and less expensive property.

When you trade down, you typically have plenty of money to put towards a smaller home, in relative terms (Chapter 14 can help you determine the amount of proceeds from a home sale). From a financing standpoint, you may be able to buy your next home outright and avoid the need for a mortgage.

Depending on your plans for retirement (and your health), however, you may want to rent rather than buy your next home. Be sure to invest the proceeds in investments that will generate the income needed to pay your rent and have a financial plan that will allow you to manage future rental increases and health costs.

REMEMBER

A home that is your principal residence is a tax-free investment. By using the money you made on the sale of your previous home to purchase another one, you're putting your money into an investment that will (hopefully) grow tax-free. If you decide to invest the proceeds from the sale of your home and rent instead, the interest will likely be taxable (assuming the money is invested outside of a TFSA or RRSP) — and can potentially take you into a higher tax bracket. Real estate appreciation is tax-free growth, but it's generally slow and steady growth, in contrast to mutual funds or stocks that generate taxable income but can be volatile in their performance.

Timing Your Move

Now it's time to sit back and let the buyers come rushing in, right? Not so fast. You have a few more details to work out — like where your next home will be and how you're going to pay for it.

Remember all the work and hassle that went into buying your current home? Well, here's the bad news: You have to go through the hassle of selling and buying now. The good news is, buying is easier the second (or third, or fourth) time around. If this is your second sell, you've already become acquainted with the fine points of coordinating the sale of your house with the purchase of another — probably the hard way. Whichever you do first, this section helps you with plenty of tips to help you balance selling with buying before you get into trouble.

Sell first and then buy, or vice versa?

Deciding whether to buy first and then sell or to sell first and then buy can be challenging. On the one hand, you can find yourself with no house, having sold your home before finding a new one of the appropriate size, style, or location. On the other hand, you can find yourself with no money as you carry two houses. You can avoid these pitfalls by basing your timing decisions on current real estate market trends and your own needs and priorities.

Riding the real estate cycle

Real estate goes through cycles. When there are a lot of buyers and not many homes available, it's a seller's market. This is also called a *hot market* because homes tend to sell more quickly and for higher prices. In a hot market, nail down the house you want — the tough part in this case — and then sell your house.

When there are more homes listed for sale than there are buyers shopping for new homes, it's a buyer's market, or a slow market. Prices tend to be lower and homes take longer to sell in a buyer's market. If the market is slow but there are lots of houses you can see yourself happy in, sell your house first — the hard part in a slow market — and then pick your next house from among your favourites.

Although trying to sell your home in a buyer's market means you may have to drop your asking price, chances are the next house you buy will also be at a reduced price, because market conditions tend to be similar within a particular region. Unfortunately, if you're moving cross-country, you can't count on being so lucky.

Market conditions within a city can be completely different, too. In any city, you'll find that one or two neighbourhoods are considered both trendy and family-oriented, and, regardless of the season, are always in high demand. Even in a recession, these neighbourhoods generate quick home sales just because of the sheer number of people who want to live there. The trick is being able to identify the type of market that your present home and neighbourhood is facing, such as the following:

- » **Check out the For Sale signs in the neighbourhood.** It's not a good sign if there are plenty of For Sale signs with no Sold signs on them.

- » **Look at recent sales.** Even if you do see a lot of Sold signs, it's wise to investigate the asking price versus the sale price. If the market is hot, properties may have received multiple offers and sold for above the asking price. However, in a buyer's market, properties may have sold only after price reductions.

- » **Watch the news.** Nothing seems to interest people more these days than housing values and monthly statistic reports. But remember, these reports describe what has happened, not what will happen. Newscasts typically run a three-minute story that will cover what they believe is happening, but often it seems that potential home buyers and sellers are only hearing headlines such as "Prices Are Falling" or "Multiple Offers Lead to Record High Prices!" What should you believe?

TIP

Ignore national trends and stick to the neighbourhood in which you're interested. For instance, even in a down market, some areas of big cities like Vancouver, Calgary, or Toronto may still experience bidding wars, whereas other neighbourhoods may see inventory languishing. That story won't make the news. Your agent will help you find out what's happening in your target area.

>> **Speak with an agent familiar with the neighbourhood.** After all, your agent is the one who is living and breathing homes every day and speaking to both buyers and sellers as well as other agents. Local agents can see the nuanced changes in market conditions long before any statistical report can.

Real estate also goes through predictable highs and lows over the course of a year. Spring is usually a peak transaction time. If you need to sell your house quickly during a slower time of the year, list your home at market value or even a smidgen below actual market value. On the other hand, if you want to get the best price possible, put your house on the market at the beginning of the peak season. Price is an important marketing tool, so you want to get it right the first time. Chapter 14 gives you the lowdown on pricing dos and don'ts.

Meeting your needs

Your needs form another important variable in the buying and selling equation. Do you need to sell your home quickly? Do you want a certain price, and if so, are you willing to wait for it? Do you want to be in your next home by a particular date?

TIP

If you want to get your kids moved into a new house before the beginning of the school year, you may decide to buy that perfect house in the new neighbourhood before you've sold your current house. The way to prevent hanging on to two houses is to price your current home to sell. For example, if you have to sell and are facing the prospect of owning two homes in six weeks' time (carrying both would probably cost you an extra $2,000 to $3,000 per month), drop your asking price. Accepting an offer, albeit below your original asking price, meets two important needs: Your kids start the new school year off on the right track, and you have only one home to carry — much more manageable. Examine your financial situation and determine your personal priorities early. But as a rule, selling before you buy is almost always better. We take a more detailed look at the financial consequences of both scenarios later in this chapter in the sections "Buying before you sell" and "Selling before you buy."

Gauging what your current house will sell for

Wanting to recoup the money you spent buying and fixing up your home when it comes time to sell is only natural. No one wants to lose money on the biggest investment they'll ever make. You're also thinking about how much money you need in order to buy your next home. Unfortunately, these factors don't determine the resale value of your home.

The cold, hard truth is that buyers determine the actual market value for your house through what they offer to pay for it. If you're working with a real estate agent or broker, ask for a *comparative market analysis (CMA)* to determine your home's market value. The report will rank your home next to similar properties in your neighbourhood based on details like size, condition, desirable features, and listing and sale prices. If you're selling on your own, you may be wise to get a professional appraisal to determine the actual market value of your home. See Chapter 14 for more on CMAs.

TIP

Consider checking out the neighbourhood competition in person. You may think that the updates that you've done to your home are more than adequate, but your five-year-old carpet may not be able to compete with the new hardwood floors in the house listed two blocks away. Likewise, your kitchen may be light years ahead of the property that still has an avocado green refrigerator. Open houses are the perfect venue for this type of investigative reporting, so set aside a Sunday afternoon with pen and paper in hand to check out what's what in the hood.

Knowing what you can spend on your next house

Figuring out how much you can afford to pay for your next house involves some basic addition and subtraction. You need to total your cash inflow and outflow, and then subtract the expenses from the income. The tricky part is making an inventory of all your sources of income and expenditure and the exact amounts associated with each.

Careful calculations will help keep you realistic about what you can afford and may help you decide whether or not you should move. When you know how much you can spend, you need to investigate whether that amount really will get you the kind of house you want while allowing you to maintain your standard of living and save for long-term financial goals. We discuss the finer aspects of personal finance in Chapter 4.

WARNING

Never assume anything when investigating what you can get for your money. The perfect home may not be in the perfect neighbourhood. The perfect neighbourhood may have listings in your price range only for properties half the size you need. You may have to make sacrifices to make improvements, so you need to know what your priorities are. Even if you can make a decent profit on the sale of your current home, you have no guarantee that you'll be better off if you sell.

Buying before you sell

So you've found the most amazing new home — it's only 20 minutes south of your new job; it's surrounded by parkland to the west; there's a gym, a huge grocery store, and a local fruit and vegetable market to the north; and the best theatre, restaurants, and shopping in town are to the east. The home is even in your price range. You know that if you wait to make an offer, someone else will snatch your dream home up, but you haven't sold your current home yet, you still owe $125,000 on it, and you don't have a spare $50,000 to make the down payment. What can you do?

Rest assured, you're not the first home seller who has been caught in the middle of buying and selling. Mortgage lenders have developed an option for precisely this situation — it's called *bridge financing,* or *interim financing.* With bridge financing, your lender lets you borrow the money you need to bridge the gap between buying a new home and selling your old one. This type of financing usually involves a personal fixed-rate loan, often one lump sum that can be repaid at maturity or prepaid at any time without penalty. Bridge financing doesn't have standard maximum or minimum amounts; your lender will decide how much it's willing to give you based on how much it thinks you'll be able to repay. Because you have already worked out the proceeds of sale and your cash flow for before and after the move, you can make an educated guess about how much your lender will be willing to give you.

WARNING

Buying first and then selling has a downside if you require bridge financing. (If owning two homes simultaneously won't put a crimp in your style, buy to your heart's content!) The downside to bridge financing is that you're paying interest on a relatively large sum of money for however long selling your current home and repaying the loan takes. With stricter lending requirements in recent years, you'll want to make sure that all your financial ducks are in a row and that you have everything in place with your lender before you tackle interim financing. No one wants to be caught owning two properties and then have their financing fall apart.

REMEMBER

Don't underestimate how long selling your home may take. If market conditions are favourable for sellers in your area, your home may sell in a week. If conditions aren't so favourable, selling can take many months (or even a few years, if the neighborhood experiences a sudden change). What if your home's value takes a nosedive? What if you simply can't sell your home at all? Murphy's Law will govern the sale of your home to some degree. Bridge financing will become expensive the longer it is required. In a slow market, buying a house prior to selling your current home may not be advisable. Buying first in a slow market is extremely dangerous. Talk to a local real estate agent about the current market conditions in your area as they relate to your home specifically.

Selling before you buy

Selling your current home before you buy the next one eliminates some financial uncertainties. You know you have enough money to buy another home. You're even luckier if a distant cousin is willing to take you and your six children in for five months while you search for a new home. What you need to have in place is a housing plan between the time you sell your house and have to move out and the time you buy a house and take occupancy.

If you're trading up, you may be counting on all the money you made on the sale of your home to go toward the purchase of a new one. However, renting a space large enough for an entire family can cost thousands of dollars per month, and renting for several months will put a significant dent in your buying power. And then there's the stress that goes along with being in limbo for an extended period of time. If you're trading down, the proceeds of the sale may be enough to cover the cost of renting for a few months, but you need to work out the financial implications beforehand.

WARNING

Selling before you buy guarantees that you'll have the proceeds of one sale to put towards another. But if you're mortgage is portable and you're planning to apply it to your next home purchase, you may face a limited window in which to do so. Many lenders allow buyers between 60 and 90 days to close on a new purchase after selling a previous property.

Cutting through the stress

Whether you decide to sell before you buy or buy before you sell, don't underestimate how long finding a new home will take. However, you can ease the stress by taking some action. This section discusses both of your options.

The safety net: Conditional subject to sale offers

One way to synchronize buying and selling when find a house you like is to make an offer subject to clause for the sale of your current house. After the conditional offer is accepted, you can place your existing house on the market. If the condition (selling your house) isn't met by a specific date, then the offer you made for the other house becomes null and void (unless you and the seller agree to extend the window for your purchase. (Refer to Chapter 9 for more information on subject to clauses.)

By writing a *subject to sale condition* into your purchase offer, you don't have to buy the house you want until you've sold the house you're living in — giving you the peace of mind and the financial security that comes with not owning two homes and not being homeless.

Here's how it works: You write into your offer a subject to sale clause that essentially states, "This offer is subject to the sale of the buyers' current residence located at [address], on or before [expiry date of clause]. However, if another acceptable offer is received, the sellers will notify the buyers in writing and give the buyers 48 hours [24 or 72 hours is also common] to remove the 'subject to sale' condition as well as all other conditions from the offer, or the offer will be considered null and void." The expiry date of the clause indicates the amount of time you have to sell your house from the time the offer is accepted and therefore to remove the condition and make your offer firm or withdraw your offer if the condition was not met. This date is usually negotiated to fall between four and six weeks after the offer is accepted, and it can be extended if both parties agree.

REMEMBER

Don't confuse the expiry date of the subject to sale clause with the completion date of the offer itself. The completion date specifies the date you'll close the deal if all the specified conditions are met. It's the day you become the legal owner of the property.

WARNING

A *conditional offer* — one that you make a purchase subject to conditions such as the sale of another property — is less attractive to a seller and therefore puts the buyer in a weak negotiating position. Because most sellers don't want to delay the sale of their home, they're often willing to accept an unconditional offer for less money.

Biding your time: Time clauses

Most sellers who receive and consider an offer with a subject to sale clause will invoke the time clause (or escape clause), the amount of time the first buyer has to either remove all the conditions from his offer — including the subject to sale condition — or withdraw his offer altogether. The *time clause,* which is negotiable, identifies how long you have to remove the subject to sale condition or withdraw your offer if the seller receives another acceptable offer before the expiry date on your clause.

Even after the seller accepts your conditional purchase offer, she'll still actively market her home, looking for a *clean offer* — an offer without conditions. If the seller receives another acceptable offer, she'll invoke the time clause and notify you in writing that you have 24, 48, or 72 hours (or whatever time period was written into the clause) to make a decision. At this point, you can remove the conditions and commit to buying the house — whether or not you have sold your own — or you can withdraw the offer.

TIP

Some sellers won't even look at offers made subject to the sale of the buyer's current house, because they don't believe the buyer is serious. Ask your real estate agent how conditional offers are received in your local market.

REMEMBER

If you've really found your dream home and your conditional offer has been accepted, price your house to sell to make sure that you don't wind up in second place. The goal with conditional offers is to satisfy the conditions as soon as possible. By being very realistic about the market value of your existing home, you put yourself in the best position to sell it before buying the next one.

For most people, putting your house on the market while you look for your next home makes sense. Doing this gives you a good sense of what buyers are willing to pay for your house and saves you from inflating the amount you think you can spend on your next home. If offers come rushing in, you can always accept the best, subject to the purchase of your next house.

Some buyers won't accept a seller's proposed counteroffer, especially if the counteroffer is conditional on the sellers' purchase of their next home. If you find yourself in this position, you have to decide what you're willing to risk. If you sell before you've found a new home, you risk becoming homeless — at least temporarily. On the other hand, if you reject the buyer's offer because you can't include the condition of buying your next house, you may wait a long time before receiving another one, depending on the market conditions and your pricing strategy.

If you have a lot of money, you can just buy your dream home and then put your current house on the market. Through bridge financing, you can use the equity in your first property to finance the purchase of the next. (We discuss bridge financing in the section, "Buying before you sell," earlier in this chapter. It's the riskiest option financially, but it guarantees that you get the house you absolutely want. You must weigh the cost of financing against having the flexibility to purchase the house of your dreams.

Buying time with the closing dates

Getting the paperwork right is the next step in making a smooth transition. When you've found a buyer for your current home and a new house to move into, you'll need to schedule each closing date, the day you transfer ownership of a property and finalize the sale. Ideally, both the sale of your current home and the purchase of your new one should close one right after the other.

Scheduling both closing dates together affords you the most security financially — and emotionally. If it simply can't be done, the next best option is to try to extend the closing date on your purchase so that it follows the closing date of your home's sale. See Chapter 18 for details on negotiating deadlines that will work for you.

TIP

Try to avoid the last day of the month or year as a closing date. These times are particularly busy for the agencies that will be registering and filing paperwork for the transfer of ownership, termination of insurance, and the like, not to mention movers.

Timing it right: The ideal selling and buying scenario

Selling before you buy tends to be less risky than buying before you sell. Unless you're moving just because you see a home you like better, you have (hopefully) put considerable thought into where and when you'll move. Assuming that you've done your homework, you'll know what to expect when shopping for a home in your new area. Even if finding the perfect home takes a little longer than expected, you know exactly how much you can afford and have the security of knowing that you're in a financial position to buy.

REMEMBER

The ideal situation is that you sell your current home and buy a new one at the same time. This entails stipulating in your offer on a new home that the offer is conditional on the sale of your previous home. Usually this clause specifies a time limit — like 30 days — for the condition to be met.

If it's a seller's market in your neck of the woods and a buyer's market in your new area, you may have enough leeway to make such stipulations. But if you're moving into a seller's market, you may not have this option. Ask yourself whether you would accept a conditional offer on your home if you thought you could get an unconditional offer easily. If you're moving into a seller's market, you may be competing with others making offers on the same home. Making a conditional offer may be just enough to tip the balance in someone else's favour. On the other hand, if you think the seller may be receptive to a conditional offer, it's a great way to buy first without taking a huge financial risk.

Changing Your Mind about Selling

Selling your home is scary business. After researching your new area, maybe you've realized that you've been taking your current location for granted — it's really not so bad; perhaps staying put and making some renovations is the best plan. (If you've already listed your house and then change your mind, you can always cancel the listing.) If you've decided to stay where you are, you have some financing options to help foot the bill. These include dipping into the equity you've built up in the home or taking on extra debt by refinancing your mortgage. We discuss both in more detail here.

Home equity loans and homeowner lines of credit

Most major lenders offer home equity loans (also known as *second mortgages* and *home equity lines of credit*) for homeowners. These options allow you to access whatever equity you have built up in your home. If you have paid off your mortgage in full, you may be able to borrow up to 80 percent of the value of your home to put towards renovations. Home equity loans are exactly like mortgages and usually take the form of fixed-rate loans with long repayment periods. Home equity lines of credit (HELOCs) usually have variable interest rates and are available as long as you like after only one application.

If you're undertaking large renovations all at one time, a home equity loan may be the best option. If you know exactly how much the renovation will cost and are planning to pay for it all up front, a home equity loan gives you the security of knowing precisely how much your regular payments will be. If you intend to make smaller renovations over many years, or if you're unsure how much renovations will cost, a HELOC may be better suited to your needs. After all, you have to pay interest only when, and if, you use it.

Many financial institutions allow you to combine home equity loans and HELOCs (for example, you may start off with a line of credit, borrowing only small amounts over a longer period, and then decide to borrow a large chunk of money for a bigger renovation project at a later date — as a home equity loan). Most financial institutions will allow you to structure your payments to suit your financial situation. Home equity plans are a great advantage to those people who decide that renovating makes more sense than selling because they allow you to borrow large amounts of money at lower interest rates than those of regular personal loans or lines of credit.

Refinancing your mortgage

Another option to pay for renovations is mortgage refinancing. If it's time to renew your mortgage and interest rates are relatively low, refinancing may be the preferred option. Some lenders will allow you to borrow up to 90 percent of the value of your home, less whatever you still owe on your current mortgage. To figure out the most economical route, talk to your lender about the products it offers for home renovators.

Reversing your mortgage

If you need extra income to help maintain your current standard of living after you retire or if you need extra income for personal care expenses, you may want a reverse mortgage. A *reverse mortgage* is an agreement between you and a lender that allows you to tap into the equity built up in your home.

Understanding how a reverse mortgage works

A reverse mortgage works in a few different ways. Your lender may provide you

>> A lump-sum payment

>> Monthly payments

>> A line of credit

>> Some combination of these options

Some standard restrictions on who can enter into a reverse mortgage agreement exist — usually, you must be at least 55 years old, have equity built up, and no liens against the property. However, you don't need to meet credit or income requirements to be eligible for a reverse mortgage. In Canada, reverse mortgages are offered through HomeEquity Bank (www.homeequitybank.ca).

The amount of money that you can access ranges from 10 to 55 percent of the value of your home, which must be worth at least $150,000. The total funds available is determined by

>> The value of your home

>> Your age

>> Current interest rates

>> The type of reverse mortgage you choose

Paying back a reverse mortgage

Unlike a conventional mortgage, a reverse mortgage doesn't have to be repaid right away; repayment starts when your home ceases to be your principal residence (a home is no longer considered a principal residence if the borrower moves elsewhere and no longer occupies the home, dies, or sells the home). Repaying a reverse mortgage involves paying the borrowed principal plus interest and any other legal or administrative fees associated with the agreement.

REMEMBER

The amount that you must repay for a reverse mortgage can't exceed the value of your home, and you can't be forced to sell your home to repay the mortgage if you still reside there. When lenders determine the amount a borrower can receive, they're betting that the home won't depreciate significantly and that the borrower won't reside there so long that the payout exceeds the value of the home.

Repayment can be made by you, your family, or your estate; it doesn't need to involve the sale of your home. If you do decide to sell your home, whatever profit you make over the market value of your home is yours (or your family's or estate's) to keep. If the sale generates less than the value of the reverse mortgage on your home, usually a third party, such as an insurance provider, is responsible for making up the difference.

Figuring out whether a reverse mortgage is right for you

A reverse mortgage isn't for everyone. If passing down your home to children or grandchildren is important to you, you may not want to consider a reverse mortgage given the risk that it may need to be sold to cover the amount advanced to you. While a reverse mortgage is never for the entire value of the home, it is nevertheless an obligation that your heirs will have to address.

Many seniors consider a reverse mortgage because they can't pay all the bills required to maintain their home. However, it's not the only option. Some municipalities allow homeowners to defer their property taxes, meaning one less hefty bill to pay each year. If property taxes are deferred, they're generally repaid when the homeowner moves out of the property or when the home is sold.

Because interest rates for reverse mortgages are generally 1.5 to 2 percent higher than a standard mortgage, a HELOC may be a competitive alternative. It will also require monthly interest payments on any money borrowed, unlike a reverse mortgage, which is paid back at the end of the term.

Before settling on a reverse mortgage, make sure you discuss your options in detail with your financial adviser and your lawyer.

Considering Estate Sales to Sell Your House

You may find yourself facing the prospect of selling a home as part of settling someone's estate. However, there's a complicating factor: from the point of view of the Canada Revenue Agency, the owner disposed of the property on the date of death. The tax implications make it important to quickly establish a fair market value for the property as of that date, because it will be critical to establishing any change in value when the estate sells the home. Even though the estate won't pay capital gains on any change in value attributed to the deceased owner, the heirs may be liable for capital gains owing on any change of value in the interim, particularly if the market is rising rapidly. This section outlines what you need to know as the executor of the estate and the person in charge of conducting the sale.

Knowing what to do as the estate's executor

Selling the home of someone who died is a lot like most other sales and requires the same amount of care and attention as if you were selling your own home. However, as the estate's executor, your primary concern will be with making sure the sale generates enough proceeds to satisfy any claims against the estate and (ideally) provide a legacy to the heirs (of which you might be one).

Besides meeting the ongoing expenses such as utilities, insurance, condominium fees (if applicable), and property taxes, you'll also want to be aware of mortgage obligations. A lender will still expect to be paid (especially if mortgage life insurance, something we discuss in Chapter 5, hasn't been purchased). The terms of the mortgage may allow it to be assumed by the heirs, but they — like any purchaser — may also be required to requalify.

Those responsible for the sale will also need to know if a reverse mortgage needs to be repaid, or if property taxes were deferred. These claims will have priority over others and may demand a faster sale of the property than not.

Knowing the window in which you must sell the property will help determine how quickly you prepare it for sale and whether you can be patient with offers or become, as the saying goes, a "motivated seller."

TIP

Just as if you were selling or refinancing your own home, take stock of the liabilities — both the ongoing operating expenses as well as debts — associated with the property and speak with an appraiser and real estate agent to determine what the proceeds might be (we discuss more about determining a home's value and sale proceeds in Chapter 14). Getting a handle on the financial situation of the property will help you maintain its value and secure the best return.

Being aware of taxes

Because the Canada Revenue Agency deems the property to have changed hands on the date of the owner's death, you, as the executor of the estate and very likely an heir, will need to be aware of your own obligations. If you don't own property and are the sole heir, then congratulations! You are deemed to have a primary residence and can take steps to arrange the transfer of title.

However, if there are several heirs and one of them doesn't own a home, then all the heirs need to decide who to pass the residence into. Doing so helps to limit capital gains exposure. However, the heirs who effectively sold their interest would face capital gains on the sale of property that's not their primary residence.

REMEMBER

To keep things simple, resolve the question of ownership and outstanding claims before taking any steps to convert an inherited property into an investment property. Avoid the temptation to undertake major renovations — other than needed maintenance — before selling it or bringing in renters for a few months until the market becomes more favourable. Your goal is to settle an estate, not build one.

TIP

Ideally, the situation you face will be simple and straightforward, which is seldom the case with estates, however, so we recommend that you consult both a lawyer and an accountant to guide you through the specifics of the situation. You may also find Douglas Gray and John Budd, *The Canadian Guide to Will and Estate Planning*, 4th edition (McGraw-Hill) a useful resource.

Chapter **14**

Setting a Price and Knowing the Cost

Y ou may be thinking, "Great! I'm selling my house, there's a big cheque coming in, and I'm gonna be swimming in cash!" Although it's true that there will be a big cheque at some point, you ought to keep in mind some costs tied to selling your house. The idea is to provide for these costs in advance, because most of them must be paid before that cheque gets cashed. Careful and informed planning can help ensure that the process of selling your house goes smoothly.

Whatever the reasons for selling your house, the process requires careful planning and advice from your real estate agent. Remove your emotions from the process in order to understand the dynamics of the market. You need to bear in mind the costs associated with selling a house and plan for these too. This chapter spells out what you need to remember when pricing your home.

Pricing Your House to Sell

Retailers know that if you price a product too high, people won't buy it. The public perception is that the product's value doesn't equate to the asking price. This same rule applies equally to big-ticket items like houses. Potential buyers are going to take on a large loan and spend a large down payment and will have some degree of stress over this. If your asking price is too high, buyers will either walk away or present a very low offer to see how motivated you are as a seller. The key is finding the balance between attracting buyers and receiving offers and a final sales price that reflect your home's true value.

Determining your home's worth

The best way to find out how much your home is worth is to ask a professional. You can hire a professional appraiser to give you an appraisal, or you can ask your real estate agent to give you a *comparative market analysis (CMA)*, sometimes also referred to as a *current market analysis* or a *competitive market analysis*. Figure 14-1 shows a sample CMA.

COMPARABLE RECENT SALES	AGE	LOT SIZE	FLOOR AREA	BDRM	BATH	BSMT	LISTING DATE	PRICE	SALE DATE	PRICE	ASSESSED VALUE (2019)
360 West Wind Street	40	33 x 120	1,956	3	3	Full	July 5/20	$700,000	July 19/20	$675,000	$650,000
410 Jack Pine Street	38	40 x 120	2,000	4	3	Part	July 16/20	$760,000	Aug. 1/20	$740,000	$750,000
290 Silver Birch Street	32	33 x 120	1,795	2	2	Full	June 30/20	$715,000	July 9/20	$705,000	$700,000

COMPARABLE CURRENT LISTINGS	AGE	LOT SIZE	FLOOR AREA	BDRM	BATH	BSMT	LISTING DATE	PRICE	ASSESSED VALUE (2019)
363 West Wind Street	40	33 x 120	1,956	3	3	Full	Aug. 11/20	$665,000	$655,000
285 Silver Birch Street	32	33 x 120	1,800	2	2	Full	Aug. 13/20	$700,000	$700,000
660 Black Spruce Drive	35	33 x 120	2,000	3	3	Full	Aug. 21/20	$680,000	$675,000
515 Sugar Maple Crescent	35	33 x 120	2,000	3	3	Part	Aug. 12/20	$660,000	$650,000

YOUR HOME	AGE	LOT SIZE	FLOOR AREA	BDRM	BATH	BSMT	RECOMMENDED LIST RANGE	RECOMMENDED SALE RANGE
269 West Wind Street	39	33 x 120	1,850	3	2	Full	$660,000-$675,000	$650,000-$670,000

MARKET VALUE: The price expected when a reasonable time is allowed to find a purchaser when both the seller and prospective buyer are fully informed.

LISTING PRICE: The price asked for a property, as set by the vendor. The vendor is urged to take into account information supplied and market conditions.

Sales representative: _____   Date: Aug. 30/20

© John Wiley & Sons, Inc.

FIGURE 14-1: Your real estate agent can give you a comparative market analysis that looks something like this.

When gauging the market value of your house, an appraisal and CMA are essentially the same. Both consider all the factors influencing the market value of your property (such as location, total floor area, general condition of the home, and amenities). They research the recent sale prices and current asking prices of similar homes in your area, compare the finer details, and adjust up or down to determine your home's fair market value. If your home has, say, an attached double garage, then it may be worth a little bit more than someone else's down the street that is also a three-bedroom two-storey house with four baths and a finished basement but only has a carport.

Most real estate agents will prepare a CMA for you free of charge. You'll always have to pay an appraiser. If you're selling without an agent, you should definitely hire an independent appraiser. The legal system, as well as most financial institutions, recognizes appraisals prepared by accredited appraisers only. (See the section "Comprehending the Basics of Appraisals for Sellers" elsewhere in this chapter to discover how they can help you as a seller.)

WARNING

The appraisal you obtain for your home isn't someone else's appraisal of a home. Although all appraisals try to determine a home's fair market value, it's entirely possible for the appraisals to differ by tens of thousands of dollars. That's because the appraisal will reflect the fair market value that best reflects the interests of the appraiser's client. Discrepancies in fair market values can create challenges when selling your property if you receive an overly optimistic appraisal of your property or run into an especially hard-nosed negotiator who intends on getting a lower price than you're offering. Your buyer may put a *clause* (a condition) into the offer stipulating that the offer accepted is subject to the confirmation of an independent appraisal. The condition is an escape clause for the buyer if the price is above market value. A price above market value may have consequences for the lender too.

REMEMBER

An appraisal by an accredited appraiser will carry more weight than a CMA prepared by a real estate agent. It will also have legal standing and will hold up in court if needed.

Recognising the three most common pricing mistakes

We know it's your home and you can ask whatever price you like for it, but proceed with caution. Your ego may tell you your home is worth $1 million, but the market may tell you something else altogether. Your listing price will be a key factor in whether or not it sells; it can determine whether your home is snapped up by eager buyers or sits on the market for months. Here we discuss the three most common pricing mistakes and how you can avoid them.

Pricing to profit

Many sellers will price their property above where the market currently is because they think they have everything to gain and nothing to lose. Their reasoning goes something like this: "If someone buys it for the high price, great; I made some money. If I have to drop the price a little to sell, then I haven't really lost anything because I still got a fair price." The problem is, it doesn't work that way. Your home gets the most attention in the first few weeks it's on the market. If you set the price too high, you run the risk of buyers ignoring your home because most won't be willing to go through the work of negotiating you down, not knowing if that's something you're even open to doing.

For example, if the market value of your home is $490,000 but you insist on listing it at $545,000, you'll discourage potential buyers in the $450,000 to $500,000 price range. If your home isn't priced to market in those crucial first few weeks, the listing might become stale by the time you do lower the price. And lowering the price won't necessarily indicate a bargain. Potential buyers will see your "price reduced" listing and think, "If it's been on the market for this long and they have to keep lowering the price, there must be something wrong with it." That line of thinking may not be true, but that's the perception. Those buyers may then turn around and purchase something else by the time you lower your price.

Furthermore, if the initial asking price is too high, buyers won't feel that there's competition for the home — which means they won't be in a hurry to make an offer. Either way, by the time you do lower the asking price, agents (and their buyers) may have lost interest in your home and you may have to sell for less than you would have gotten had you priced your house realistically in the beginning.

REMEMBER

Canadians have a reputation for being polite. Most buyers will respect your listing price and won't present offers that are substantially lower than what's being asked, even if their offer reflects fair market value. You may think that you can ask for a high price for your home so that someone will bring you a low offer and then negotiate a deal, but chances are, you won't get any offers (or interest) at all.

The only real circumstance where you can be optimistic in your asking price is in an overheated seller's market where there are few, if any, homes that directly compete with yours. In this dream-come-true scenario, you can ask a higher price than your CMA indicates. Better yet, you may get offers from competing buyers that drive the price higher than what recent sales indicate your house is worth.

Pricing for your needs, not the buyer's

Many sellers have a new location (or even a new house) in mind and know how much money they need to make on the sale of their current home in order to purchase a new one. Other sellers may be planning to trade down as a way to make money they can then invest for retirement. Frankly, buyers don't care about your needs. Buyers have their own needs to worry about, two of which are affordability and paying fair market value for their new house. If all the similar houses in your neighbourhood sell in a certain price range, buyers will likely offer a similar price for your home. Surveying the asking prices and recent sale prices of comparable homes in your neighbourhood gives you a basic idea of what price you can expect to get. If you keep the sale price too high because you need the money, you won't be able to sell your home.

Pricing based on past expenses

Spending a load of money on your property doesn't mean it's going to repay you. In other words, spending $30,000 on renovations won't translate to a $30,000 increase in the market value. Yes, some improvements will add value to your home far beyond their own value; for example, kitchen and bathroom renovations often deliver the best return. On the other hand, some improvements, such as painting, will be minor. And if the upgrades reflect your personal tastes rather than the market's, they may actually cost you money. A standard upgrade will have broader appeal than one that transforms your 18th-floor apartment into a rustic farmhouse.

Cosmetic improvements, such as a fresh coat in an attractive but neutral paint tone, are always good investments. Although they won't increase the value of your home by a significant margin, basic home touch-ups are relatively cheap and extremely important for making a good first impression on buyers. A good agent knows what counts and what doesn't, and so do most buyers. See Chapter 8 to find out which renovations are the most likely to deliver value when it's time to sell.

If you had to spend a ton of money maintaining the property just so it held its value, or you paid more in mortgage interest than you expected, don't expect to recoup it all when you sell the property. A home helps you build equity and long-term wealth, but owning a home will still cost you money. Don't expect the final sale price to give you back everything you spent. However, we can promise you that you'll likely have more at the end of the day than if you had been throwing away thousands on rent.

Comprehending the Basics of Appraisals for Sellers

If you're selling privately — that is, without an agent — an appraisal makes a lot of sense. You obtain a professional, objective assessment of what your house is worth on the current real estate market. Based on your appraisal, you can realistically set the price for your home. (See the previous section, "Recognising the three most common pricing mistakes," for more on the perils of pricing.) An appraisal can also make sense in certain circumstances if you're selling your home through an agent.

Be sure to hire an accredited appraiser. Whatever identification is presented to you should indicate that the appraiser holds the designation AACI (Accredited Appraiser Canadian Institute) or CRA (Canadian Residential Appraiser). Work only with an appraiser you trust. Refer to Chapter 2 for tips on selecting an appraiser.

Here we dive deeper into what you need to know about appraisals when you're selling your home.

Knowing if your home requires an appraisal

Whether or not you, as a seller, have your home appraised, buyers almost always need to have an appraisal when they apply for a mortgage. If your buyer doesn't need a new mortgage — for example, if your buyer is assuming your mortgage — then you don't need to worry about appraisals.

Several scenarios may warrant having your home appraised before you put it on the market. The chief benefit of having a professional appraisal performed before you list your home is knowing a realistic price range for your home. This is especially important if you're making plans for a larger purchase and are trying to determine the best way forward. An appraisal helps you know whether or not your plans are financially viable. In addition, if your home offers special features that makes it difficult to draw comparisons with others in the market, a professional appraiser can help establish a reasonable value.

TIP

Home sellers typically don't commission an independent appraisal before listing their homes for sale unless they're selling privately. Most real estate agents are well versed in the factors that influence the market value of a home and can provide you with an accurate estimate of your home's worth (see the section, "Determining your home's worth," earlier in this chapter). They'll also do it free of charge, usually using the same methods and information available to an appraiser.

There are differences between the assessments offered by a real estate agent and an appraiser. A real estate agent is a professional sales agent, and the opinion of an experienced and reputable agent may take into account intangibles — the "Wow!" factor — because the agent knows a certain type of buyer will pay big bucks for your home. By contrast, an appraiser isn't a sales professional and will provide an expert, unbiased opinion that takes into account not only the intrinsic value of the land and buildings, but also the development or redevelopment potential and the impact of local zoning bylaws that could impact the price. It will be grounded in fact, not "Wow!"

Exploring how an appraisal is performed

A standard home appraisal (say, a bungalow in a neighbourhood with a fair amount of owner turnover) can run you anywhere from $200 to $500, depending on the size and location of the property and the depth of the assessment. The fee is determined by how much work the appraiser has to do to figure out the value of your property. It's a fairly easy job if there have been plenty of comparable sales in the recent past. But if the last time a house sold in your neighbourhood was 2002 and it was nothing like yours, an accurate appraisal will be more complicated and thus more expensive.

What will I get for my money?

Appraisers will be very quick to tell you that they aren't home inspectors. Having said that, they do look at a lot of the same things. Here's a list of some of the things an appraiser notes about your home:

>> **Size:** What is the total square footage of the home, including basement, if there is one? What are the lot dimensions?

>> **Age:** What is the age of the home? The roof?

>> **Condition:** Does the home need repairs that will affect its value?

>> **Upgrades, finishing:** What work have you put into the home recently that will increase its value? Bathrooms and kitchens are usually the focus here.

>> **Infrastructure:** Heating, A/C, plumbing, and electricity. Do they all function properly? Or are there costly repairs needed?

>> **Amenities:** Especially in condos, but in houses too — sauna, pool, hot tub, deck, garage, and so on.

>> **Neighbourhood:** Schools, shopping, transportation, safety, and so on.

>> **Immediate surroundings:** What does your yard back onto, a park or a high-rise apartment? Which way does your condo face, south for the best light, or east for the morning sun?

>> **Anything that makes your home special:** Unique features can boost the value of your home.

The appraiser's work is limited to a visual inspection of the property, but the site visit may double-check the property dimensions to ensure they're accurate. Photos may be taken to document the condition and situation of the premises. The appraiser will document signs of problems or potential problems, like cracks in the walls that can indicate excessive settling.

TIP

Many appraisal firms focus on specific types of real estate, so be sure to make sure the expertise you're hiring matches your property. Don't hire an appraiser to assess your century-old character home if he specializes in suburban properties built after 1980. Choose someone who's familiar with the special attractions a home like yours offers prospective buyers.

An appraiser may use one of three methods to evaluate the subject property:

>> **A comparative market analysis (CMA):** This evaluation is based on a comparison of your home to the recent sale prices and current asking prices of comparable homes in your neighbourhood, taking the condition, amenities, and other particulars associated with your home into account to adjust that figure up or down. See Chapter 15 for an example of a real estate agent's CMA.

>> **A replacement cost approach:** This method determines the value of your home based on how much it would cost today to rebuild your exact home. This approach is used less frequently than the CMA because it provides a less accurate picture of how much buyers are willing to pay for your home.

>> **A rental income approach:** This is used for homes that include rental units and is essentially a CMA that factors in the income and expenses generated by those units.

How long will an appraisal take?

Believe it or not, an appraisal doesn't take much time. For an ordinary home, the site visit may take as little as 10 to 15 minutes (we've seen it happen), but a comprehensive assessment should take about an hour, depending on how many unique features the home has. After the visit to your home, the appraiser researches other sales in your area in the recent past to compare what other homes similar to yours have sold for. This helps determine the market value of your home as well as the replacement value (a useful figure to have for insurance purposes). The research process takes a little longer, but you can expect the report in a day or two for a standard home. If your home is in an old-money, leave-it-to-the-grandkids neighbourhood where sales are uncommon, the research will be harder and will definitely take longer. The more complex a property is, the longer the appraisal will take, both on site and back at the office.

Appraising condominiums

The appraisal process is almost identical for condominiums and houses (go back and read the preceding section if you skipped on to this one). The costs are the same, although a really posh condo may run you a little more. One thing that does make a difference in condos is the maintenance fee. A very high monthly fee that clearly supports extras like a concierge, swimming pool, and meticulously maintained property won't detract from the value assigned to a condo. However, a high monthly fee on a condo without a lot of frills reduces the price that a buyer is willing to pay.

WARNING

Be aware that the appraisal may not take into account the status of the condominium corporation — and this factor significantly affects how much a buyer offers for your home. (Refer to Chapter 6 for more information on condominium corporations.) Even though the state of the building corporation's finances and the state of the common areas have a bearing on the value of each unit, appraisers don't usually have access to this information. For example, if there's no money in the building's reserve fund, underground parking upkeep or security may be neglected, possibly decreasing the value of the property. To ensure a more accurate estimate of your unit's value, you can provide your appraiser with a copy of your condominium's documentation, which will include all the relevant information about maintenance, finances, and the legal obligations of the condo corporation. In some provinces, this documentation is referred to as the estoppel certificate, condominium certificate, status certificate, or information certificate.

Preparing for an appraisal

You can take a few steps to make a favourable impression on any appraiser:

>> **Showcase your home.** Although, technically, cleanliness and tidiness (or lack thereof) shouldn't affect the appraiser's "objective" opinion, appraisers are human, so showing off your home for the appraisal never hurts. If the appraiser thinks you're a conscientious homeowner, he may give you the benefit of the doubt and place your home at the upper end of a range of values.

>> **Make sure the appraiser has all the relevant information about your home.** Everything from appliance warranties and inspection reports to receipts for any recent work done on structural, electrical, heating/cooling, or plumbing systems should be available. Feel free to give the appraiser any information you have on recent asking prices or sale prices in your area, especially any private sales that may not show in sales statistics. Even though the appraiser will research the most up-to-date information, making sure she has all the information she needs never hurts.

>> **Be available while the appraiser tours your home.** Be on hand for questions, but don't interfere. Feel free to discuss factors that you, or the appraiser, feel influence the value of your home, and make notes. This will help you understand why the appraiser may or may not agree with your own assessment of the value of your home.

REMEMBER

Get a written copy of any appraisal performed on your property, if you can. You'll receive a copy of any appraisal you commission, but if you're the seller, you won't have automatic access to the buyer's appraisal (in fact, if a bank commissions an appraisal on behalf of the buyer, the buyer may not receive a copy, either, especially if the bank covers the cost). It's important to counter any incorrect facts an appraisal serves up, because these could seriously, and negatively, influence the value and perception of your property. You can't argue for an adjustment if you don't have a copy of the appraisal, however.

If an accredited appraiser refuses to correct factual errors, you can file a complaint with the Appraisal Institute of Canada (www.aicanada.ca).

Sum Fun: The Math of Selling Your Home

You may think you're going to make a bundle off your bungalow, but selling your home brings a whole lot of expenses. We recommend doing some simple math before you start dreaming about what you're going to do with all that cash. This exercise is just as important as tallying the closing costs when you purchase a home, something we discuss in Chapter 4.

Estimating the costs of selling

On the surface, the economics of selling your home seem pretty simple. You sell your home, and hopefully, you make enough money to cover the purchase of another one. If the sale price of your current home is greater than what you pay for your new home, you may feel like you'll come out ahead. Unfortunately, a few steps in the middle of the process may shrink your profits from the sale. With proper planning, you can accurately estimate the proceeds of the sale to find out for sure. This section takes you through the expenses you're responsible for as a seller.

Agent's commission

Unless you have time and energy to burn, chances are you'll hire an agent to handle the listing and sale of your home. Your agent receives a commission when you sell — usually a percentage of the sale price — as does the buyer's agent. And guess what, you're responsible for both! A typical total commission expense may be between 2.5 and 6 percent of the selling price, but rates are negotiable. Some agents will charge you a flat fee for listing your home: these tend to be discount agents, so you may find that you'll have to handle some responsibilities yourself, such as showing the home. Many flat-fee agents won't pay for local advertising or hold open houses. If you decide to sell privately, you'll probably still deal with buyers who are using an agent, so you may get stuck with some commission fees no matter what.

Legal fees

The sale of a home requires legal documentation. You may need a lawyer (or notary) to draw up or check over all the paperwork. The legal fees will reflect the amount of work involved. Talk to several lawyers to get an idea of how much your situation may cost, but a budget of $600 to $1,200, including fees for conveyance (the transfer of title to the property), should cover the most common scenarios. However, the sum may be more if you need the lawyer to draft specific documents, depending on your circumstances and the particular residence changing hands.

Repairs or renovations

Most homes will *not* require major renovations to ensure a sale. If you've kept your home in good shape or if your home is relatively new, you may need to do only minor repairs. First impressions go a long way — no matter how new your home is, pay attention to cosmetic details (chipped paint, leaky faucets, loose doorknobs, and so on). The better your home looks, the quicker it will sell. Consult with your agent about the best way to present your home and what details need to attention and be ready to spend some money to address any recommendations.

Property inspection

Your buyer will have a home inspection (for plumbing and structural problems, and so on) to find out what deficiencies need to be addressed. The cost of repairs may be deducted from the sale price, likely with a margin of error that will benefit your buyer. You may wish to have your home inspected prior to listing if you suspect there is a serious problem or to provide assurance to potential buyers that the property is in good shape (of course, they may commission their own inspection, too).

If you're selling a condominium and the building has a positive engineering report, you have an excellent selling point — use it. A glowing inspection report from a reputable agency provides an incentive to potential buyers. However, if the inspection reveals any serious liabilities, you're legally obligated to disclose that information to potential buyers.

An inspection should cost $300 to $800. We discuss property inspections for sellers in Chapter 15.

Mortgage discharge fees

If you don't have a mortgage, give yourself a pat on the back and skip ahead to the next point! However, many people still have a mortgage when selling their home, which can create challenges with respect to timing, as we discuss in Chapter 13. Most lenders will charge legal and/or penalty fees when you discharge your mortgage prior to the end of its term, and you need to be aware of these fees at the time you take the mortgage out. Typically, fees are relative to the outstanding loan amount.

However, the frequency with which people move means lenders have several options available for handling your mortgage when you sell. The mortgage may be portable, allowing you to take it with you to your new home; alternatively, you may be able to let the buyer assume it, or you may be able to pay it off early.

Check your mortgage agreement to see what is permitted, and ask your lender about the fees you may incur (sites such as www.ratehub.ca provide calculators to determine the penalties for early discharge). Although fees are sometimes negotiable if you've been a long-time client of your lender, don't hold your breath. Many lenders have a policy where the penalties for early discharge aren't negotiable. Your lender and lawyer will help you to understand the finer points of the mortgage.

Property taxes and prepaid utilities

The day you usually pay your property taxes is not likely to coincide with the day you sell your home, nor the day when utilities are due (and there's even less of a chance of all three happening on the same date). That means the sale contract will specify an *adjustment date* (the day the buyer assumes all responsibility for paying property taxes, and so on). Usually the adjustment date is the same day as the *possession date*, or the day you hand the buyer the keys. In effect, your buyer may owe you a refund on a portion of your annual property taxes, or you may owe the buyer some money if you don't prepay your property taxes.

Likewise, any prepaid utilities, condo fees, or assessments need to be reviewed. Your lawyer will work out exactly how much is owed to whom and adjust the taxes as part of the conveyance or statement of adjustments. The statement of adjustments shows the net result for the seller or purchaser of the home, taking into account the purchase price, deposit, real estate commissions, legal fees, property purchase tax, property taxes, and all other adjustments.

Moving costs

How much it costs to move depends on how much stuff you're moving, how far you're moving it, and which moving company you hire. Several variables will factor into moving costs, including the time of year and any items you may be moving that require special care (such as your baby grand piano). Do your research. Find out exactly how much stuff you've accumulated over the years and how much getting it to your new home is really going to cost.

An extra few hours assessing the contents of your basement and garage, plus a phone call or four, are a lot less hassle than under-budgeting your moving costs by several thousand dollars or finding out too late that your one-bedroom home has three bedrooms' worth of memorabilia (two-thirds of which won't fit into the moving truck). We provide tips on weeding out items that you don't need to move in Chapter 12.

Appraisal fees

You need to know the value of your home before you set the selling price. If you're not using an agent, you may want to hire a professional appraiser for an expert opinion of how much your home is worth. (Your buyers will probably still have a second appraisal done — their mortgage lender may require it, or they may simply want to be certain they're getting a good deal.) If you're using a reputable and experienced agent, you may not bother with a pre-listing appraisal. For more information, see the section "Comprehending the Basics of Appraisals for Sellers" earlier in this chapter.

REMEMBER

Don't confuse an appraisal with an inspection. An inspection reveals any major structural or systems-related problems with your home that will need to be fixed before you sell; an appraisal investigates what the market value of your home is. The appraiser may take into account any of the same problems that the inspector looks for, but will focus on the impact these have on the fair market value of the property.

Location-specific expenses

Some geographic regions come with their own unique set of housing issues. As a seller, you may be responsible for extra costs associated with your particular region.

Believe it or not, Canada has termite hot spots. If you know you live in a hot spot, you may want to have a termite inspection performed. Insects and other pest problems may be part of a standard home inspection. If you live in a region notorious for pest infestations, such as southern Ontario, you may have to pay for a separate inspection. In some cases, getting a termite warranty is possible. If you have one, and keep it active; it may cover the cost of the inspection.

If you live in the country, regular testing of well water is advised as well as regular servicing of the septic system. You may need to hire a landscaping company for mowing acres of lawn and plowing several feet of snow on the driveway. Maybe you live on a fault line, or maybe you live on a flood plain. Wherever you live, be aware of the extra expenses you'll incur because of your location (see Chapter 19 for more on regional concerns).

GST/HST

Regardless of whether the sale of your home is exempt from GST/HST, the federal goods and services tax that's harmonized with provincial sales taxes in some provinces applies to most services you'll use in selling your home. The fees you pay to real estate agents, lawyers, appraisers, building inspectors, surveyors, and anyone else will apply GST/HST on top of their service fees.

Selling your home is an expensive endeavour, but the old saying that "time is money" certainly applies when selling your home. You're also going to spend time — lots of it. This brief overview gives you a sense of the common costs, but every situation is different. Just remember that anything you pass off to someone else will cost you money; anything you don't will cost you time.

Tallying it up

When you have an idea how much selling your home will cost, you can estimate how much money you will make (we assume the best) on the sale of your home.

If you have investigated the anticipated market value of your home and each of the costs we outline earlier in this chapter, then you've already done the hard part. Just fill in Table 14-1 to determine the net proceeds you'll realize from selling your home. Start with your home's estimated sale price and then subtract the associated costs. What you're left with are the net proceeds from the sale.

TABLE 14-1 **Calculating the Net Proceeds from the Sale**

Item	Amount
Estimated sale price	_____
– Agent's commission/and or flat fees	_____
– Legal fees	_____
– Repairs or renovations	_____
– Discharge of your mortgage	_____
– Property taxes and prepaid utilities +/–	_____
– Moving costs	_____
– Survey fees (if applicable)	_____
– Appraisal fees (if applicable)	_____
– Location-specific expenses (if applicable)(termite inspection, well water inspection)	_____
– GST/HST (if not already included)	_____
Net proceeds from sale =	_____

Some Good News about Taxes

The money you make on the sale of your home (remember, we're assuming the best!) and the money you spend moving to your new home may be tax deductible (it's true!). Here's how it works.

Principal residence exemption

If you have lived in your home the entire time you have owned it, all proceeds of the sale are tax exempt — this is known as the *principal residence exemption*. If, however, you bought a residential lot and waited a while to build on it, or the home was not your principal residence for a period of time while you owned it, then some tax may apply.

Since 2016, the federal government requires disclosure of the sale of a principal residence on your personal income tax return to ensure the sale wasn't speculative in nature (or what's technically known as "an adventure in the nature of trade"). There are exceptions. For example, you can use your primary residence as a rental property for up to four years under certain circumstances and still retain your capital gains exemption.

However, if you fear losing your capital gains exemption, your accountant may be able to provide guidance as to the possible scenarios for you. And there is some good news:

>> If the home sells for a price that's less than what you paid originally, the proceeds are nontaxable (no gain, no pain!).

>> However, if the sale price is greater than the original purchase price, a portion of that money may be taxable.

The following example gives you an idea of how much of how the CRA will view your situation. In early 2009, Jesse and Danielle bought a beautiful lot for $75,000 just outside Guelph. They had one daughter and were hoping to have more children after they settled into their new house. They spent two years renting while they built their dream home, which was completed in 2011 for $225,000. The family lived happily in their new home, and as the economy boomed, so did their family. They had twins, then a fourth child ("a bonus," says Danielle). They decided to sell and move to an acreage near Fergus where Jesse could work from a home office, Danielle could have a huge garden, and the children would have plenty of room to roam. Owing to the large influx of new residents in their area, housing prices had skyrocketed. They managed to sell their home in 2018 for $750,000, more than double the $300,000 they paid for the lot and construction. Using the principal residence exemption formula, Jesse and Danielle did the math to figure out the taxable gain on the sale when they filed their tax return for 2019:

8 years as principal residence (2011 to 2018, plus one*) ÷ 9 years that they owned the property (2009 – 2018) = 0.89

* One year is added for the purposes of the capital gains exemption calculation to account for the use of the property as a principal residence in 2018 even though they technically owned two in that tax year, and Jesse and Danielle were residents of Canada in 2009, the year they purchased the property.

0.89 × $450,000 (net change in value) = $400,000

The calculations show that because the home was the principal residence for Jesse and Danielle for almost 90 percent of the time they owned it, close to 90 percent of their capital gain (the difference between what they spent to acquire the property and the gross sale proceeds) — or $400,000 — is tax-free! That means just $50,000 is subject to capital gains taxes. Because the couple was joint owners, the taxable capital gains could be further divided between them, further mitigating the pain.

WARNING

If you've owned your principal residence since before 1982, you need to use a slightly more complex formula than the principal resident exemption formula — due to a change in the taxation policy in 1981. The procedure for long-time home-owners is the same, only you have to calculate the exempt portion twice, under the hypothetical assumption that you sold your home on December 31, 1981, at its FMV for that year, and reacquired it on January 1, 1982.

Moving tax credits

If you're an employee relocating for a new job (or being transferred), if you're self-employed and relocating for professional reasons, or if you're moving to become a full-time post-secondary student, your moving and selling expenses are tax deductible! These expenses include all the selling costs listed in Table 14-1, except repairs or renovations, and your personal travel costs, including food and lodging. They also include the cost of shipping and storing your belongings and up to 15 days of temporary room and board near either your current home or your new home. Even legal fees and transfer taxes (affectionately known as "the welcome tax") incurred on the purchase of your new home count as moving expenses. The only catch is that your new home has to be at least 40 kilometres closer to your new school or place of business (so if you're moving from one part of the city to another, it probably doesn't count).

REMEMBER

Tax rules are constantly changing, so be sure to research current policies via the Canada Revenue Agency website (www.cra-arc.gc.ca) and double-check the rules with your accountant to make sure there are no surprises.

IN THIS CHAPTER

» Inspecting your home for deficiencies

» Deciding what renovations to make, if any

» Using successful marketing strategies

» Ensuring your home makes a lasting first impression

Chapter **15**

Making Your House Shine

After you're set on selling your old place and finding a new place to call home, your attitude towards your current house will change. Your home — the place where you've relaxed, slept, worked, ate, raised kids, and cuddled pets (and maybe let dust bunnies accumulate in the corner) — will slowly become a commodity, a house. And if you get top dollar for this house, you'll be in a better position to buy a great new home.

In this chapter, we work with you to take a good, hard look at your house that helps identify what needs to be done to improve it and what improvements are unnecessary. After you've decided what needs to be done, we give you tips on how to make it the shiniest house on the block. A good place to start is a property inspection, which can pinpoint the improvements that need to be done to make the home a safe bet to a potential buyer.

Taking a Closer Look at Inspections for Sellers

We know what you're thinking: "Why would I want to pay hundreds of dollars for an inspection when the buyer will have one done anyway?" You're right, your buyer will, almost certainly, have an inspection performed on your home. Some lenders will approve a buyer's mortgage only subject to the home passing a full inspection, and most buyers' offers are also contingent on the seller's home passing a full inspection.

If your house is well maintained, then an inspection generally isn't necessary — don't waste your money. However, if the real estate in your vicinity is affected by common problems — like radon in the Maritimes, contaminated well water in rural areas, or leaky condos in British Columbia — having an inspection done may be advisable. A positive prelisting inspection report can be a great tool to relieve buyers' concerns. (Refer to Chapter 10 for tips on choosing an inspector.)

Having your home inspected: The why

If you have your home inspected before you put it on the market, you stand to realize the following benefits:

» **An inspection alerts you to any defects that require repair.** You may want to do the repairs to help raise the value of your home, as well as to prevent haggling with buyers over the cost of repairs that, in turn, affect the asking price for your home. Also, by doing the necessary repairs before you list the home, you cut down on the amount of time your home may spend on the market — an important consideration when trying to attract prospective buyers. Remember, many buyers don't have the interest, the energy, or the excess cash to make repairs. An increasing number of buyers expect move-in ready premises that are as good as new, particularly in active urban markets like Toronto and Vancouver. You may save a sale by doing what your buyer isn't interested in undertaking herself.

» **Commissioning a professional home inspection before you list may save you from having to redo any cosmetic improvements.** For example, if an inspection reveals you have to take out part of the walls of your home office to update the wiring, then you want to find this out before you add a fresh coat of paint.

>> **Providing a full inspection report to potential buyers gains their respect.** It fosters trust in both you and your home.

>> **If you're selling your home privately, a professional home inspection may help you determine the value of your home.** In turn it enables you to set the right list price for your property.

Having your home inspected: The why not

We have to point out the two main drawbacks to having your home inspected before putting it on the market:

>> **If your inspection reveals any serious problems, you're legally obligated to disclose that information to potential buyers.** You're also obligated to tell your agent, if you're required to sign a disclosure statement — refer to Chapter 16 for details on disclosures. You may prefer the "ignorance is bliss" approach, but chances are your buyers (and their lawyers) won't share this point of view.

>> **An inspection costs $300 to $800.** Any buyers who make you an offer will have their own inspection performed, regardless of whether you offer one.

If you don't feel you need an inspection report to inspire buyer confidence, and you're certain that your property meets safety standards, don't waste your money on an inspection. If you just want to make sure that your plumbing and wiring are in good condition, you may just want to get a plumber or an electrician to take a look around. Ditto for a roof: Knowing how much life is left in your roof can be very important when selling a home. Having your home inspected before putting it on the market can eliminate one more uncertainty from the selling process, and that means one less thing you have to worry about. The real benefit of a prelisting inspection is *peace of mind*.

Knowing what your inspector looks at

Similar to when you bought the property, an inspector will closely examine all the major functional systems in your home, including the following:

>> **Structural components:** Roofing, foundations, floors, walls, columns, and ceilings

>> **Exterior components:** Exterior wall cladding, doors, windows, eaves, balconies/decks, and vegetation

>> **Interior components:** Walls, stairways, counters, cabinets

>> **Heating and cooling systems:** Furnace, air conditioning

>> **Electrical systems:** Wiring, outlets, and GFCIs

>> **Plumbing:** Condition of pipes, faucets, and drains

>> **Insulation and ventilation:** Insulating materials, ductwork

Refer to Chapter 10 for more information on inspections.

Preparing for the inspector

The inspector isn't authorized to turn on any systems that aren't already operating at the time of the inspection. So you need to have all your home's systems turned on and ready for the inspector's visit, including gas, water, electrical, heating, cooling, and plumbing systems. Be on hand to help if the inspector needs to rearrange your personal property in order to gain access to blocked-off areas. You can take a few steps to make sure the inspector can do the job easily and thoroughly:

>> Make sure electrical panel boxes are unblocked.

>> Remove clutter blocking access to electrical panels, the attic, basement crawl spaces, the foundation, heating and cooling systems, water heaters, and pipes.

>> Restrain your pets and watch your children so they don't interfere with the inspection.

>> Have a copy of each of the following:

• Any service records, warranties, or information on age and performance for appliances that will come with the home

• A written list with the age of all major structural components and systems components, and any service records and warranties

• Your utility bills for integrated systems (for example, electric or gas)

REMEMBER

The inspector doesn't evaluate your home — if you want an evaluation, hire an appraiser (refer to Chapter 2 for tips on selecting an appraiser). An inspector merely reports. For example, your house may be of the "they don't make 'em like they used to" variety, but the inspection report states only that your furnace is 48 years old and is functional and presently operational, not how well it heats. If you want a report that includes how well your systems function, hire the necessary heating or plumbing contractors to evaluate these systems.

Undertaking Home Improvements

If you're addicted to home renovation reality shows, you're not alone. Just stroll down the aisle of any home improvement store, and you'll run into do-it-yourselfers as well as contractors shopping for their clients. A surge in online tutorials has also helped boost the ranks of people keen to fix up their homes.

As a seller, renovations mean more to you than just making the place more livable. Hopefully you're increasing the resale value of your home, too. Lots of people feel that way. However, one of the most common selling mistakes is to make major renovations before a sale. Pouring thousands of dollars into renovations doesn't result in an equivalent increase in the market value of your home. Some renovations are good and others are bad in terms of a return on your investment, and you need to know which is which before jumping in with both feet. Renovations that would have fallen into the good category or the bad category can, if poorly executed or done without recognizing what buyers in your neighbourhood expect, can knock money off your sale price.

If you're a homeowner who has maintained your home properly, you're likely far less concerned with needing to do any last-minute renos or repairs. Regular upgrades can pay off into the future, and cut down the work needed to create curb appeal and attractive interior spaces. Plus, you get to enjoy the benefits before you move, too!

Keeping future returns in mind

When you're getting ready to sell your house, focus on improvements that will save your buyer money as a new owner and make it more desirable. For example, making your home more energy efficient means your buyer saves on heating and cooling costs. However, this renovation probably won't return more than 30 to 50 percent of your investment. In fact, there are few, if any, renovations for which you'll get back all of what you put in. Here are some guidelines to follow as you spruce up your home to sell it:

>> **Inexpensive cosmetic improvements, such as repainting, are always your best bet.** Select colours from a neutral, conservative palette to repaint your house inside and out. (You may think that a magenta living room is warm and inviting, but most buyers won't.) These colours will make your house look brighter, larger, and well maintained. Statistics show that when you sell your house, you'll recoup at least 60 to 65 percent of the money you spent on painting.

>> **If interior or exterior structures of your home need improvement to make it saleable, then larger renovations may be worth the time, money, and hassle.** For example, if you neglected to add an extra bathroom to go with those two extra bedrooms you built back in 2005 and your daughters have grown up having to run across the house when nature calls, then adding one now may make sense. As a general rule, kitchens and bathrooms are good places for renovations. Upgrading the features of existing kitchens and bathrooms make good selling points, too, and return about 65 to 75 percent of the money spent.

But if you'll never make back the money you spend, why would even consider renovating? The fact is, if buyers recognize your home needs work, they'll factor the expense into their offering price as well as a generous margin of error. You can either sell your home *as is*, which means the buyers will negotiate a lower price and undertake renovations and improvements themselves, or you can undertake some strategic renovations yourself before you sell. Although you may never get a 100 percent return on the money you spend renovating, you may lose less than if you were forced to drop the sale price into the "as is" category.

TIP

Sometimes renovations simply aren't warranted. Even though your 50-year-old bungalow could badly do with sprucing up, renovating may not be worth it if all the houses on your street were sold and redeveloped. If people are buying local homes to rebuild them, let others do the improvements.

TIP

If you're thinking about renovating, talk to your real estate agent. If you aren't using an agent, good places to go for information are the Canada Mortgage and Housing Corp. (www.cmhc.ca) or the Canadian Home Builder's Association (www.chba.ca). If you're curious about how much (or how little) a renovation will add to the resale price of your home, the Appraisal Institute of Canada (www.aicanada.ca) has a guide sizing up returns from the 20 most popular home renovations in Canada. The guide isn't meant to replace a professional appraisal, but you'll get a rough idea of the value of your renovations. (A quick overview of the payback on common renovations also appears in Chapter 8.)

WARNING

Remember all those people you saw in the aisles at the home improvement stores? Well, a lot of them are attempting to do home renovations themselves. Although many of these home improvement stores now offer in-house classes on how to do things like tiling, a level of skill and patience is still required. Are you really up to the task of replacing the tub or the backsplash in the kitchen? You may end up having the job done twice: the first time when you mess it up, and a second time when a professional has to come in to do it right. Shoddy renovations can end up costing more money in the long run and will be detected when the home inspector pays you a visit. They also make potential buyers suspicious. If buyers notice that the new dimmer switches you installed spark when they're turned, they'll wonder what else wasn't done properly. If you need to upgrade plugs or switches, call an electrician. Keep yourself and your family safe, and the next family who will be moving in.

TIP

Ideally, if you have time to plan, consider renovating gradually so that you're able to get some benefit out of the improvements before you sell. That way, they'll have some worth to you rather than be a last-minute investment to boost your home's value. But if you're looking to sell immediately, leave significant renovations to the next owners. They'll know what they want.

Creating curb appeal

Making a good first impression is crucial to selling your home. Potential buyers don't walk up your driveway blindfolded; their first view of your property is from the street. Your home has to look good outside as well — this is often called curb appeal. You never know who's going to drive by your front yard, so consider it part of your marketing strategy.

PRETTY ON THE OUTSIDE

In case you're wondering where to begin, here's a checklist of tasks to help enhance the exterior of your home and yard:

- Clean out the garage, and put any large, infrequently used items into storage (or better yet, sell them if you won't need them).

- Clean windows, shutters, eaves, doors, and mailboxes.

- Replace damaged window or door screens.

- Do any necessary repairs, and touch up paint.

- Get out the gardening gloves: Trim hedges, trees, and shrubs; rake leaves; mow the lawn; weed gardens; tend to flowers.

- Clean oil marks and stains off the driveway; it may even be worthwhile resealing your driveway to make it look like new.

- Ensure the garage door opener is working properly.

- Clear and clean paths, patios, and patio furniture.

- Make sure your house number is visible from the street.

- Do last-minute tidying to get rid of any clutter that's accumulated over the past week.

- Pick up all junk mail regularly.

A big For Sale sign in front can go a long way to getting your home noticed, but you want to make sure the next reaction will be "And it looks great!" You have to draw buyers in before you can dazzle them with the stunning reclaimed hardwood floors and huge master bedroom with en-suite bathroom. Getting the right kind of attention requires a plan of attack.

Take a good look at the exterior of your home. Is the hedge overgrown, and are the shutters peeling paint? Is your garage jam-packed to the rafters with ten years' worth of outgrown hockey equipment and broken toys? Take the time to trim those hedges, repaint the shutters, and clean out that garage. If you don't have room to park your cars, your potential buyer will assume you don't have enough storage space — not a good impression, and that can cost you a sale.

Alluring interiors

Inside your home you must be concerned about two extra qualities: neutrality and ambience. Being organized and spotless isn't enough. Buyers who are touring your home need to be able to see themselves living in it, which means you have to erase, as much as possible, your personality from the interior. A neutral setting lets buyers start to think seriously about your house as "my new home," which is the first step toward an offer. This neutrality doesn't just mean toning down personal touches: It also means removing family photos from the mantle, and all the finger-painted masterpieces from the refrigerator. After you've visibly neutralized your house, you need to take care of all the other senses that create ambience — the smells, sounds, and feels that make your home comfortable and inviting. The sidebar "An inviting inside" helps make sure you've covered all your bases.

TIP

If you plan to repaint, or if you're replacing countertops or fixtures, choose light, neutral colours. Painting is better than wallpaper — it's much easier for a buyer who doesn't share your design sense to repaint than to strip wallpaper. Light, neutral paint will make rooms brighter and feel larger and will remove some of your personality from the decor. Simple cosmetic improvements are relatively inexpensive and can make a big difference to the appearance of your home. Make sure all light fixtures are operational and that the lighting is appropriate for the environment — a dangling lightbulbs may be okay in an unfinished basement, but soft task lighting around the kitchen and attractive fixtures in the bedroom will set the right tone in those spaces.

Be prepared to show at any time of day or night and on short notice. Keep things clean and have a contingency plan for your family and pets in case your agent calls unexpectedly.

AN INVITING INSIDE

Hardly know where to begin? Take a look at this list, and plan to perfect your home's interior appeal:

- Undertake needed renovations (see "Keeping future returns in mind" earlier in this chapter for guidance on "good" and "bad" renovations).

- Repaint or touch up paint and repair cracks in the plaster.

- Fix or replace leaky faucets, loose wobbly doorknobs and cupboard handles, and squeaky hinges or floorboards.

- Clean draperies and upholstery; shampoo carpeting.

- Move excess furniture and belongings (especially toys) into storage — buyers will have an easier time walking around, and the rooms will appear larger.

- Purge closets.

- Get rid of any unwelcome visitors, such as the pantry moths in the kitchen, the family of mice in the crawl space, or the earwigs that congregate around the back door and venture into the family room.

- Wash inside windows, walls, panelling, and any other surface that may have smudges or fingerprints.

- Put away all small appliances on kitchen countertops, and clean any large appliances that are included in the sale.

- Put jewellery and valuables in a safety deposit box.

- Add comforting touches like candles or flowers; light the fireplace (if you have one, if it's clean and functional, and if it isn't August).

- Have fresh towels in bathrooms.

- Empty all garbage cans, and make sure that all sinks are clean and all toilets are flushed.

- Clean out inside kitchen and bathroom cabinets, especially under sinks.

- Be aware of potentially offensive odours, such as from pets or your favourite brand of incense, and take appropriate countermeasures. Putting a few drops of vanilla in a warm oven just before a showing is a common ploy, as is baking bread or some other comforting treat. If you're a smoker or have one living in your home, take your habit outside, at least while your property is on the market (and give the walls a good scrub; one solution to eradicating an accumulation of smoke in the walls is washing them down with a mix of water and ammonia).

(continued)

(continued)

- Weather permitting, open windows to let in as much fresh air as possible.

- Place any inspection reports, records, or information sheets outlining the features of your home in plain view, with enough copies so that buyers can take one with them.

To make sure the steps you've taken have made the interior of your home more appealing and less offensive to the senses, ask a trusted friend if any bad odours or other negative elements are present.

Clearing out your clutter

You may think that your collection of international beer cans is a work in progress, but chances are your prospective buyer thinks of it as junk. Decluttering is a combination of cleaning, clearing, and organizing before showing your house. With each item, ask yourself, "Do I really need this?" Be honest. If you don't need it, get rid of it. If you do, figure out exactly where the item should go and then keep it there. Clutter-free rooms look more spacious and make the house more appealing to potential buyers. Plus, you'll have less stuff to pack up, move, and unpack. Chapter 12 offers specific guidance about what to move and what to ditch and tips to make the decluttering process go a little more smoothly.

Home staging: Cue the professionals

Home staging professionals prepare your home to be shown to buyers, making sure to show all its finest qualities in the best possible light. You can't argue with the reasons why people stage their homes: The better a house looks, the better a price it'll fetch. If the market is a little slow when you list your home, home staging can speed up the selling process by making your home the star attraction among the others on the market. If your home has languished on the market for a couple of months, you may want to call in a staging company and let its team work their magic instead of reducing your asking price. Your agent may be able to make the arrangements as part of the marketing strategy.

Staging enhances your home's best features with appropriate colours, furnishings, and props to make it all the more alluring to potential buyers. A home staging professional will evaluate every room in your house (yes, even the back area where you keep your lava lamps) and make recommendations on how to make the rooms look bigger and better, highlighting the good and hiding the bad and the ugly. Apply the same process to your yard.

Staging can be an especially strategic move for a vacant home. A fully furnished home usually looks more attractive than a vacant space, so a properly staged vacant property will often sell more quickly — and hopefully at a higher price — than a vacant property that looks empty and neglected. The staging company will bring in furnishings, artwork, and plants (temporarily, of course) to give the home a polished look. Better still, if you're busy and a bit stressed, like most people selling their homes, they'll come in and do all the work for you.

WARNING

Home staging can be fairly expensive. Depending on whether you want a simple consultation, major rearranging, or a complete staging, you'll need to think about how much you can afford to spend. Most staging companies will offer an à la carte range of services, ranging from a quick rearranging of furniture to a total redo with rented furniture and accessories. Many staging companies have a minimum term of contract (60 days or 90 days, for example), and at the end of that term, you can decide if you want to keep the staging furniture or pay for the decorating and consulting done to date and move on . . . hopefully, your home has sold in the initial staging period.

Should you hire a home staging professional? It depends on your budget, the type and current condition of your home, and your neighbourhood, as well as how quickly you need to sell. Although staging your home isn't guaranteed to sell your home for above the asking price, it can give you a huge advantage over homes that are only so-so in appearance. To identify a staging company that's a good fit, ask your real estate agent and friends for recommendations, research the options, and interview at least three candidates before making a choice.

Going to Market

So your home sparkles inside and out and you're ready to spread the word that you want to sell. From the sign on your front lawn to your open house, your marketing techniques are a key part of the home-selling process. Although you may be able to advertise a garage sale with a flyer posted at the end of your street, we suspect selling your home will take a bit more effort. To sell your home with the least amount of hassle — and for the highest price — you need to have a marketing plan.

The more professional you are about your advertising, the more trusting your buyer is likely to be. If you're selling with the help of a real estate agent, you automatically benefit from the image and credibility of the company your agent works for and its marketing expertise.

If you're selling your house on your own, take a page from the real estate agent's book: A coordinated effort is better than a haphazard one. An agent explores all avenues for sale and acts like a salesperson. You should, too. Prepare information sheets that look professional (not handwritten), use clean, professional signage, and be polite to buyers. If you're technically adept, take top-quality photos of your property and possibly even develop a short video that tours buyers through your home.

The following sections outline the basics of promoting, also called exposing, your home to the largest number of potential buyers.

Your basic For Sale sign

If you have a yard, posting a For Sale sign in it is one of the best ways to attract buyers. If they're interested in your neighbourhood, buyers will tour the area looking for potential homes. Don't let them miss yours. Your sign should be prominently displayed (perpendicular to the road) and list a number where your real estate agent or you, the homeowner, can be reached. If your house is on a corner lot, maximize your exposure by putting a sign facing each road, providing local bylaws allow more than one sign.

Unless you put the words "by appointment only," your buyers may come knocking at any time of the day or night. (In fact, they may come knocking any time, regardless. Be forewarned.)

TIP

If you're selling on your own, give yourself an edge by investing in a quality For Sale sign. Make sure that the sign will withstand weather conditions and has a solid post or spike so that it can be easily secured out front of your home. A quick search online should help you find a quality sign maker at a reasonable price. The sign should say "Private Sale" or "For Sale by Owner" and include a number where interested buyers can call or text you.

Advertise, advertise, advertise

Real estate agents are a home seller's best marketing tool because they're constantly in touch with potential buyers and other agents. The majority of home sales are completed through agent-to-agent contact, not by advertisements or For Sale signs. Nevertheless, an advertisement is part of a well-rounded marketing plan. Your goal is to get people to phone and book an appointment, so you want to cast as wide a net as possible.

A good advertisement gives the basic information — the general location, kind of house (bungalow, split-level), and key selling features such as the number of bedrooms and bathrooms. Be sure you include the price, which will help buyers know if the property is in their price range. A good ad will tempt, but not give away everything. After all, you want to entice buyers to actually come by and see your home.

Whether you're working with an agent or going solo, keep these elements in mind when developing your ad:

» A list of the top five or ten reasons you bought the home and that you think would appeal to others

» Key local amenities or features, such as top-ranked schools, a waterfront location, or unbeatable view

» The way you're selling. If you're selling privately, make sure you're clear about the advertisement saying "Private Sale" or "For Sale by Owner," because many buyers will see an opportunity for a good deal through shared savings on the commission.

TIP

When people phone you, ask them how they heard about your house, so that when it comes time to review your progress, you can stop advertising in places that aren't getting results. Advertising will cost money, but missed buyers will cost you more.

Reaching beyond newspapers

The rise of online media outlets has virtually displaced the local newspaper as a key venue for real estate listings. Many may feature a page of listings, but that's a fraction of what's available online through both the Multiple Listing Service (www.mls.ca) and For Sale by Owner sites.

If you're working with a selling agent and have an MLS listing, you're well on your way to reaching a wide audience. If you're selling on your own, you'll want to try to get as much online attention for your home as possible. There are the "For Sale by Owner" sites, but don't forget places like Facebook, Craigslist, and Kijiji, either.

If you're selling your home yourself and you're relatively tech savvy, you may want to create your own website. If you don't have the gadgets, your local web design company can help you out, or you can just ask your favourite techno-geek. You can register a domain for your property's address — www.33CreweAvenue.ca, for example — and make it as simple or extravagant as you want (just make sure it's functional and doesn't take eons to load). Keep in mind what you'd want to get out of the website if you were a homebuyer. Would you want entertainment or straightforward information about the house? Most likely the latter. Remember, if people are turned off by the site's appearance, they probably won't give a darn about your house.

Be sure to include the website URL in any print marketing materials. You may not be able to include a video on a piece of paper, but by directing people to the site you can take potential buyers on a virtual tour that gives them a 360-degree view of each room. But be sure to keep your tour professional, and make your home look as good as it would if someone was doing an in-person walk-through. Avoid fancy camera tricks, no matter how fun the zoom and the fade-out features are — they'll just distract, or worse, annoy viewers. If you're including narration, write a script, don't improvise.

TIP

Always, always check for spelling mistakes or typos in your advertisement or website. People may be frightened to see you've got a "1,500-square-foot mouse for sale."

Making sexy feature sheets

A *feature sheet* is the classy, older sibling of the newspaper ad. It's essentially a flyer that you or your agent hands to potential buyers who come to view your home. It includes the same basic information — type of house, number of bedrooms and bathrooms, total floor area, neighbourhood, price, and contact information — but it also uses colour and strong design elements to make an impressive pitch for your house.

Selling with the help of an agent? If so, chances are your agent will prepare the feature sheet for you. If you're selling privately, here are some suggestions for making up your own feature sheet:

>> **Attend some open houses and ask for their feature sheets.** If you see a well-designed form, model your own in the same manner. Of course, you can't use any copyrighted text or illustrations, so don't plagiarize, but do take note of what information is specifically outlined and how it's presented most effectively.

>> **Put a great photograph of your house looking its very best on your feature sheet.** If you don't already have the right shot, hire a photographer or get a talented friend to take photos using a wide-angle lens. You may even want to use pictures of your house at different times of the year, so that prospective buyers can see how cozy your home looks with a dusting of snow, and how magnificent the gardens are in the summertime.

>> **Ensure the pages of the feature sheet are detailed, but also readable.** Don't feel you have to fill the page completely — white space allows people to focus on the important elements of your feature sheet without feeling

overwhelmed and leaves room for taking notes. Stick to a standard, easy-to-read font for the text and a simple, bold headline. If the elements of good typography are beyond you, ask a design-savvy friend to help or pay a professional to do the job.

If you have a scanner and a colour printer, you can print your own feature sheet. If you don't, most copy shops will print from a digital file you send them or bring from home. Keep copies handy to give to prospective buyers. You may even want to attach an information box to your lawn sign so that prospective buyers can pick up a copy when they drive by. The feature sheet provides a good reference when buyers are comparing homes and gives them a reminder of all the features your house offers. The feature sheet is a marketing tool that will keep selling your house even while you're on the golf green or taking a nap.

Showing (Off) Your Home

Showing your home can be a painful experience. If the reality of moving out of the beloved family home hasn't hit yet, it certainly will now. Try to focus on the excitement of what lies ahead, not the criticisms people are leveling at the house you're in. If you're selling on your own, find a balance between showing all the features of your house and letting people move through it at their leisure. Nothing annoys a buyer more than a seller hovering nervously over her shoulder.

If you're working with a real estate agent, he'll show your home to potential buyers for you. If you're selling privately, you may still allow other agents to show your home.

If you're selling privately, make it easy for buyers to reach you. Put your cell phone number on your sign and make sure to keep the phone with you so you can receive and return calls promptly. If your voice mail greets callers with the singing efforts of your 3-year-old, it's time for a change! Your outgoing message should state that the house is for sale and that you'll return calls as soon as possible.

The next few sections outline how to work with potential buyers, cultivating their interest and helping to get offers on the table.

LOCK-BOXING — NO PUNCHES PULLED

Some agents will use a *lock box system* to facilitate showings when you can't be around. A lock box contains your key and is secured with a coded lock system. If a buyer's agent wants to bring prospective buyers into your home, she can access the lock box and then return the key to it when the buyer leaves. All entries may be recorded so that you know who has gained access to your home, and when. In areas that do not have such systems, a numbered "punch code" might be used. If this is the case in your area, make sure the code is changed frequently by your agent to avoid unexpected or unscheduled intrusions.

The lock box system makes life infinitely easier for you. You don't have to automatically drop what you're doing as soon as you get wind of someone else who wants to see your house. Let your agent take care of the showing — that's one of the reasons you hired her. Your agent will leave a key to your house in an outdoor lock box. This allows other agents to show your house when your own agent can't be there. Now, pluses and minuses to this setup exist. On the one hand, your house may get shown to more buyers because the lock box is really convenient. However, it also means that your agent won't be there to point out the fantastic features your house has to offer and draw buyers' attention to the built-in bookcases in the study, the breakfast nook that gets the morning sun, and the short walk to the local school and shopping centre.

Nevertheless, buyers often want to look at homes with their own agent, not the seller's. A good agent chooses the right buyers to show the home to and doesn't need to go over each feature point by point with an overeager listing agent.

If your agent recommends a lock box, find out what security precautions are taken. Most companies verify the identity of the agents who want to show your house before giving them an access code to the lock box. Many lock box systems used in major metropolitan areas rely on a lock box "key" (which may be like a swipe card) that is issued only to agents, has a code known only to that agent, and must be updated daily. This means that if the key is lost, it's useless to anyone else, ensuring the safety and security of your home.

Nevertheless, you aren't obliged to use a lock box if you prefer to have your agent present at every showing. In fact, you can make it a condition of the listing that your agent is present at every showing of your house. Remember, you pay the commission, and you call the shots.

Fielding the calls

If you're selling privately, you take all the calls from people interested in your home. Handle phone calls as professionally as you can. Get back to buyers as quickly as you can and have all the information they may request on hand so that you can let them know you're serious about selling your home.

Many people, both buyers and sellers, find the initial phone call a bit awkward. You'll quickly find ways of putting yourself and your callers at ease, so don't be annoyed or defensive if the caller sounds wary at first. Keep these tips in mind:

>> **Always, always have a pen and paper by the phone.** Try to engage callers in a regular conversation so they don't feel as if they're being grilled. Respond to their questions frankly, and ask them questions as well. Find out as much as you can about your callers. Open-ended questions work best. What are they looking for in a house and neighbourhood? How familiar are they with the neighbourhood? Do they have school-aged children? Will they have to sell their own house before they buy?

>> **Demonstrate the ways your house may fit their needs as you answer their questions.** For example, if they have children, you'll want to emphasize the excellent reputation of the local schools, the recreational facilities in the nearby park, and the polite, well-adjusted teenagers down the road.

>> **Find out as much as you can about the callers.** You want to find out where they work and if they can give you a number you to reach them at there. This is useful for checking the identity of callers, and if you need to reschedule at the last minute, you know where to find them. Also, ask how they heard about your house, and make a note for when you review your marketing plan.

>> **Don't negotiate with buyers over the phone.** If they say the price is too high, urge them to come and look at the house. If you think they are serious buyers, ask them when they want to come to see your house. Make the time specific: "Would Thursday evening or Saturday morning be better for you?" Try to line up successive appointments, maybe 45 minutes apart, so that as one set of prospective buyers is arriving, the earlier one is leaving. This way, buyers get a sense that there is a fair bit of interest in your property . . . and you have to get your house ready only once.

>> **Call to confirm all appointments.** People are less likely to stand you up if you've called to confirm.

>> **Be prepared for a potential buyer to walk through the door on short notice.** One of the joys of cell phones is that someone may be standing on your front lawn asking when she can see your house. If you're working with an agent, he will schedule the appointment at a convenient time. If you're selling on your own, you'll have to get buyers to come back when it's convenient for you or let them in on short notice. You'll also have to keep your home in tip-top shape on a full-time basis. Even though all this may seem inconvenient (it is!), it'll all be worth it when you close the sale.

COOPERATING WITH AGENTS

If you're willing to cooperate with buyers' real estate agents, put "courtesy to agents" or "will cooperate with agents" in your ad. Some buyers won't deal directly with a seller and prefer to have their agent contact you to coordinate a showing. Some agents will call with prospective buyers for your house, and others will be interested in listing your house. Whether or not you decide to use an agent's assistance in selling your home, take the time to talk with one. An agent can offer you great advice on competitively pricing your home and potentially assist in the sale of your home.

Many real estate agents will be pleased to work with you. If an agent brings you a buyer and you can negotiate a commission fee, you may just have a deal. And because you want to sell your house, make sure you consider cooperating with an agent.

Staying secure

Real estate agents work with buyers all the time and become very good at screening people who either aren't serious about buying or are genuinely creepy. Likewise, if your home's showing is with another agent, that buyer's agent will have prequalified the buyers to make sure they can afford the house and ensure that they are ready to buy the right house if it comes along at the right time.

REMEMBER

When you're selling privately, you do have to talk to strangers, but you don't have to let them into your home. Trust your instincts. For your own safety, don't allow anyone who just knocks on your door to tour your home right away. If someone shows up without an appointment, speak to them at the door, and cover the same topics you'd discuss if they called to arrange to see your home. Take their names, phone numbers, and any other details. Explain that you can't show your home immediately, but you can make an appointment for later.

You may want to establish a safety system with a family member or friend. This could include providing a friend or neighbour with the names and phone numbers of everyone who has scheduled an appointment. Notify the friend or neighbour before each appointment, and make sure you check in again after the prospective buyer leaves. Conversely, you may want to have the friend or neighbour present with you for showings. In almost no other situation would you let a stranger in your home. Watch out for your own personal safety.

Make sure to take precautions against being robbed. Ask people to sign a visitor information sheet so that you know exactly who has been in your home, when they came in, and how long they stayed. This list will be useful for assessing the amount of interest in your house and for keeping track of prospective buyers with whom you'll want to follow up. However, in the event of theft or damage, you'll also have some information about everyone who has been through your home. (Keeping such lists became common practice for the purposes of contact tracing following the outbreak of COVID-19.)

Holding an open house

The open house is your home's big day. The basic idea is that your home is open for showing on certain designated days (usually during the weekend). An open house may cut down on the number of private showings you have to give, thereby reducing the disruption to your daily life. Also, many buyers feel more comfortable and leisurely being "one of the crowd" rather than touring on their own. Even though open house protocols have changed since COVID-19, resulting in smaller, often prequalified groups of buyers during a designated viewing window, open houses remain a primary option for exposing your home to a relatively large number of prospective buyers in a short amount of time.

The more people who see your home, the more chance there is that someone will fall in love with it. Someone who wasn't even thinking of moving may wander in and fall in love with your property! Your home should be at its best on the day of the open house, so follow our preparation tips in this chapter. If you haven't already overhauled your home, make sure you do so before the open house.

If you're selling privately, announce the times and dates of your open houses in your advertising materials and post an Open House banner on your For Sale sign with the hours showing. Buyers who happen to drive by and see the notice will think it's their lucky day. Make sure everyone who comes to the open house gets a copy of your feature sheet. Try to avoid booking an open house on a long weekend — it will probably be a waste of time. If you're not selling privately, you can rely on your agent to take care of all the organizational details of your open house.

TIP

All your neighbours — and your neighbours' friends — may troop through your home during your open house. Maybe they are just being nosy, but remember that word of mouth can be a great marketing tool, too. So let them talk. Give them a reason to talk! The more people who know about your fabulous home, the more potential buyers you may attract.

Whatever you do at the open house, here are four basic rules to observe:

>> **Don't negotiate the price verbally.** Be firm that you'll seriously consider all written offers.

>> **Don't give a particular reason why you're selling your home.** A good standard response is, "We've enjoyed this house, but it's time to move on."

>> **Don't indicate you're under time pressure to leave.** This gives potential buyers an edge when negotiating.

>> **Don't take things personally.** You want to sell your home, not defend your love of brown appliances. Don't lose your cool; you may lose a sale.

TIP

Many agents are encouraging video tours and other multimedia marketing tools since the outbreak of COVID-19. If you aren't comfortable with the idea of an open house, remember that technology offers a number of novel ways to interest buyers in your house without them having to visit it.

BUT NOTHING SEEMS TO BE WORKING!

If you've taken all of your real estate agent's expert advice (not to mention ours), had plenty of open houses, and still haven't received any offers, you must be wondering, what's gone wrong? The problem can be one of many things, but the following are the most common:

- The asking price for your home is too high.

- Your home is in poor condition.

- Your home is located in a less-desirable neighbourhood.

- Buyers don't know about your home.

Don't give up. Get feedback from potential buyers, either directly or through your agent. If you've heard from several buyers that they love your home and it's in great shape, but it's just a bit beyond their budget, you may consider lowering the price. If the general feeling among buyers is that the price and location are great, but the property feels dated, you may want to get out the paint and spruce up your home's appearance.

Make sure you talk to your agent about how many buyers have come through your home and what they're saying. You can drop your asking price, refresh your advertisements, or do some home improvements, but whatever the problem is, you can fix it only if you take the time to figure out what's stopping your home from selling.

6

Sealing the Deal

Chapter **16**

Examining Listings and Disclosures

I f getting ready to sell your house or condo meant only a fresh coat of paint and waiting for your agent's call, the process would be a lot less stressful. But like so many other major events in life, selling your home involves lots of details and decisions that need recorded.

This chapter focuses on one very important set of papers — the listing documents and the disclosures you need to make to buyers, so they can't come back and say, "You *didn't* tell us so!" The information guides you through the paperwork, helping you to breathe easy again, confident that you've lived up to your legal obligations while presenting your home in the best possible light to buyers.

Getting the Lowdown on Listing Contracts

Reaching potential buyers is the purpose of a good marketing campaign. Marketing your home involves listing it either on your own or through an agent. If you're listing through an agent, you'll need to fill out and sign a listing contract. The listing contract gives authorization to at least one agency to sell your home and specifies how much you'll pay for its services. We delve deeper into a listing contract here and discuss the different types.

Understanding the listing contract

A *listing contract* is a legal document that must be signed by both you and your agent, usually via standard forms that your local real estate board supplies. All the particulars about your home appear on the listing contract; it also states under what conditions you're willing to sell and you and your agent's obligations to each other. Make sure you obtain a copy of your listing contract related to the purchase and sale of your home.

If it makes you more comfortable or if you're concerned or confused about something in your contract, you can have your lawyer review it before you sign. Remember that although you're listing with an individual salesperson, the listing contract is with the salesperson's agency. (So if Suzanne Smith, your real estate agent, works for Sell That House Realty, your listing contract is with Sell That House, not with Suzanne.)

A listing contract deals with three sets of issues:

>> **The exact details of the property for sale:** Your home's lot specification, size, building materials, heating and air conditioning systems, number and description of rooms, and other details are included in the listing contract. Any extra items (movable things, such as appliances or furniture) or chattels included in the sale are also shown on the listing contract.

>> **The financial particulars relating to your home:** The listing contract establishes the asking price for your home and may (depending on your jurisdiction) disclose information concerning your mortgage (such as the balance, payment schedule, or maturity date) as well as the property taxes and any legal claims on your property.

>> **The precise terms of employment for your agent(s):** Your listing contract specifies who's allowed to market your home and in what manner as well as stating the time period in which your home can be marketed by the agent and what you'll pay the agent for marketing your home.

Contracts for Multiple Listing Service (MLS) listings include a standard disclosure statement that cover off all these three areas. We discuss disclosure statements in detail in the next section.

REMEMBER

Your listing contract doesn't require you to accept an offer on your home, even if the buyer fully meets the conditions of sale stipulated in the contract. A listing contract simply creates an agency relationship between you, the seller, and your selling agent. Throughout the sales process, your real estate agent acts on your best interests to sell the home, without misleading or making any misrepresentations to potential buyers. Refer to Chapter 2 for more information on agency relationships.

Selecting your listing type

You have three key options for listing your home if you're working with a traditional real estate agency:

>> **Multiple Listing Service listing:** Authorizes your agent to work with other agencies

>> **Exclusive listing:** Gives a single agency the right to market your home for a specific period of time

>> **Open listing:** Gives you the right to sell the property yourself while allowing other agents to present offers to purchase

When choosing the kind of listing that's right for you, consider all the variables. For example, what are the general market conditions? How well are other homes of the same size, price, and location selling? Do you have the time to be searching for buyers on your own? And exactly how easy should it be for buyers to find you? When you know what your needs are and you know the market conditions for homes like yours, you're in a good position to decide on your listing strategy.

REMEMBER

People who are serious about selling their homes list their homes via the MLS system because it gives their homes maximum exposure on the market. Because of this, many buyer's agents don't consider open or exclusive listings to be serious efforts to sell the property. The following sections take a closer look at these three options.

Multiple Listing Service

Multiple Listing Service (MLS) listings authorize the agent representing you to work with salespeople at other agencies. MLS listings are the most common kind on Canada and provide exposure to agents and buyers from coast to coast, reaching a huge network of real estate agents.

The Canadian Real Estate Association's MLS website (www.realtor.ca) allows access to nearly all the MLS listings in Canada through its links to local real estate boards across the country. Together with the local real estate boards that maintain it, the MLS system has very specific requirements regarding cooperation between real estate agents, protecting the interests of both buyers and sellers. The listing contract and the MLS data indicate what portion of the total commission is payable to the buyer's agent — that is, the agent who brings along a ready and willing buyer for the property.

TIP

MLS listings provide the fastest route to maximum exposure to the market for your home. If you need to sell quickly, you'll want to take out an MLS listing. And if you want the best possible price for your home, the surest way to get the right bid is to advertise to as many people as possible that your home is for sale. MLS listings achieve this, while allowing prospective buyers to see how your home stacks up against comparable properties.

Exclusive listing

An exclusive *listing* authorizes an agency to market your home for a specified period of time. A property with an exclusive listing won't appear on the MLS system and doesn't get the exposure the MLS system provides. As such, the commission for an exclusive listing may be less than the commission for an MLS listing. The reduced commission is the key advantage to the seller.

IF YOU EVER THINK OF SELLING, WOULD YOU LET US KNOW?

If a neighbour or friend expresses an interest in your home, you can add an exclusion to the listing contract (in exclusive and MLS listings only) that states you don't have to pay your agent a commission if that neighbour or friend — identified by name in the contract — buys your house. After all, you are the one who got them thinking about your home in the first place — not your agent!

Put the exclusion in writing before you sign the listing. Give the names of the excluded parties to your real estate agent before the listing documents are finalized. Your agent will prepare a letter stating the exclusion, which is signed the manager or broker. The letter should read something like this:

> "This letter is to confirm that XYZ Realty acknowledges that the following parties are excluded from the listing contract dated May 1, 20__, and should any of the parties purchase the property at 123 Main Street, Brandon, there will be no commission payable to XYZ Realty.
>
> Mr. and Mrs. Neighbour,
>
> 125 Main Street, Brandon
>
> Aubrey McCousin,
>
> 18 Showoff Lane, Moneysville
>
> Signed by both the agent and the agent's manager"

In some cases, an exclusion may have a time frame attached. For example, "No commission paid if either party purchases the property by May 30, 20__." Your agent may want this time frame included, because he'll be investing his time in the listing, so it's unreasonable to permit the neighbor or relative a lot of time to make a decision, not to mention the fact that the time frame usually encourages the excluded parties to make a decision sooner rather than later.

WARNING

Because an exclusive listing occurs outside the MLS system, your agent isn't under any obligation to show your property to other agents. Usually the listing agent cooperates with other real estate agents, but with an exclusive listing the listing broker has exclusive responsibility for marketing. (Refer to Chapter 2 for an explanation of the role of a real estate broker.) Because most sellers want the extra exposure and agent cooperation guaranteed by the MLS system, they'll opt for an MLS listing agreement.

Open listing

An *open listing* authorizes one or more agents to sell your home but protects your right to sell it yourself. Open listings are common in commercial real estate where properties or businesses are made available without being actively listed through an agent. They're less common in residential real estate. The most common type of open listing in residential real estate is in a For Sale by Owner scenario. The owner lists the property without an agent but entertains offers that arrive through an agent. Because you don't have an agent, you save on the commission and aren't obligated to pay one to an agent you presents you with a buyer. Instead, the buyer will typically pay the buyer's agent a finder's fee for locating the property. (The buyer's agent has an agency relationship with the buyer, but the seller has no agency representation.)

The downside, however, is that your listing may not appear on the MLS system, reducing its exposure. Because you're effectively the listing agent for the property, you'll have to put in more time and energy marketing the property and presenting it to potential buyers. Refer to Chapter 15 where we discuss what you need to know about For Sale by Owner listings.

Grasping the Importance of Disclosure Statements

When you sign the listing contract, you'll likely be required to fill out a *disclosure statement*, also known as a *property disclosure statement*, or in Ontario, a *seller property information sheet (SPIS)*. The disclosure statement is a legal document in which you describe your property and all other items included in the sale to the best of your knowledge. Depending on where you live, the disclosure statement may be viewed by the buyer prior to making an offer, or be provided to the buyer after you accept the offer. Regardless, the disclosure statement is usually incorporated into the contract (signed and acknowledged by the buyer) and becomes part of the contract. For MLS listings in Canada, disclosure is usually mandatory; for *most* exclusive listings, disclosure is recommended.

The disclosure statement informs the buyer and your agent about the condition of your home and protects you and your agent from any litigation in the event that a buyer discovers some dreadful problem with your property that you weren't aware of. By providing detailed information on the condition of your home, you ensure that your agent accurately represents your property to potential buyers.

WARNING

A disclosure statement won't protect you if you fail to disclose information about the property that misleads the buyer about its true condition. You are responsible, in short, if deliberately concealed information about your property comes to light after you've signed and submitted the disclosure statement. For example, if you commissioned a property inspection or appraisal of the property prior to proceeding with the listing and failed to disclose the faulty wiring or the fact that the guest room was a nonconforming suite, you could expose yourself to legal proceedings.

Knowing who sees your disclosure statement

Disclosure statements are designed for the benefit of all parties in the transaction. You disclose what you know about your property, and the buyer receives the disclosure statement, often using it as a starting point for a professional home inspection. Both the buyer's and seller's agents refer to the disclosure statement while viewing your home, and they may point to any disclosed deficiencies when negotiating the contract.

The disclosure statement puts the onus of accuracy on you, the seller, and any misrepresentation is potentially dangerous. As the seller, you must disclose everything you know about your home, and you're obligated to disclose anything that you should have been reasonably expected to know. For example, if there's a minor water leak in your basement that appears only once a year under heavy rains, you should disclose that there's potentially a problem with the drain tile or foundation. Buyers will inevitably find small problems you try to hide. In other words, if you're not sure whether to disclose, disclose.

By signing a legal document that states you have disclosed all knowledge of the condition of your property, you (the seller) are responsible for any concealment — usually not *your agent* — if a buyer pursues legal action after becoming aware of some previously undisclosed information. You are liable, however, only if you intentionally conceal information. If you don't disclose information because you aren't aware of the issue (and would have been just as surprised to discover it as the buyer), it's simply a case of bad luck. Your agent would be liable if *she* misrepresented any details provided by you, the seller.

Bear in mind that most buyers will do a building inspection, and by doing so, the buyer assumes some responsibility for the condition of the house. Buyers will do their due diligence as they inspect and investigate a house. If you complete a disclosure statement to the best of your knowledge, and a problem surfaces that you were unaware of and the home inspector missed, the buyer's dispute will likely be with the home inspector, not you.

TIP

In many areas, sellers may have the option to simply draw a line through the disclosure statement and state "the seller makes no representations regarding the subject property, and the buyer is to do their own due diligence." This option is common in several instances. The seller may have owned the property as an investment and rented it out, perhaps never having lived in it. Or it may be an estate sale, in which case the executor has no direct knowledge of the condition of the property. Or the seller may be unable to fill out the disclosure statement because of health issues or age. In these cases, buyer should be especially diligent with the home inspection, knowing that the seller hasn't provided any information.

Identifying what you need to disclose

The disclosure statement deals with all aspects of your property. It asks you about both land and structures. A typical disclosure statement deals with these three categories of information.

General information

This section is geared toward the land areas surrounding your property. You include information about the following, if applicable:

>> **Water and sewer:** Is your home connected to public water and sewage systems, and are you aware of problems with either of these systems?

>> **Rental units:** Do you have rental units, and are they authorized?

>> **Encroachments, easements, and rights-of-way:** Are there any that aren't registered in your title?

>> **Ownership issues:** Any notices of claims on the property need to be disclosed, alerting potential buyer to issues such as infringements on other properties or site issues like contamination that may need to be addressed.

Structural information

Here, you disclose information specific to your home itself. You may include any or all of the following:

>> **Insulation:** What kind of insulation do you have? When was it installed and are there any problems with it?

>> **Ventilation:** What kind of ventilation system do you have? Are bathrooms properly ventilated? Have there been issues with mould?

>> **Electrical, plumbing, heating/cooling systems:** Again, are there any problems you are aware of?

>> **Structural damage:** Is there any (unrepaired) damage from flooding, fire, or wind to the home?

>> **Pests:** Have you had any insect or rodent infestations? Have they been addressed? How and when?

>> **Inspections:** Has your home passed a full inspection? Do fireplaces, security systems, and safety devices meet local standards?

Additional information

This section provides blank space for any extra information that is relevant to the condition of your property, or for explaining any problems or conditions that have previously been mentioned, or repaired in the past.

If you're selling a condominium, you need to include information about current restrictions (regarding pets, children, rentals, or use of the condominium unit), and any future restrictions you're aware of (for example, new bylaws or proposals). You also need to disclose information about anticipated repairs or major construction projects planned for the building. Many of these potential issues will be addressed in the minutes of the condominium council, depreciation report, and other materials that sellers must provide to buyers and which buyers should review closely.

TECHNICAL STUFF

Some buyers may want to know about nonstructural issues, also known as *stigmatizing issues*, associated with a property. These can include a death either by natural or unnatural causes; criminal activity, paranormal activity, or even poor feng shui. Although some real estate associations recommend the disclosure of these factors, you aren't legally required to disclose them because the properties are generally habitable and structurally sound. Only factors that compromise the material structure or use of the building must be disclosed.

IN THIS CHAPTER

» Grasping the basics of sale contracts

» Knowing which parts of the sale contract concern you (the home seller) the most

» Taking into account important differences in condominium sale contracts

» Learning about legal terms and documents involved in transfer of ownership

Chapter **17**

Understanding the Legal Stuff

After you find a buyer, you need to take care of all the legal stuff. And though sale contracts, deeds, and titles may just seem like minor details compared to when you bought the property, taking them very seriously is vitally important. One slip-up can send your sale sideways. Selling your home is a great accomplishment, but you have to make sure it's done right. This chapter can help you figure out the ins and outs of the important legal documents.

Cooking Up a Recipe for a Successful Contract

Most home sellers were once home buyers, so more than likely you already know plenty about the purchase side of the *contract* (or *agreement*) of purchase and sale (take a look at Chapter 9 for more information). Here, we review the contract from a seller's point of view.

When the excited and happy buyer decides that she wants to buy your home, she fills out a contract of purchase and sale that includes

>> The offer price

>> Conditions to which the sale is subject

>> The intended possession date

The buyer's agent may give the contract to your agent, and you'll review the offer with your agent (or lawyer, if you're not using an agent). The buyer's agent may also choose to present the offer to you and your agent in person and give you some background information about the buyer, including how she arrived at the proposed purchase price. At this stage, the contract is called an *offer*.

You can discuss the offer at your house, but if there are too many distractions at your house (kids, pets, in-laws), you may want to meet at your agent's office or at the buyer's agent's office. Wherever you meet, you should feel comfortable and relaxed as you review the offer. Your agent will take you through the offer step by step and point out the key features, while the buyer's agent explains how or why the buyer made the offer subject to various terms and conditions.

If you and the buyer agree on all the terms and conditions, you'll have an accepted offer, subject to the agreed-upon terms in the offer. For example, if the offer is subject to the buyer receiving and approving an inspection report on your home by a certain date, your home won't be sold until the buyer has had a chance to review and approve the inspection report by that date. All conditions must be removed from the contract before your house is considered sold — that is, sold unconditionally with a firm and binding contract in place.

TIP

Keep in mind that you're entitled to negotiate the offer, so keep your emotions in check. The process need not be stressful, which is more easily accomplished with a calm approach.

Reading the Recipe: Basic Contract Know-How

Sale contracts are a bit like pancakes. Basic pancakes need flour, eggs, and milk, but beyond that you can add blueberries, bananas, cinnamon, maple syrup, and anything else you like, whether it's in the batter itself or on top. Great pancakes have no set recipe, but they all use some common ingredients. The same goes for real estate sale contracts. Most real estate agents have software that generate a standard form contract of purchase and sale. However, these programs also allow for the customization of the contract through the insertion of additional phrases and clauses that reflect the particulars of your situation. Because we can't tell you exactly what your recipe should be, this section outlines the sorts of things that will be of particular concern to you, the seller, in some key areas.

Real estate laws differ from province to province. Consequently, no single standard contract exists for all of Canada exists. Most home sales use a contract supplied by the provincial real estate board or association or its local affiliate. Be prepared to receive a lengthy document. The offer — the partially completed contract you receive from the buyers — may be six or seven pages, or longer.

Don't worry if your sale is particularly complex or unique. The standard forms are only a guide — they can be modified to suit the particulars of your sale, and you can add as many schedules, also known as *addendums*, as you need. These add-on forms specify all the clauses and conditions of sale that simply don't fit in the space allotted on the standard agreement. Some come with pre-printed clauses; others require you and your agent to fill in the particulars.

A contract of purchase and sale has a typical structure with three main sections: First it lays out the legal property description and terms of the offer, then the conditions of sale and any restrictions or obligations involved in the ownership of the property (known as *covenants*), and finally the signatures for acceptance. In the next sections, we explain all these contract components in detail.

A pound of offer

The buyer's agent prepares the offer to purchase and has a three-fold function. First, it identifies the parties involved in the transaction:

>> You (the seller)

>> Your buyer

>> The agent(s) acting on behalf of the buyer and seller

If your home is owned jointly by you and another party (perhaps your spouse or partner), both owners are identified in the seller section. Second, the offer identifies the home as it's registered with the local land registry office, including the lot and plan numbers, and sometimes the approximate dimensions of the lot. All this information is taken from the listing contract or from the title search that either you or the buyer (or your agents) have obtained. Last, the offer sets out the major financial details — usually consisting of the offered price and amount of the deposit.

Every offer has some common elements. Make sure that all this information is present:

>> The name and address of the buyer (in some provinces, supplied only upon acceptance of the offer)

>> The amount of the initial deposit accompanying the offer or payable on acceptance of the offer

>> The civic and legal address of the property being sold

>> The amount of the buyer's initial offer

>> Subjects and terms and conditions of the offer

>> Items included and excluded from the sale

>> Completion, possession, and adjustment dates (which may be the same day in some provinces or circumstances)

>> Time that the offer is open for acceptance (also referred to as *irrevocable time* in some provinces)

>> The buyer's signature (witnessed, where necessary)

An ounce of buyer

The name (or names) and address(es) of the buyer(s) let you know with whom you're dealing (in some provinces, the buyer's address is obtained only upon acceptance of the offer). If the offer is made by a corporate entity, you'll need to know the position the buyer holds in the company and whether or not the buyer has signing authority on behalf of the company.

WARNING

Be very careful if the buyer's name is followed by "and/or nominee" in the offer to purchase. The buyer may intend to assign the contract to a third party, and ideally the buyer should specify who that third party (or nominee) is on the contract. If the name of the third party isn't specified in writing, it may create ambiguity in the contract and possibly make the contract unenforceable. Your agent or lawyer can explain the proper way to assign the contract and deal with any potential problems.

A pinch of deposit

A *deposit* is an initial amount of money to confirm that the buyer is serious about the offer to purchase your home. The deposit will form part of the down payment when the sale is completed. We recommend that the deposit be made by certified cheque or bank draft. Indeed, in some parts of Canada, the deposit must be presented in this fashion.

No standard figure for the deposit exists, but from the seller's perspective, the bigger, the better. If the deposit is substantial, your buyer will be less likely to consider walking away before the sale is completed. A reasonable and substantial deposit is about 5 to 10 percent of the purchase price, depending on price range, although in competitive situations the buyer may offer as much as 15 percent, which can amount to the entire down payment. If you're buying another house based on the sale of your current home, the deposit gives you assurance that your buyer is committed to the purchase of your current home. You don't want to commit to buying a new house unless you feel secure that your buyer's offer is sincere and the sale of your home will complete on schedule.

Initially, the offer may be presented with a small deposit ($500 or $1,000) that the buyer will increase when all the conditions are removed from the contract. In some provinces, no initial deposit is required; the buyer makes only one deposit of about 5 percent or even as little as 2 percent. If the buyer doesn't make a sincere effort to satisfy and remove the conditions, thereby collapsing the offer, she risks forfeiting the deposit. If the buyer breaches the contract after conditions have been removed and you suffer damages, you may be in a position to sue.

The buyer's deposit can be placed in an interest-bearing trust account, so that at least the buyer will earn interest on the money until the sale completes. Real estate agents will have a company trust account in most cases, and there may be a small surcharge involved for holding the deposit in trust.

A dash of address details

Your *home's address* is included to make sure you're selling the right property. The legal address isn't that much of an issue in towns and cities, but if you're selling vacant land, you should always verify the legal description at the land registry office, especially where there may not be a street number and address. If you're unsure about your home's legal description, check your property tax notices or contact the land registry office in your area.

Pricing to taste

The *price* is your starting point for negotiations and probably the first thing you'll check when the offer comes in. If the buyer's initial price is at least reasonable, you can probably negotiate an acceptable final price in short order. In an ideal world, the initial offer will be at exactly the price you asked for or better, and you can skip to the part where you negotiate the other terms of your sale contract. If the offer isn't everything you hoped for, see the negotiating tips in Chapter 18.

A handful of covenants and a sprinkle of conditions

One of the most important parts of the agreement is the sale conditions. We know what you're thinking: "Can sale conditions be of greater concern than the price?" Yes. The financial details contained in the "Offer to Purchase" portion of the sale contract are easily and quickly verified. The conditions of sale necessitate careful review.

In Chapter 9, we discuss the various conditions (or subject to clauses, or subjects) that are common in contracts of purchase and sale. The subjects are noted in the body of the contract and, in essence, state that the buyer will purchase your house if it passes an inspection and if she can get a mortgage. The onus is on the buyer to satisfy these conditions within a reasonable time frame. Other subject to clauses or conditions of the contract require the seller to do some work. These clauses may require that you remove the broken-down car in the garage or repair a loose handrail before the buyer will commit to buying the house.

REMEMBER

All terms and conditions included in an offer to purchase your home are negotiable; both parties (you and your buyer) must agree to them. You'll almost never see an offer that doesn't contain any subject to clauses. Sometimes, in a very active market with competing offers, buyers keep the subject to clauses to a minimum to make their offers as attractive as possible to sellers. Even with a plethora of competing offers, you'll usually find a quick *subject to inspection clause* inserted in an offer. You can choose to reject one or all these clauses the buyer has attached to the offer, but if you do, you risk losing the offer altogether. Use good judgment; if you think the buyer's requests are reasonable, then accept them and let the buyer go about fulfilling the conditions. If one or two of them seem questionable and without foundation, talk to your agent about making a counteroffer that excludes the conditions that you find unacceptable. Of course, if you're selling privately, you have to take care of this yourself, but do consult your lawyer for help so that your counteroffer clearly states your terms.

Regardless of who inserted conditions into the offer, both you and the buyer need to confirm that all conditions of purchase and sale have been met. After you and the buyer acknowledge that the conditions have been met, you must remove them from the offer. In effect, you're saying that yes, the buyer has secured financing or that you've cleaned up the property in accordance with subject to clauses in the contract.

Procedures vary from province to province for removing subject to clauses from an offer. In Nova Scotia, for example, clauses are typically worded so that if no written notice from the buyer to the contrary is received by the seller, the seller can assume the buyer is satisfied. In most provinces, a standard form is attached to the offer stating that X, Y, or Z condition has been satisfied; in Ontario, you attach a waiver; in Saskatchewan, you attach a condition removal form. In British Columbia, subject to clauses are removed using a separate amendment. Subject to removal documents are usually prepared by the agents on the applicable standard forms. Standard contracts and add-on forms are suitable for about 99.9 percent of home sales and are mandatory in some provinces. Your real estate agent supplies these standard forms. If you aren't using an agent, your lawyer will have these forms available.

Some of the most common subject to clauses of importance from the seller's perspective include the following.

Subject to financing

This is the condition that the buyer includes in the offer basically as a safeguard until obtaining financing. In some cases, the buyer's financing can require that the home be appraised at an equivalent or greater value than the purchase price. With mortgage preapproval offered by most lenders, many of today's buyers come to the negotiating table with the security of financial backing. Even if they have a preapproved mortgage, most buyers will make their offer subject to financing to allow the lender to do an appraisal and confirm that the accepted offer is fair market value. If your buyer doesn't have a pre-approved mortgage, five to seven business days should be adequate for a buyer to arrange financing.

Like all subject to clauses, the *subject to financing clause* must include a date by which it must be removed. A commonly worded subject to financing clause reads like this:

> "Subject to new first mortgage being made available to the buyer by_____, in the amount of $_____ at an interest rate not to exceed ___% per annum calculated semi-annually, not in advance, with a ___-year amortization period, ___-year term and repayable in blended payments of approximately $____ per month including principal and interest (plus $\frac{1}{12}$ of the annual taxes, if required by the mortgagee). This condition is for the sole benefit of the buyer."

TIP

Subject to financing clauses require the buyer to make a true effort to arrange the required financing. The buyer isn't permitted to just sit at home and say, "I couldn't get it." If you think that a buyer didn't make a good-faith effort to get financing, and can prove it, you may be in a position to refuse to return the initial deposit if the offer falls apart because this condition hasn't been met. This type of situation is where lawyers get involved, but keep in mind that a clearly worded subject to financing clause and a true concerted effort by the buyer eliminates the need for lawyers and disputes related to financing subjects.

Subject to inspection

Most offers these days have a *subject to inspection clause*. Even though you have maintained your home, the buyer has every right to commission a full inspection. If you had your home inspected prior to listing and disclosed all relevant information (see the discussion of disclosures in Chapter 16), the buyer's inspection shouldn't hold any surprises for you. Moreover, if your home is relatively new (no more than three to five years old) and passed an inspection before you purchased it and you haven't seen any evidence of problems, you probably don't need to worry, either. However, if you own an older home in which the major operating systems and structural components haven't been updated or replaced in decades, this condition may become an issue. Even if your home seems to be running smoothly, you may be in for some unpleasant surprises come inspection time.

Typically, the clause will read something like this:

> "Subject to the buyer, at their own expense, receiving and being satisfied with an inspection report from a certified building inspector of their choice on or before _____. This condition is for the sole benefit of the buyer."

REMEMBER

If a prelisting inspection reveals any problems, as the seller you must disclose those problems. It's to your advantage to be aware of the problems and making repairs ahead of listing the house.

Subject to sale

Buyers often make an offer conditional on the sale of their previous home prior to an agreed-on date. It's your call whether you should accept an offer with this sort of condition or wait for an offer that has no such condition, but understand that you have control of the sale process. If you agree to the condition, the clause in the offer to purchase will read like this:

> "Subject to the buyer entering into an unconditional agreement to sell the buyer's property at 123 Main Street, Outlook, Saskatchewan, by _____. This condition is for the sole benefit of the buyer.
>
> However, the seller may, upon receipt of another acceptable offer, deliver a written notice to the buyer or the buyer's agent [enter name of the buyer's agent and company name] requiring the buyer to remove all conditions from the contract within 12/24/48/72 hours [choose one] of the delivery of the notice. Should the buyer fail to remove all conditions before the expiry of the notice period, the contract will terminate, and all deposit monies will be returned in accordance with the Real Estate Act."

The portion of this clause from the word "However" on is known as the *time clause*. This clause is extremely important if you think that you may receive other offers while this buyer is trying to sell her home. The length of the notice period is negotiable and can be as short as 12 hours, but this puts a lot of pressure on the buyer, and you'll find that many buyers won't agree to this. If you're in a seller's market, you'll want to keep the notice period as short as possible, because this will allow you to deal with a backup offer relatively quickly if one comes in. From the buyer's point of view, the longer the notice period, the longer she'll have to arrange interim or bridge financing while she tries to sell her house.

If you need to invoke the time clause, you may want to get confirmation that the notice was actually delivered at a certain time. Although technically this isn't necessary to make the notice valid and enforceable, it helps keep everyone clear on the process. The delivery can be witnessed by someone, or the buyer or the buyer's agent can sign a copy of the notice to acknowledge receiving it. At this point, there is no negotiating and you're just waiting to see who will buy your home. The notice to invoke the time clause will look like this:

> "This notice constitutes written notice from the seller to the buyer requiring the removal of all conditions (or condition) from this contract within (24/48/72) hours or this contract will terminate at the end of the (24/48/72) hour period and the deposit will be returned to the buyer. This time clause will start running on delivery of this notice to the buyer or [the buyer's real estate agency], which will be at _____ o'clock a.m./p.m. on (date), 20__. Therefore, the [24/48/72] hours will terminate at _____ o'clock a.m./p.m. on [date], 20__."

TIP

In some provinces, you may have to exclude Saturdays, Sundays, and statutory holidays from the time clause. In this case, the clause will read "24/48/72 hours, excluding Saturdays, Sundays, and statutory holidays." Your agent or lawyer will know local provincial regulations.

Escape clauses

Another category of subject to clauses depends on a third party or requires the approval of one party to the contract. These third-party subject clauses are often called *escape clauses* or *whim-and-fancy clauses*, because either party can simply withhold approval and walk away from the contract.

One of the most obvious escape clauses is subject to a relative or friend reviewing the contract. This is very ambiguous and hard to enforce, and you should do everything you can to avoid such a condition. Another escape clause is subject to the buyer obtaining financial advice. The buyer should have received financial advice before writing the contract — this is an extremely obvious escape clause and may indicate a buyer who isn't serious.

You or your agent should recognize escape clauses and try to keep them to a minimum, and where they're necessary, keep the time frame as short as possible. Generally, a contract with an escape clause is unenforceable until the subject is removed.

Clauses introduced by the seller

Few sellers are concerned with what happens to the property after it has been sold. However, in some cases the seller may want to place restrictions or obligations on the new owners of the property. For example, when history buffs and activists Pierre and Marie decided to sell their home in the Old Quebec district of Quebec City, they wanted to stipulate in the contract of purchase and sale that the new owners respect the home's historical significance. Its heritage status had narrowly missed having legal protection conferred by government, and they wanted to make sure future buyers knew what they were buying and showed the property due respect. So they introduced a clause stating that the new owners were forbidden to undertake any major additions or renovations to the original structure other than restoration projects to preserve the character and historical importance of the building.

WARNING

Most clauses of this sort come with the land and aren't the prerogative of the seller to introduce. Remember, too, that a clause of this nature will in many cases severely limit the number of interested buyers who will consider purchasing your home.

If your property has municipal or provincial conditions restricting the use of the property, they should be clearly outlined in the contract to protect you from any future actions by the buyer. If there were no restrictions or obligations placed on you when you bought the property, you shouldn't attempt to introduce these sorts of clauses.

SUBJECT TO SELLER'S PURCHASE

A clause that you as a seller may need to include is a *subject to purchase clause*. This condition stipulates that the buyer's offer to purchase will be accepted only if the seller's offer to purchase another home is in turn accepted.

For example, Lars and Jorge wanted to sell their house, but only if they could get the house of their dreams. They did find one house that fit the bill, but their offer, subject to the sale of their own house, was rejected. The couple decided that in such a busy market, they had better list their house and keep an eye on their dream home. After a couple of weeks, they got an offer on their house and notified the prospective buyers that they would sell only if they could come to an agreement on their dream house. The buyers appreciated the advance warning and were in no rush, so they accepted the subject to purchase clause. It was written into the contract of purchase and sale as follows:

> "Subject to the seller entering into an unconditional agreement to purchase the property at _____ by _____. This condition is for the sole benefit of the seller."

TECHNICAL STUFF Subject to purchase clauses aren't very common, and in a situation like Lars and Jorge's, letting the buyer know the seller's plans in advance is always a good idea so that the buyer won't be surprised to see a seller's condition added to the contract.

WHAT'S INCLUDED — FIXTURES AND CHATTELS

Anything that is fixed to the structure of your home (known as a *fixture*) is assumed to be included in the purchase price unless otherwise stated. Anything movable — appliances, furniture, and the like, known as *chattels* — is assumed to be excluded from the sale. Nonetheless, in some provinces, appliances are typically included in the sale price. Find out early in the process what the conventions are for your area. Now is the time to exclude from the sale anything buyers may think they'll be getting, whether it's your fabulous new and astonishingly silent dishwasher, or the antique chandelier from your great-grandmother. Conversely, removing that beautiful chandelier and replacing it with something suitable may prevent a lot of squabbling later.

The contract of purchase and sale will list exactly what is, and what is not, included in the sale. How would you like to buy a home in Moose Jaw and take possession in February only to discover the furnace had been ripped out of the basement? These kinds of events aren't common, but they have been known to happen. Clearly this section of the contract is of greater importance to the purchaser — the one likely to get the short end of the stick. But you need to do a quick review of this section as well, just to ensure that everything you want to take with you will still be yours come moving day.

TIP Breaking out the chattels may also be a wise move in terms of the sale price. By listing and assigning a value to the chattels separate from the real estate, the value assigned to the real estate can be reduced. This could result in certain tax savings, potentially reducing capital gains for you and giving the buyer a little more leverage with his lender.

Time frame of the offer

The time frame of the offer, or the *irrevocable date*, is one of the most important elements of your contract of purchase and sale. This element states that the offer is valid only for a certain length of time. If this length of time expires before the offer is accepted, the offer is null and void and the deposit is returned to the buyer unless both parties agree to extend the time for acceptance.

The completion date is the date on which the deal is firm and the house is registered in the buyer's name. The possession date is the date the buyer assumes possession of the property. If all conditions haven't been met by the subject removal date, the offer can be withdrawn and the transaction terminated.

Pay extremely close attention to these dates. Most contracts hold the seller responsible for the property until the completion date. If a fire ravages your home the day before the completion date, it's your problem. From 12:01 a.m. on the completion date, the property and all included items are at the risk of the buyer, but a condition of mortgage financing is that the property is insured.

TIP

Arrange to have your insurance policies terminated on the closing date and not before. If possible, avoid the last day of a month or year as a closing date. These are busy days for banks, creditors, insurance providers, and most administrative staff that will be involved in processing the new information generated by the sale. This means you're at an increased risk of otherwise avoidable delays in registering the sale of your home.

If you have rental units

The contract of purchase and sale becomes considerably more complex if your home has rental units and your buyer intends to continue renting out these parts of your property. This aspect is typically a larger headache for the buyer than for the seller. However, if you have tenants at the time of sale, here is some general advice.

If you have a rental unit and are selling to a buyer who intends to continue renting the unit, speak to your agent or lawyer about the legal and contractual consequences before signing the contract of purchase and sale. If you're getting close to an agreement on price and you want to keep negotiating, you can go ahead and accept the offer, but make it subject to consulting with your lawyer if you have concerns. In many parts of the country, a copy of the rental agreement may become an addendum or schedule to the contract. If the buyer wants to terminate the tenancy, the buyer will request in the contract that the seller give legal and binding termination notice to the tenants in accordance with provincial tenancy legislation.

Top with acceptance

This final section of the contract is quite simple. When the contract has been negotiated to the satisfaction of both you and the buyer, all that remains is to sign on the dotted line (as well as fill in the appropriate dates and seals). Doing so will indicate that the offer has been accepted subject to the terms and conditions outlined. You must make sure that both parties have initialled any changes made to the contract and that all signatures have been witnessed where necessary.

Keeping Condo Owners Covered

The legal considerations of selling a condominium are slightly different than those for selling a house. First of all, condos may have separate standard legal forms. In essence, these forms are similar to the standard contract of purchase and sale for a house because both kinds of forms cover the details of the offer, the conditions of sale, and the acceptance. But two very important elements are specific to condominium sale contracts: the financial status of the condominium corporation and its bylaws. In many areas you use the standard forms, and then add the condo clauses just as you would add financing clauses to the contract.

In most provinces, these details are included in a document known as the condominium certificate, estoppel certificate, information certificate, or status certificate. It lists the expenses for a specified unit, discusses the status of the complex in its entirety, explains the regulations and procedures for the administration of the complex, outlines the rules governing the behaviour of residents and the corporation, and stipulates all financial obligations (we discuss these documents at length in Chapter 6).

Making sure your buyer has had a chance to carefully review the condominium certificate or equivalent documentation before removing the subjects from the offer is extremely important. The buyer's lawyer can also review any aspect of the information package that concerns the buyer. The lawyer may also want a copy of the building's insurance policy to make sure the building has adequate coverage.

Be a proactive seller and provide your agent with all relevant documents, and have copies to give to potential buyers at showings. You must make all these documents available to the buyer, and if you can provide everything promptly, it may help to solidify a trusting relationship with potential buyers and speed up the process. The condominium corporation must provide you with a copy, but it often takes quite a while to process requests. The moral of the story is, send in your written request for all the required documents well in advance. Keep in mind that fees may be attached when ordering these documents, if in fact they're coming from a building management company.

IS EVERYTHING IN ORDER?

In B.C., under the Strata Property Act, the strata corporation (the condominium corporation) prepares a package for the seller or the seller's agent to give to potential buyers. This package, usually put together by the property manager of the condominium, includes

- An information certificate

- Current financial statements and bylaws for the building

- Minutes from the building's meetings for the past two years

- Any rules or regulations regarding the use of the suite

All of these items are specified in the contract, and the offer is subject to the buyer receiving and approving all of these documents.

Check with the relevant legislation in your province governing condominiums or ask your agent to understand what the condominium corporation must make available for the seller to provide prospective buyers in your province.

Your buyer will also be interested in the state of the condominium corporation's reserve fund. This is the fund that supplies money for structural repairs and any renovations or work needed on the complex. This information is generally contained in the condominium certificate or the financial statements for the building. Your agent will need this information as she presents your unit to potential buyers. You can win points with potential buyers by being knowledgeable about the status of the corporation and the procedure if repairs are needed on the building.

Examining Deeds and Titles

You have some great buyers lined up who plan to keep feeding the hummingbirds that hang out in your garden. Oh, and they've also offered you a great price for your home. Time to call the moving truck, right? Well, before you sign the contract and hand them the keys (and the bird feeders), you have to prove to them what it is you really own — and then legally transfer this ownership to them. You may think of that gurgling stream out back as yours, but is it your property? Do you owe anything to anyone in relation to your house? You're not on the road to your fabulous new home yet — but read this section, and you soon will be.

Conveyance

The process of transferring ownership is known as *conveyance*. When you sell your home, whether it's a house or a condo, your lawyer prepares a legal document called a deed. The *deed* certifies that all the conditions of sale have been met, and transfers ownership of the property to your buyer. A deed may not always transfer full ownership; it may transfer partial ownership, or any other specified interest in the land.

TIP

Duhaime's Law Dictionary (www.duhaime.org) is an indispensable online source of legal terminology. The definitions are reader-friendly, and it's free! Use it to look up any legal terms you find baffling.

Any claims or encumbrances against a property, such as Crown grants or rights-of-way, can also be transferred along with ownership. The term conveyance also applies to the transfer of these encumbrances. When your lawyer has dealt with all aspects of conveyance, the information becomes collectively known as the title to the property. The *title* identifies the property and the owner of the property and lists any debts or claims against the property.

Transfer of title has to be registered with your province (generally at the land titles office) in order to guarantee that you will no longer be held responsible for that property. The drafting of the conveyance documents is the responsibility of the buyer. When the documents are submitted for registration, the buyer is issued a certificate of title, and you no longer have any claim to the property.

Usually the buyer (or, more precisely, the buyer's lawyer) is responsible for doing the title search. The title search ensures that you do in fact own the property and that no debts or claims exist against it that you haven't disclosed. Most provincial registry offices are now automated and current transactions take place digitally, but many original documents are stored in a variety of formats, including microfilm, bound volumes, and paper. If your property is more than 100 years old, the original documents may have been archived. Restricted access to documents means that your lawyer and your buyer's lawyer may have to meet in the local registry office to perform some of the necessary tasks.

TECHNICAL STUFF

Some areas of the country, particularly older neighbourhoods and subdivisions developed prior to the Second World War, may have exclusive covenants on title. These covenants limit ownership of the property to those of a specific ethnic group or race, or bar ownership or conveyance of the property to those of specific ethnic groups. Although these covenants no longer have force or effect, they remain on title as part of the property's history. Because they regularly crop up, causing embarrassment to sellers and distress to buyers, many jurisdictions allow them to be removed at no cost. In fact, many are proactive about this measure as a matter of social justice. If such a covenant or other embarrassing element affects the title of your property, be sure to work with your lawyer and the buyer's lawyer to address it so that you're the last seller who has to deal with it.

Land registries

Just as the various provinces and territories support distinct real estate laws, they also support many different systems of land registration across the country. It isn't always the same department or division of government that is responsible for registering land titles. For example, in Alberta, Land Registries is a division of Alberta Municipal Affairs; in Saskatchewan, Information Services Corp., a public company, is the provider of registration services. In the Northwest Territories it's the Legal Registries division of the Department of Justice, and in Newfoundland and Labrador it's the Commercial Registrations division of Government Services and Lands.

Different provinces and territories have divided the land differently. This means that the identification information for your property will take a form dictated by your provincial government. If you desperately want to know exactly how it works in your area, you can contact your provincial or territorial government or the land surveyors' association, but there's no pressing need to be an expert on systems of land registration.

You do, however, need to know about the documents that are typically required for registration. In all cases, these include the transfer deed (prepared to change the registered ownership of the home) and your mortgage discharge statement (instructing your lawyer regarding the paying of applicable funds back to the bank). If your buyer is assuming your mortgage, you must register the conveyance and your buyer must register the new mortgage on the property, as well as any new rights-of-way or minor easements for utilities. In those cases involving properties with outstanding debts or claims, these must be registered or discharged as well (if they have not been already). Should an up-to-date survey be required, it may be registered, too.

WARNING

Almost every registration or service provided by your local registry office comes with a separate charge. Registering the transfer of land usually entails a base fee plus $1 or $2 per every $1,000 of the value of your home. For example, if your home sold for $350,000, you may have to pay a $35 base charge plus $350 to register the transfer deed. Registration of a mortgage discharge will carry a separate fee, as will the survey plan and any other documents. If you need to obtain copies of official documents, you'll have to purchase them, usually for around $10 a copy. The cost of any registrations that your lawyer makes on your behalf will filter down to you as disbursements — in other words, you'll pay for them as part of your legal bill. When you get a quote from a lawyer for your conveyance, make sure the price includes all fees and disbursements.

Clearly, the registration of some of these documents falls to your buyer. However, they may become of interest to you if the documentation for your title to the land wasn't registered properly.

Western Canada primarily uses the Torrens System of land registration. This system holds that regardless of the existence or status of any previous titles, the certificate of title that you possess is indefeasible. This means that so long as you have a certificate of title, ownership of your land can't be taken away from you under any circumstances. Claims, debts, or other ownership issues not spelled out in your certificate are irrelevant to your title.

In other parts of the country, your title must be validated before you can transfer it to another party. If there happen to be any previous titles with unresolved ownership issues, they can affect your right to ownership. The Torrens System was adopted to make the validation of titles unnecessary, and therefore to make transfers of titles simpler and easier to record. But even under the Torrens System, there can be hindrances to a smooth title transfer.

TIP

Even though title insurance offers good protection for buyers, the risk of selling a property with a compromised title is also a good reason for obtaining title insurance. Some owners discover when it comes time to renew a mortgage or sell a property that they've been swindled out of title, something title insurance protects owners against. Although the use of title insurance is more common in some parts of Canada than others, consult with your lawyer to determine if this protection is worth obtaining in your particular case. For example, if you've purchased a property with a difficult history (such as survey errors and liens), you may wish to hold title insurance against any further challenges. Alternatively, if the property was recently subdivided from a larger one, you may wish to obtain title insurance against any oversights or mistakes during the subdivision process.

Many companies provide of title insurance in Canada, one of the largest is First Canadian Title (www.fct.ca).

IN THIS CHAPTER

» Getting ready to negotiate

» Identifying your bargaining chips and playing them wisely

» Navigating your way through the negotiating process

» Using success tactics when receiving multiple offers

» Accepting a backup offer

Chapter **18**

Being Cognisant of Negotiating Tricks and Bargaining Chips

H ammering out a final deal with the buyer of your home involves several elements. Yes, price will be the first thing on your mind, but pay attention to other key details, such as the possession date, conditional clauses and their expiry dates, the extras you'll include in the sale (chattels like your washer and dryer), and the amount of the buyer's cash deposit (we discuss all of these items in Chapter 17). Everything is negotiable, so have a clear idea of what is most important to you and be flexible in everything else. This chapter gives you some tips to help the negotiating process.

REMEMBER

Ideally, all parties to the sale (if there are more owners than just you) should be present when you're negotiating the offer to purchase because all signatures are required to seal the deal. If you and your spouse (or your sibling, or parent, or other partner) jointly hold title to your home, for example, then both of you should be involved in the negotiations. Turn the ringers off the phones, keep children and pets out of the way, and focus on the job at hand.

Keeping Your Eye on the Prize: What's Really Important

Emotions have no place in negotiations. You love your home. You may have raised your kids there and decorated it to your taste and style, making it a reflection of you. And we know you're a wonderful person, so who in their right mind won't love your home, too? Imagine your horror when you find out that the couple making an offer on your home wants to rip out everything — the red velvet wallpaper and even the orange shag carpet! You may feel so offended that you want to throw their offer in the garbage, but if the dates are perfect, the offer is subject only to inspection, and their initial deposit is a fair starting point, you'd better give the negotiations a try.

REMEMBER

The point here is to sell your home — for a fair value, as quickly and simply as possible. Just because your potential buyer doesn't appreciate your retro tastes doesn't mean that a deal can't be reached. No one-size-fits-all negotiating strategy exists, but you should have an unemotional, business-like game plan that allows you to make rational decisions as you go through the buying and selling process. Unfortunately, your buyer may not share your negotiating style and approach. Try not to take the proceedings personally. You're working on a business deal, and you share a common goal — the buyer wants to have your home, and you want her to buy it (if the price is right, anyway). If you've received a fair offer from the buyer, put personalities aside and deal with the terms of the offer!

Work out your strategy in advance, taking into account whether you're in a buyer's or a seller's market, and therefore whether you're negotiating from a position of relative weakness or strength. (Refer to Chapter 13 for market definitions.) If you're negotiating in a buyer's market, purchase offers can be scarce and you may have to take a lower price for your home than you had hoped for. In a seller's market, you may be able to capitalize on the competitive conditions and hold out for a bigger and better offer if your negotiations go poorly.

TIP

Even the most stoic of sellers may find themselves getting worked up at the negotiating table. Stay cool, and act calm. You're making big decisions here, and you don't want to do anything rash. This is particularly important if you're selling privately, because you won't have an agent at your side to keep you grounded with their sage reassurance and sober second thoughts.

Getting an Overview of the Negotiating Process

Many factors come into play in a negotiating process. The asking price will influence a buyer's negotiation strategy. Is the asking price aggressive and at the top of the market? You can reasonably expect to negotiate so that you and the buyer reach a deal that is fair to both sides. There are also the conditions, terms, and clauses to work through.

REMEMBER

Don't begin the negotiation process until you get a written offer. And don't sign anything until you've consulted with your real estate agent or your real estate lawyer (or notary, if you live in Quebec). You need a professional to make sure the contract is legally binding and the terms and conditions represent you properly. This is tricky stuff. If you have even a signature in the wrong spot, the contract may be null and void.

TIP

Don't dismiss early offers. Houses often generate the best offers when they're fresh on the market . . . and you never know when, or if, the next serious offer will come. Sometimes your first offer is your best offer. Remember that an offer represents an opening bid to start negotiations. Both the buyer and the seller want the same thing: the best possible price and terms of sale. Each party can make certain concessions and expect gains. (Of course, your list price should anticipate the direction of the market, representing a price that you'll be happy to receive, or providing room for a lower offer in a buyer's market.)

COUNT ON THE COUNTEROFFER

After her husband passed away, Mary realized that she didn't need the large family home that they had lived in for the last 20 years. In a buyer's market in Vancouver, she listed the home for $1,695,000 (not outrageous in Vancouver, by any means).

About a month later, a couple who had visited the home several times submitted an offer that was more than $300,000 below the asking price. She felt the offer was insulting and told her agent that there was no sense in responding to the offer. But her agent convinced her that she shouldn't take the number on the contract personally and that she should counter. Sure enough, the buyers came up in price by almost $200,000. After some more negotiating, with concessions made on both sides, the final sale price was just $50,000 below the list price, a substantial difference from the initial offer.

The offer may seem to be overly detailed and specific, but to ensure you have a binding contract with no misunderstandings, every detail should be written into your purchase agreement. Including little things like remote openers for the garage door. Attention to detail will impress the buyer.

When you get an offer, your options are to accept it, reject it, or sign it back, that is, return it to the buyer with a counteroffer proposing a different price or different terms. Review the offer with respect to each of the following considerations.

Knowing how low you will go

First and foremost, most people are interested in the prices they pay for their purchases. Your home isn't just a purchase, though; it's an investment — and if you've cared well for your home, you should be able to count on a reasonable profit when it comes time to sell the place. Determining what your home is worth in the current housing market takes a bit of analysis. In Chapter 14 we provide you with detailed information on estimating a realistic sale price for your home. But after you've figured out your listing price, you also need to decide what is the lowest offer you'll accept.

Remember that the initial offer is the buyer's starting point, just as the list price is your initial bargaining position.

TIP

Entertain any and every offer you receive. Don't reject anything out of hand, unless your lawyer or real estate agent strongly advises you to do so; make a few changes to the agreement and counter your buyer's offered price. If a buyer is interested enough to write up the paperwork, you have a better-than-decent chance of negotiating a price you're willing to accept.

Remember that negotiating requires give and take. If you don't give buyers an idea of your flexibility, they won't take the time or effort to pursue an agreement. A buyer may be truly interested in getting your house, but may put in an offer that cuts $25,000 off the asking price. Don't tear it up; he may be following the "You can't blame a guy for trying" philosophy. The response to your counteroffer may surprise you by being, "Yeah, okay."

Negotiating the subject to clauses

Subject to clauses are a buyer's safety hatch — a way to escape the contract of purchase and sale if something goes wrong. If a buyer needs to sell his home before he can afford to buy yours, he may make her offer *subject to sale*, meaning that her offer to buy your home will be confirmed only when she's been able to secure the sale of her own current residence.

The following clauses are common in an offer to purchase and offer a seller room to negotiate.

Subject to financing

The *subject to financing clause* allows the buyer to step away from the purchase if he can't obtain the required financing. This type of clause doesn't offer much room for negotiation. A buyer can't remove this subject clause during the offer/ counteroffer process unless he has a lot of equity and doesn't really need a mortgage or requires a small mortgage that's easily secured. (But remember, if the buyer didn't need a mortgage, he likely wouldn't have made the offer subject to financing in the first place.)

You can try to negotiate a shorter time limit for the buyer to arrange his mortgage, however. A buyer who inserts this clause will often have a preapproved mortgage, one that usually only requires an appraisal of the property in question to finalize. If this is the case, then allowing the buyer to insert this clause may put you in a better position to negotiate other things. You'll also be sure the buyer has the means to pay you if this clause is satisfied!

Subject to inspection

There are many good reasons for including a *subject to inspection clause* in the contract. The chief reason for accepting it is that it protects the buyer against any hidden issues in the fabric of the building (if you haven't commissioned an inspection report prior to listing, it may also be helpful to you). It should take no more than two or three days to arrange an inspection. Most inspectors can deliver a copy of the inspection report at the end of the inspection.

As with the subject to financing clause, however, you can try to negotiate a shorter time frame for the inspection's completion to speed things up. Keep in mind that most buyers won't want to pay for an inspection until they have their financing in place. Why inspect something if it turns out that you can't buy it?

Subject to sale

The *subject to sale clause* gives the buyer time to close the sale of his existing home before completing the purchase of the home you're selling. A buyer who already owns a home probably can't afford to carry the expense of two homes at once, so it pays to be reasonable.

This clause offers a key opportunity for negotiation and concessions that could be quite valuable, given the potential savings in financing costs. No matter how anxious you are to move, allow the buyer a decent amount of time to list and sell his home. Usually four to six weeks is considered fair, and (depending on how badly you want to sell to this particular buyer) you can agree to extend the time period if he can't meet the original deadline.

TIP

In conjunction with the subject to sale clause, also include a time clause to keep your options open. If you're waiting for your buyer to secure financing or sell his residence, your time clause can release you to pursue another offer that arrives in the meantime.

The time clause gives the first buyer a specified time period to remove all the subject to conditions from the contract and close the sale. If the first buyer can't remove all the subjects in time, your time clause releases you from the contract and allows you to pursue other offers. Refer to Chapter 13 for more about the time clause.

REMEMBER

If you extend the subject to sale clause, you'll probably have to extend the completion and possession dates stated on the contract of purchase and sale. Whatever dates you choose, they'll probably change when your buyer has a buyer for her own house. Your closing date for the sale may depend on your buyer's yet-to-be-negotiated closing dates on the sale of her house.

Other conditions

If you've found a house you really want to purchase after selling your own, you can try to add a subject to purchase clause that makes your home's sale conditional on whether you can still get the house you want. But be prepared: Your buyer may not be happy with this condition and he may not accept its inclusion in the contract. This clause isn't common, but it can give you peace of mind that you won't be homeless if your dream house was snatched up before you had a chance to sell.

If you're selling a condominium, you may encounter a subject to viewing condominium bylaws and financial statements clause. In many provinces, the law requires that a condominium corporation provide the buyer with full information on the condo complex and its regulations. Your buyer must acknowledge in writing that the information's been received and approved. You won't have too many negotiating points here, except for the time frame and how far back into the building's history the buyer wants to go.

Expect some regional differences and extra information to be required in different parts of the country. For example, around Vancouver (where there have been a number of leaky condominiums), the buyer may ask for any engineering reports or building envelope studies that are available (or for rainscreen warranty information if the building has been repaired), and the seller must provide the information to the buyer.

REMEMBER

In most provinces, when conditions in the contract of purchase and sale have been met, they're formally removed from the contract with a written *waiver*, *amendment*, or *condition removal form*. These legal documents are usually signed by both parties (the buyer and the seller) to confirm that a condition has been fulfilled and is no longer part of the offer.

Including appliances and household decor: "I never liked those drapes anyway"

Anything permanently attached to the property is considered to be part of the package. So any built-in cabinets, built-in appliances, or wall decorations — legally considered fixtures — are things you'll be leaving behind for the next owners. Anything portable, on the other hand, is yours to keep, if you want it. Under this logic, the drapes are still yours, but the tracks they hang from aren't; Grandma Bertha's bedside lamp comes with you to your new home, but the beautiful chandelier in the entrance hall belongs to the new owners.

Anything portable that you do want to leave behind (the drapes, the refrigerator, the pool-cleaning accessories you won't need in your new condo) must be written into the contract specifically and listed item by item. Something else to keep in mind, though: Anything you don't want to leave behind is best removed before showing the house. If you can't do that, be sure to make it clear to everyone who walks through the door that those items aren't part of the deal. You don't want prospective buyers to fall in love with an antique light fixture that you'd never consider parting with and make an offer that turns on whether or not it's included in the sale. And build everything (exceptions and inclusions) into the property section of the contract. If you include a built-in vacuum system, make sure you also include the attachments and powerhead for the system.

TIP

Even though some chattels, like the major appliances, will usually be advertised as part of the sale, others may be negotiable. These could include garden equipment that you won't need at the next place or would rather not move. You can sell them to anyone, but they can also be valuable bargaining chips when dealing with potential purchasers of your home. Hold back and don't include the snow blower or lawn tractor in the contract. If you need to sweeten the deal, you can offer them — saving you the burden of moving them while making your buyer feel better about the price he's paying.

WARNING

Don't include any leased items, such as a security or water filtration system, as part of the sale. The buyer may assume she's purchasing these items. The last thing the buyer wants is to get a bill for a security system she thought she'd bought outright with the house. Specify in writing that the buyer agrees to assume the lease on the security system if there is a lease.

OF COURSE, SOMETIMES PEOPLE SURPRISE YOU

Jed and Daisy were relocating to the southern United States and needed to list and sell their home fast. They didn't have a chance to clean up the really big problems around their house like the car-on-cinder-block flower planters in the front yard. So they trimmed, weeded, watered, and crossed their fingers. Most of the prospective buyers turned around without even getting out of their cars, and Jed and Daisy were just about ready to give up. But — surprise! — the next couple to view the house weren't put off by the dead car museum out front. In fact, they asked that it be included in the sale contract! You just never know when someone will want to keep what you can't bear to take with you.

Buyers may also specify that certain items be removed as a condition of the offer. Consult with your agent (if you're using an agent) and determine if this type of request is reasonable. Do you really want to be burdened with removing old carpeting, for example? If the buyer has allergies and you have pets, the request may indeed not be unreasonable. If you need to hire a service to do the removal, the cost should be factored into the agreed purchase price.

Deciding on the closing date

After having spent a couple of hours reviewing the price, the subjects, and all the inclusions and exclusions, the dates may seem relatively minor. Give yourself a breather from the contract, and then refocus. The dates will be the most important factor when moving time comes around. If you can negotiate a sensible and relaxed set of dates now, your move will be much easier at a time when stress will be at an all-time high. Again, if you can get ideal dates scheduled, you may consider dropping a little bit off the price in return for the buyer's flexibility.

The closing date (or completion date) is the day when the money changes hands and legal title is conveyed to the buyer. The possession date is the day you receive (or give) the keys to the other party. The adjustment date is the day that property taxes, condominium fees, and any other annual municipal fees and utility bills are adjusted to. These last two dates should be one and the same: You get the keys, you start paying the bills.

Ideally, give yourself a one- or two-day overlap where you have the keys for your new house as well as the keys for the house you've sold. The following would be a perfect scenario, starting on a hypothetical Monday:

>> **Monday:** Completion date on your present house (that you're selling).

>> **Tuesday:** Completion date on the house you're buying.

>> **Wednesday:** This is the possession and adjustment date for the house you're buying. You get the keys for the house you're buying at noon (the usual time of key transfer) unless you negotiated an earlier time.

>> **Thursday:** This is the possession and adjustment date for the buyers of your house. You give the keys to the buyers of your old house at noon.

This scenario gives you a chance to have a relaxing move and still go back to clean up your old house Thursday morning before you give the keys to the buyers. The downside is that the buyers pay their money on Monday but don't get their keys until Thursday noon. This is fairly common in some provinces and, for the right price, the buyers will accept the dates after they have negotiated with you on all the terms of the agreement.

In provinces such as Ontario, it's common for the closing date and the possession date to be identical. If this is the case, it may be worth arranging interim/bridge financing to close the purchase of the house you're buying a couple of days before your present home's closing date so that you don't have to store all your possessions, especially if something is delayed.

WARNING

Discuss with your real estate agent or your lawyer how many days you'll need for the closing. If you're working with a real estate agent, you may still want one or two days to run the contract by a lawyer. In some provinces, legal documents can't be signed on Sundays or statutory holidays.

The transfer of title officially closes the contract when you file the paperwork at the land titles office. These offices are typically open from 9 a.m. to 3 p.m. weekdays, though in some provinces they keep longer hours and filing can be done electronically. If at all possible, don't try to officially close two contracts on the same day. (If you must, make sure both sides of the transaction are aware of the situation, and have a contingency plan discussed with your legal team.) Leave at least one day to close the sale of your current house and transfer money before you (or your lawyer) return to the land titles office to close the purchase of your next house (for more information on the logistics of closing dates from the buyer's perspective, see Chapter 12).

Racing against the clock: Open for acceptance until . . .

When you realize how many changes can be made to the contract, you may find you'll need more time to reach an agreement. If both you and the buyer agree, the offer can be extended until an agreement is reached on all the terms. If the offer expires before you reach full agreement with the buyer, it should be rewritten with a new time frame for acceptance.

Signing on the dotted lines

Both the buyer and the seller have to sign the contract and usually have their signatures witnessed on each page. In some jurisdictions, having one page of the contract signed and witnessed (such as the first page or third page), and then having both parties initial the bottom of every page, is sufficient. Your agent or lawyer can advise you on the proper way to sign or initial the contract.

Contending with Multiple Offers

If you're lucky enough to be selling your home in a red-hot seller's market, you may get competing offers on your home. This embarrassment of riches has to be treated carefully to ensure you secure the offer you want without inadvertently selling the house to two different people.

Keep these guidelines and practices in mind to ensure everything goes smoothly:

>> **Keep everyone informed.** If more than one buyer is interested in your home, making sure everyone is kept up to date when offers start being written is in your best interest. In the ideal scenario for the seller, the eager buyers enter into a bidding contest and pay up to, or more than, the asking price.

>> **Act in good faith.** Many buyers won't compete with another buyer when making an offer. Remember that what's good for the seller isn't always good for the buyer. If a seller tries to get greedy and delay one offer hoping to get a second competitive offer and cause a bidding war, this plan may backfire and both potential buyers may cancel their offers.

Imagine Ken and Sue list their fabulous heritage house for sale. It's a seller's market, meaning buyers outnumber sellers, and the low inventory of homes means Ken and Sue should get close to their $499,000 asking price.

Buyers A, B, and C all see the house the first day it's listed for sale, and all come to the same conclusion: The house is gorgeous, the house is well priced, and they want it.

Ken, Sue, and their agent get together to review the offers. Buyer A is the first to notify the listing agent that she has an offer, so her offer is presented first, followed by the offers from B and C. Before making changes to any offer, Ken and Sue discuss all three offers with their agent and decide which offer has the most potential. Buyer C is offering $475,000, which is all he can afford. Both A and B are offering the full price of $499,000, with similar terms and conditions.

Ken and Sue decide to deal with offers A and B. A's offer is $499,000 and subject only to inspection. The dates are perfect, and the $50,000 deposit is attractive. B's offer is $499,000, but it's subject to financing (with B stretching to afford the price) and inspection, with a $25,000 deposit.

Ken and Sue have a couple of options: They can choose to accept one offer as is, or with minor changes that both parties agree to, and hope that the conditions go through and the contract is fulfilled. Or, they can reject both offers as presented and ask A and B to present better offers and hope for an even more advantageous offer. In the end, Ken and Sue decide to accept A's offer. But they actually have a third option: Accept B's offer as a backup offer, a scenario we discuss in the next section.

Dealing with Backup Offers

In some provinces, a second offer can be accepted as a backup offer, subject to the collapse of the first offer. Your agent or lawyer will advise you what is acceptable in your province. The offer is worded something like this:

> "This is a backup offer only and is subject to the seller being released by the buyer from all obligations under the previously accepted Contract of Purchase and Sale by _____, 20__. This condition is for the benefit of the seller."

Looking at Ken and Sue's situation from the previous section, they could accept B's offer as a backup offer subject to A's offer collapsing. B has nothing to lose by being a backup offer for a couple of days while A has an inspection done. If A isn't thrilled by the inspection, then B has the chance to purchase the house, subject to her own inspection and financing. If A buys the house, then B's offer won't proceed and B will get any initial deposit money returned to her.

The other common situation for a backup offer is when the buyer has added a subject to sale clause to the offer and a second offer comes in, subject to the collapse of the first offer. In this scenario, the first offer should have a time clause in it, giving the buyer 24, 48, or 72 hours (or whatever was negotiated) to remove all subjects from the contract. If the seller gets a second acceptable offer, the seller gives written notice to the buyer who placed the first offer to remove all subjects within the prescribed time frame, or step aside so that the backup offer will be the offer in effect.

REMEMBER

In the best of both worlds, the seller wants to achieve the listing price or higher, and the buyer wants to pay no more than he needs. Negotiating is what falls in between, but with patience, persistence, and old-fashioned determination, both sides can come to an agreement.

7

The Part of Tens

Be aware of regional concerns when buying a home in Canada, a country of many regions and cities with diverse and distinct neighbourhoods.

Understand what makes condominium ownership a unique proposition versus other kinds of residential real estate.

Know how to position your home for sale, so that you can get the deal you want (and don't upset the neighbours or tenants).

Protect your home with ten tips that will maintain and even enhance its value and your peace of mind.

Chapter 19

Ten Regional Concerns When Buying a Home

Canada is the second largest country in the world in terms of its geographic area, but its population is on par with Tokyo, the world's biggest city. And, just like a major city, it has a lot of neighbourhoods, each one with its own rules, geography, and climate. Just think of all the differences in the provinces and territories, from the temperate climate of Vancouver, British Columbia to the frigid conditions of Inuvik, Northwest Territories and the dynamic, sociable character of the Atlantic region. The incredible variety present in such a huge country can make homeownership very different from region to region. Moving to a new part of Canada can be the best thing you'll ever do. But before you peel off your "I Love Toronto" bumper sticker and head for Wolfville, or ditch Swift Current for a retirement home in Kelowna, keep these tips in mind.

Check Transportation Routes in Cities

The fact that a city has a public transportation system doesn't necessarily mean that everyone in the city can get from point A to point B with ease. When researching an urban property, check out the city's transit system. Know when buses, subways, trains, streetcars, and even ferries run, and make sure they'll fit the kind of schedule you expect to have. Some organizations issue annual reports on the state of traffic congestion and transit use in major cities, and this information can help you understand the issues you'll face getting around. Walk Score (www.walkscore.com), a private company, scores cities, neighbourhoods, and specific addresses based on walkability. If the townhouse you're eyeing has streetcar access only, realize that getting anywhere may take you longer than it would from a property with bus or subway access. If you move to a suburb outside the city and have to be at your place of employment at 6 a.m., you can find yourself out of luck if the train or bus service doesn't start until 5:30 a.m. Your research may lead you to locate closer to one form of transit rather than another, or to make cycling or walking your commuting method of choice.

Be aware of the potential downside of being too close to a transit stop: the noise of regular vehicle traffic and the potential for loiterers and strangers to the neighbourhood being outside your door (with a quick escape route if they're up to no good). Although you want access to transit, you also want to have peace of mind (and property).

Be Cautious about Industrial Sites

You may have heard of horror stories about people developing illnesses that turn out to be directly related to the emissions from a factory half a kilometre away or to the pollutants contained in that dumping ground over the hill. If your new home is anywhere near large power generators, factories, or dump sites, or on reclaimed industrial land, start by doing some research on the impacts these sites have had or are likely to have on local health.

Have there been articles in the local media, disputes, or letters to the editor about the site? Are there plans to remediate the site? More important, are there any impacts for which you might be held liable? Because many pollutants leach into the soil and groundwater, seriously consider running tests to determine if this is the case with your property, particularly if you're primary water source is a well drawing from the local aquifer. You may wish to make your purchase subject to these tests (we discuss subject clauses in Chapter 9).

Stay Away from Major Roads If You're Noise-Sensitive (Or Nose-Sensitive)

Buying into that new subdivision along the highway can be extremely tempting if you're a commuter. But has the subdivision been adequately soundproofed against the noise of rush-hour traffic? Get the whole family to do a sound check. Stand in the yard, close your eyes, and listen. Will you be able to handle what you hear day in and day out? Repeat the check in all rooms of the house with the windows open and closed.

The same applies for a property on any major road in a town or city. The hum of traffic can seem gentle at first, but over time it can become extremely disruptive. If your idea of the perfect summer afternoon is lounging in the backyard reading a book or having friends over for a barbecue, having to wear earplugs to concentrate or yell to be heard may ruin the fun.

REMEMBER

Traffic may include emergency vehicles. Check to see if the property you're thinking of is near a local hospital or a key roadway. Although double-paned windows and white noise can help reduce the potential impact of sirens, you'll also want to research where those routes are. You may find an equally good deal a block or two away, which can make a significant difference in noise levels.

TIP

Try to check neighbourhood noise levels at different times of the day. See how loud the noise is at night when you may be trying to go to sleep.

Be sure to do a smell test of your new neighbourhood. Vehicles emissions can have a significant effect on local air quality, as can nearby industrial sites. Keep in mind that a home that's in a noisy or smelly area may be a great deal, but when the time comes to sell, the pollution issues may put off potential buyers. Some helpful tools to gauge local air quality include an interactive mapping tool from Environment and Climate Change Canada (www.canada.ca/en/environment-climate-change/services/environmental-indicators/interactive-maps.html) and the World Air Quality Index Project (https://waqi.info).

Be Certain Your Street's on the Level

Research the property where your house stands to know if there are — literally — any underlying issues that may not be apparent. Whether it's an improperly filled excavation, a peat bog, or reclaimed floodplain, it pays to know where you stand. The site conditions could affect the condition of your house, and the amount of maintenance you'll have to do in the future. And if your house is on the level, knowing the site conditions will give you the confidence to make improvements.

For instance, Melody found a beautiful house in a good area of a major city. As she stood on her side of the street, she noticed something odd. The houses across appeared to have different heights, and some even looked like they'd been built with a slight tilt.

Melody called the municipal planning office, who explained that the houses on the opposite side of the street had been built on the site of a reclaimed gravel pit. Unfortunately, the builder hadn't taken precautions against the fill settling. Fortunately, the building department had on file the exact perimeter of the old gravel pit and it turned out that the house Melody wanted to buy was on solid ground.

Make Sure You're in a Good School District

If you have children or are planning to have them in the next little while, do some research into the school catchment area for your new home. The *catchment area* is the geographical boundary that determines which children go to what school. Catchment maps are available online from the local school board or district. If you're outside the catchment area of the school you want your children to attend, contact the school. It will sometimes allow children outside its catchment area to enroll, especially if there are too few students in its own area. If you live outside the area served by the school's buses (if transportation is provided), you'll be responsible for getting them to school and home again every day.

TIP

The Fraser Institute (www.fraserinstitute.org) publishes an annual report card that rates and ranks primary and secondary schools in British Columbia, Alberta, and Ontario as well as secondary schools in Yukon and Quebec.

Be Sensitive to How Local Climates Can Affect Your Lifestyle

Anyone who has lived in Vancouver can tell you stories about the interminable stretches of rain. On the upside, living in a coastal area can be mild; when the sun does come out, you can play golf in December. So a little rain may be a setback you need to live with. At the same time, you may love the hot, humid summer in Toronto, but can't stand the long, snowy winters. That's where some research can pay off.

TIP

Go online to a site like www.climatedata.ca to discover the average temperatures and precipitation in the area where you're planning to move; the site also gives future projects to help you understand what lies ahead in a world where the weather is becoming more variable and extreme.

Watch Out for Waterways

Homes by a river, lake, or stream can be real showstoppers. But if the waterway is prone to flooding each spring, your rose bushes may become waterlilies. In the case of extreme rainfall or storms, you, your partner, and Spike the hamster may have to vacate. Local authorities (or the seller) can tell you if the property you're interested in has historically been prone to flooding.

Catastrophic flooding in recent years has also prompted both the federal and lower levels of government to update floodplain maps. These new maps can help you determine whether the property is a good risk and whether insurers will think it a good enough risk to insure. Overland flooding commonly isn't covered, and some provinces have embarked on buy-back programs to prevent people from putting themselves at risk on vulnerable properties.

Many provinces and municipalities also have setback requirements for development near water. Check what local planning regulations allow and restrict. A decades-old cottage may be closer to the water than existing regulations allow, meaning it could never be rebuilt as it is. Similarly, if a stream runs through your acreage, you may have a lot less developable land than you think. Also, water safety is an extremely vital lesson to teach your children; after all, a potentially dangerous element will be a part of their backyard.

Only You Can Avoid Wildfires

To protect residents, many provinces and local governments have embraced fire-smart planning principles that aim to reduce the risk of *interface* fires — fires that put homes and communities at risk. If you're in a community that borders on a forest or that has faced devastating wildfires in the past, check to see how local protocols have adapted and what they require. You may need to pay special attention to removing brush from your property, or, if you're planning to build on the property, you may need to pay special attention to setbacks, buffer zones, and the like to ensure adequate separation from nearby trees and grasslands.

REMEMBER

Even though many municipalities have their own fire departments, rural areas sometimes rely on volunteer fire services. In both cases, however, check to make sure what kind of coverage you'll be able to count on. Some rural homes fall outside the local fire service district, which may make fire insurance very expensive or impossible to obtain.

Research Services in Rural Areas

That charming lakefront cottage out on Route 845 may seem to you like a promise of pastoral bliss, but there's a chance it can leave you in no man's land. Check with the town hall or your region's public works office to find out which services, if any, are available. How often is garbage pickup? Where do recyclables go? Do you have an emergency 911 locator on the property? Does the highways department maintain the road in winter? Will you have to get propane delivery or pay through the nose for electricity to heat your house? You can find most of this info online, even in rural areas. Your real estate agent should also be able to give you the inside scoop on what you'll be facing so that can make an informed decision about the properties you're considering.

Think Twice about Leased Land

Many recreational properties across Canada are built on land leased from a provincial government or First Nation. However, a growing number of urban communities are also built under some kind of lease arrangement. Most of the recent long-term lease deals struck are prepaid and end decades after you've moved on — to the next property, or the next life — but some older lease deals hold surprises. Check to make sure any lease underlying your property isn't about to come up for renewal or renegotiation. Also, make sure the lease doesn't include a provision for the rent to increase in the near future.

Dangers of leasehold properties include the risk that your lease may not be extended, and you may not receive any compensation for any buildings you've constructed if you're forced to leave (this could be one time where you wish you *could* take it with you). Although compensation may have been stipulated in the original lease, changes in the intervening years may mean you receive no compensation whatsoever, even after a costly, stressful court battle.

TIP

Before putting your money down, do your research and have a lawyer carefully review all aspects of the lease to ensure you know what you're getting into. For more information on leasehold and freehold properties, see Chapter 6.

Chapter **20**
Ten Tips for Condo Buyers

Condominium comes from two Latin words: *con*, which means "with," and *dominium*, which means "ownership." And when you think about it, the name really fits what you're about to invest in. A condominium gives you all the privileges that come with owning your own home, while allowing you to share many of the responsibilities of ownership with others.

But before you sign your purchase offer with starry-eyed notions of moving into a ready-made community, think of this: If you make an ill-informed decision, a condominium can make you suffer the very worst of both worlds. You can get locked into owning a cramped, restrictive unit in a building with irresponsible owners you can't stand. (As the philosopher and writer Jean-Paul Sartre famously wrote, "Hell is other people.")

Because we want you to have the best of both worlds just as much as you do, here are some tips that can help you avoid becoming a prisoner of your new home.

Insist on Seeing and Reading Documentation

When your offer has been accepted, you should receive — promptly — the condominium certificate (also known as the strata documentation package), which makes full-disclosure of all the details about the condominium complex that the laws in your province require you to know. The documents may have different names from province to province, but the package should include variations of a sample deed, a strata plan (equivalent to a land survey), building bylaws, and a budget. Keep a copy and get the originals to your lawyer ASAP if you're not using an agent. Then, dive into everything yourself. This stuff is so boring it'll guarantee you a good night's sleep, but persevere and read it! You may find out that your five silverpoint Persian cats aren't permitted (or worse, just two of them are welcome), or that the giant barbecue you planned to perch on the balcony isn't permitted.

The condominium's financial status is of the utmost importance to you. If you read the financials and the meetings of the building council's meetings and notice that the complex needs a new roof but the contingency fund falls short of what's needed to pay for repairs, you'll know you're in line for a major levy (a "special" one at that!) down the line. A well-managed condominium will have a financial plan that takes into account the building's future maintenance and repair costs.

Have the Condo Inspected

Buying a condo is just as significant a financial commitment as buying a house. The unit might be cheaper and more affordable, but it still comes with a mortgage and some major responsibilities. For this reason, get an inspector on your team before you remove the subjects from your offer to buy. The inspection should cover most of the same things that a standard home inspection would cover (as we detail in Chapter 10): the exterior upkeep of the building, the basement, the heating, water, and ventilation systems, and interior problems such as possible leakage in your unit.

Just as if you're buying a stand-alone house, a condo inspection can give you a heads-up on any immediate repairs that are needed and any issues that could result in damages to other units. Those damages are ones that you'd be on the hook for, and because condos are typically multifamily developments, more than one unit will likely be involved. Preventative maintenance on your suite can prevent remediation of several suites down the road and the added cost that entails.

Use Your Measuring Tape If You Buy New

The centrally located condo development is selling out quickly. The catch? It's not built yet. To get the condo of your dreams, you may have to invest in an unfinished project. But if you do, make sure you know the differences between the spacious, pristine model unit that prompted you to buy and the unit you're actually buying — the one that built from the floor plan that the condo developer's sales team thrust into your eager little hands.

This floor plan is also called a condominium plan — the owner's equivalent to a land survey. The strata plan will give you the exact dimensions of your condo, as well as its situation in the building, the number of condos on your floor, and whether that beautiful bay window you'll have in your living room has a northern or southern exposure. You should also get the plans for the parking areas, basement, laundry, gym, and any other of the building's common areas in which you'll have a share.

TIP

Take a thorough look at the condominium plan and compare it to the actual unit. It's not uncommon to hear people raving about how well laid out the floor plan of their new condo is — until they realize that they've bought a 900-square-foot two-bedroom unit that's actually smaller than advertised (the original description could have been based on measurements to the outside walls rather than the finished, inside walls). Figure out if the rooms in the unit will really be big enough for you. How does your prospective new condo's "spacious" master bedroom compare with your current, humble boudoir? You may be surprised to find that it may look larger but actually be significantly smaller.

Keep in mind that a presale condo may have you waiting a long time before it completes. What happens if your new condo won't be ready for up to two years? Are you prepared to sit it out? What if market conditions or your financial situation changes? You may have fallen in love with that condo and entered into a contract when you were footloose and fancy free, but that one-bedroom condo may now be too small for you, your new husband, and the Great Dane puppy you just adopted.

Get to Know the Board of Directors

Taking the time to get in touch with the directors of your building's council will give you an idea of the kinds of people that you'll have to deal with once you take possession. The most recent copy of the building minutes should allow you to run the directors' names through an online search. Give a couple of them a call to see what the building's like, being clear that you're a potential purchaser looking for a straight-up opinion on what you're getting into.

Bear in mind that building councils change over time. You may have concerns about who's on council now, but if you become an owner, you'll have an opportunity to stand for council yourself and offer a new vision. Other owners may also feel the building needs a fresh direction, and you may be able to make the complex a better place for everyone.

Stay Away from High-Rental Developments

If you buy a house, you want to make sure your new neighbourhood is made up of people who really make a commitment to the upkeep of their homes and the safety of their street. That's why it's not the best idea to move onto a street where most of the homes are rented. The same goes for condos.

When you're thinking of buying into a condo development, ask the board of directors what percentage of units in the development are rented. The higher the percentage, the more concerned you should be. Renters typically aren't invested in — and investing in — long-term improvements, like extensive roof repairs, landscaping, or plumbing, which can compromise the condition of the building and in turn your own unit.

WARNING

The ownership mix in new a development may not be finalized until building completion and occupancy. The mix of residents may take even longer to pin down, as the investors who bought units hoping to rent them out take time to source and locate prospective tenants. As a result, you may be one of a few resident owners for several months, which can make hammering out bylaws with respect to tenants that much harder. A condo development owned largely by investors aiming to be landlords is unlikely to adopt bylaws placing heavy restrictions on renters. You may find that you're more comfortable buying in a building where some of these unknowns have been settled long before you buy.

Watch Out for Maintenance Fees That Are Too Good to Be True

If you're looking into a new building, don't jump to buy if you see low monthly maintenance fees. It's possible the developer is providing an artificially low estimate based on a best-case scenario. Although the projections may support it, the low-ball estimate also serves to lure in unsuspecting buyers. Be a suspecting buyer and do your due diligence on the projections yourself.

To prevent getting duped when buying a condo with unusually low maintenance fees, compare the developer's stated maintenance fees with the actual maintenance fees of an established building of similar size and with similar systems. Make sure you know exactly what your maintenance fees cover, so you can make a fair assessment.

Ask about the Building's Commercial Property

If you're thinking of buying into a new building, ask how many commercial properties there will be, if any. Then, ask to see documentation of what share of the maintenance fees the commercial businesses will be expected to pay and any perks they may be getting, such as extra parking. The nature of the businesses will be important to you as well: You'll likely feel better if the business are shops that complement your lifestyle rather than a dance club that closes at 2 a.m.

For example, Alyssa was overjoyed when the salesman in the condo showroom told her that there would be a convenience store, dry cleaner, and dental clinic on the first floor of the building. However, her joy turned to anger at a homeowners' meeting six months later, when she discovered that these properties paid ludicrously low maintenance fees and were given extra parking places for free.

Share as Few Walls as Possible, Especially If You Crave Quiet

The more walls you share with other units, the greater your chance is of hearing the odd voice or thump. It's true in concrete buildings as s in wood-frame construction. Sound transfer is a key concern for many residents, whether it's hammering in the elevator — the vibrations travelled through the floor and reverberated into adjacent units).

Typically, your unit will be quieter with just someone below you than with people above and below you. (Anyone who's lived underneath a Tae Bo video addict can attest to this.) It also explains why corner suites are usually more expensive, and why top-floor corner suites are the *crème de la crème*.

Own Your Locker and Parking Space

When you're told that you'll have a big storage locker and a parking place, make sure you determine whether you own them or are given exclusive use of them. If they're for your use exclusively, you don't own them, you can't sell them, and you may not be able to transfer use of them to someone else. If you own them, you can make a little side money by renting them out or selling them if you decide to give up your car or have a big garage sale.

If you own your locker and parking space and choose to rent them out, you may be limited to renting to other residents of your building. You'll also want to make sure that your rate isn't undercutting whatever the building council might be charging for any lockers or parking spots it owns.

WARNING

Given the cost of providing locker and parking space, many developers are seeking ways to cut these costs. This means many new units don't come with storage space, forcing owners to seek space at public storage facilities. Parking spots are generally mandated under local building bylaws, but older buildings may not have the charging stations needed by the new generation of electric vehicles that are growing in popularity. Be sure to check that the storage and parking space fit your needs.

Check for Signs of Aging

The conversion of charming, century-old apartment buildings has a certain appeal, especially if the modern towers of glass and cement resemble a monochrome forest. But make sure that the old-fashioned vibe you get from the building won't put you in the Middle Ages after you move in. If you're looking at a condo in an older apartment building, research the conversion process and how the building was retrofitted to become a condo.

Check for signs of deterioration, such as crumbling walls or roof that show the building's age, not the date of its conversion. Also, check to see whether the heating, cooling, ventilation, and security systems are up to date. If they're not, you may soon be paying extra maintenance fees to fix a big breakdown. A property inspector should be able to pick up on these issues, flagging them for your consideration prior to purchase.

IN THIS CHAPTER

» Spiffing up the place

» Deciding where to advertise

» Spreading the word

» Gathering documents

Chapter **21**

Ten Tips for Home Sellers

Y ou undoubtedly have a lot of pride in your home, and you want that pride to show. No matter what type of home you have, you want to make a great first impression that tells a buyer that your home has been well cared for and is bright and clean. The message you want to send to the buyer is that the home is their dream home, just like it was your dream home. Here are our ten tips to help you prepare your home for sale.

Sell When Your Home Is at Its Peak

You never get a second chance to make a good first impression. If you're the owner of a home behind a white picket fence in the suburbs, wait to sell until spring when the leaves are on the trees and the scent of flowers and cut grass give the neighbourhood an appealing freshness. Better yet, if you can put a new coat of paint on the outside and reseal the driveway, the house will be as good as new.

Condo dwellers can't do much about their building, but if the council plans to paint it in the next month or so, you may want to wait until after the work is completed. The external improvements will make a good first impression on potential buyers. Similarly, if you know major roadwork is planned for the summer, aim to list your home when the neighbourhood will be the most appealing. The more welcoming the neighbourhood and building seems, the better the price you're likely to see.

REMEMBER

A new building will see the sharpest gain in value in the first ten years of its life. After the warranty runs out and regular maintenance begins to be required, the rate of appreciation will plateau as the cost of future repairs begins to be factored into purchase prices.

Prepare Your Home for Sale

If a house looks cramped and small due to unnecessary clutter, you can only imagine how small a condominium can look when it's crammed with lots of stuff. Your first impulse may be to just chuck everything in the closet or basement, but buyers will want to see these important features of your home, and they don't need to see them stuffed with, well, stuff.

Before you list your house is a great time to clean out the clutter (see our decluttering tips in Chapter 12). Declutter all areas of the house, including the basement, the storage locker (if you're in an apartment or condo), and the garage. Get rid of all those old clothes that no longer fit as well as the kids' toys your teenagers have outgrown.

Disposing of your stuff can be as simple as hosting a yard sale (also a chance to let people know your home's for sale) or, if you're in a condominium, taking items to the local thrift shop. Facebook Marketplace, Kijiji, Craigslist, and other online tools can help you sell items for a few extra dollars. You can recycle the rest and throw out what you can't recycle.

If you're getting ready to downsize, you may be able to determine what can go into a storage unit for the long term or what can go to your kids or other family members. Rent a storage unit near your future home if possible, ideally in a facility that allows you to upgrade or downgrade according to your space requirements (you may only need a small unit now and after the move, but you may need to buy a month's worth of time for the dining room set and fitness equipment). On the other hand, if you have family or friends nearby, you may be able to call them up and ask if you can throw some boxes into their basement or garage.

Fix the Little Things

Whether you're in a mansion or a tiny one-bedroom suite, the little things that don't work properly can drive you crazy. The sound of a dripping tap can resonate throughout the entire suite, or the front door that never seems to close without an extra push can make you want to pull out your hair. They're not enough for a full-on renovation, but with a bit of effort you can eliminate them and maybe even give a fresh look to the area in question.

A dripping tap, for example, may be an excuse to upgrade the bathroom fixtures. The wonky door could prompt you to sand down the door and install some weatherstripping that makes for a more energy-efficient home. Regardless of what annoys you, you don't want it annoying the next buyer. Now is the time to get around to doing the little maintenance tasks you've been putting off.

If you can't fix them yourself, ask friends or family members for the name and contact information for a trusted handyperson to help.

Light It Up

Most buyers are attracted by the words "Bright and spacious . . ." Real estate ads often start by highlighting (pun intended) the amount of light a space gets. Even if you don't have a southern exposure or picture windows, you can still shine a light on what makes a bright and welcoming place. A few strategically placed lamps (corners work well for spreading light) can help buyers feel the cheerful atmosphere, plus the brighter it is, the bigger it looks. Keep your curtains or shades open and use mirrors to reflect light and space.

Let Your Neighbours Know

If you live in a very desirable neighbourhood with low turnover, let your neighbours know that you're thinking of selling. You may be able to sell your home privately to someone who has a friend who's always wanted to live in the neighbourhood (we discuss private sales in Chapter 15). The same goes for condo units. If you list with an agent and your building doesn't allow for sale signs, make sure you get a feature sheet up in the building's bulletin board ASAP to let everyone in the building know your unit is for sale. In great buildings, a lot of units will sell by word of mouth from neighbours within the building.

Whether you're selling privately or working with an agent, you may want to consider doing a mailing with a feature postcard of your condo, including the basics like total floor area, number of bedrooms and bathrooms, and of course, the asking price. Don't forget posting the listing to your social media channels, too! This lets people who know you know that you've listed your condo, and they can tell their friends, too!

Know Where to Advertise

You're not just selling your home, you're also selling a lifestyle. If you don't have an agent to help you out, the first thing you need to figure out is what type of person would be happy living in your neighbourhood and building. Then you need to figure out how to reach that person.

If your neighbourhood is full of young families with toddlers, make potential buyers aware of amenities for children and parents. You may be able to place an ad on Facebook for very little money compared to other forms of advertising (the big developers do this all the time). If your condo building is full of active seniors who play miniature golf and have cocktail parties a few times a week, the local coffee shop may have a bulletin board or a seniors centre may have a newsletter willing to carry an ad. Check with your neighbours to see if they know like-minded people who may be interested. You need to figure out how to target your market, advertising not just to the kind of resident who's there now but also to people who want to *become* that kind of resident.

Get Your Documents in Order

Even though appraisal and inspection reports may be the starting point for the average resale home, the seller of an undeveloped building lot may want to have information on what's possible under local zoning, copies of any permits and approvals received, and a report on the local soil and water. (It's amazing how many people buy a rural lot thinking it's a great place to start a farm, only to realize that keeping chickens isn't allowed.)

Condo sellers are required by law to present a more comprehensive set of documents (we discuss disclosure requirements in Chapter 16). Ideally, you have the minutes from the building's meetings for the last couple of years and recent copies of the building bylaws as well as the depreciation report. If you list with a real estate agent, she'll need these documents, and it will save her time and money if she doesn't have to order them from the management company. Many of these documents are now available electronically, making providing them a simple process. However, you may want to order up all the proper documentation from the management company regardless. A chance always exists that, through no fault of your own, you haven't received a recent update on the building bylaws or you've misplaced minutes from two years ago. Having complete and accurate documentation is essential and will prevent problems for you down the road.

Regardless of the type of property you're trying to sell, most provinces require you to complete a disclosure statement at the time of listing (we discuss disclosure statements in Chapter 16). The *disclosure statement* requires you to answer to the best of your knowledge. The more you know about the building, the better you can complete the form, and avoid the embarrassment of not knowing the answer.

If your property includes a rental unit, have the documentation demonstrating that it's a legal suite and provide the lease agreement and a statement of cash flows so that prospective buyers can see what kind of help the mortgage helper will give and at what cost in terms of operating expenses. (This information may buy them some extra room on their mortgage.)

Prequalify Buyers

It's not uncommon for homeowners to receive letters from real estate agents saying how wonderful their home is and that they have qualified buyers ready to buy it. Although flattery might get them nowhere, when it comes time to selling your home you'll want to have those qualified buyers.

If you're working with a real estate agent, he'll target his marketing efforts and field most of the calls so that only serious contenders put in offers. But if you're selling your home yourself or helping get the word out in any way, know how to filter out the duds from the hot prospects. An interview with a potential buyer is likely to confirm whether his interest is sincere or if he's just looking in the area. What is his timeline for purchasing the property, and why is he purchasing it? Perhaps the buyer is recently divorced and is putting the proceeds from the settlement towards the new home; perhaps the buyer is relocating for work and has a steady job that will help pay for the purchase (you want to make sure the buyer qualifies for financing).

Remember that you have a selling strategy and that your time is valuable, so don't waste it on potential buyers who have a low level of interest.

Tighten Security

When you advertise that your home is for sale, not just buyers will be interested. Crooks may take a shine to the property, too, using open houses as a chance to scout out their next break-and-enter prospect, or even lifting some prize pieces from the home while the agent's eyes (or yours) are looking elsewhere. (This is a very good reason to stage a property so that the home staging company's property is at risk, not yours!)

TIP

To reduce the risk of property crime during the sales process, be discreet and be alert. Avoid giving prospective buyers a long lead time on open houses and always have viewings by appointment. Doing so gives you time to collect contact information, vet the identities of visitors (again, search online; social media platforms can be valuable allies), and make sure you have at least two people on hand for the showing.

If your home is going to be vacant for any length of time during the sales process, make sure some kind of security program is in place, such as a card access system and surveillance cameras or even regular checks (a wise move for insurance purposes). Putting lights on timers or employing other measures to make the home looks lived in is also important. Because you're responsible for the property until it's sold, you also want to make sure it's safe until you pass it off to the new owner.

Send Notifications: My Dear Tenants . . .

If you're selling a suite that is tenanted, check with your provincial tenancy agency to make sure you're respecting the rights of the tenant as you sell the suite. Ensure the tenant is aware the suite is for sale and assure the tenant that the new owner will honour the lease (and if that's not the case, give the tenant adequate time to find new lodgings). Let the tenant know that any damage deposit and accrued interest owed and being held by you in trust for the tenant will be delivered to the new owner. Procedures will vary from province to province regarding giving notice to the tenant to show the suite, so make sure you're in compliance. If you're listing with an agent, the agent should be familiar with the local procedures and regulations.

If the tenant is messy, you can ask him to clean it up. He may just need an incentive, in which case you can always offer a discount on the rent in return for a cleaner suite and a little extra accommodation for showings. You can't go into the suite and start cleaning up the tenant's stuff, but you're within your rights to ask him to keep things clean and help you out in other ways.

Of course, if your tenant is an out-and-out slob, you may have a bigger problem on your hands. Tenanted properties often sell for less than those occupied by owners. The tenant doesn't have a financial interest in the property and may be worried that he'll be out of a home when the unit sells. Consequently, he doesn't have much interest in making sure your condo shows to the best of its ability.

Chapter **22**

Ten Ways to Protect Your Investment

M any people have an "if it ain't broke, don't fix it" approach to home upkeep. But repairing water damage is much more expensive than checking the roof for loose or damaged shingles every six months. Just as you should change your car's oil every 5,000 kilometres or so, you should change your furnace's air filter at least twice a year. If you dote on your car, pay even closer attention to your home, a much larger investment that is many times more costly to replace!

Skimping on regular maintenance can significantly reduce your home's value. You may even be able to prevent damage altogether. Whether it needs to be done monthly or yearly, take time to inspect and repair your home's interior and exterior. We guarantee you'll enjoy living in your home much more, and you're more likely to be happy with its resale value. This chapter points out key areas to watch.

Inspect the Exterior

Do an exterior inspection twice a year. Check your home's foundations for signs of cracking, bulges, or deterioration. If you have a brick home, you should watch for deteriorating bricks or masonry; aluminum siding should be checked for dents, cracks, or warping. If you have any retaining walls, make sure that they're well maintained with no signs of cracks or erosion.

Clean and check your eavestroughs at least once a year in the fall. Trim vegetation away from gutters and downspouts to prevent blockage. When it rains, check to make sure they're draining properly and not overflowing. Downspouts should direct water away from your home, not toward the basement. Water constantly draining against the side of the house can eventually find its way into the house.

A roof inspection doesn't require you to put yourself at risk. A pair of binoculars will help you spot damaged or missing shingles. Don't forget to check the *flashing* (the metal or plastic reinforcing the angles and edges on a roof) for deterioration. Call a roofing specialist in to do a full inspection if you notice anything. Watch chimneys for loose or deteriorated mortar, and examine the flashing around the chimney. Look for birds' nests in them, too.

Know Your Surroundings: Landscaping, Yard, and Deck

Inspect the property around your house before and after winter. Have a look at the trees — are they healthy? Branches that lack leaves while others are in full bloom are probably dead and should be removed. Have a look at any exposed tree roots near the house; they can lift up walkways or driveways around the home or disrupt the water and sewer lines. Trim any shrubs around your doorways and windows so that prowlers can't hide behind them. Make sure tree branches don't brush against your house — trees are a great way for squirrels and other rodents and insects such as carpenter ants to gain access to your home.

If you have a lawn sprinkler system, check it in the spring for leaky valves or exposed lines. Get rid of any garden debris that can attract wood-eating insects — you don't want your home to be a termite hotel! Check out your pool and hot tub and look for leaks or damage. Pool liners should be in good repair, and if water is in the pool, it should look like water you'd want to swim in, not a slimy, green science experiment.

Check your walkway for unevenness, which can be a result of a tree root, the settling of earth, or moisture either creating channels underneath or expanding in the depths of winter (a phenomenon known as *frost heaves*).

Finally, don't forget to inspect the foundation, roof, and the walls of the garage. In the summer, if you have an asphalt driveway you should check it and patch up any cracks.

Maintain Heating and Cooling Systems

It's cleaner and also easier on your wallet if the system is working at its highest efficiency. Have your system inspected and serviced once a year — a good time to do it is just before you start using it for the winter. If you have a forced-air system, clean or change your furnace filters at least twice a year. Have the ducts cleaned out, too, so that the air can travel freely around the home without moving lots of dust around, too. If you have in-floor or radiant heat, make sure that those systems are checked on a regular basis and baseboard heaters show no signs of wear. Include the chimney on your "to clean" list: A blocked chimney is a big fire hazard.

A central air conditioning unit should also be serviced once a year. Remember to cover it before the winter when not in use. If you rely on window air-conditioning units to keep you cool in the summer, make sure to store them in a safe place for the winter (not on your garage floor where de-icing salt can leak onto them) or protect them from snow with plastic sealed with duct tape. When window units are in place, make sure to fill any gaps between the window and the unit — gaps reduce the unit's efficiency and stability.

Stay Warm: Insulation

If you've ever had frozen pipes in the winter, you know the importance of having good insulation. Even if you live in Victoria and aren't particularly worried about frozen pipes, insulate your hot water pipes to keep them from losing heat when in use. If you notice small drafts around your home, you may be able to block them with the addition of spray foam insulation. Ask at your local hardware store for tips on convenient mini-insulation materials. Watch for drafts especially near electrical outlets and light switches on exterior walls, under baseboards, around window and exterior door casings, and around entrances to uninsulated areas in your home, like the cold storage room.

TIP

Good insulation makes your home more efficient, keeping your heating and cooling costs low. Insulation can now be blown into hard-to-reach areas in attics, walls, and basements, creating that extra barrier your home may need.

Breathe Easy: Ventilation

Clean air makes for a healthy living space, especially if you or anyone else in your family suffers from allergies or asthma. Be sure there's an adequate exchange of air inside your home, allowing it to breathe. Sealing all your doors and windows may also allow moisture or harmful gases to build up inside your home. Built-in air exchange systems help keep clean air flowing, but other options include attic fans, heat recovery ventilators, and balanced mechanical ventilation systems — or keeping windows open.

REMEMBER

Similar to the heating/cooling systems in your home, have your ventilation system serviced yearly. Your home's ventilation includes kitchen exhaust hoods, bathroom fans, and dryer exhausts. On the outside of your home, check around the ventilation openings for any cracks, leaks, or damage. On the inside, clean or replace ventilation screens or filters, and turn on your fans and fume hoods at all settings to make sure they work properly. Dryer ducts are a particular concern; the accumulation of lint and other particles so close to a heat source is a genuine danger. We've known more than one person who's lost their home to a dryer fire. You don't want to be that person.

Sleep Soundly: Home Safety

Here are ten things to do regularly to safeguard your home:

>> Replace batteries in smoke detectors at least twice a year.

>> Test all your smoke detectors, fire alarms, and carbon monoxide detectors once a month.

>> Don't leave any flammables near the furnace, water heater, or space heaters.

>> Pay attention to the condition of stairways and their railings; make repairs if they are unstable.

>> Plan out fire escape routes for your home, and make sure your children know how to get out if they can't use regular doorways.

>> Test locks on all the doors and windows, and change them if you've had a break-in or lost a key.

>> Ensure extension cords are tucked away from people's feet and pets' teeth.

>> Check any exposed wiring — including those extension cords, phone cords, cable lines, and appliance cords — for broken or frayed wires; replace them if you find anything.

>> Test your circuit breakers every six months.

>> Update that list of emergency numbers and information on your fridge, especially if you have a caregiver.

Keep an Eye on Your Doors and Windows

Inspect all window and door screens for rust, holes, and tears, and mend or replace them. Give the screens and windows a good wash. Replace any broken or cracked panes of glass. Open and close all doors and windows: Do they stick? Oil door hinges where they bind or squeak. Test window locks. Look at your windowsills for signs of water damage. If the wood framing feels damp or looks warped, rainwater may be getting through.

Check window trim, seals, putty, caulking, and weather-stripping on both the exterior and interior for deterioration. If you notice problems, fix them immediately. The longer you allow water damage to occur, the more expensive the repair cost. An alternative danger is heat; some older windows on the eastern, southern, and western sides of high-rise condos have been known to fracture after years of exposure to the sun. Because the window is considered part of the common property, you'll need to inform your building council to arrange the repair, usually at no cost to you as the owner.

Test outdoor lighting to make sure your entrances are lit adequately in particular from an insurance point of view as well as a deterrence to property crime and a way to facilitate visits by delivery companies and first responders.

Cook Up a Storm in a Safe Kitchen

The kitchen is a prime place for water problems, so inspect the sink and around the dishwasher for leaks and make sure to reseal vulnerable joins around the sink and faucet. Every outlet near the sink should be a GFCI receptacle that will protect you from being electrocuted if it comes in contact with water. You should test it every six months (press the little test button; it's that easy!).

Clean out the fridge and freezer. Get rid of the dust that builds up on the refrigerator coils and make sure the seal on the fridge door is tight. Give your stove and oven a thorough cleaning, especially if you use them often. You'll find the cooking elements produce less smoke and odours and have less chance of causing a grease fire if you keep them clean.

Check the burner operation on your stove to prevent fire hazards. Make sure your fire extinguisher still works and that it's within easy reach in case of an emergency. You should also have a kitchen exhaust hood above your stove that is properly vented outside to remove odours and smoke while you cook. Change or clean the filter every month or two.

Get Away in a Leak-Free Bathroom

Every six months, you should inspect your bathrooms. As in the kitchen, test the GFCI receptacles in your bathroom. Check for water leaks around the faucets, toilets, and pipes. Watch for water damage (typical signs include brown patches, warped wood, and mould) in the flooring, walls, and ceiling. Re-grout what you need to, especially in the corners of your shower and where the tub meets the wall. Make sure that the toilet flushes properly, that the handle doesn't stick, and that it seals properly after a flush. For plumbing repairs, consult a professional; if you're a novice, you may make a minor problem into a major one.

Into the Dark: The Basement and Attic

You may not spend much time in either your basement or your attic, but don't ignore them altogether. Although you may use both areas for storage, go through them once a year and get rid of unnecessary clutter; if you've left paint, varnish, or oily rags about, make sure you properly dispose of them — they're a major fire hazard.

Basement and attic leaks are the major cause of water damage, so inspect these areas carefully. Watch for water leakage in crawl spaces, on ceilings, on walls, and around windows. A brown patch on a white wall is a bad sign but use your nose, too: A damp, musty smell points to water leakage, even if you can't see it.

Look for signs of termites or other pest infestations: Hollow-sounding beams, holes in wood, droppings, and bite marks are a good indication that you're not living alone. In the summer, look in the attic for bigger freeloading visitors. You may be able to set a few mousetraps yourself, but if you discover a raccoon or some other large varmint, call a professional pest control specialist.

Glossary

acceleration clause: A clause written into a mortgage agreement to allow the lender to accelerate or call the entire principal balance of the mortgage, plus accrued interest, when the borrower is delinquent with payments.

adjusted cost base (ACB): The value of real property established for tax purposes. It's the original cost plus any allowable capital improvements, certain acquisition costs and any mortgage interest costs, less any depreciation.

adjustment date: The date on which adjustments for items such as condominium fees, taxes, utilities, and other items are made.

agreement of purchase and sale: A written agreement between the owner and a buyer for the purchase of real estate for a predetermined price and terms.

amenities: Generally, those parts of the condominium building that are intended to beautify the premises and that are for the enjoyment of occupants rather than for utility.

amortization: The reduction of a loan through periodic payments in which interest is charged only on the unpaid balance.

amortization period: The actual number of years it will take to repay a mortgage loan in full, which can be well in excess of the loan's term. For example, mortgages often have 5-year terms but 25-year amortization periods.

analysis of property: The systematic method of determining the performance of investment real estate using a property analysis form.

anniversary date: One year from the interest adjustment date for a mortgage, which is less than one month before the first payment. The anniversary date is the same date each year during the term of the mortgage. Often, a lump sum payment can be made on or before the anniversary date each year to accelerate payment of the mortgage.

appraised value: An estimate of the property's fair market value, usually determined by an accredited appraiser. This value will guide a lender's decision to extend credit to a mortgage applicant.

arbitrator: A person chosen to settle a dispute between two or more parties, often through an alternative dispute resolution process or when directed by the courts.

arrears: The overdue payments owing on either a mortgage or a lease; it also refers to the state of being late in fulfilling the obligations of the mortgage or lease agreement.

assessed value: The assessed value is a property's value for the purposes of property taxes. It may differ significantly from both the appraised value and the actual value — what a buyer is willing to pay — in a given market.

assessment fee: A monthly fee that condominium owners must pay, usually including management fees, costs of common property upkeep, heating costs, garbage-removal costs, the owner's contribution to the contingency reserve fund, and so on. Also referred to as the *maintenance fee.*

assign: The act of transferring ownership of or responsibility for a property to a purchaser; usually a step that occurs prior to the original owner completing the purchase. The assignee assumes the right to purchase a property.

assumption agreement: A legal document signed by a home buyer that requires the buyer to assume responsibility for the obligations of a mortgage made by the previous owner.

backup offer: An offer on a property received by the seller and held in reserve should an initial offer be withdrawn or collapse.

balance sheet: A statement that indicates the financial status of a condominium corporation at a specific point in time by listing its assets and liabilities.

blended payments: Equal payments consisting of both a principal and an interest component, paid each month during the term of the mortgage. The principal portion increases each month, whereas the interest portion decreases, but the total monthly payment doesn't change.

breach: The violation of a law, contract, or obligation.

broker, mortgage: An individual, typically accredited by Mortgage Professionals Canada, who assists borrowers in obtaining financing.

broker, real estate: An individual licensed to engage in the purchase and sale of real estate on behalf of another in exchange for a fee.

budget: An annual estimate of a condominium corporation or apartment building's expenses and the revenues needed to balance those expenses. There are operating budgets and capital budgets. See also **capital budget.**

Canada Mortgage and Housing Corporation (CMHC): The federal Crown corporation that administers the National Housing Act. The CMHC services include providing housing information and assistance, financing, and insuring home-purchase loans for lenders.

Canada Revenue Agency (CRA): The federal agency responsible for collecting taxes on behalf of the federal government; formerly known as Revenue Canada, a name many people (and even some agency staff) continue to use when referring to it.

Canadian Real Estate Association (CREA): An association of members of the real estate industry, principally real estate agents and brokers.

capital budget: An estimate of costs to cover replacements and improvements, and the corresponding revenues needed to balance them, usually for a 12-month period. Different from an operating budget.

capital gain: Profit on the sale of an asset that is subject to taxation.

capital improvements: Major improvements made to a property that are written off over several years rather than expensed off in the year in which they are made.

charge: A document registered against a property, stating that someone has or believes she has a claim on the property.

chattels: The movable (and removable) elements of a property, such as appliances, tools, drapes, lamps, door knobs, and other items. These may be included in the total purchase price or itemized in a separate list for the sake of clarity regarding the price paid for the property itself.

closing costs: The expenses over and above the purchase price of buying and selling real estate.

closing date: The date on which the sale of a property becomes final and the new owner takes possession.

closing: The actual completion of the transaction acknowledging satisfaction of all legal and financial obligations between the buyer and seller; acknowledges the deed or transfer of title and disbursement of funds to appropriate parties.

collateral mortgage: A loan backed up by a promissory note and the security of a mortgage on a property. The money borrowed may be used for the purchase of a property or for another purpose, such as home renovations or a vacation.

common area: The area in a condominium project that is shared by all the condominium owners, such as elevators, hallways, and parking lots.

common-area maintenance fee: The charge to owners to maintain the common areas, normally due on a monthly basis.

condominium certificate: A written statement of a condominium unit's current financial and legal status. Different names may apply from province to province; in Ontario, the term is *certificate of estoppel.*

condominium corporation: The operating company automatically created at the time a condominium project registers with provincial authorities. It is called a strata corporation in British Columbia. Its shareholders are the unit owners in the building and any judgment against the corporation for the payment of money is usually a judgment against each owner.

condominium: A housing unit to which the owner has title and of which the owner also owns a share in the common area (such as elevators, hallways, swimming pool, and land).

condominium council: The governing body of the condominium corporation, elected at the annual general meeting of the corporation.

conventional mortgage: A mortgage loan that does not exceed 75 percent of the appraised value or of the purchase price of the property, whichever is the less. Mortgages that exceed this limit generally must be insured by mortgage insurance, such as that provided by CMHC and Genworth Financial Canada.

conversion: The changing of a structure from some other use, such as a rental apartment to a condominium apartment.

conveyancing: The transfer of property, or title to property, from one party to another.

cooperative: A form of property ownership in which each individual owner holds an equal share in the entity that actually owns the property rather than in the property itself. The co-op owner has a right to live in a housing unit by means of a lease from and often at the discretion of the co-op.

court-ordered sale: The formal term in Canada for a foreclosure, the situation when a lender exercises its right to sell a property when a borrower is in default of his or her obligations. Court-ordered sales may also occur to settle claims related to a divorce, settlement of an estate, and other situations.

credit bureau: An agency that maintains credit files, such as Equifax and others.

credit check: A report typically run to review the credit history of an individual to assist in determining whether or not the individual is worthy of receiving credit.

credit file: A history of past credit granted, debts owed, and the manner in which those debts were repaid. The file may also include information on a party's places of residence and employment history.

credit rating: The score — usually expressed as a number — calculated using information in an individual's credit file. The credit rating is typically used to determine credit worthiness. The better the score, the more worthy of credit an individual is.

damage deposit: Also known as a tenant's or security deposit, the damage deposit is the amount of money given to a landlord when a tenancy begins to cover the expense of any damages to a property over the course of the tenancy. It is returned to the tenant on departure if the property has been left in good condition. Quebec is the only province where landlords cannot collect a damage deposit.

debt service: Cost of paying interest for use of mortgage money.

deductions: The expenses that the Canada Revenue Agency (CRA) allows one to deduct from gross income.

deed: This document conveys the title of the property to the purchaser. Different terminology may be used in different provincial jurisdictions.

default: The state of being noncompliant with mortgage obligations, usually by missing payments.

depreciation: The amount by which a property owner writes off the value of a real estate investment over the life of the investment. Depreciation is not applicable to the value of land.

down payment: An initial amount of money (in the form of cash) put forward by the purchaser. Usually it represents the difference between the purchase price and the amount of the mortgage loan.

encumbrance: See also **charge.**

equity return: The percentage ratio between an owner's equity in a property and the total of cash flow plus mortgage principal reduction.

equity: The difference between the price for which a property could be sold and the total debts registered against it.

estate: The title or interest one has in property such as real estate and personal property that can, if desired, be passed on to survivors at the time of one's death.

eviction: The removal, by force, of a tenant and his or her effects. The due legal process provided for this in each province must be followed.

fair market value (FMV): The value established on real property that is determined to be one that a buyer is willing to pay and for which a vendor is willing to sell.

fee simple: A manner of owning land, in one's own name and free of any conditions, limitations, or restrictions.

financial statements: Documents that show the financial status of the condominium corporation at a given point in time. Generally includes an income-and-expense statement and a balance sheet.

fiscal year: The 12-month period in which financial affairs are calculated.

floating-rate mortgage: Another term for variable-rate mortgage.

foreclosure: A legal procedure whereby the lender obtains ownership of, or the right to sell, the property following default by the borrower. In Canada, it typically takes the form of a court-ordered sale.

freehold: The outright ownership of land, or land and buildings; differs from leasehold.

Genworth Financial Canada: A private company providing mortgage insurance in Canada.

goods and services tax (GST): A value-added tax charged on goods and services, including all supply of "real property" (except residential rents and in other well-defined circumstances), in Canada. Sometimes harmonized with provincial sales taxes. See also **harmonized sales tax.**

gross debt service (GDS) ratio: The percentage of gross annual income required to cover payments associated with housing: mortgage principal and interest, and potentially (but not always) taxes, heating and a portion of condominium fees. Most lenders require the GDS ratio be no more than 30 percent to 32 percent, but this can vary from lender to lender and according to individual circumstance.

guarantor: A party that guarantees to pay the debts of an individual in the event the individual is unable to pay the debts.

guarantor's letter: A legal document by which the guarantor agrees to assume the debt of another party.

harmonized sales tax (HST): A value-added tax combining both federal and provincial sales taxes in Ontario, New Brunswick, Nova Scotia, PEI and Newfoundland and Labrador. Charged on goods and services, including all supply of "real property" (except residential rents, and in other well-defined circumstances). See also **goods and services tax** and **Quebec sales tax.**

high-ratio mortgage: A conventional mortgage loan that exceeds 75 percent of the appraised value or purchase price of the property. Such a mortgage must be insured.

high-rise: Any multi-unit residential building of six or more storeys.

Human Rights Code: The federal and provincial laws that define the basic rights of citizens. The code most commonly protects individuals to freedom from discrimination.

income, gross: Income or cash flow before expenses.

income, net: Income or cash flow after expenses (but generally before income tax).

interest averaging: The method of determining the overall average interest rate being paid when more than one mortgage is involved.

interim financing: The temporary financing by a lender during the construction of real property for resale or while awaiting other funds.

joint tenancy: Ownership of property by two or more people, typically providing for the right of survivorship (meaning that the death of one of the owners increases the ownership share of the surviving owner or owners).

judgment: The official outcome of a lawsuit or other legal proceeding. The judgment may be financial or otherwise.

key money: Typically, the fee charged to secure or cut the keys at the start of a tenancy or to replace the keys in the event of loss. It may also refer to a fee required to secure a spot on a waiting list for accommodation.

landlord: The party that rents or leases a premises to another party, called the tenant.

lease: The agreement between a landlord and a tenant. Also, the act of securing rights to use a property for a given term under such an agreement. A sublease is the assignment of rights under the lease agreement to another party.

legal description: Identification of a property that is recognized by law that identifies that property from all others.

lessee: The tenant in rental space.

lessor: The owner of the rental space.

letter of intent: Used in place of a formal written contract with a deposit. The prospective purchaser informs the seller, in writing, that he is willing to enter into a formal purchase contract upon certain terms and conditions if they're acceptable to the seller.

leverage: The use of financing or other people's money to control large pieces of real property with a small amount of invested capital.

lien: A claim for the payment of money registered on a property's title.

listings, exclusive agency: A signed agreement by a seller in which he agrees to co-operate with one broker. All other brokers must go through the listing broker.

listings, multiple: A system of agency and subagency relationships. If broker A lists the property for sale, A is the vendor's agent. If broker B sees the MLS listing and offers it for sale, B is the vendor's subagent. See also **Multiple Listing Service.**

listings, open: A listing given to one or more brokers, none of whom have any exclusive rights or control over the sale, by other brokers or the owner of the property.

marginal tax rate: That point in income at which any additional income will be taxed at a higher tax rate.

MLS: See also **Multiple Listing Service.**

month-to-month: A tenancy that renews each month, often under a commonly under-stood agreement between the landlord and tenant. Typically exists when tenancies continue after the term of a formal lease agreement.

mortgage wraparound: Sometimes called an *all-inclusive mortgage.* A mortgage that includes any existing mortgages on the property. The buyer makes one large payment on the wraparound and the seller continues making the existing mortgage payments out of that payment.

mortgage, balloon: A mortgage amortized over a number of years, but that requires the entire principal balance to be paid at a certain time, short of the full amortization period.

mortgage, constant: The interest rate charged on a mortgage consisting of both the rate being charged by the lender and the rate that represents the amount of principal reduction each period.

mortgage, deferred payment: A mortgage allowing for payments to be made on a deferred or delayed basis. Usually used where present income is insufficient to make the payments.

mortgage, discounted: The selling of a mortgage to another party at a discount or an amount less than the face value of the mortgage.

mortgage, first: A mortgage placed on a property in first position.

mortgage, fixed: A conventional mortgage, with payments of interest and principal. Fixed terms with a fixed rate can vary from 6 months to 10 years or more.

mortgage, insurance: Insurance provided by the lender as an option for the borrower. It would pay out the balance outstanding on the mortgage in the event of the borrower's death.

mortgage, interest only: Payments are made only of interest; the payment doesn't reduce the principal of the debt.

mortgage, points: The interest rate charged by the lender.

mortgage, second: A mortgage placed on a property in second position to an already existing first mortgage.

mortgage, variable: A mortgage with an interest rate that fluctuates with the Bank of Canada interest rate. The mortgagee just pays the interest, with optional pay-down on the principal. Different from a fixed-rate mortgage. See also **mortgage, fixed.**

mortgage: The document that pledges real property as collateral for a debt.

mortgagee: The lender.

mortgagor: The borrower.

multiple listing service (MLS): A service licensed to member real estate boards by the Canadian Real Estate Association. Used to compile and publish information in guides and online concerning a given property to a large number of agents and brokers.

National Housing Act (NHA) loan: A mortgage loan that is insured by Canada Mortgage and Housing Corporation to certain maximums.

Normal wear and tear: The damage to a property that results from its normal use by tenants, and for which they can't be held liable.

Notice: The written notification the landlord or tenant gives to the other announcing the end of a tenancy.

NSF cheque: A cheque for which there aren't sufficient funds. The cheque is said to *bounce* because the bank returns the order for the transfer of funds, typically at a charge to the party trying to cash the cheque.

offer to purchase: The document that sets forth all the terms and conditions under which a purchaser offers to purchase property. This offer, when accepted by the seller, becomes a binding agreement of purchase and sale once all conditions have been removed.

option agreement: A contract, with consideration, presented to a purchaser of a property giving her the right to buy at a future date. If the individual chooses not to purchase, the deposit is forfeited to the seller.

PI: Principal and interest due on a mortgage.

PIT: Principal, interest, and taxes due on a mortgage.

possession date: The date that one legally obtains possession of a real estate purchase.

post-dated cheque: Any cheque written with a future date for the purposes of delivering payment on the date for which it's written.

postponement clause: The agreement of the second or subsequent lender allowing the borrower the right to renew or replace a first mortgage that becomes due before the second or subsequent mortgage.

prepayment penalty: A penalty charge written into many mortgages that must be paid if the mortgage is paid off ahead of schedule.

principal: The amount the purchaser actually borrowed, or the portion of it still owing on the original loan.

project documents: The documents required to create a condominium corporation, often including the declaration, plan, description, and bylaws.

property manager: A manager or management company hired to run an investment property for the owner.

prospectus: A written presentation prepared by the developer that outlines material facts about the offering to induce offers from prospective buyers.

purchase-and-sale agreement: See *agreement of purchase and sale*.

Quebec sales tax: A harmonized sales tax (HST) similar to provincial sales taxes in Ontario, New Brunswick, Nova Scotia, PEI, and Newfoundland and Labrador that are harmonized with the federal goods and services tax (GST). Unlike the HST, it's administered by Quebec under a separate agreement with the federal government. However, as with the GST and HST, it applies to goods, services, and the supply of real property. See also **goods and services tax.**

recission period: The period of time following the sale during which the buyer can change his mind, cancel the purchase agreement, and get a refund of monies paid on deposit. The length varies from province to province, but typically runs from three to 30 days.

renew: The act of entering a new lease or mortgage agreement following the end of a previous lease or agreement with the same party. A residential lease may renew automatically at the end of its term, whereas a mortgage is typically renegotiated.

rent: The amount owing pursuant to a lease agreement for the use of a property; also the act of using a property under the terms of such an agreement.

rental agreement: An agreement under which one party, the landlord, agrees to lease premises to another party, called the tenant.

rental application: Filled out by a prospective tenant and often including an authorization to conduct a credit check, a landlord uses the application to determine the suitably of renting a unit to the individual. Questions on the rental application cannot violate the applicant's rights.

rental authority: The organization, usually appointed by a province or territory, established to oversee landlord-tenant issues in the said province or territory.

RRSP: Registered Retirement Savings Plan, a tax-sheltered investment arrangement designed by the federal government to encourage people to save for retirement. First-time homebuyers can tap these funds to supplement a down payment.

security deposit: See also **damage deposit.**

stress test: A tool to determine a homebuyer's borrowing capacity. Typically the contracted mortgage interest rate plus 2 percent or the Bank of Canada's current 5-year benchmark rate, whichever is greater.

survey: A document that illustrates the exact quantity of land, the position of major improvements on the property, any registered or visible easements or rights of way, any building setback requirements, zoning, or encumbrances.

tax shelter: The tax write-off possible through the depreciation benefits available on investment real estate ownership.

tenancy: The term for which a tenant has agreed to lease and occupy property; also the act of leasing the property.

tenant insurance: The insurance a tenant purchases to protect property contained in a rental unit from loss.

tenant: The party who rents an investment property from the landlord.

TFSA: Tax-Free Savings Account, a tax-sheltered federally registered savings vehicle on which no tax is owing on any increase in value. Tax has been paid on the deposits and funds may be withdrawn at any time to supplement a down payment or other housing expenses.

title insurance: This insurance covers the purchaser or vendor in case of any defects in the property or title, that existed at the time of sale but which were not known until after completion of the sale.

title: Generally the evidence of right that a person has to the possession of property.

total debt service (TDS) ratio: The percentage of a borrower's gross annual income required to cover payments associated with housing and all other debts and obligations, such as payments on a car loan. Most lenders prefer a TDS ratio of 40 percent or less.

trust account: The separate account in which a lawyer or real estate broker holds funds until the real estate closing takes place or other legal disbursement is made.

trust funds: Funds held in trust, either as a deposit for the purchase of real property or to pay taxes and insurance.

unit: Normally refers to the rental suite or that part of a condominium owned and occupied or rented by the owner.

useful life: The term during which an asset is expected to have useful value.

utilities: Any one of the array of services that allow a property to function, and which typically deliver a basic social good, such as heat, water and electricity, or phone and television service. The landlord may provide access to utilities for a fee, or the tenant may be responsible for arranging a connection to the utilities.

vacancy allowance: A projected deduction from the scheduled gross income of a building to allow for loss of income due to vacant apartments or other rental units.

value, assessed: The property value as determined by local, regional, or provincial assessment authority.

vendor take-back: A procedure wherein the seller (vendor) of a property provides some or all of the mortgage financing in order to sell the property. Also referred to as *vendor financing*.

vendor: A person selling a piece of property.

week-to-week: A tenancy that renews each week, typically under a commonly under-stood agreement between the landlord and tenant. It usually exists when tenancies continue after the term of a formal lease agreement.

zoning: Rules for land use established by local governments.

Index

documentation *(continued)*
- pricing as component in, 333
- renegotiating, 209
- rental units as component in, 340
- seller on, 195
- time frame of offer in, 339–340
- lawyers reviewing, 204–206
- from lenders, 111
- mortgages and, 206–207
- for preapproved mortgages, 111
- preparing, 376–377
- signing, 236–237
- warranty and, 232

doors, 382

Douglas Gray, 281

down payment
- boosting, 89
- cheque, 236
- closing costs and, 80–81, 237
- debts and, 70–71
- increasing, 70
- mortgages and, 9
- savings and, 72–73
- scenarios of, 88

drainfield, 170

dual agency, 22, 24

due diligence, 11, 140–141, 200–201

due process, 204

Duhaime's Law Dictionary, 343

duties
- of appraisers, 37
- of executor, 280
- of inspectors, 208–209
- of lawyers, 41–44
- of real estate agents, 30–32

dwelling, 224–225

E

easements, 195, 327

eaves, 213

eavestroughs, 184–185

education facilities, 150–151

electrical systems
- aluminum wiring in, 168
- disclosures agreements and, 328
- ground fault circuit interrupter (GFCI) in, 168
- inspecting, 185, 216, 302
- maintaining, 188
- service amps in, 168
- urea formaldehyde foam insulation (UFFI) in, 169

electricity, 123, 164

emergency services, 150

encroachments, 327

encumbrances, 36

endorsements, 228

Environment and Climate Change Canada, 363

Equifax, 71

equity, 262

e-savings accounts, 70

escape clauses, 197, 337–338

established broker/office manager, 21

estate sales, 279–281

estimating costs, 292–296

estoppel certificate, 83

ethics, 21

ethics, code of, 21

exclusion principle, 226

exclusions, 226

exclusive listing, 324–325

expenses, 74–76, 287

experience, 20

extending
- coverage, 228
- lines of credit, 181

exteriors
- components, 301
- considerations with, 57, 144
- inspecting, 188
- walls, 213

external stairs, 188

F

feature sheets, 160, 312–313

Federation of Law Societies of Canada, 45

About the Authors

Douglas Gray, LLB, is one of the foremost experts on real estate in Canada. He's written more than 25 books on real estate and personal finance, all of them best-sellers. They include ten books on real estate, such as *Making Money in Real Estate, 101 Streetsmart Condo Buying Tips for Canadians, Mortgages Made Easy,* and *The Canadian Landlord's Guide.* He brings to this book 35 years of experience investing in residential properties as well as many years as a lawyer representing buyers, sellers, lenders, borrowers, and developers. Doug is a consultant and columnist and regularly gives seminars on real estate across Canada for both professional Realtors and the public. His website is www.homebuyer.ca.

Peter Mitham has written on Canadian real estate for publications in Canada and abroad for more than 20 years. A long-time real estate columnist for Business in Vancouver (www.biv.com), he also covers rural property issues as associate editor of *Country Life in BC* (www.countrylifeinbc.com). Growing up in Quebec, he was fascinated with the catalogues of property listings and mortgage applications in the home office of his father, an appraiser. He has also collaborated with Douglas Gray on *Real Estate Investing For Canadians For Dummies* and *The Canadian Landlord's Guide: Expert Advice for the Profitable Real Estate Investor* (both by John Wiley & Sons, Inc.).

Authors' Acknowledgements

The authors gratefully acknowledge the invitation John Wiley & Sons senior acquisitions editor Tracy Boggier extended to them to undertake this edition. The opportunity to refresh and update the original text of Tony Ioannou benefitted from the close reading of editor Chad Sievers and technical editor Don Loney. Don has been Doug's muse and mentor on real estate books for almost 19 years and is a consummate and talented professional in the publishing business; this latest collaboration furthered his esteem for the excellent guidance he provides.

Peter appreciates the many conversations he's had with homeowners and professionals in the course of covering the Vancouver real estate market for Business in Vancouver Media Group. He acknowledges his debt to those who have shared with him their real estate adventures, stories that have spurred many of the anecdotes, and some of the advice offered in these pages (names have been changed to protect the innocent). He gratefully acknowledges the support of family, in particular his parents who instilled in him an appreciation of both good writing and residential real estate.

Publisher's Acknowledgments

Senior Acquisitions Editor: Tracy Boggier

Project Editor: Chad R. Sievers

Technical Editor: Don Loney, MA, B Ed

Production Editor: Mohammed Zafar Ali

Cover Image: © Maxx-Studio/Shutterstock, © alexsl/Getty Images

Take dummies with you everywhere you go!

Whether you are excited about e-books, want more from the web, must have your mobile apps, or are swept up in social media, dummies makes everything easier.

Find us online!

dummies.com

dummies
A Wiley Brand

PERSONAL ENRICHMENT

Staying Sharp

9781119187790
USA $26.00
CAN $31.99
UK £19.99

Facebook

9781119179030
USA $21.99
CAN $25.99
UK £16.99

Guitar

9781119293354
USA $24.99
CAN $29.99
UK £17.99

Investing

9781119293347
USA $22.99
CAN $27.99
UK £16.99

Beekeeping

9781119310068
USA $22.99
CAN $27.99
UK £16.99

Digital Photography

9781119235606
USA $24.99
CAN $29.99
UK £17.99

Meditation

9781119251163
USA $24.99
CAN $29.99
UK £17.99

Pregnancy

9781119235491
USA $26.99
CAN $31.99
UK £19.99

Samsung Galaxy S7

9781119279952
USA $24.99
CAN $29.99
UK £17.99

iPhone

9781119283133
USA $24.99
CAN $29.99
UK £17.99

Crocheting

9781119287117
USA $24.99
CAN $29.99
UK £16.99

Nutrition

9781119130246
USA $22.99
CAN $27.99
UK £16.99

PROFESSIONAL DEVELOPMENT

Windows 10

9781119311041
USA $24.99
CAN $29.99
UK £17.99

AutoCAD

9781119255796
USA $39.99
CAN $47.99
UK £27.99

Excel 2016

9781119293439
USA $26.99
CAN $31.99
UK £19.99

QuickBooks 2017

9781119281467
USA $26.99
CAN $31.99
UK £19.99

macOS Sierra

9781119280651
USA $29.99
CAN $35.99
UK £21.99

LinkedIn

9781119251132
USA $24.99
CAN $29.99
UK £17.99

Windows 10 All in One

9781119310563
USA $34.00
CAN $41.99
UK £24.99

SharePoint 2016

9781119181705
USA $29.99
CAN $35.99
UK £21.99

Fundamental Analysis

9781119263593
USA $26.99
CAN $31.99
UK £19.99

Networking

9781119257769
USA $29.99
CAN $35.99
UK £21.99

Office 2016

9781119293477
USA $26.99
CAN $31.99
UK £19.99

Office 365

9781119265313
USA $24.99
CAN $29.99
UK £17.99

Salesforce.com

9781119239314
USA $29.99
CAN $35.99
UK £21.99

Coding

9781119293323
USA $29.99
CAN $35.99
UK £21.99

dummies.com

dummies
A Wiley Brand